hojo Beat

Yurara™

Volume 2

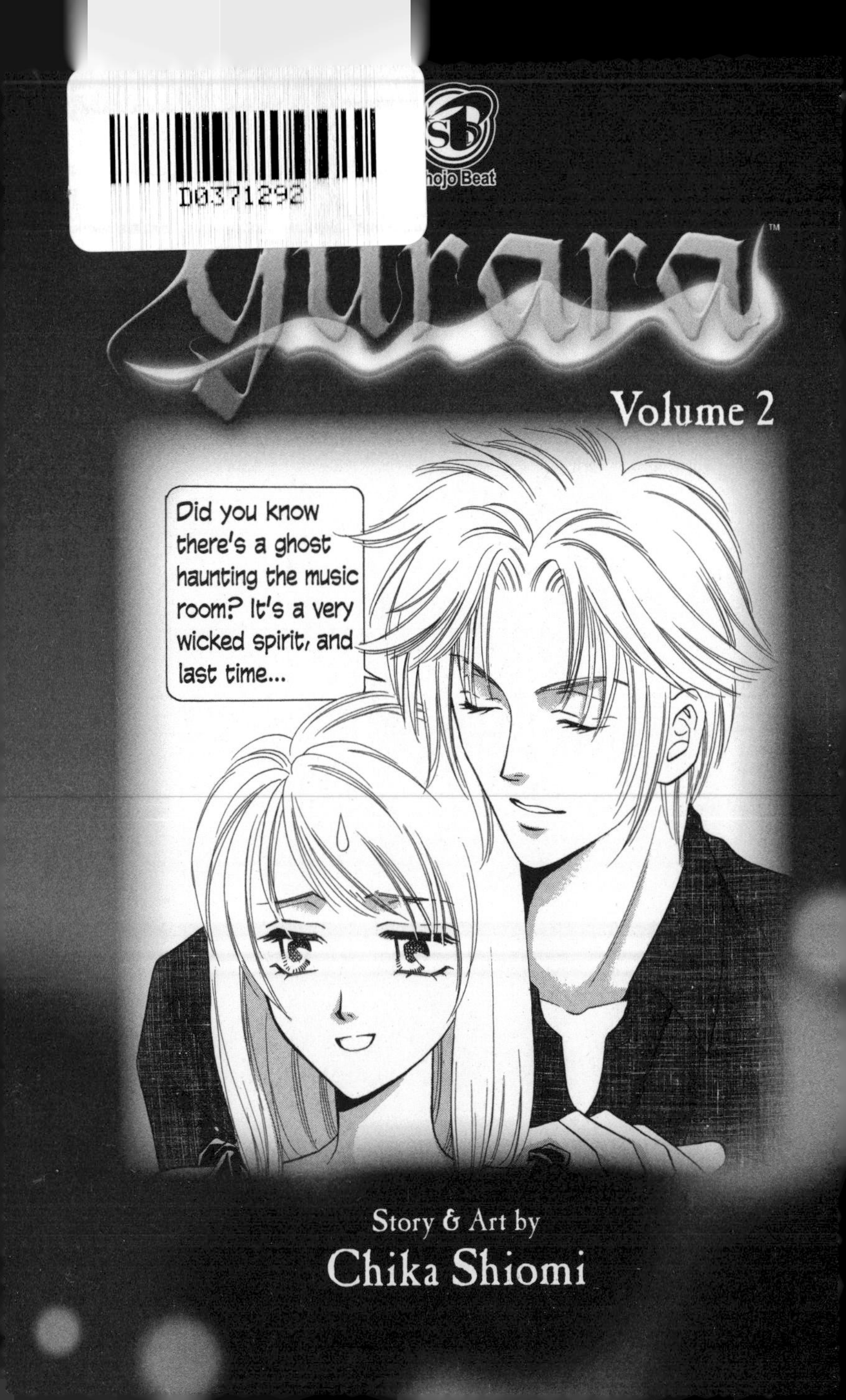
Did you know there's a ghost haunting the music room? It's a very wicked spirit, and last time...

Story & Art by

Chika Shiomi

Contents

Chapter 5 ················· 3

Chapter 6 ················ 47

Chapter 7 ················ 97

Chapter 8 ················ 139

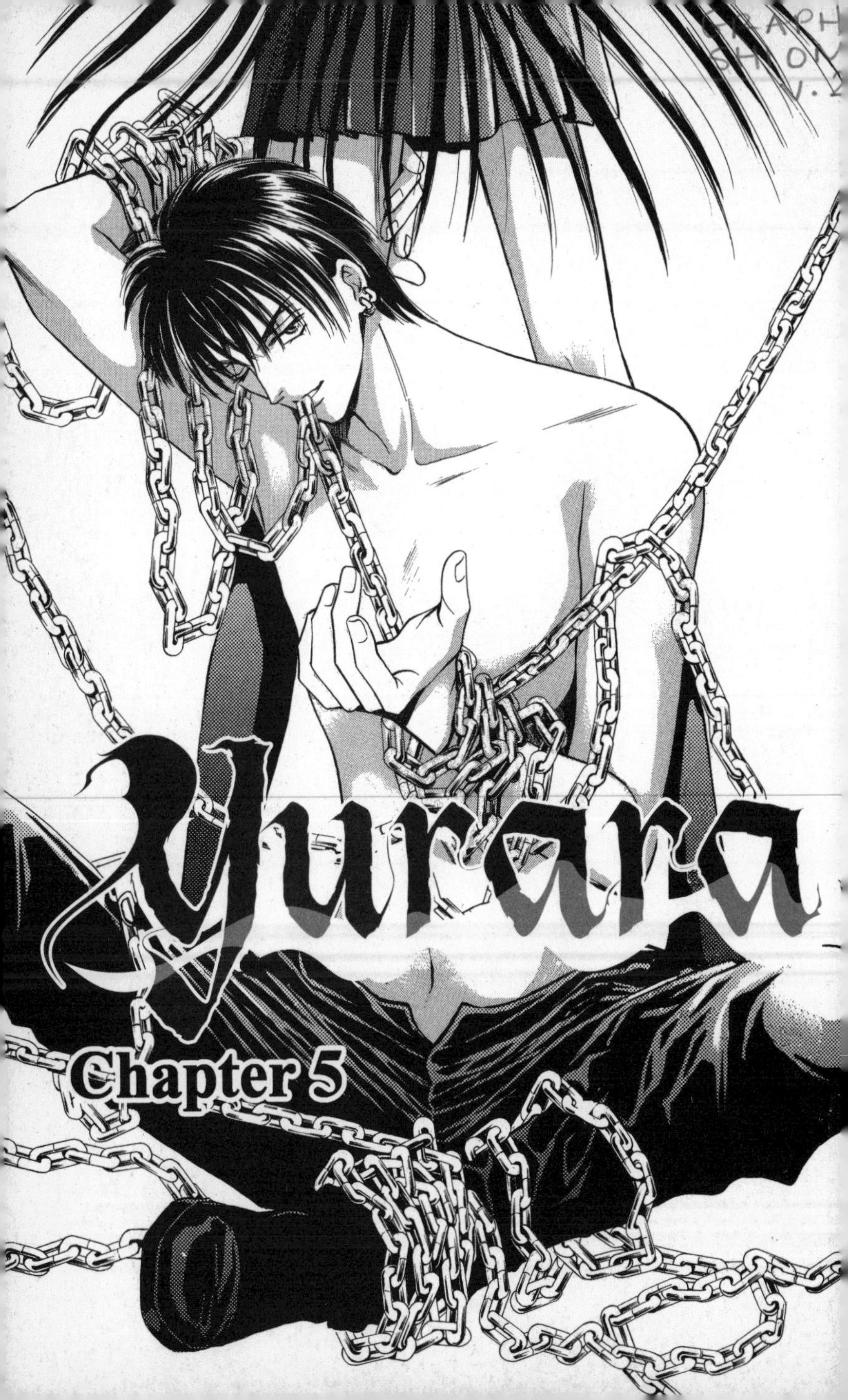
Yurara
Chapter 5

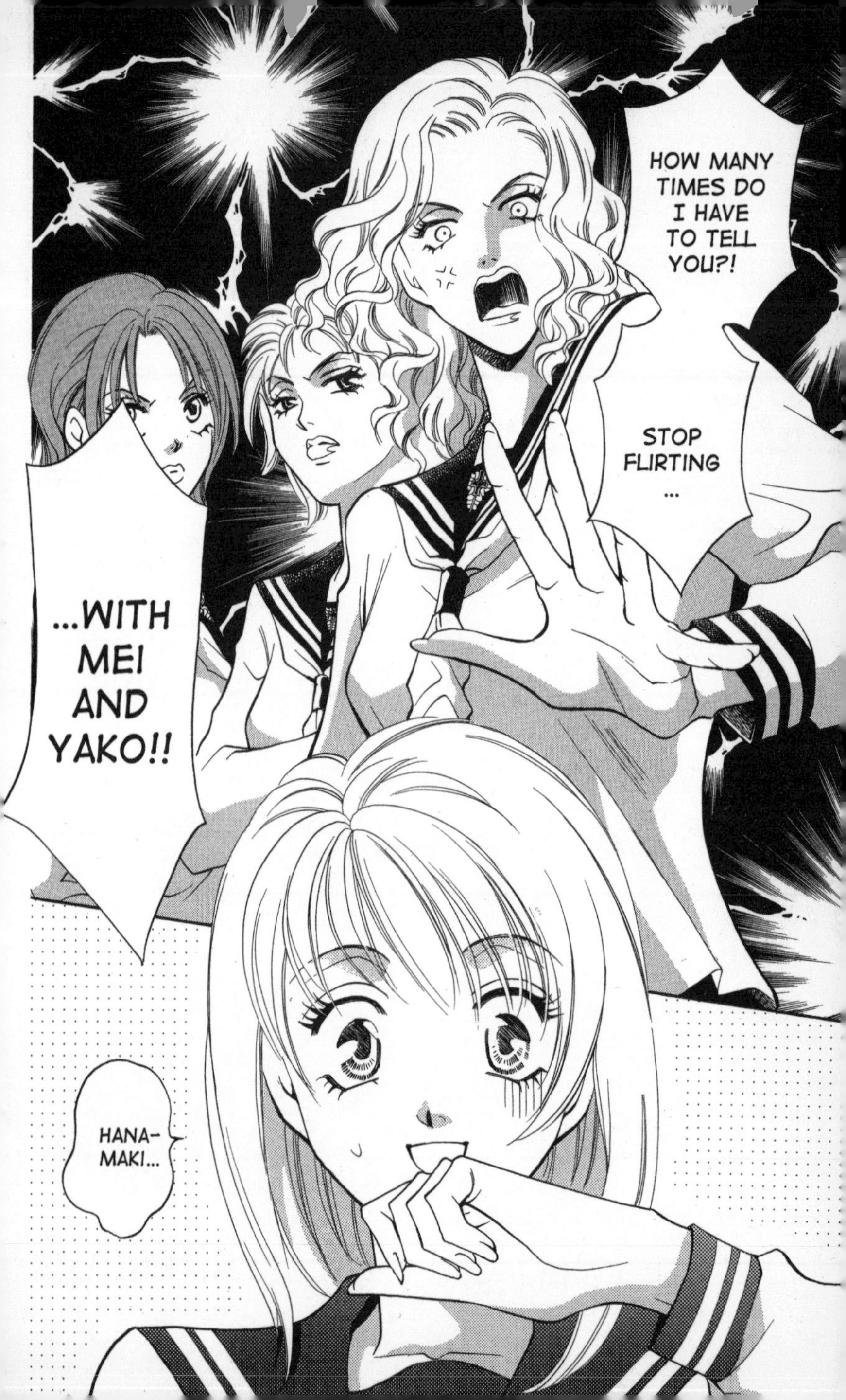
HOW MANY TIMES DO I HAVE TO TELL YOU?!
STOP FLIRTING ...
...WITH MEI AND YAKO!!
HANA-MAKI...

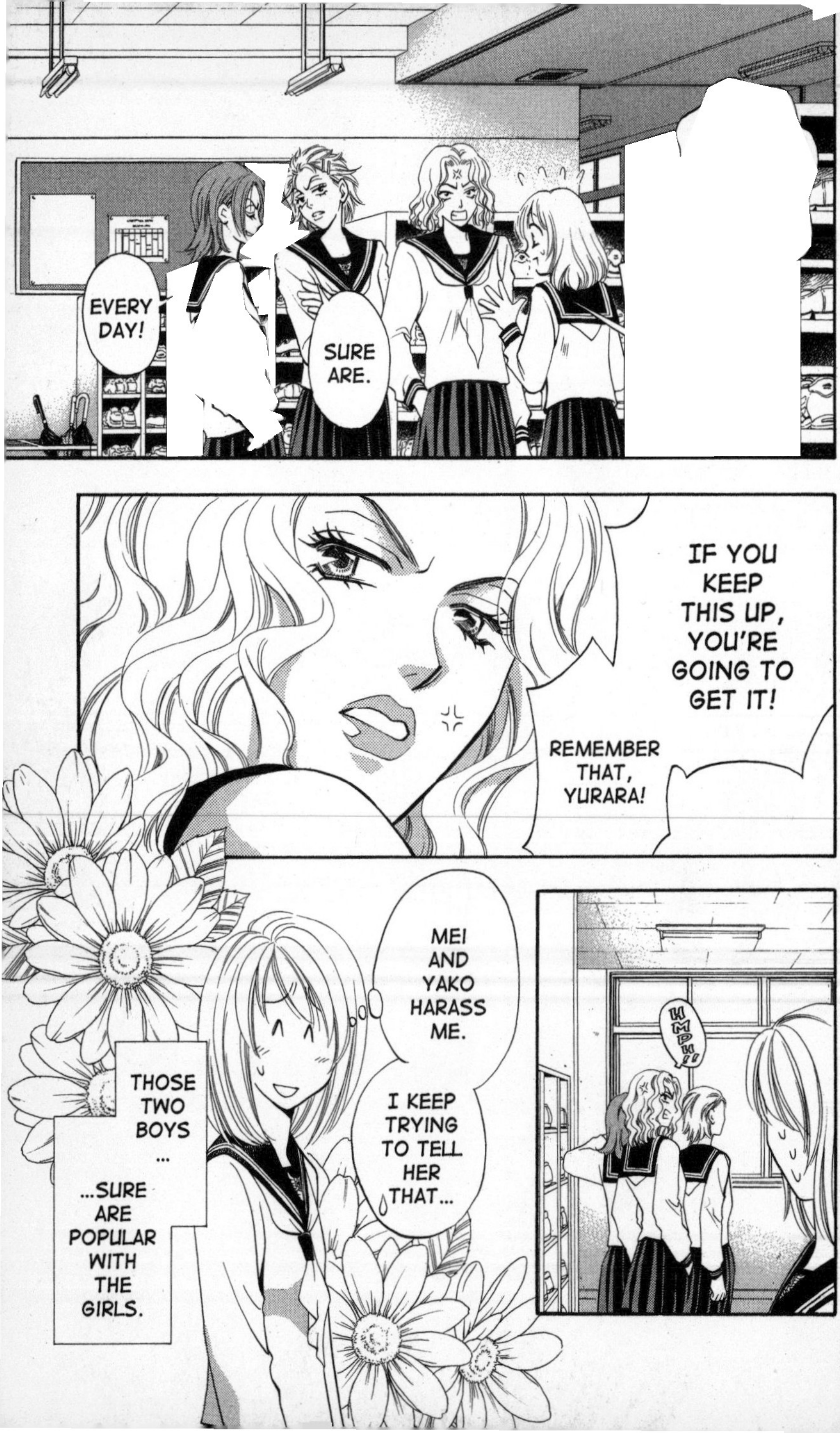

SURE ARE.
EVERY DAY!
IF YOU KEEP THIS UP, YOU'RE GOING TO GET IT!
REMEMBER THAT, YURARA!
HMPH!!
MEI AND YAKO HARASS ME.
I KEEP TRYING TO TELL HER THAT...
THOSE TWO BOYS ...
...SURE ARE POPULAR WITH THE GIRLS.

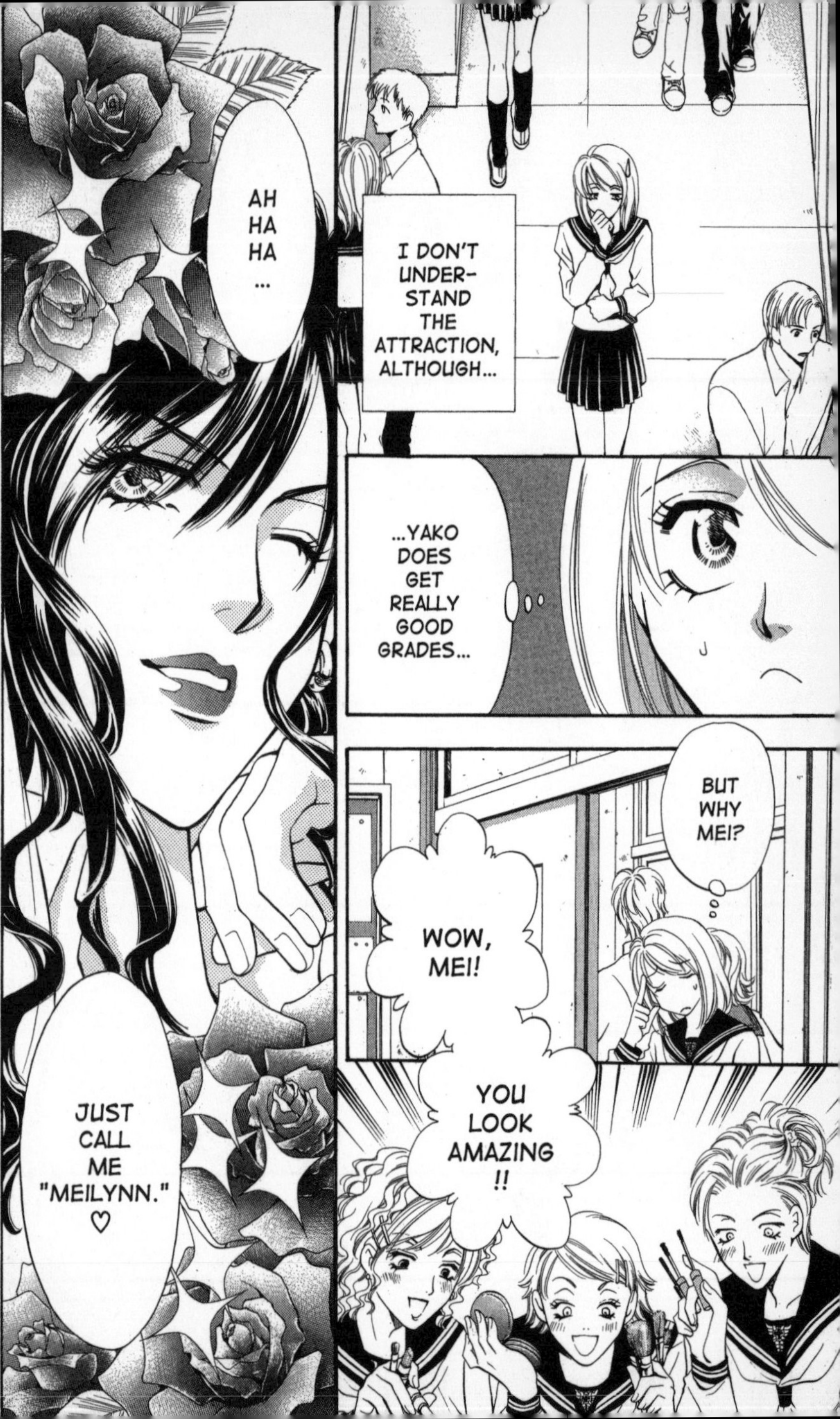
I DON'T UNDERSTAND THE ATTRACTION, ALTHOUGH...
...YAKO DOES GET REALLY GOOD GRADES...
BUT WHY MEI?
WOW, MEI!
YOU LOOK AMAZING !!
AH HA HA ...
JUST CALL ME "MEILYNN." ♡

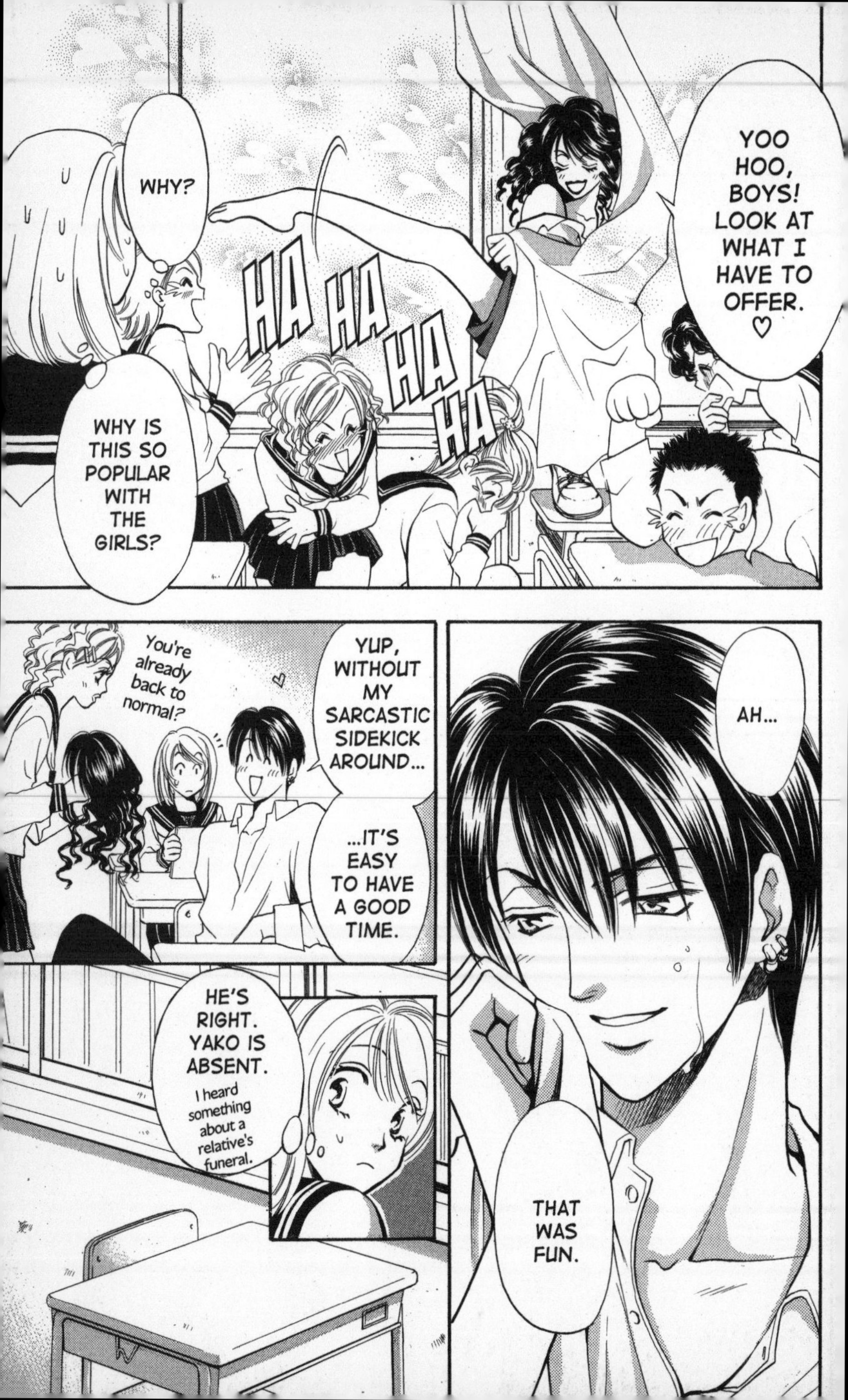
YOO HOO, BOYS! LOOK AT WHAT I HAVE TO OFFER. ♡
HA HA HA HA
WHY?
WHY IS THIS SO POPULAR WITH THE GIRLS?
AH...
THAT WAS FUN.
YUP, WITHOUT MY SARCASTIC SIDEKICK AROUND...
...IT'S EASY TO HAVE A GOOD TIME.
You're already back to normal?
HE'S RIGHT. YAKO IS ABSENT.
I heard something about a relative's funeral.

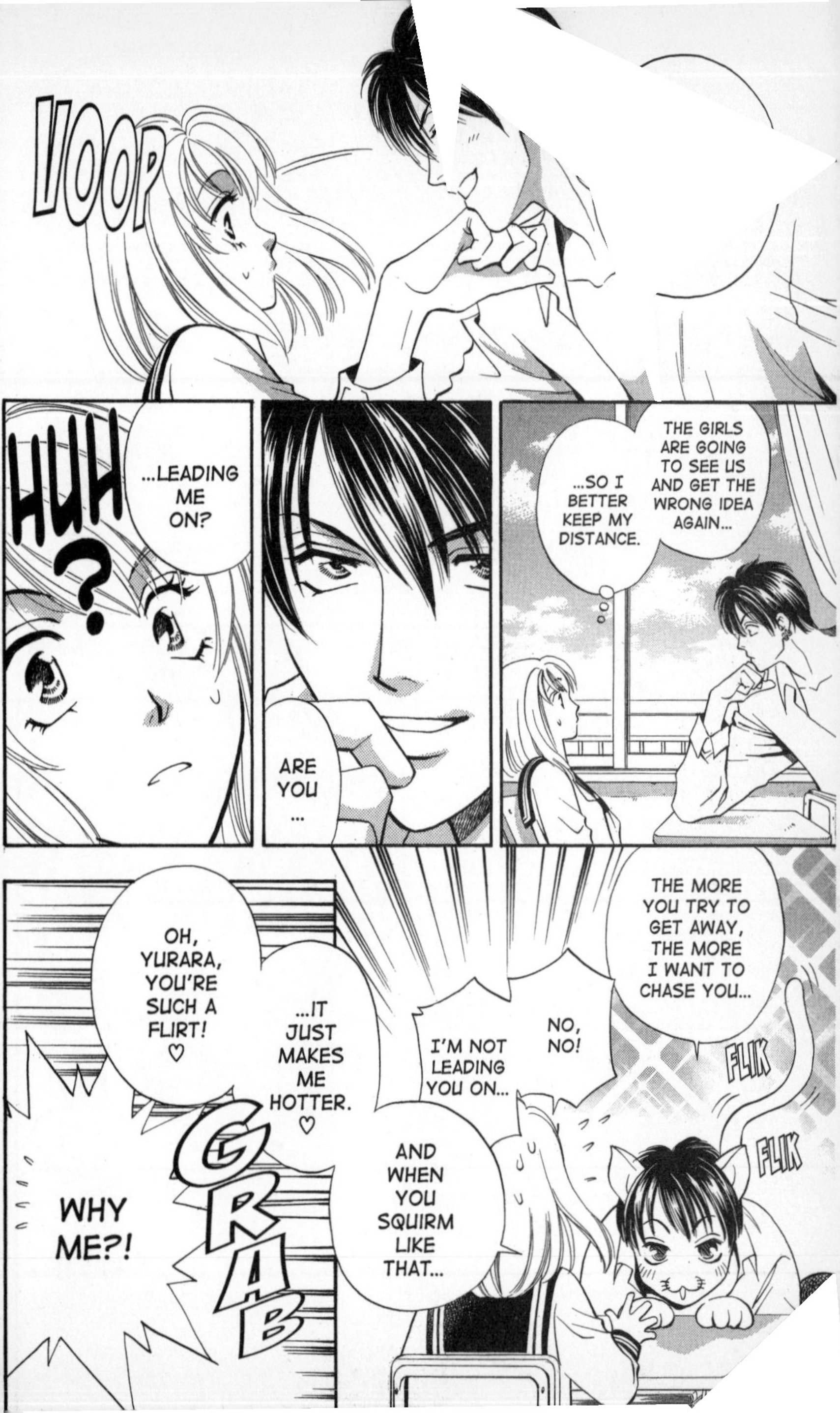
VOOP
THE GIRLS ARE GOING TO SEE US AND GET THE WRONG IDEA AGAIN...
...SO I BETTER KEEP MY DISTANCE.
ARE YOU ...
...LEADING ME ON?
HUH ?
THE MORE YOU TRY TO GET AWAY, THE MORE I WANT TO CHASE YOU...
FLIK
FLIK
NO, NO!
I'M NOT LEADING YOU ON...
AND WHEN YOU SQUIRM LIKE THAT...
...IT JUST MAKES ME HOTTER. ♡
OH, YURARA, YOU'RE SUCH A FLIRT! ♡
GRAB
WHY ME?!

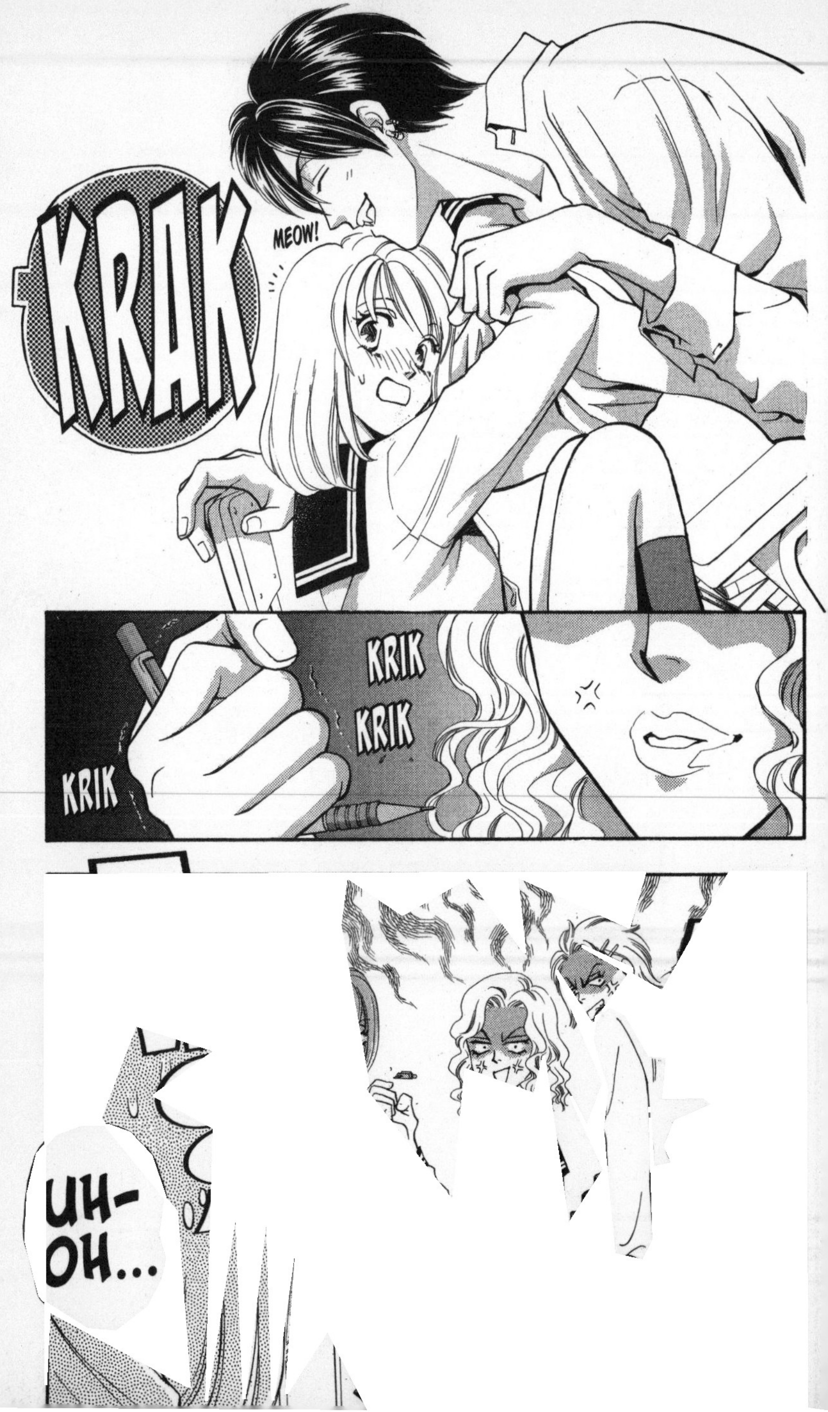
MEOW!
KRAK
KRIK
KRIK
KRIK
UH-OH...

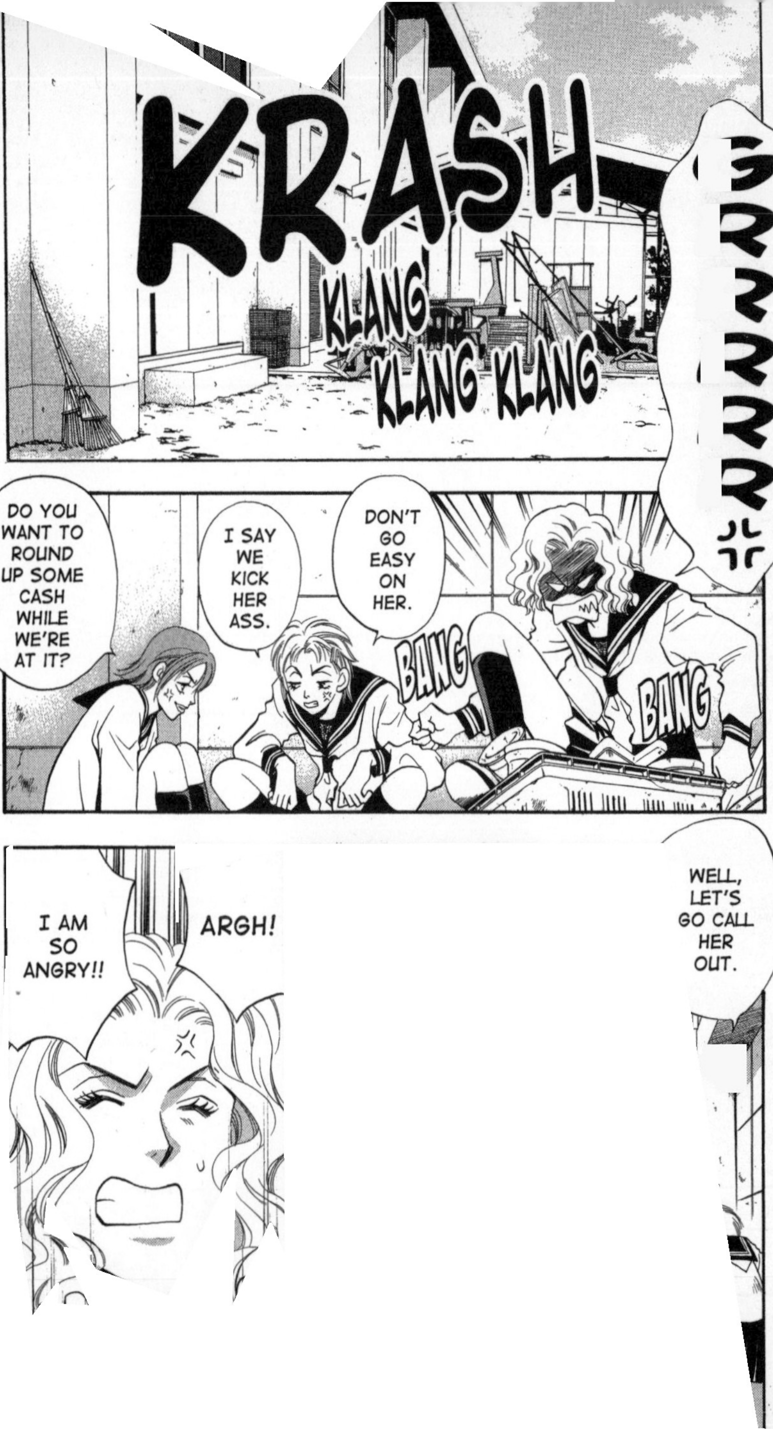
KRASH
KLANG
KLANG KLANG
GRRRRR
BANG
BANG
DON'T GO EASY ON HER.
I SAY WE KICK HER ASS.
DO YOU WANT TO ROUND UP SOME CASH WHILE WE'RE AT IT?
WELL, LET'S GO CALL HER OUT.
ARGH!
I AM SO ANGRY!!

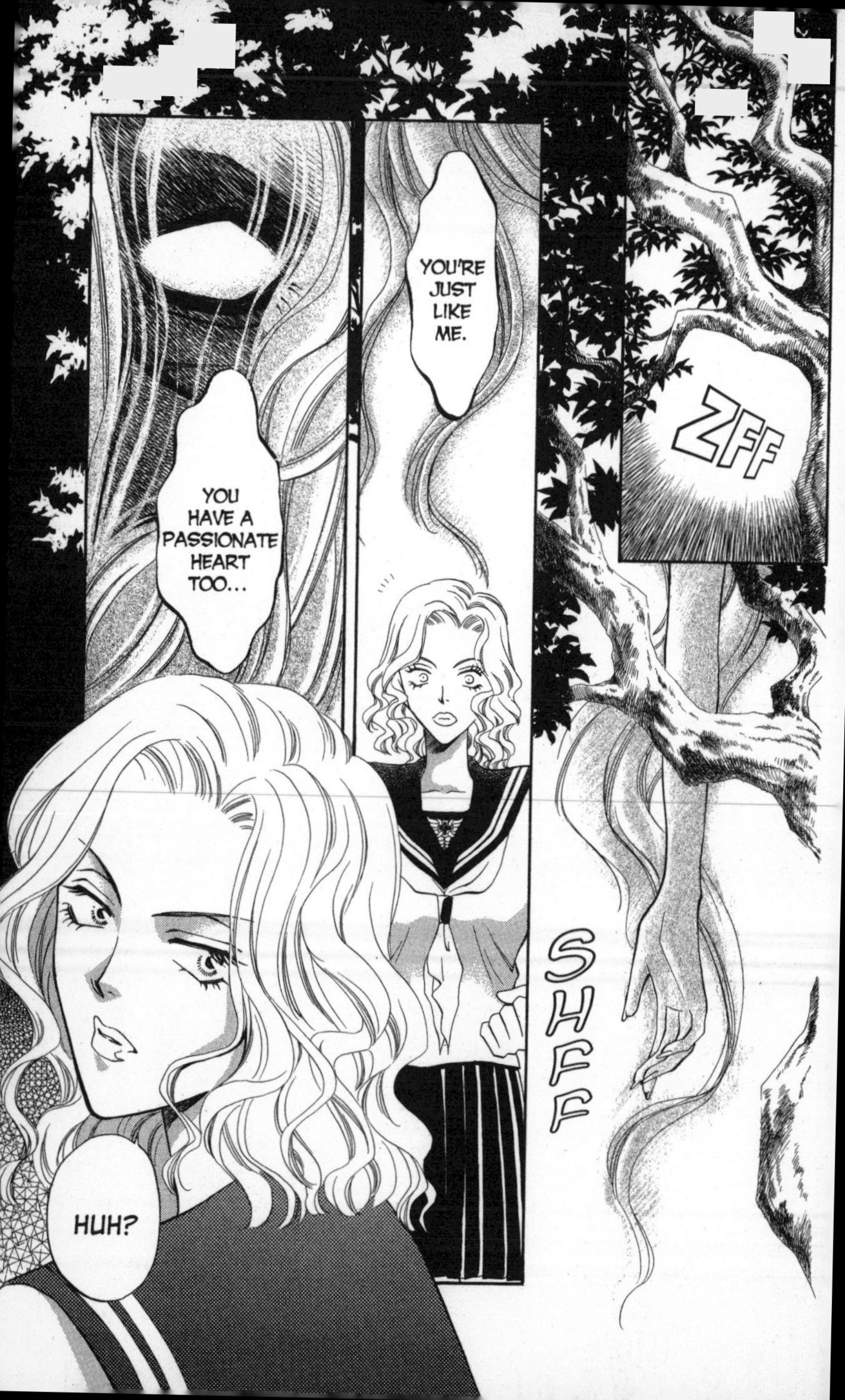
ZFF
YOU'RE JUST LIKE ME.
YOU HAVE A PASSIONATE HEART TOO...
SHFF
HUH?

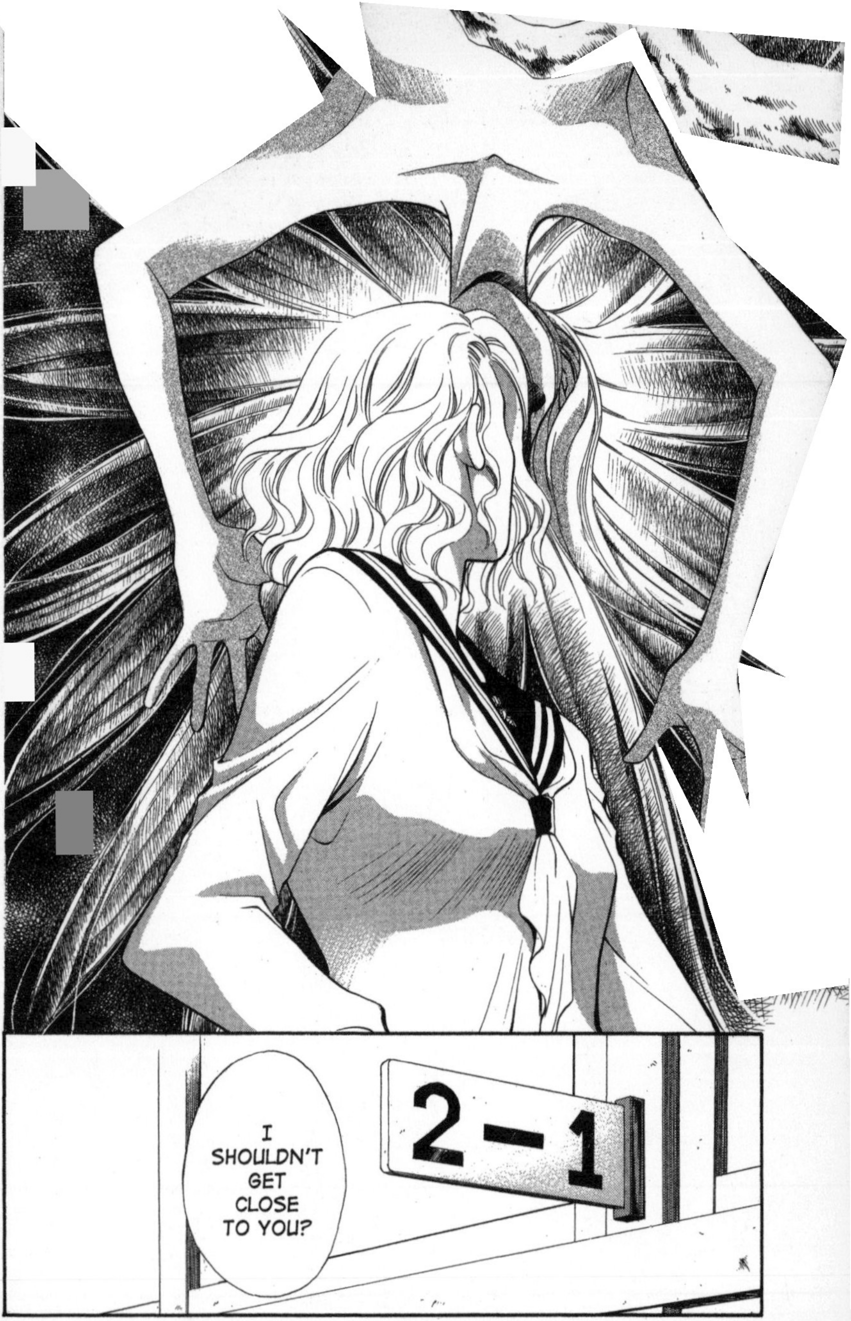
2-1
I SHOULDN'T GET CLOSE TO YOU?

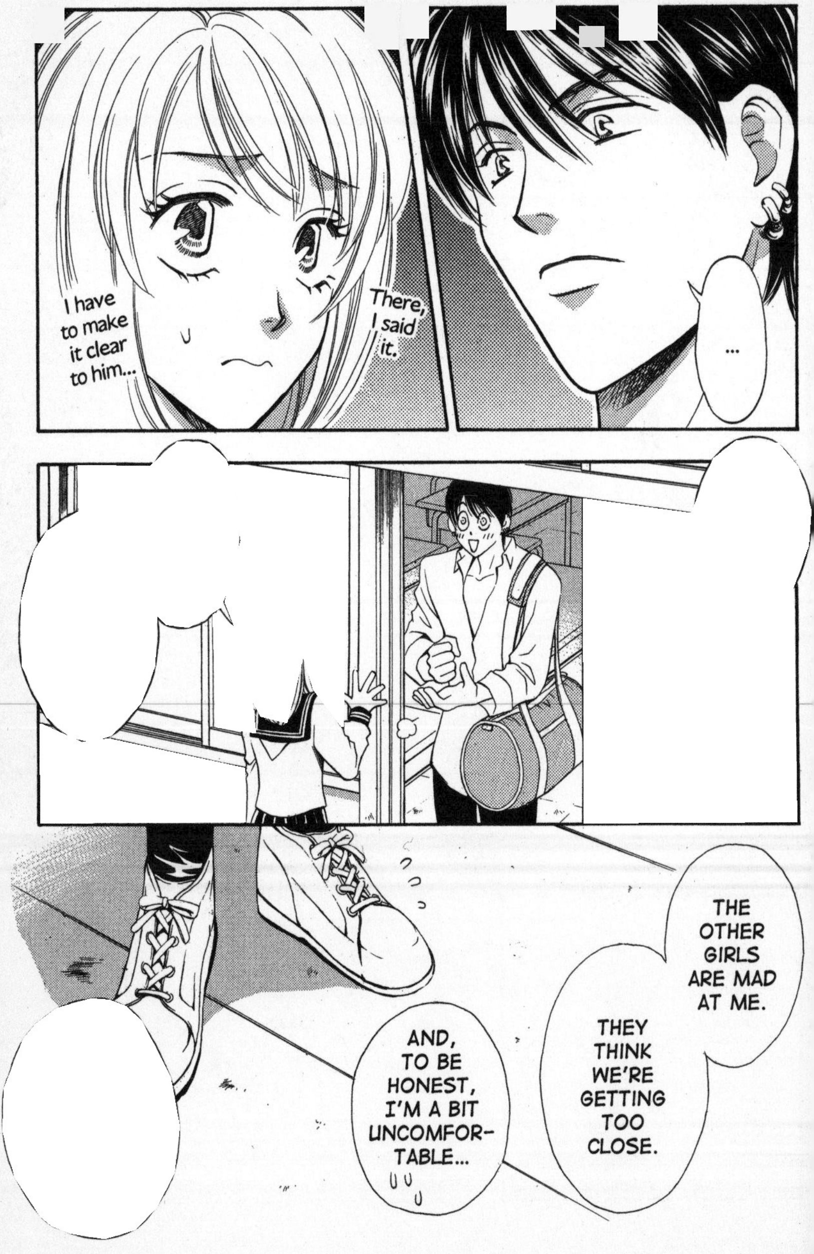
...
There, I said it.
I have to make it clear to him...
THE OTHER GIRLS ARE MAD AT ME.
THEY THINK WE'RE GETTING TOO CLOSE.
AND, TO BE HONEST, I'M A BIT UNCOMFOR-TABLE...

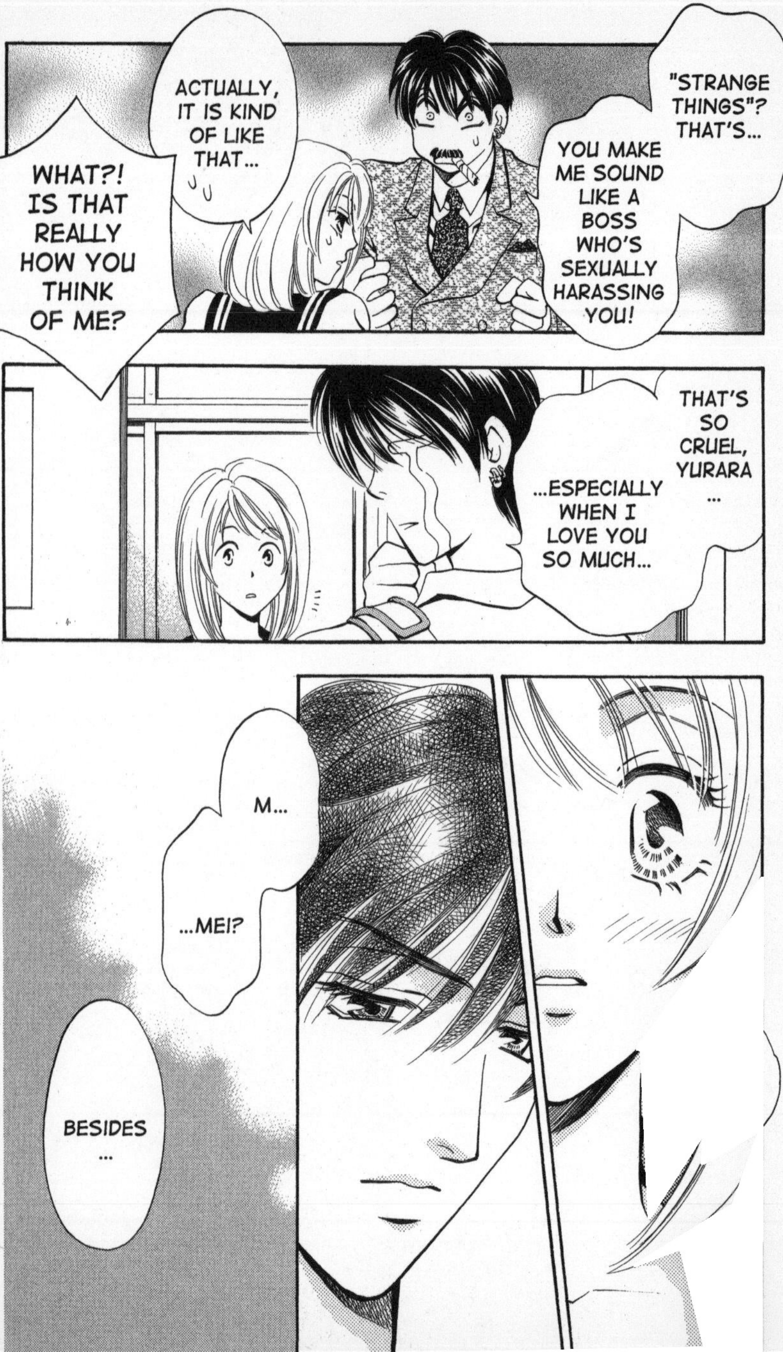
"STRANGE THINGS"? THAT'S...
YOU MAKE ME SOUND LIKE A BOSS WHO'S SEXUALLY HARASSING YOU!
ACTUALLY, IT IS KIND OF LIKE THAT...
WHAT?! IS THAT REALLY HOW YOU THINK OF ME?
THAT'S SO CRUEL, YURARA...
...ESPECIALLY WHEN I LOVE YOU SO MUCH...
M...
...MEI?
BESIDES...

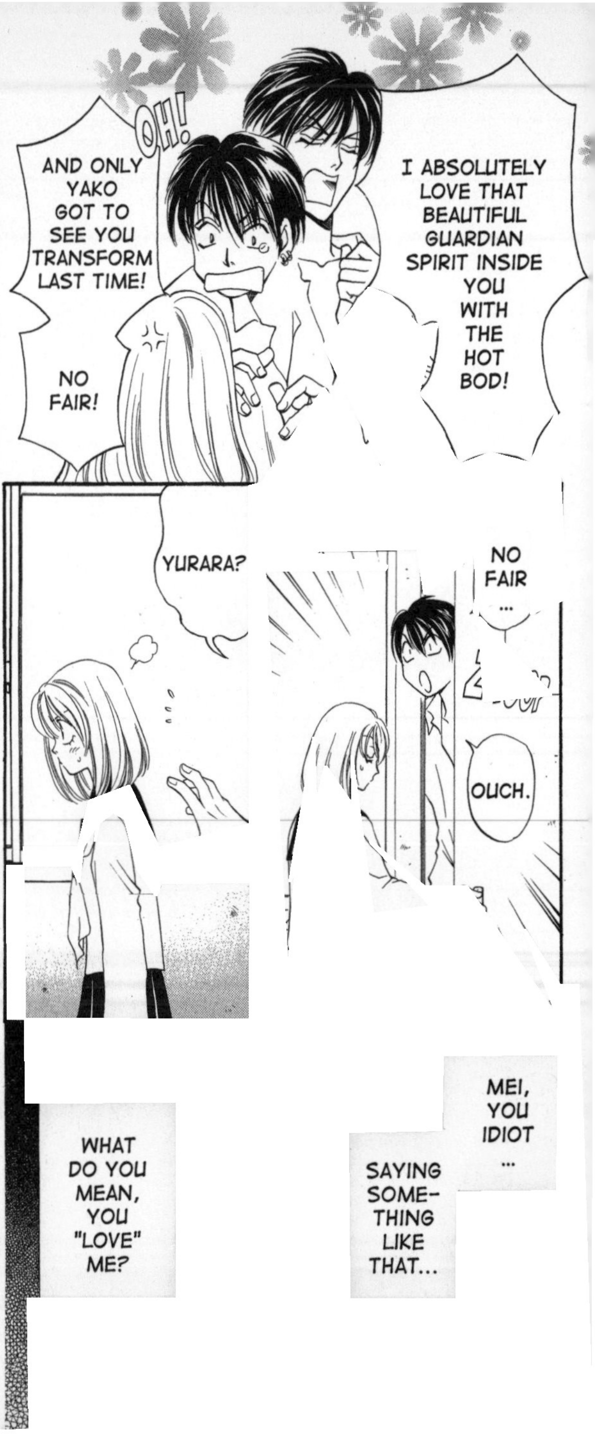
I ABSOLUTELY LOVE THAT BEAUTIFUL GUARDIAN SPIRIT INSIDE YOU WITH THE HOT BOD!
OH!
AND ONLY YAKO GOT TO SEE YOU TRANSFORM LAST TIME!
NO FAIR!
NO FAIR...
OUCH.
YURARA?
MEI, YOU IDIOT...
SAYING SOMETHING LIKE THAT...
WHAT DO YOU MEAN, YOU "LOVE" ME?

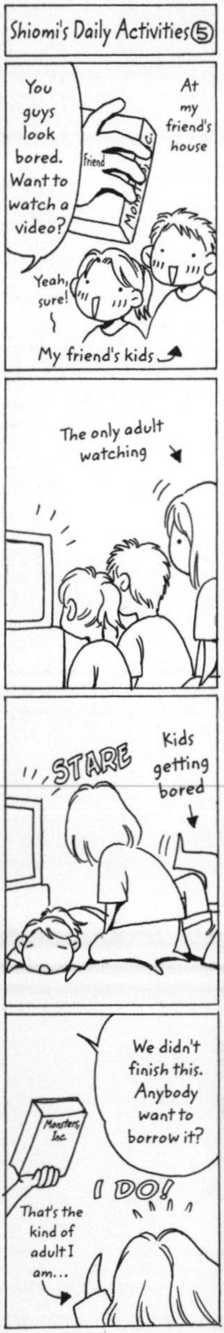
Shiomi's Daily Activities ⑤
At my friend's house
You guys look bored. Want to watch a video?
Yeah, sure!
My friend's kids
The only adult watching
STARE
Kids getting bored
We didn't finish this. Anybody want to borrow it?
Monsters, Inc.
I DO!
That's the kind of adult I am...

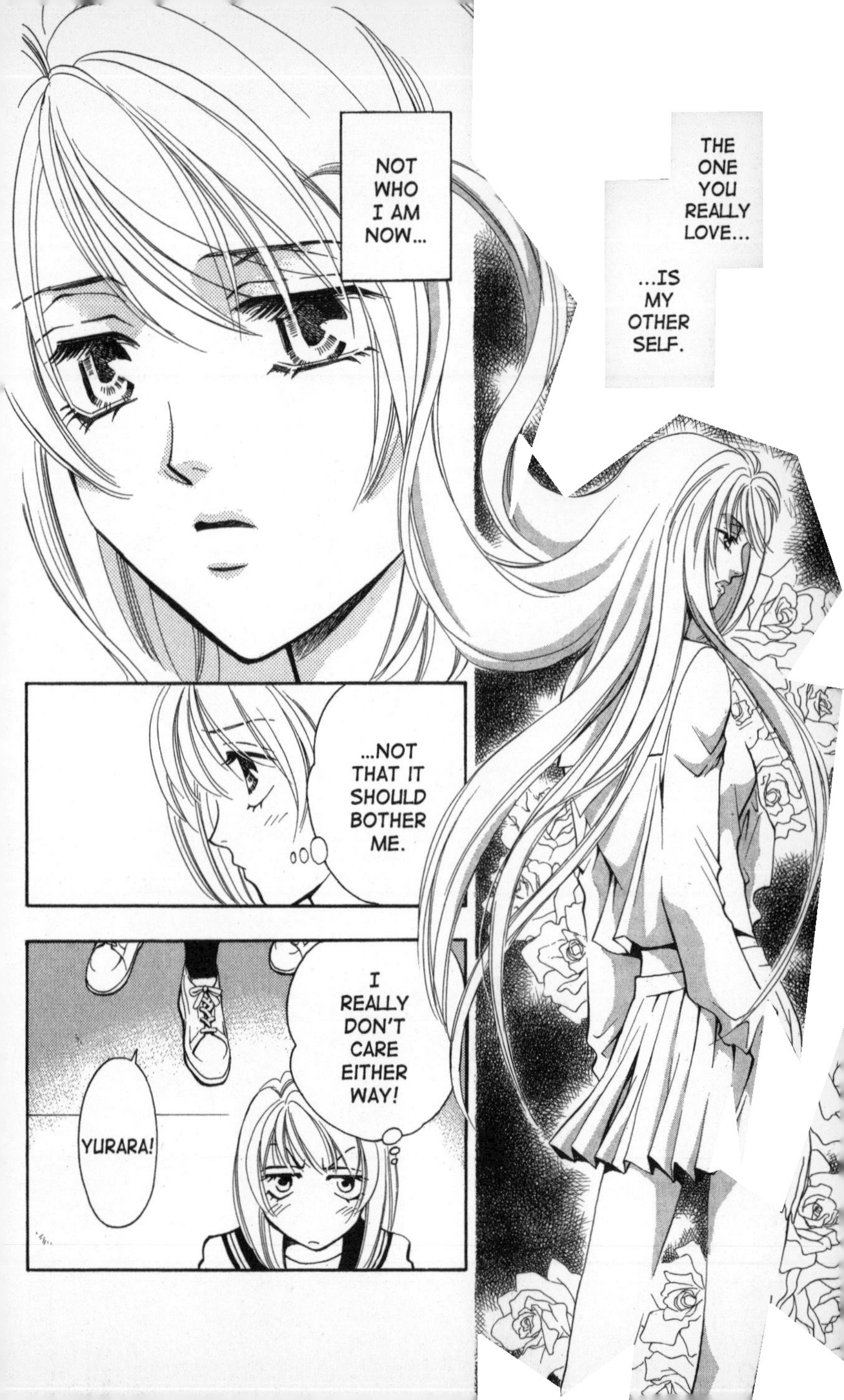
THE ONE YOU REALLY LOVE...
...IS MY OTHER SELF.
NOT WHO I AM NOW...
...NOT THAT IT SHOULD BOTHER ME.
I REALLY DON'T CARE EITHER WAY!
YURARA!

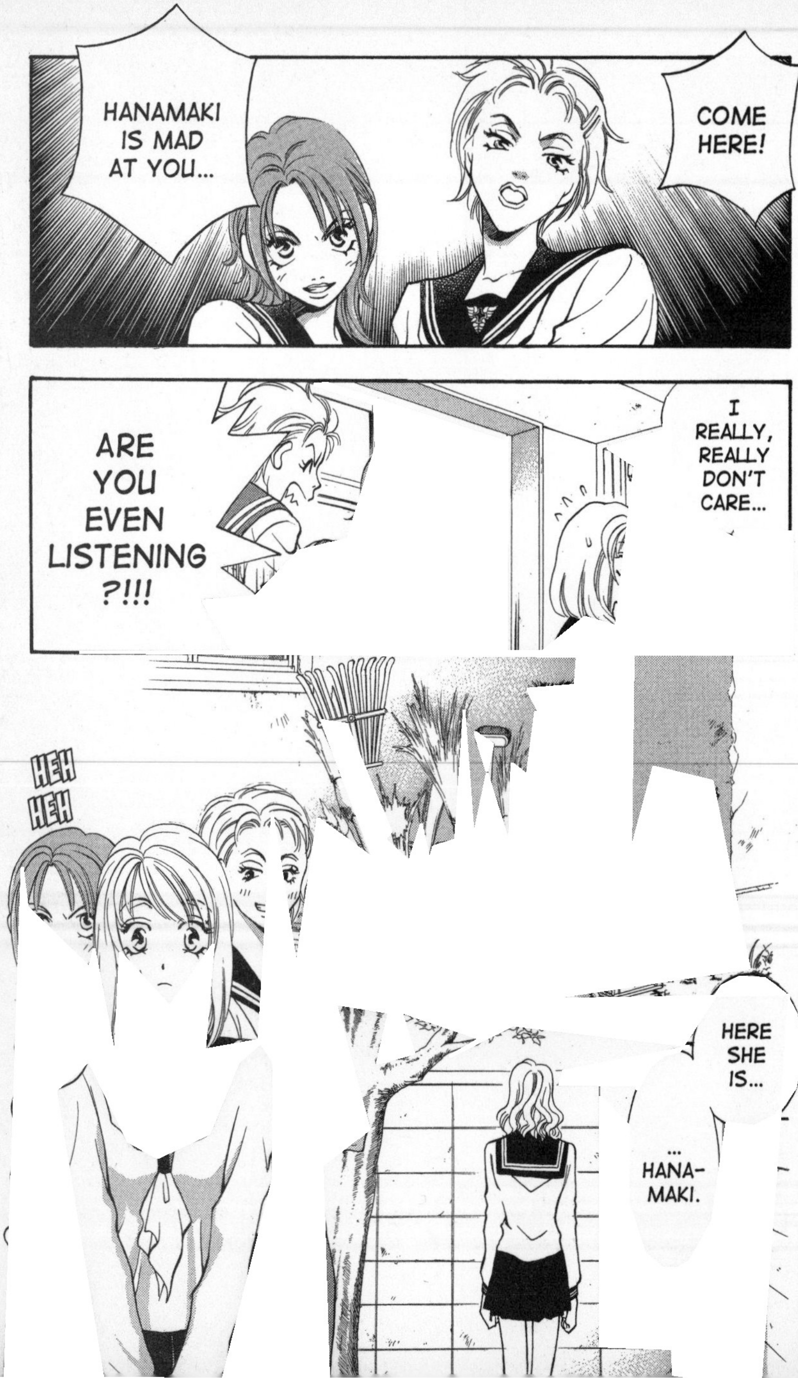
COME HERE!
HANAMAKI IS MAD AT YOU...
I REALLY, REALLY DON'T CARE...
ARE YOU EVEN LISTENING ?!!!
HERE SHE IS...
...HANA-MAKI.
HEH HEH

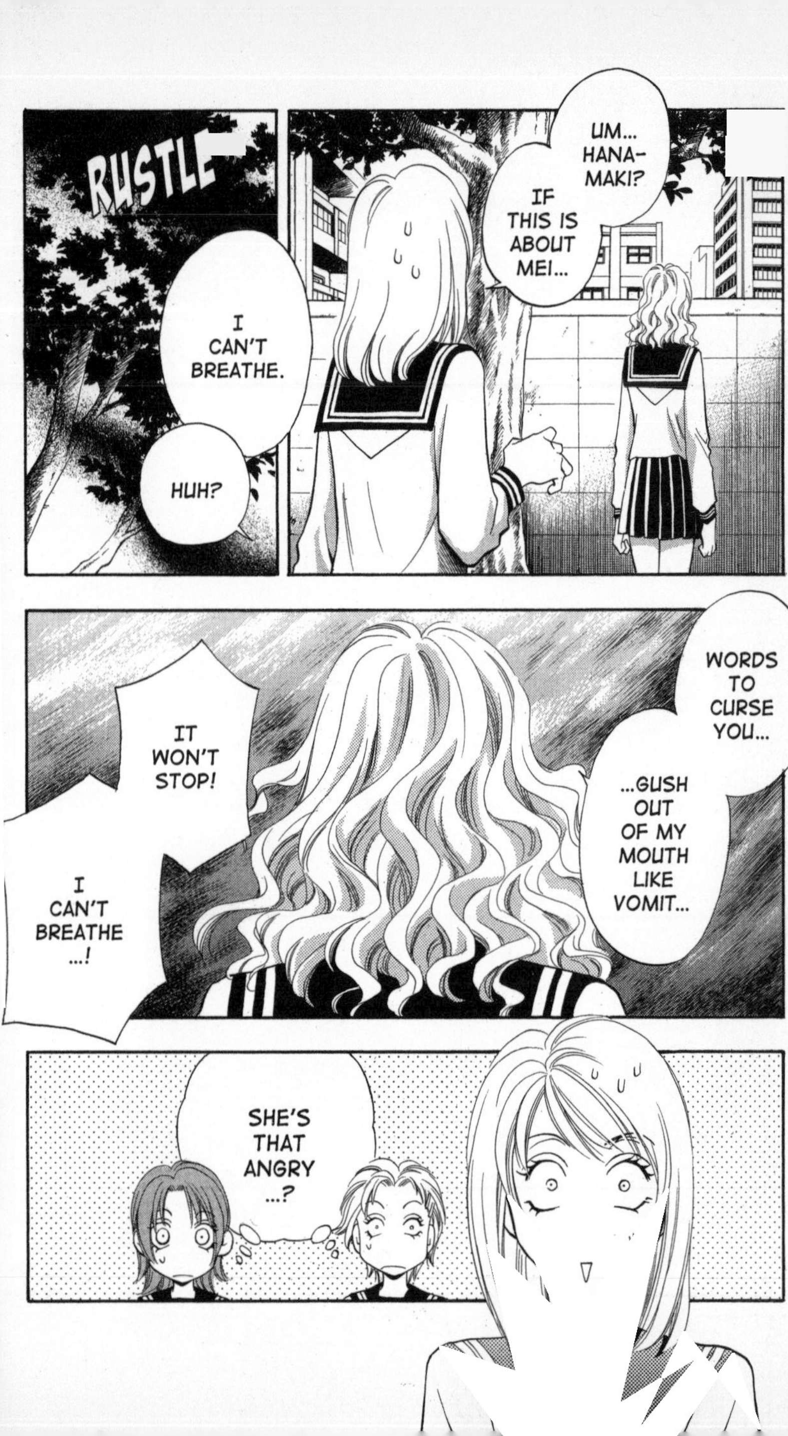
UM... HANA-MAKI?
IF THIS IS ABOUT MEI...
RUSTLE
I CAN'T BREATHE.
HUH?
WORDS TO CURSE YOU...
...GUSH OUT OF MY MOUTH LIKE VOMIT...
IT WON'T STOP!
I CAN'T BREATHE...!
SHE'S THAT ANGRY...?

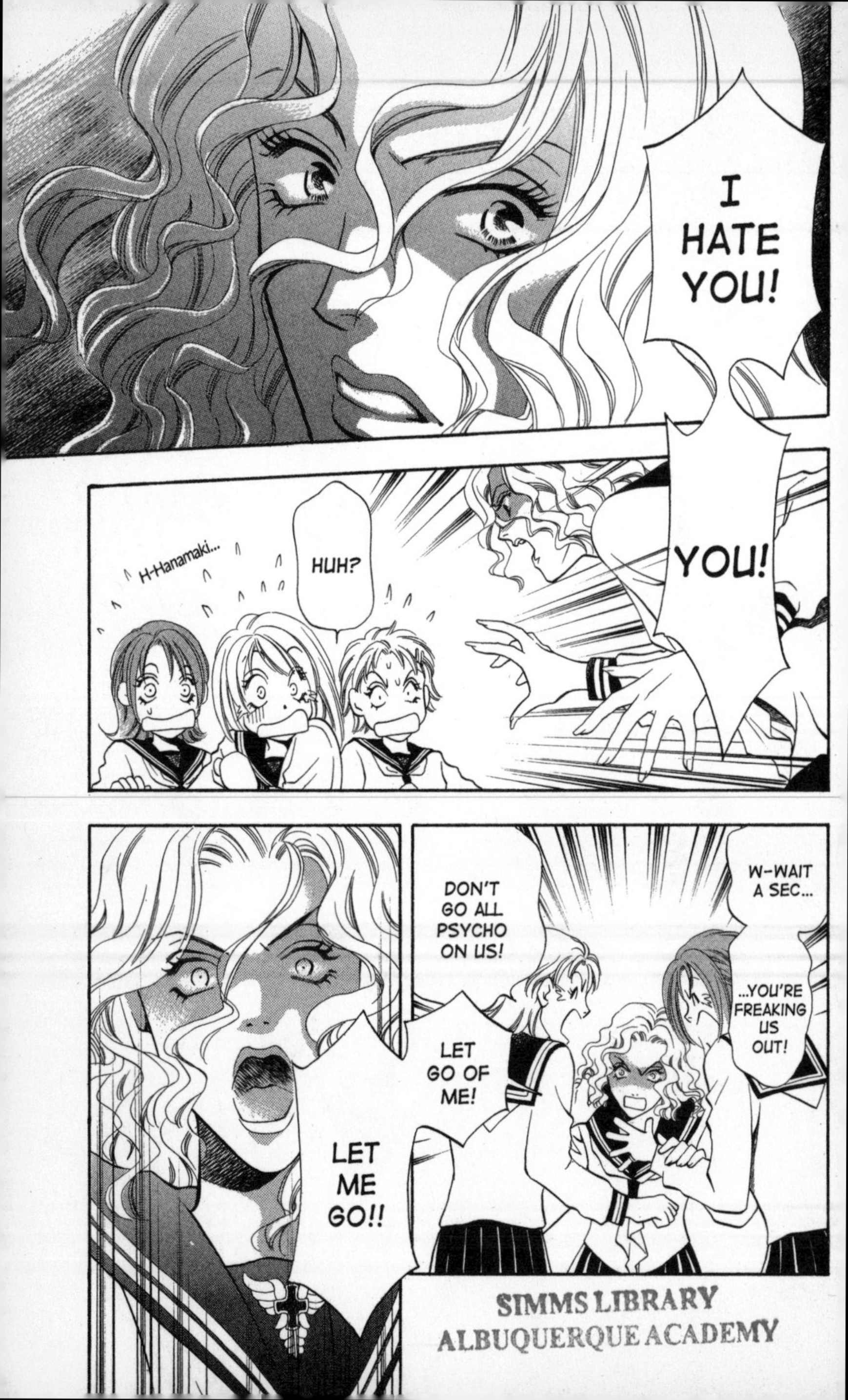
I HATE YOU!
YOU!
HUH?
H-Hanamaki...
W-WAIT A SEC...
...YOU'RE FREAKING US OUT!
DON'T GO ALL PSYCHO ON US!
LET GO OF ME!
LET ME GO!!

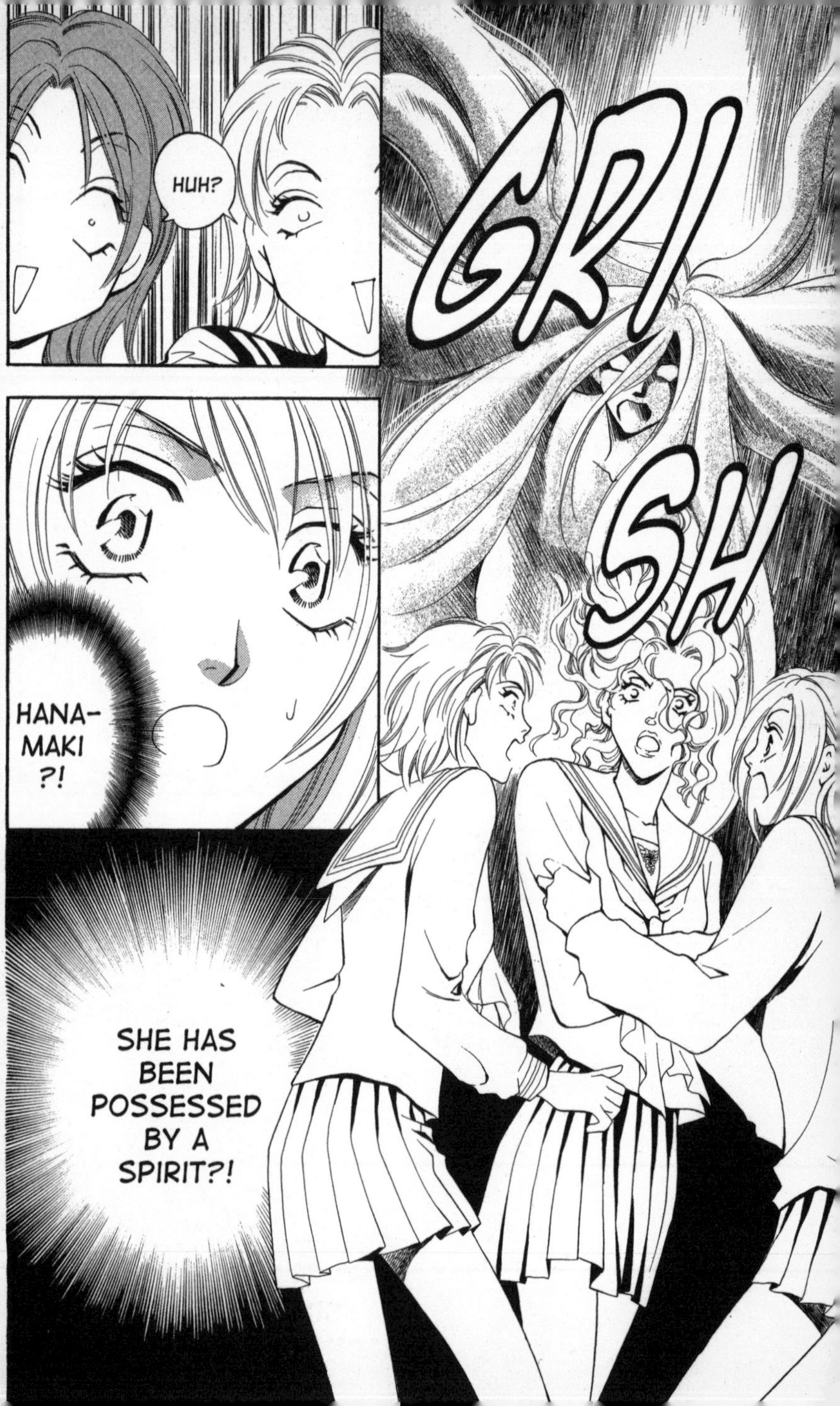
GRISH
HUH?
HANA-MAKI?!
SHE HAS BEEN POSSESSED BY A SPIRIT?!

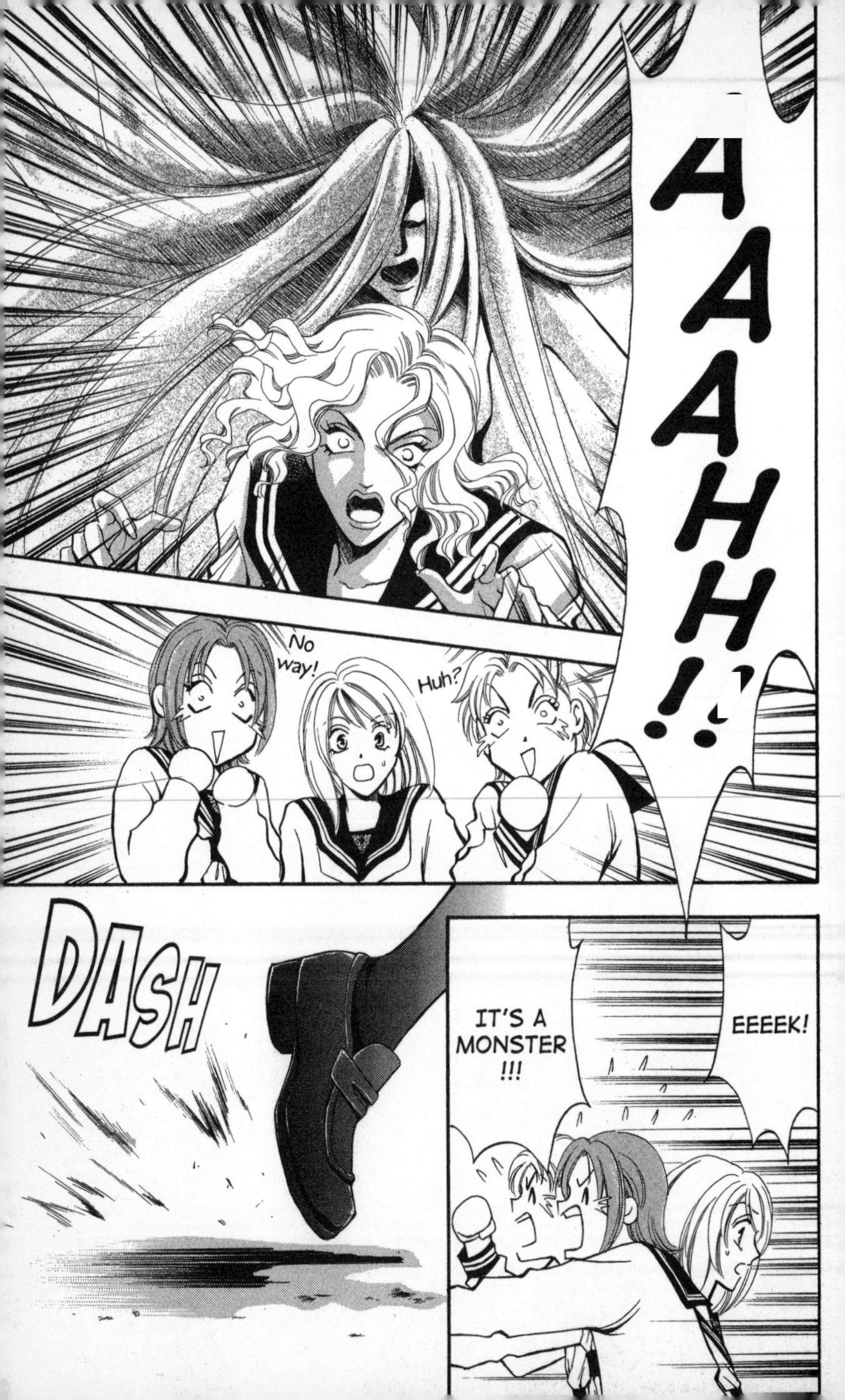
AAAHH!!!
Huh?
No way!
EEEEK!
IT'S A MONSTER !!!
DASH

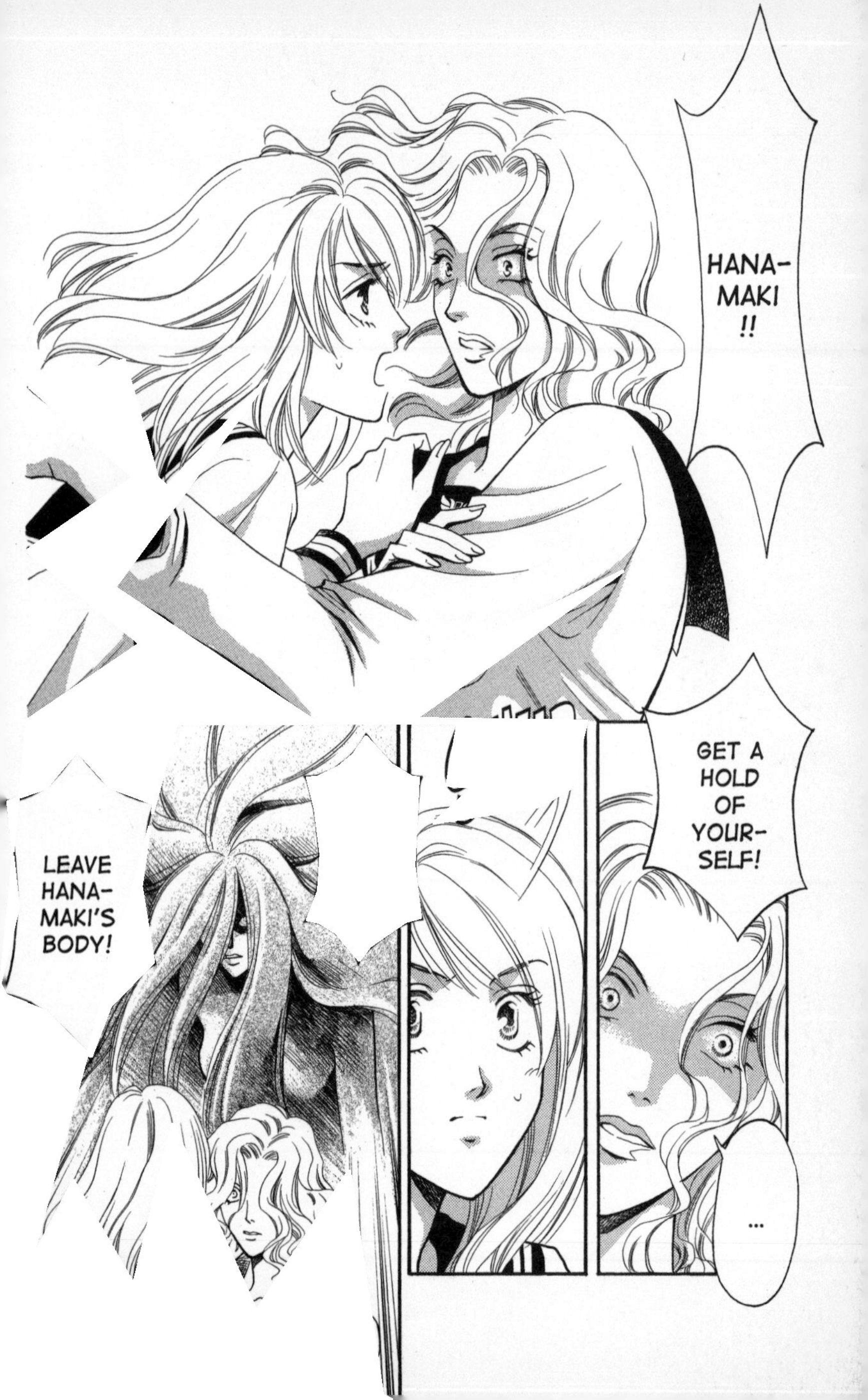
HANA-MAKI !!
GET A HOLD OF YOUR-SELF!
...
LEAVE HANA-MAKI'S BODY!

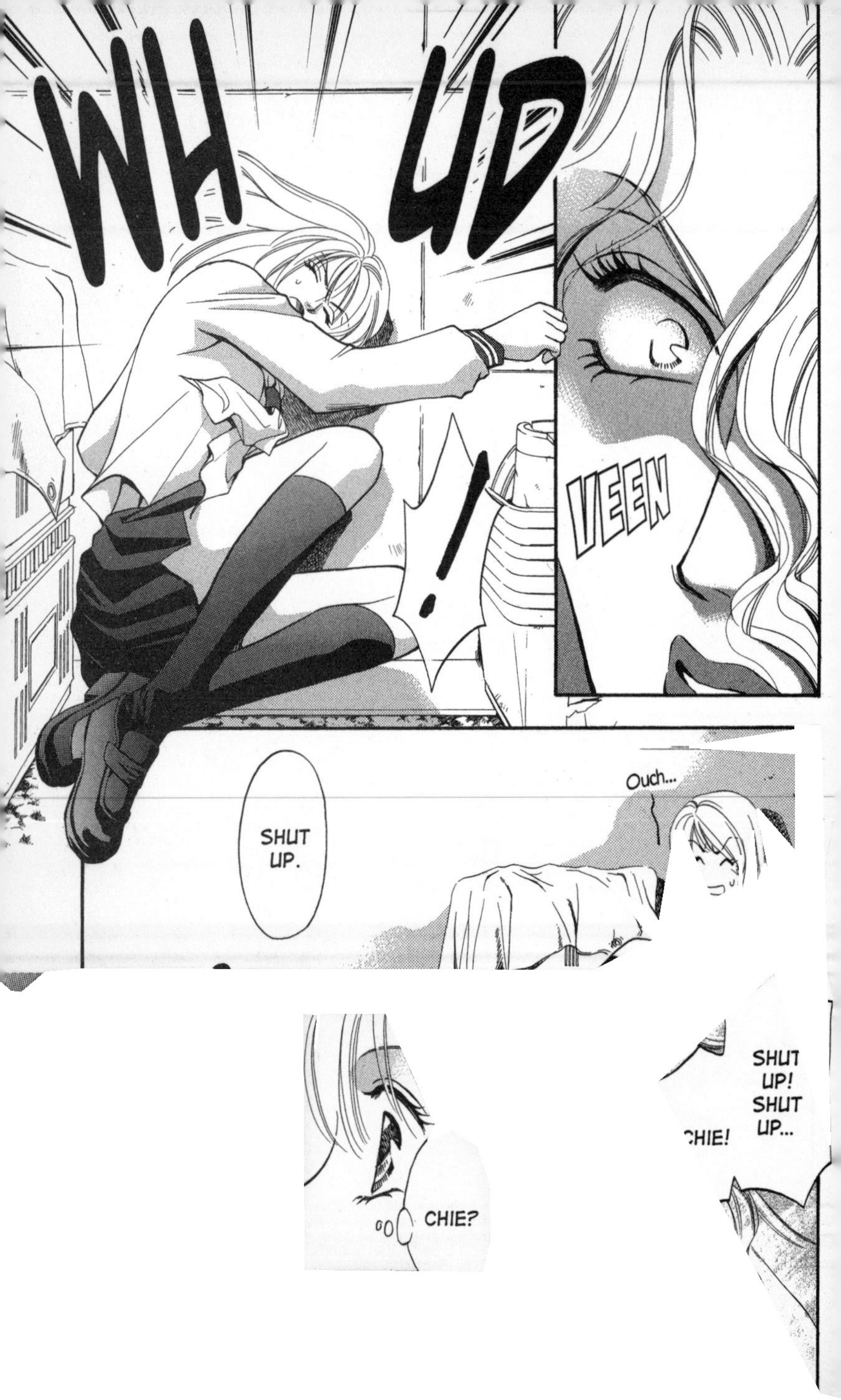
VEEN
WHUD
!
Ouch...
SHUT UP.
SHUT UP! SHUT UP...
CHIE!
CHIE?

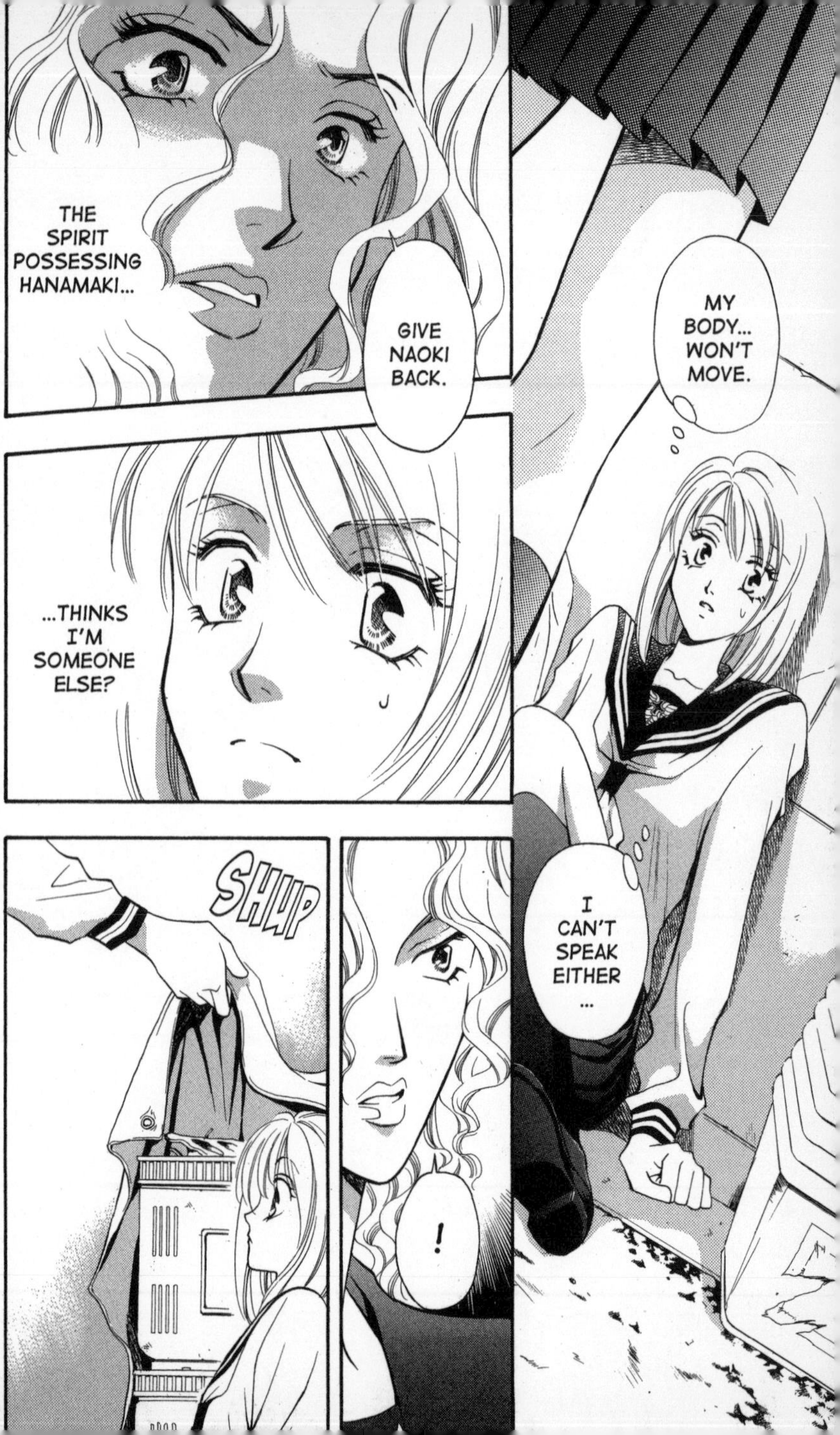
MY BODY... WON'T MOVE.
I CAN'T SPEAK EITHER...
GIVE NAOKI BACK.
THE SPIRIT POSSESSING HANAMAKI...
...THINKS I'M SOMEONE ELSE?
!
SHUP

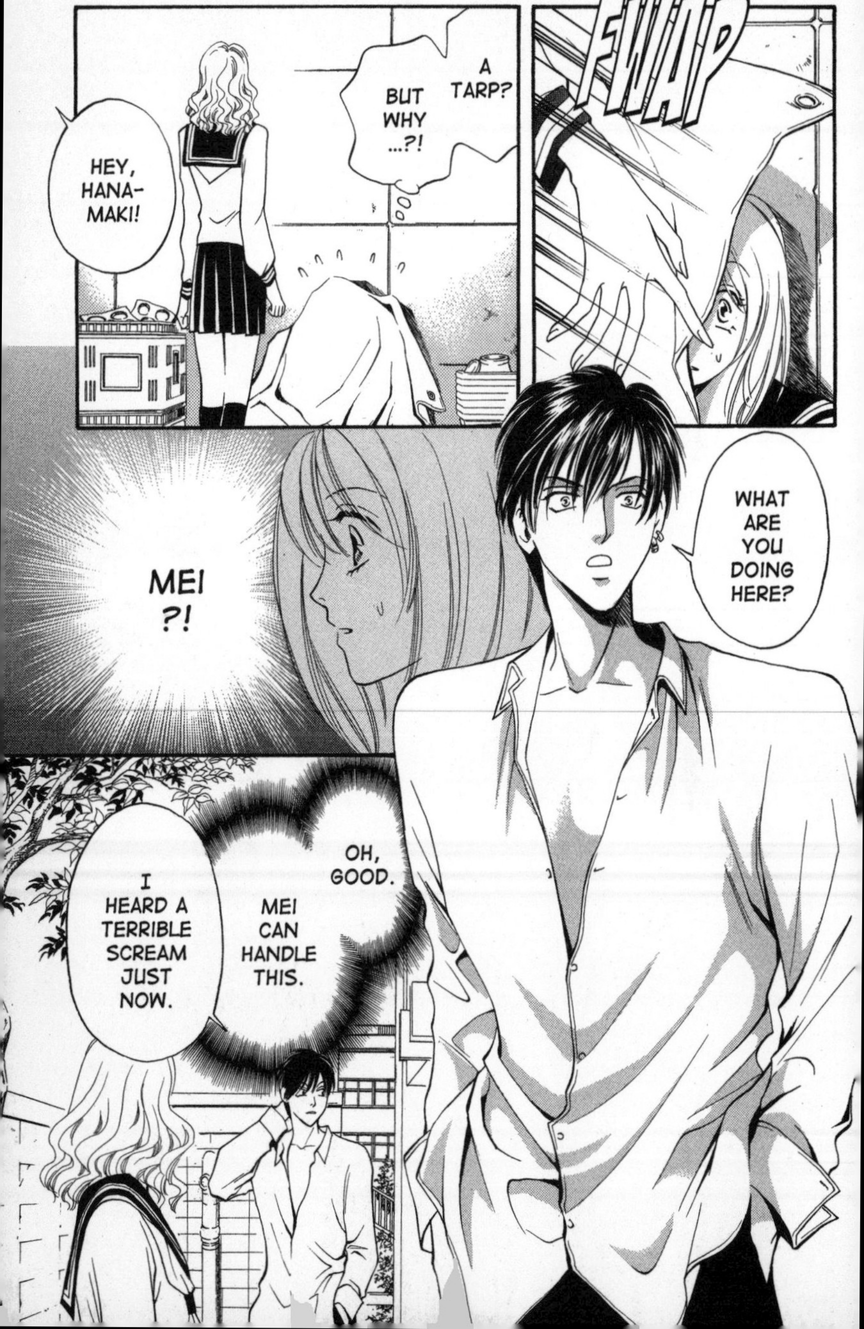
FWAP
A TARP?
BUT WHY ...?!
HEY, HANA-MAKI!
WHAT ARE YOU DOING HERE?
MEI ?!
OH, GOOD.
MEI CAN HANDLE THIS.
I HEARD A TERRIBLE SCREAM JUST NOW.

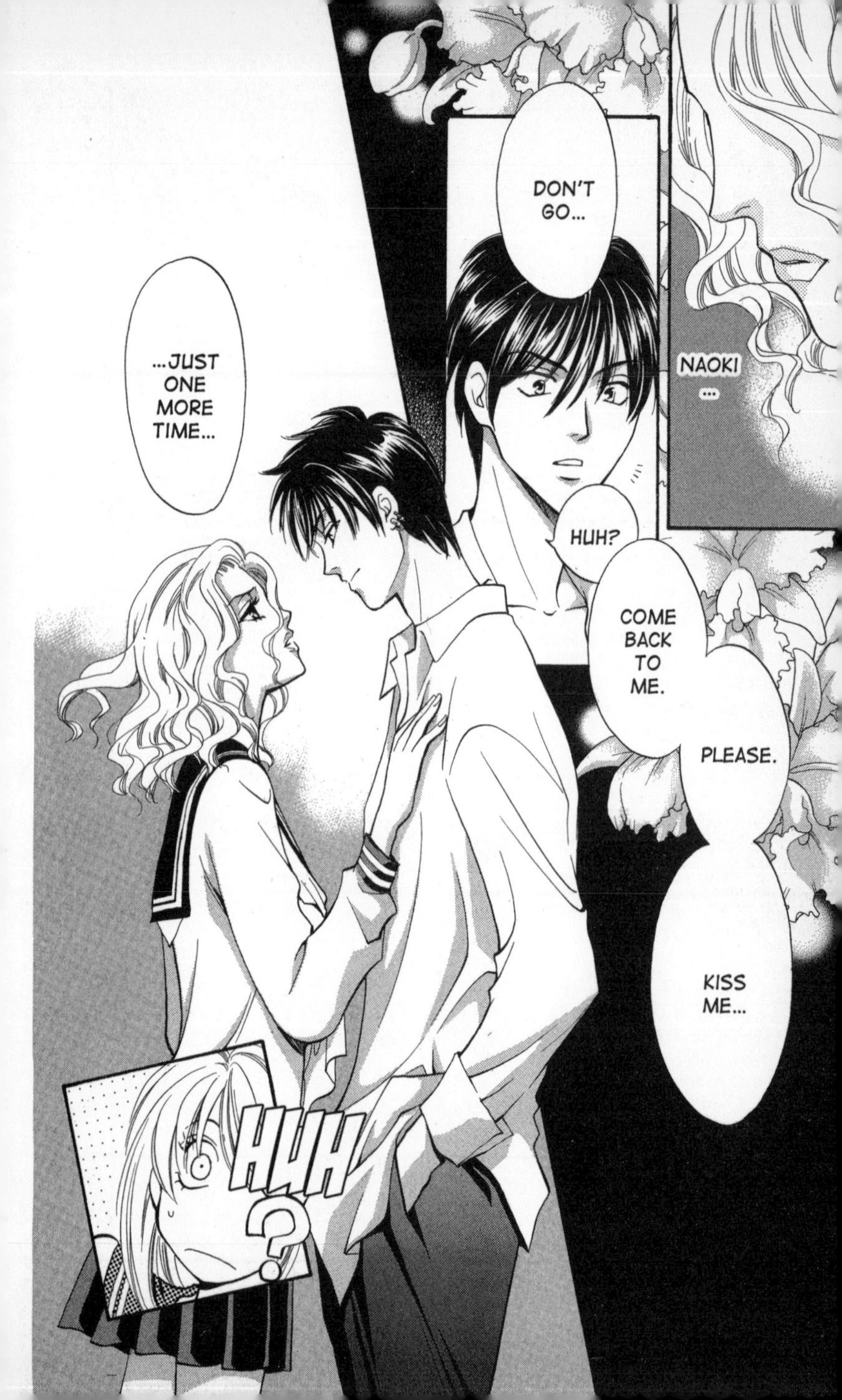

NAOKI ...
DON'T GO...
HUH?
COME BACK TO ME.
PLEASE.
KISS ME...
...JUST ONE MORE TIME...
HUH ?

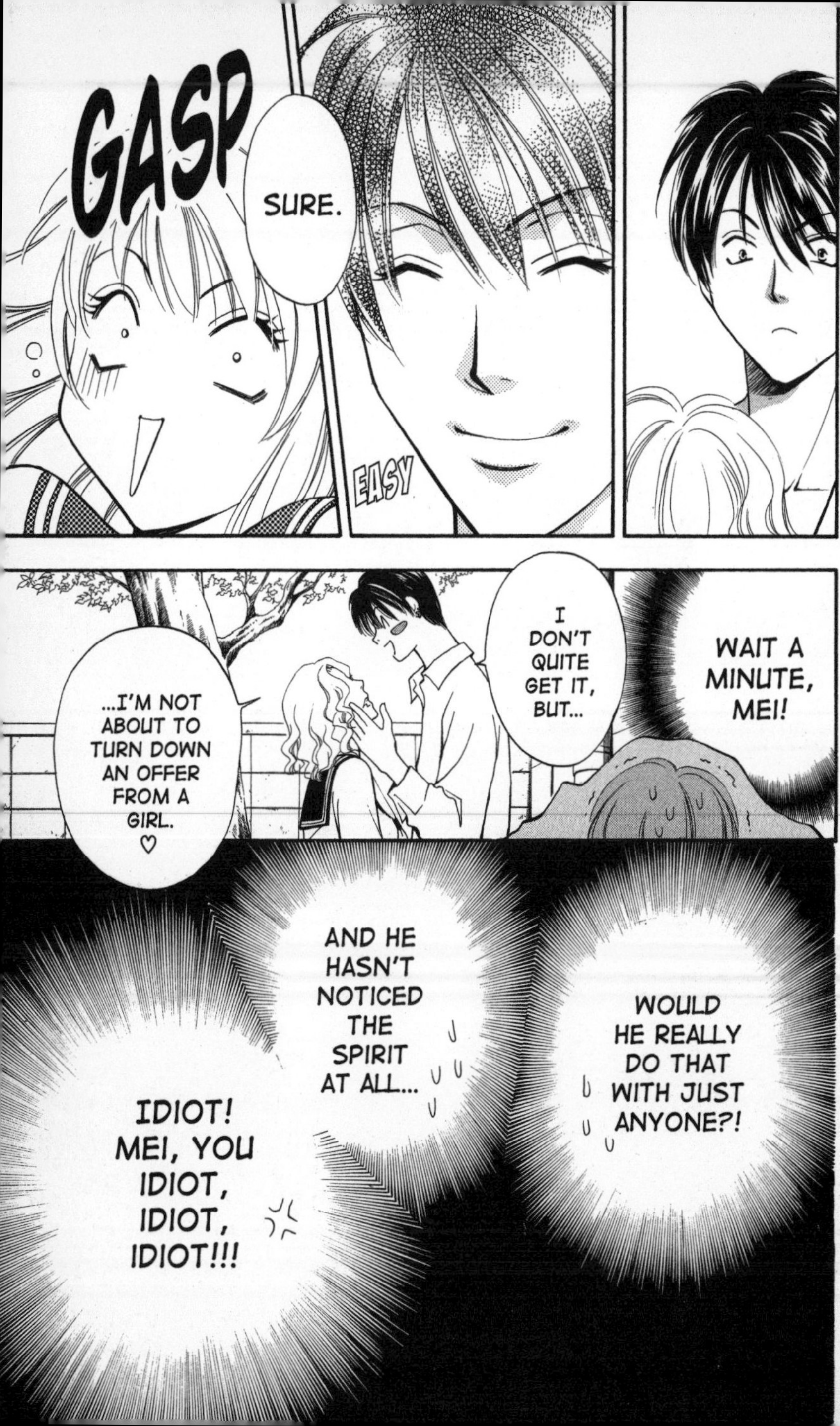
SURE.
EASY
GASP
WAIT A MINUTE, MEI!
I DON'T QUITE GET IT, BUT...
...I'M NOT ABOUT TO TURN DOWN AN OFFER FROM A GIRL. ♡
WOULD HE REALLY DO THAT WITH JUST ANYONE?!
AND HE HASN'T NOTICED THE SPIRIT AT ALL...
IDIOT! MEI, YOU IDIOT, IDIOT, IDIOT!!!

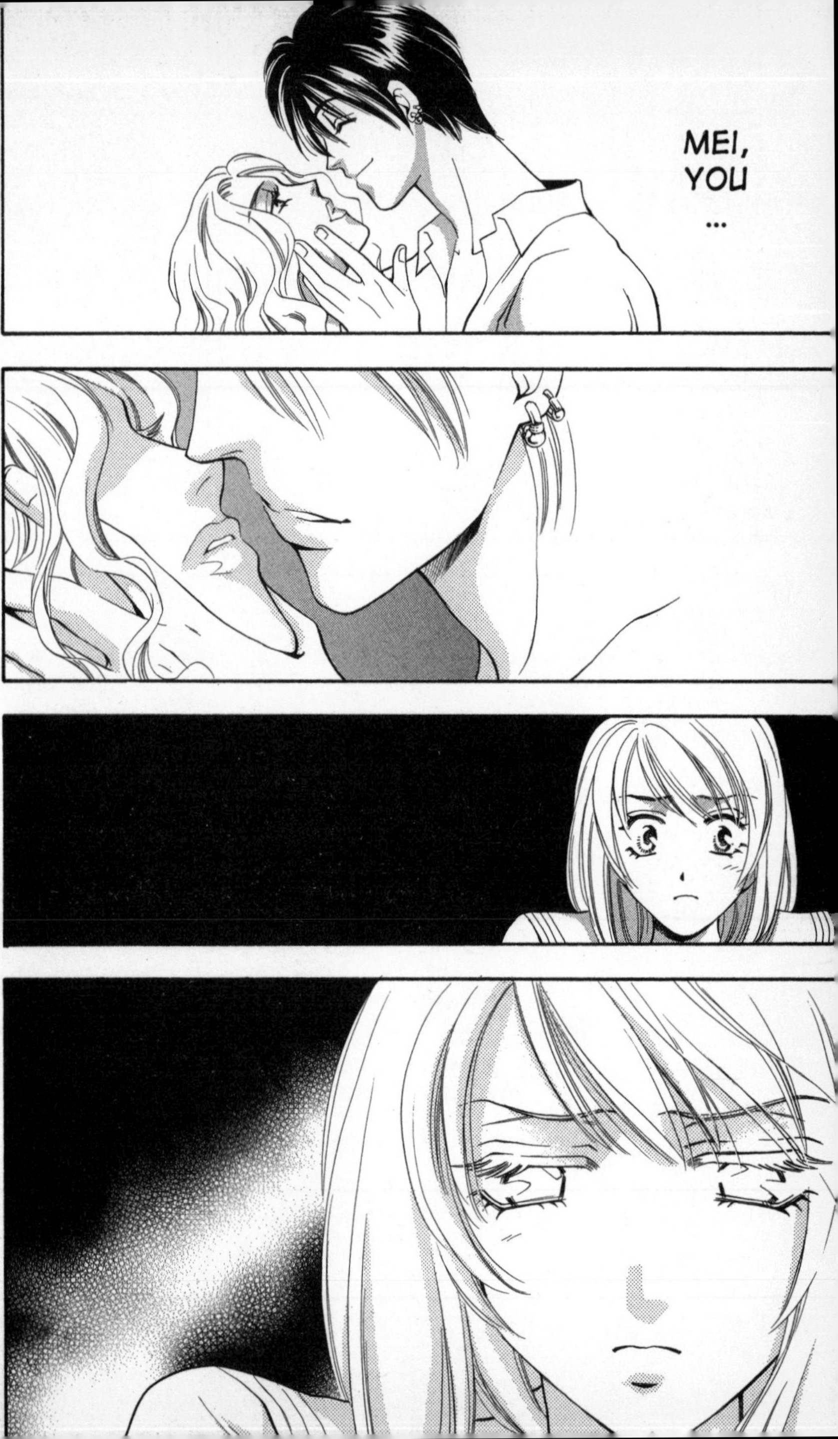
MEI, YOU ...

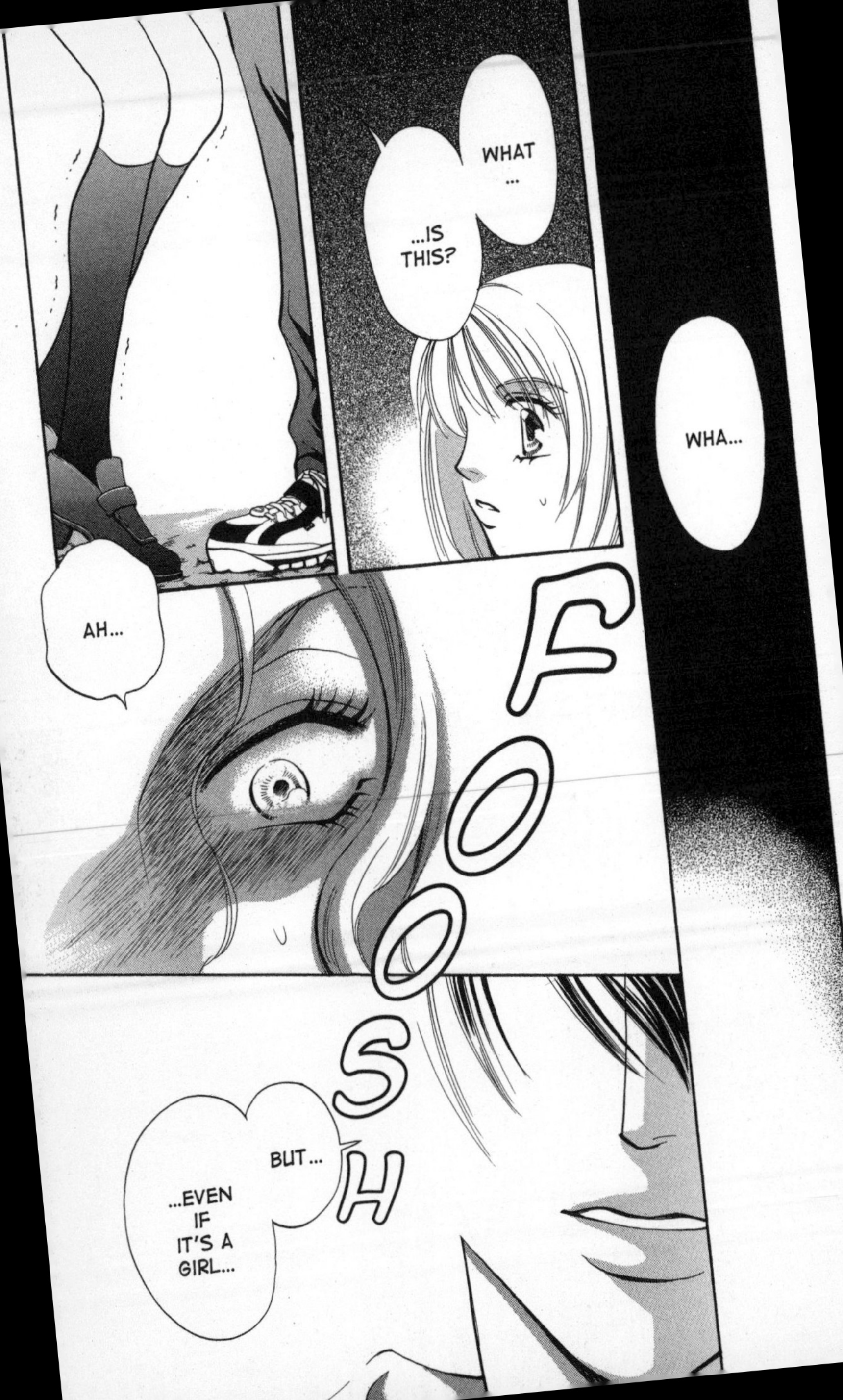
WHA...
WHAT...
...IS THIS?
AH...
FOOSH
BUT...
...EVEN IF IT'S A GIRL...

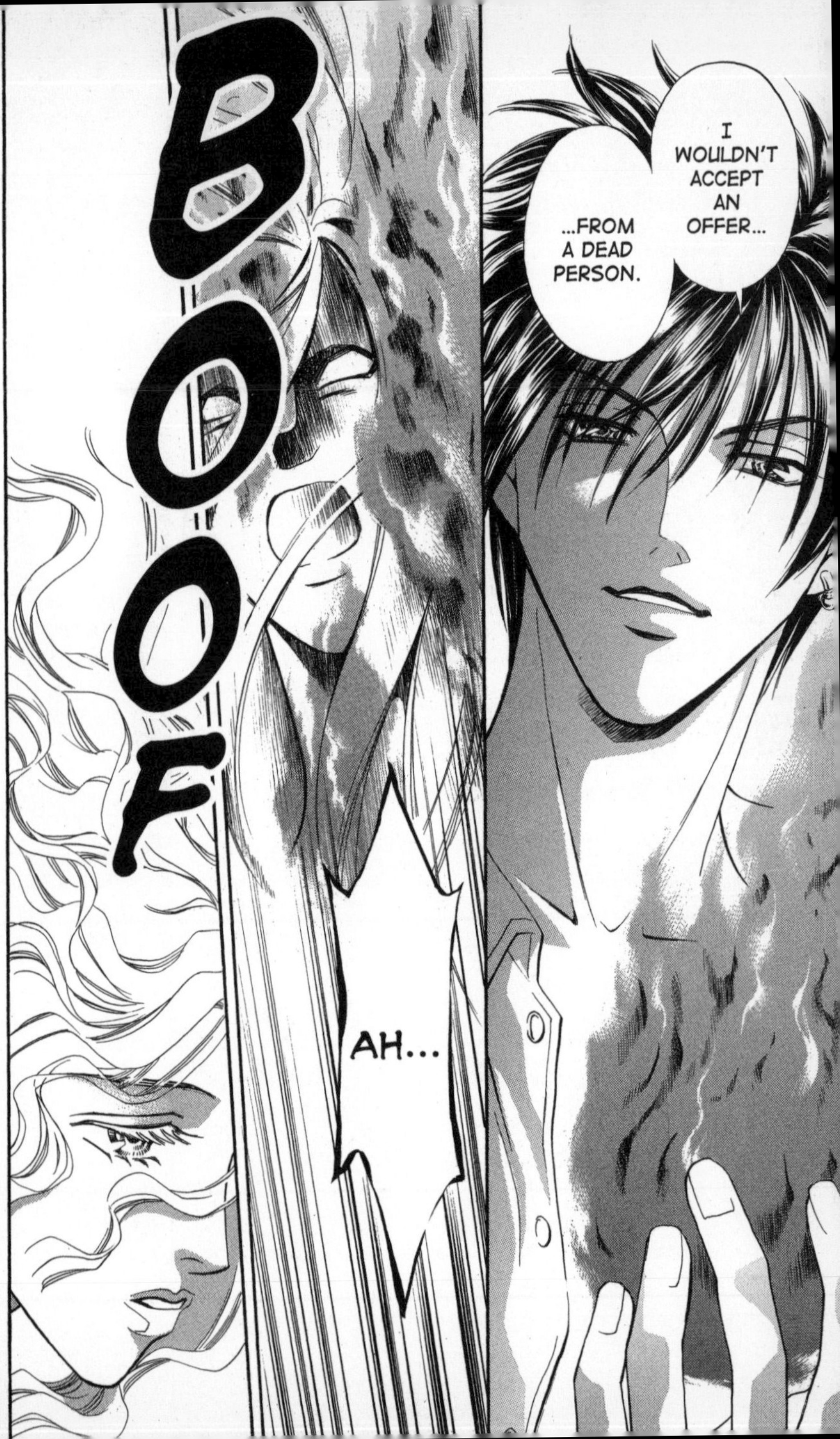
I WOULDN'T ACCEPT AN OFFER...
...FROM A DEAD PERSON.
BOOF
AH...

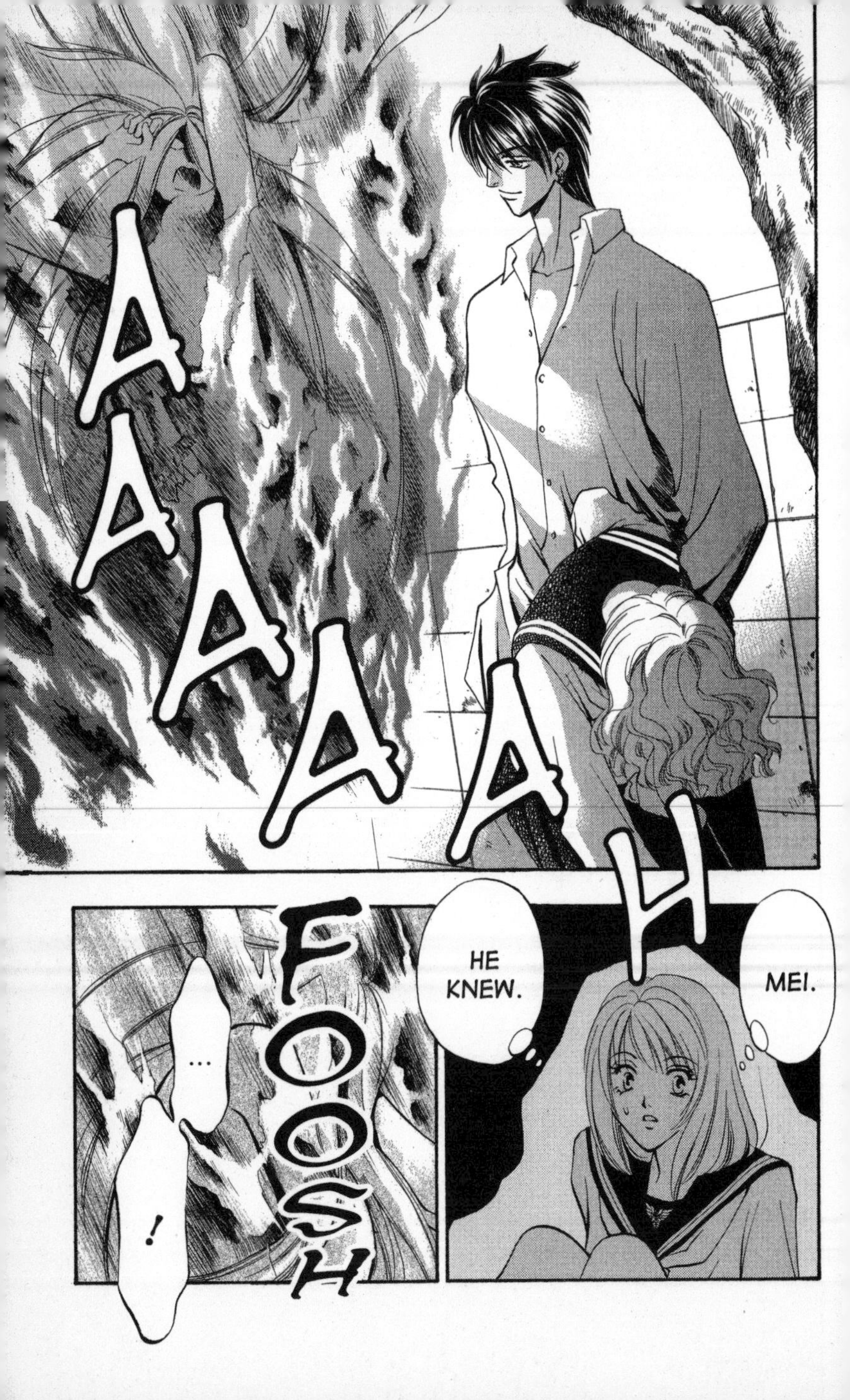
AAAAAH
MEI.
HE KNEW.
FOOOSH
...
!

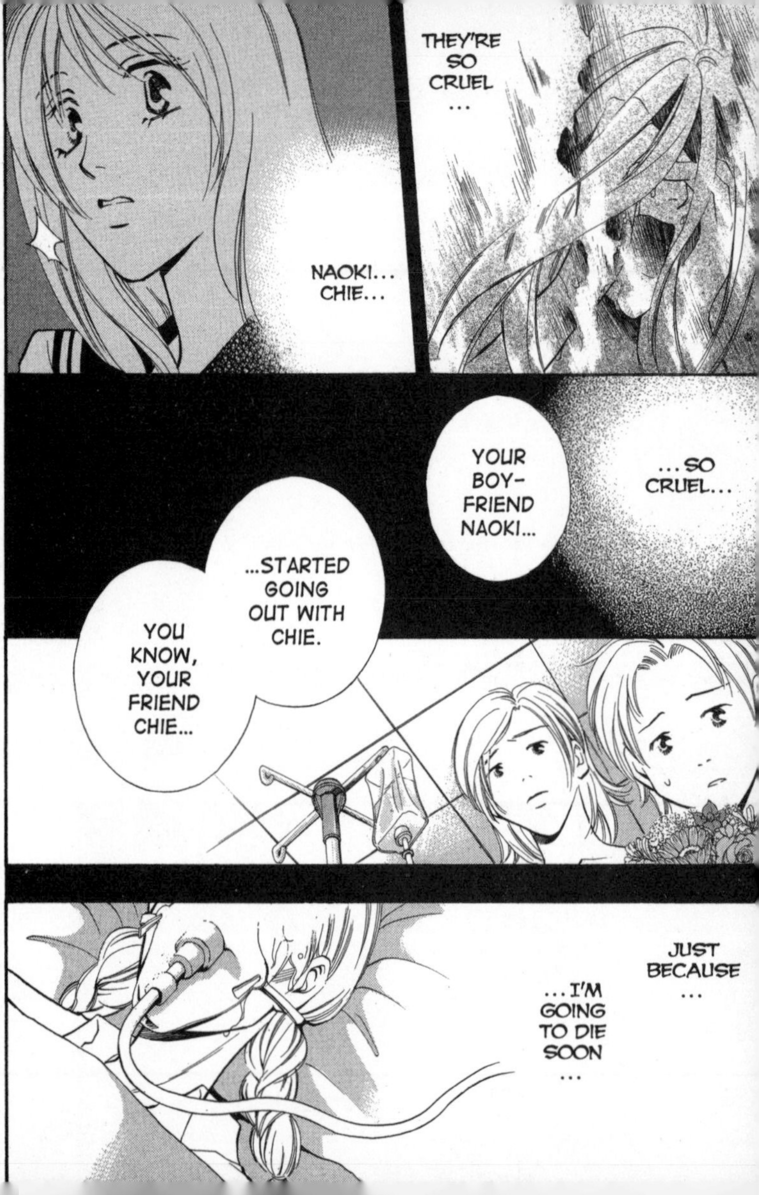
THEY'RE SO CRUEL ...
NAOKI... CHIE...
...SO CRUEL...
YOUR BOY-FRIEND NAOKI...
...STARTED GOING OUT WITH CHIE.
YOU KNOW, YOUR FRIEND CHIE...
JUST BECAUSE ...
...I'M GOING TO DIE SOON ...

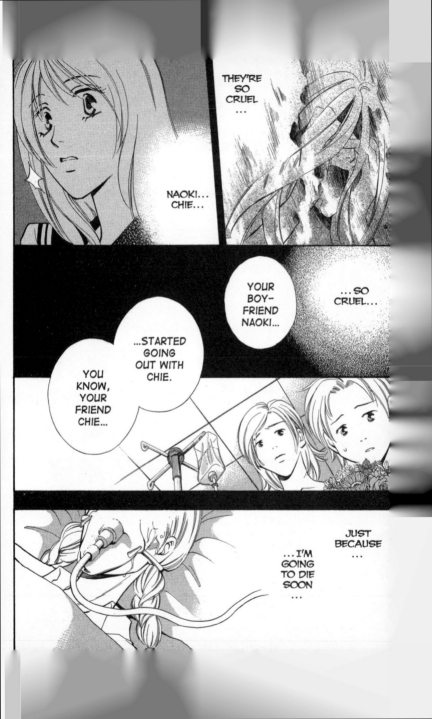

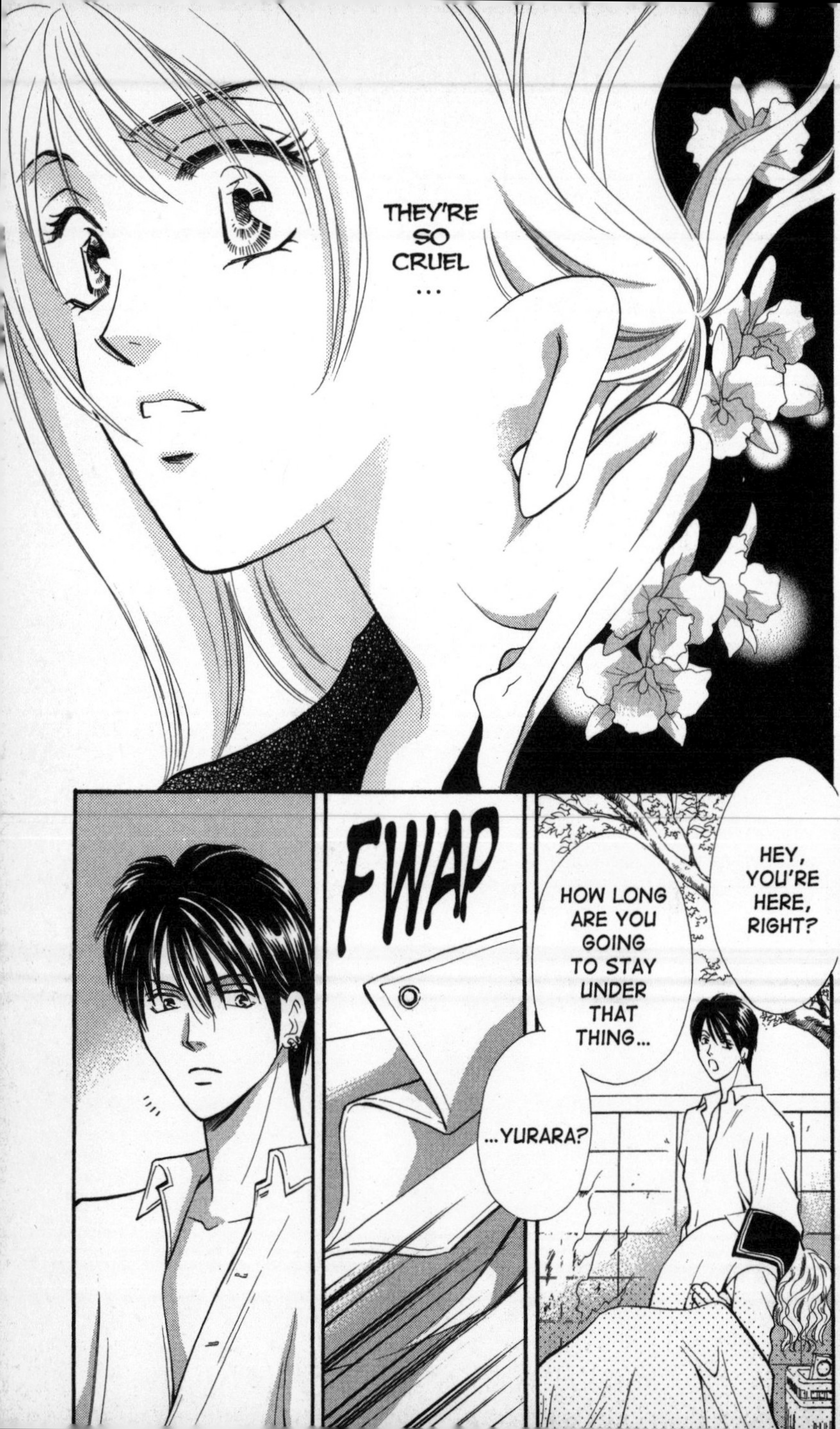
THEY'RE SO CRUEL ...
HEY, YOU'RE HERE, RIGHT?
HOW LONG ARE YOU GOING TO STAY UNDER THAT THING...
...YURARA?
FWAP

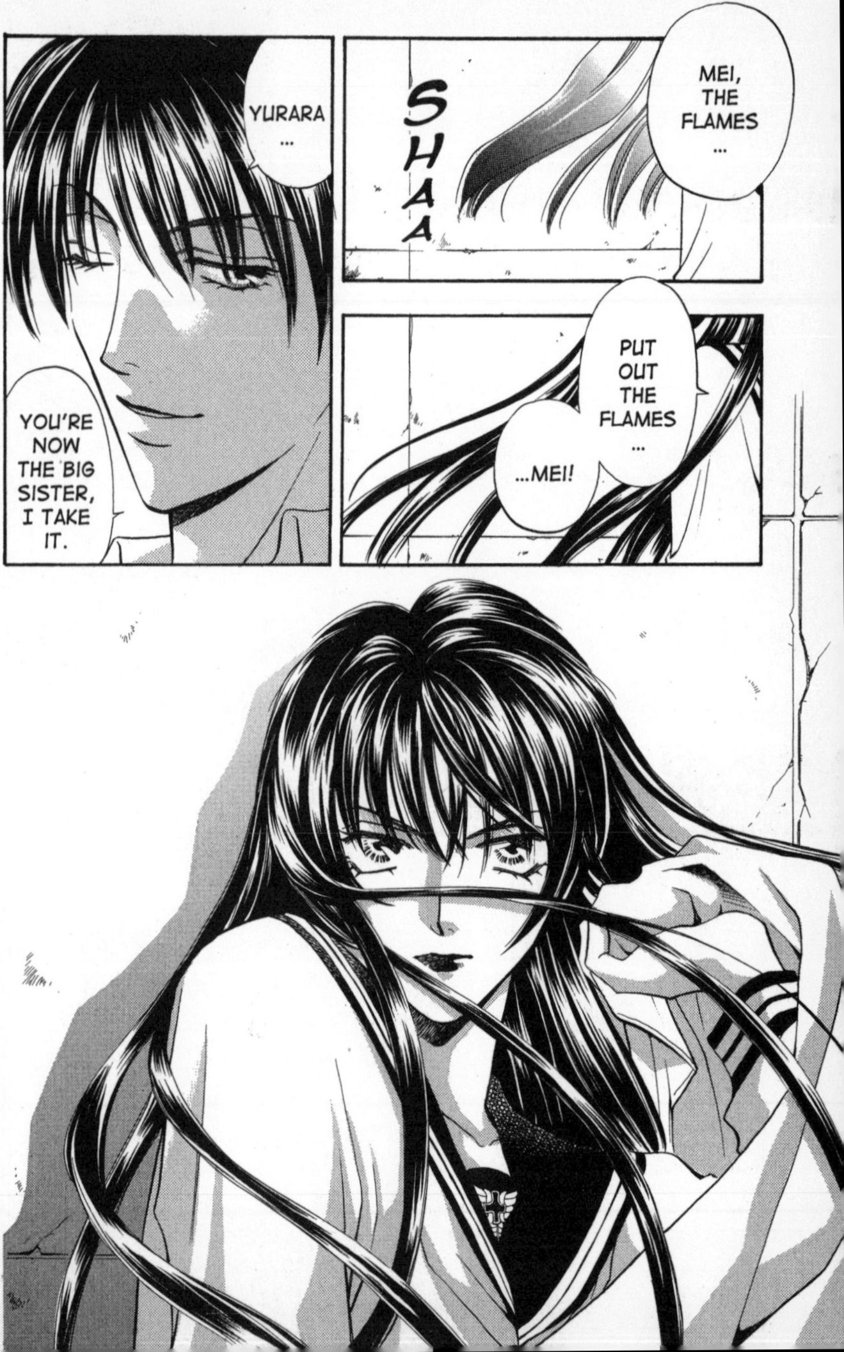
MEI, THE FLAMES ...
SHAA
PUT OUT THE FLAMES ...
...MEI!
YURARA ...
YOU'RE NOW THE BIG SISTER, I TAKE IT.

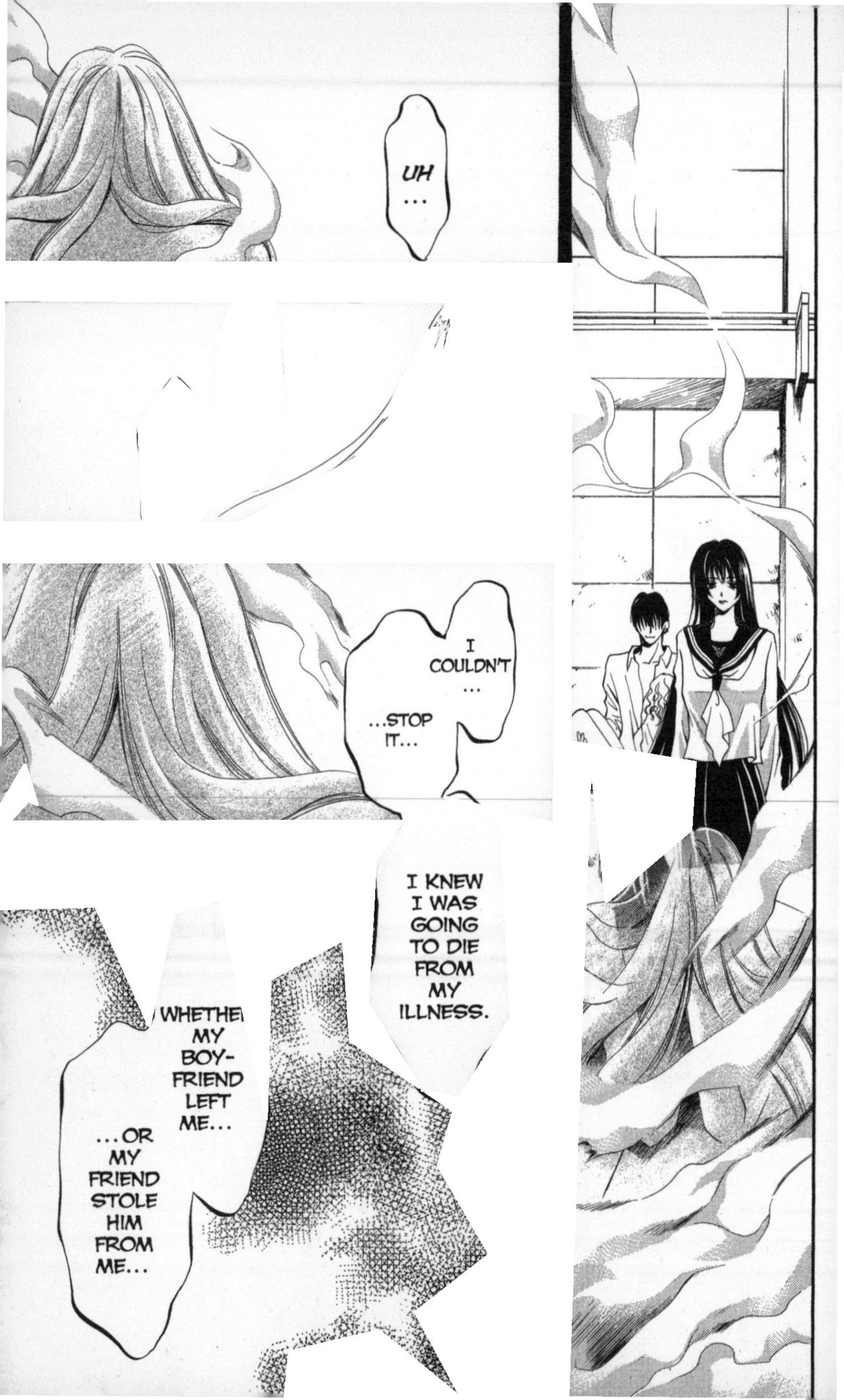
UH ...
I COULDN'T ...
...STOP IT...
I KNEW I WAS GOING TO DIE FROM MY ILLNESS.
WHETHE MY BOY-FRIEND LEFT ME...
...OR MY FRIEND STOLE HIM FROM ME...

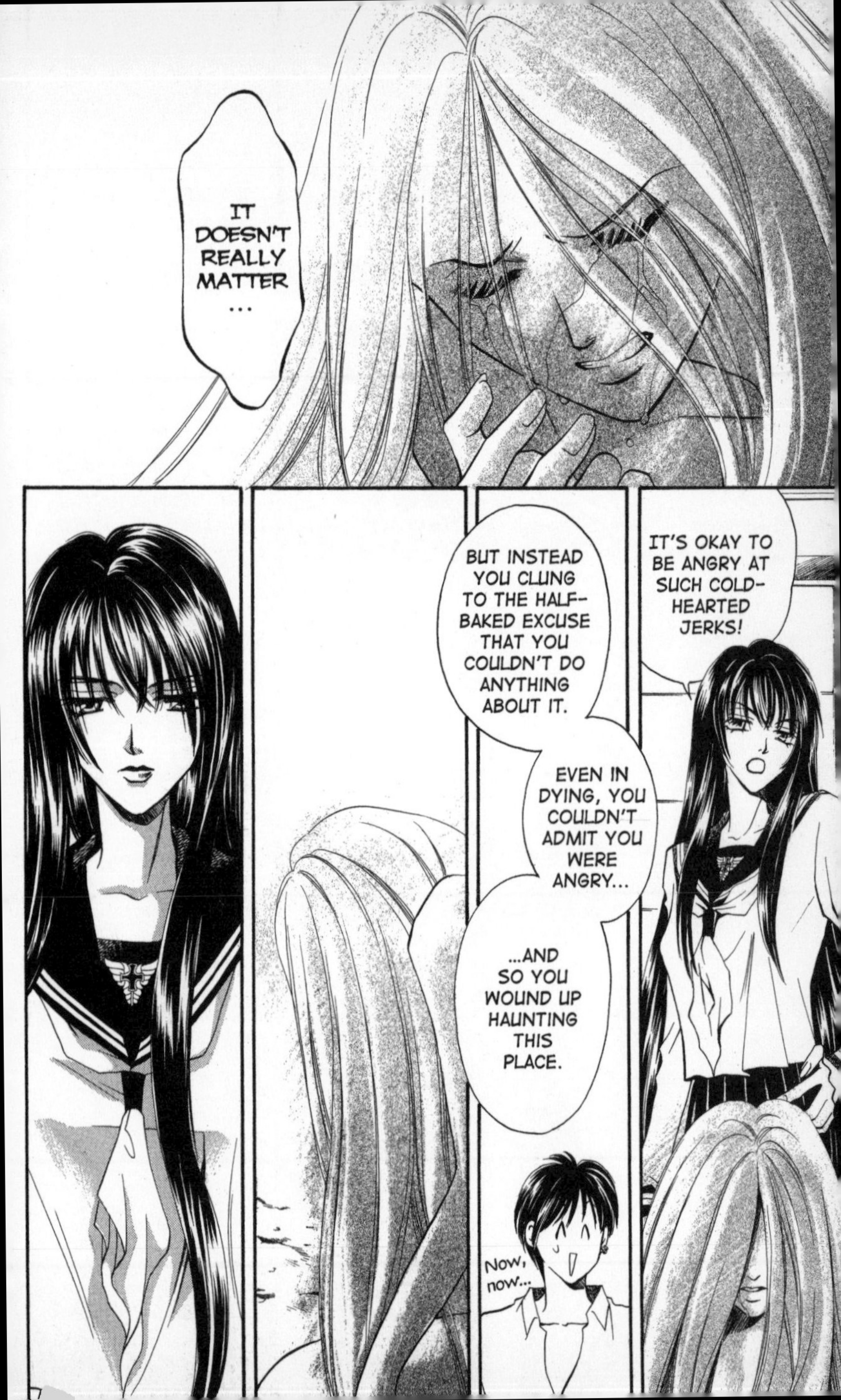
IT DOESN'T REALLY MATTER ...
IT'S OKAY TO BE ANGRY AT SUCH COLD-HEARTED JERKS!
BUT INSTEAD YOU CLUNG TO THE HALF-BAKED EXCUSE THAT YOU COULDN'T DO ANYTHING ABOUT IT.
EVEN IN DYING, YOU COULDN'T ADMIT YOU WERE ANGRY...
...AND SO YOU WOUND UP HAUNTING THIS PLACE.
Now, now...

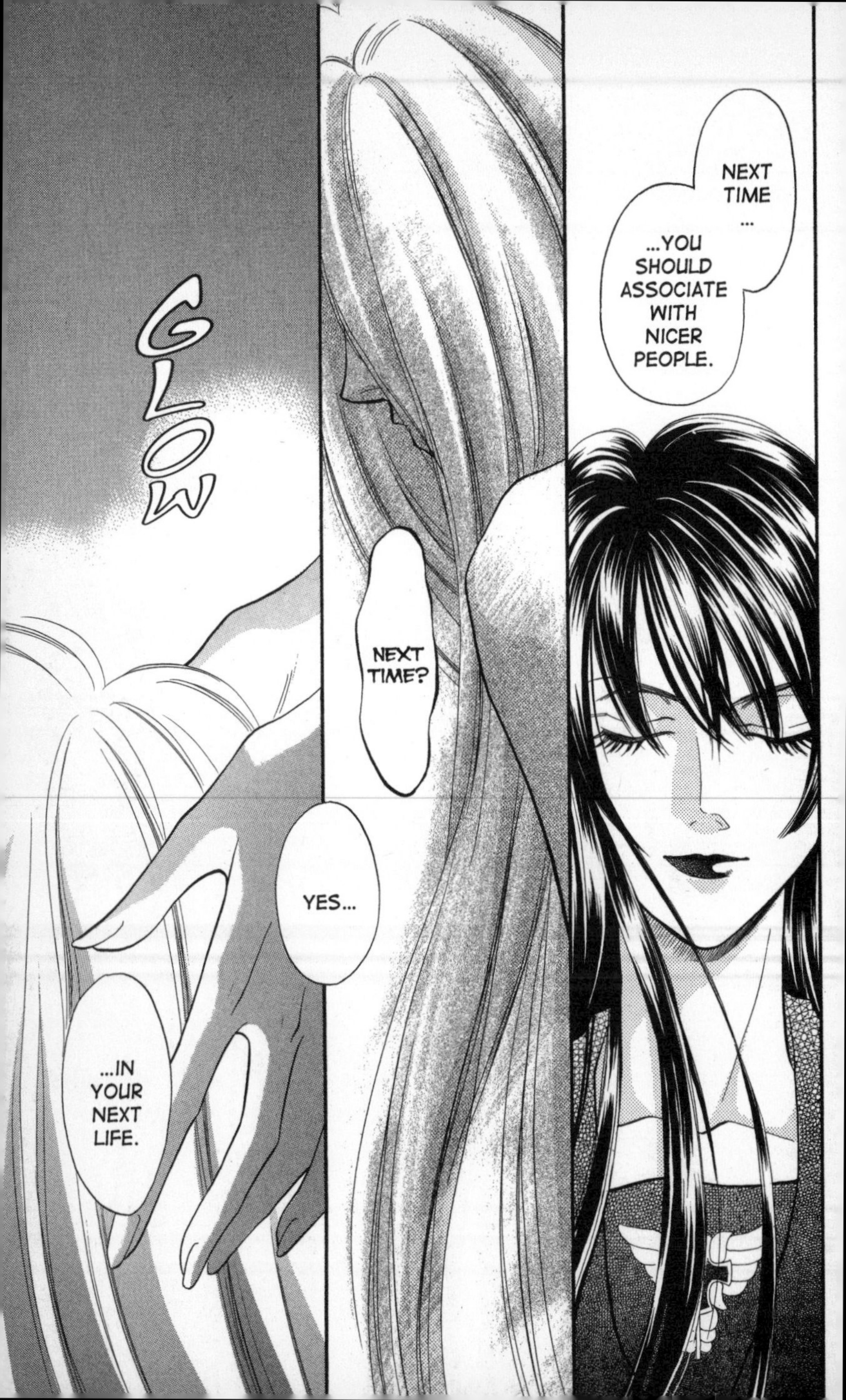
NEXT TIME ...
...YOU SHOULD ASSOCIATE WITH NICER PEOPLE.
NEXT TIME?
GLOW
YES...
...IN YOUR NEXT LIFE.

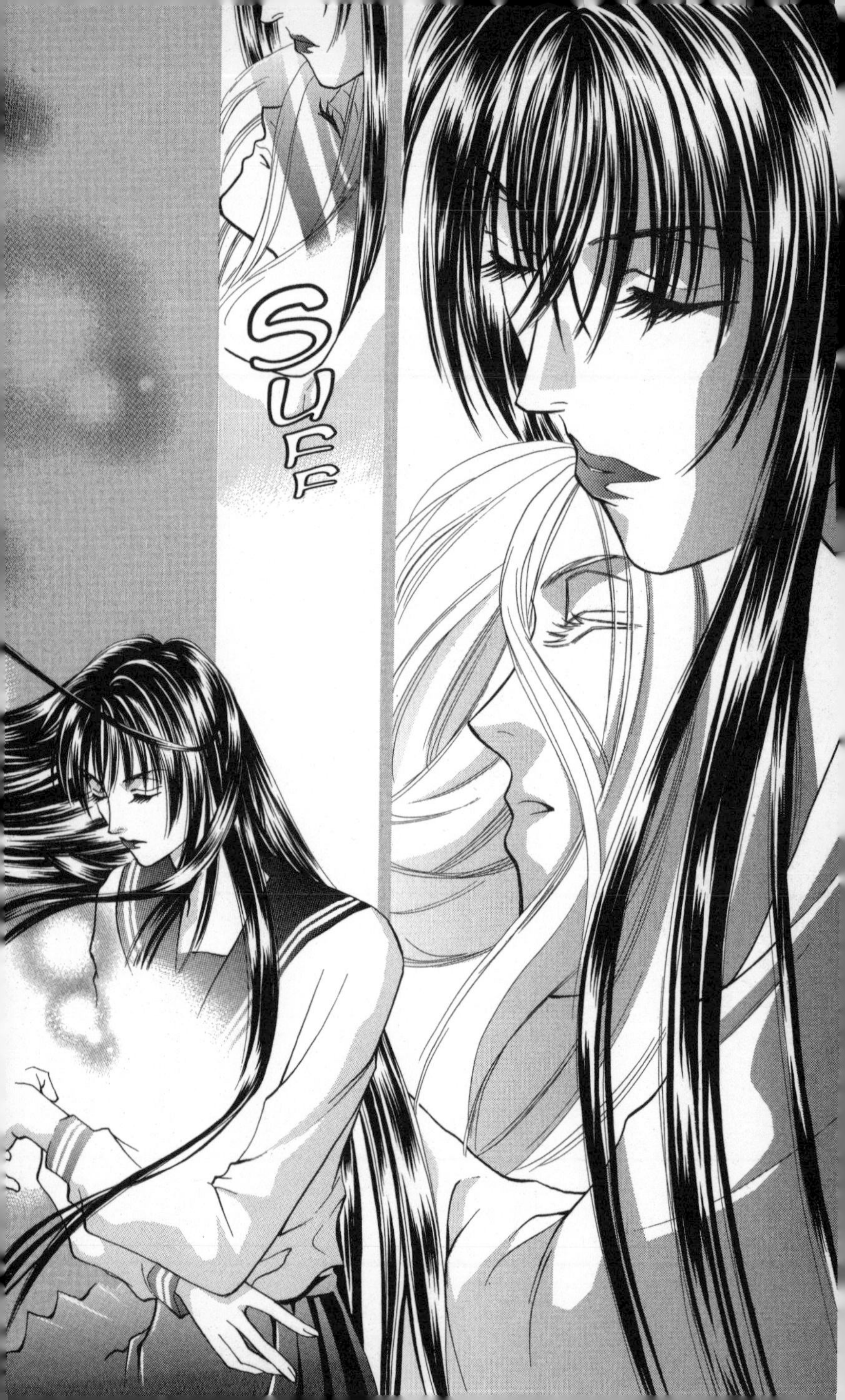
SUFF

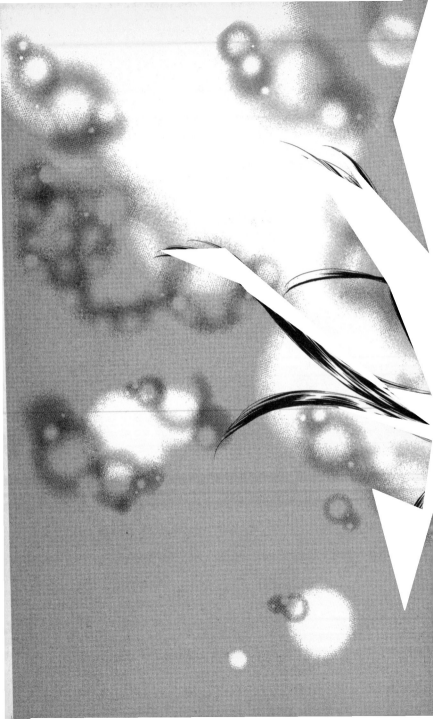

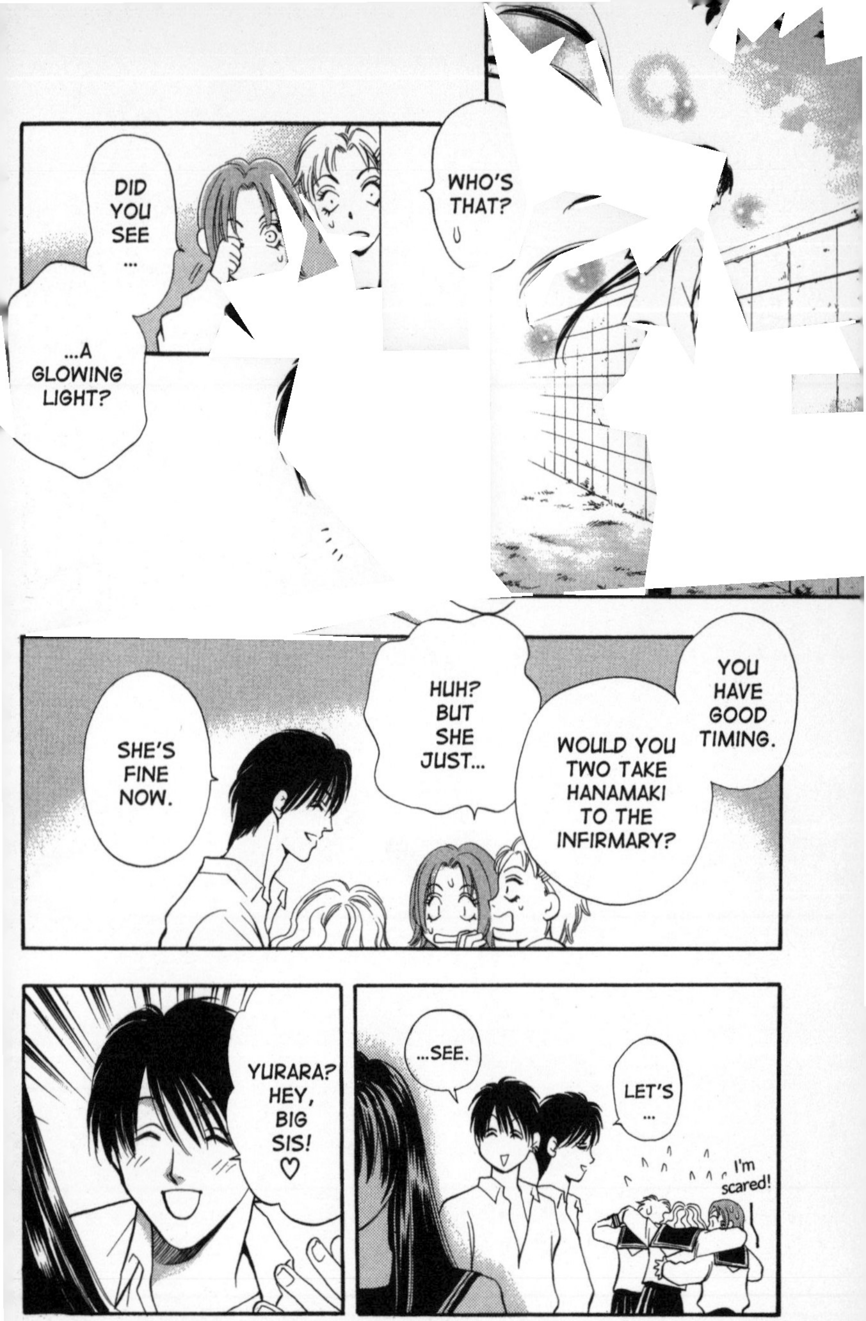
WHO'S THAT?
DID YOU SEE ...
...A GLOWING LIGHT?
YOU HAVE GOOD TIMING.
WOULD YOU TWO TAKE HANAMAKI TO THE INFIRMARY?
HUH? BUT SHE JUST...
SHE'S FINE NOW.
LET'S ...
...SEE.
I'm scared!
YURARA? HEY, BIG SIS! ♡

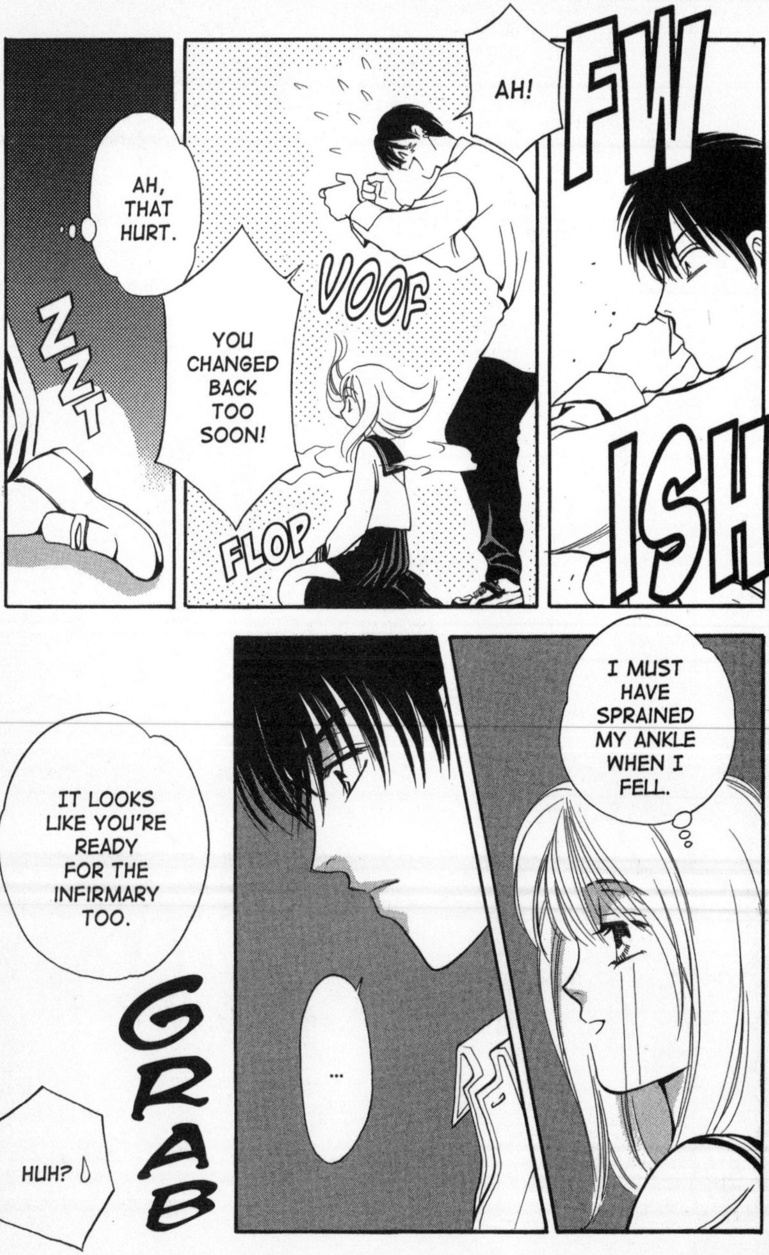
FW
ISH
AH!
VOOF
YOU CHANGED BACK TOO SOON!
FLOP
AH, THAT HURT.
ZZT
I MUST HAVE SPRAINED MY ANKLE WHEN I FELL.
...
IT LOOKS LIKE YOU'RE READY FOR THE INFIRMARY TOO.
GRAB
HUH?

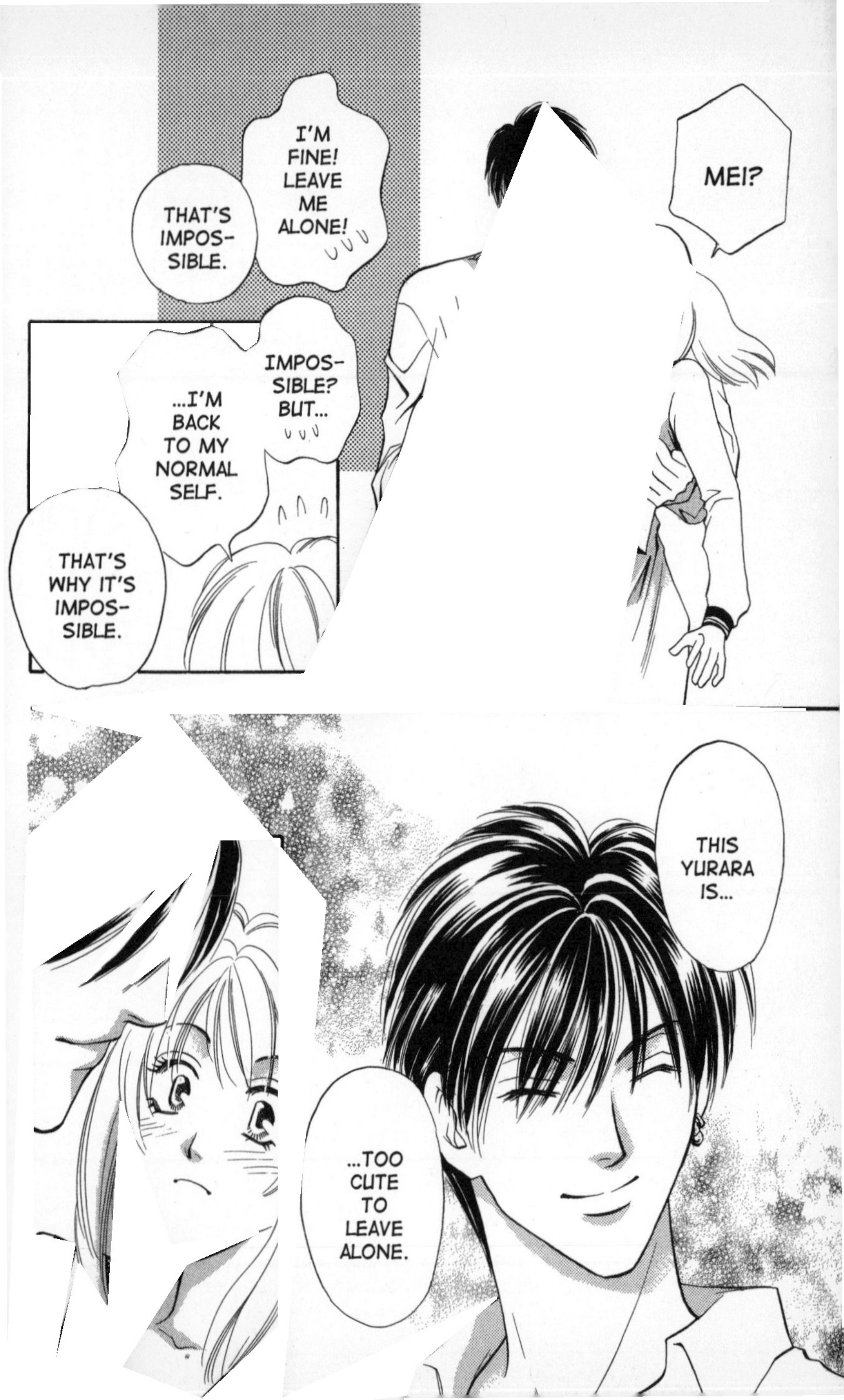
MEI?
I'M FINE! LEAVE ME ALONE!
THAT'S IMPOSSIBLE.
IMPOSSIBLE? BUT...
...I'M BACK TO MY NORMAL SELF.
THAT'S WHY IT'S IMPOSSIBLE.
THIS YURARA IS...
...TOO CUTE TO LEAVE ALONE.

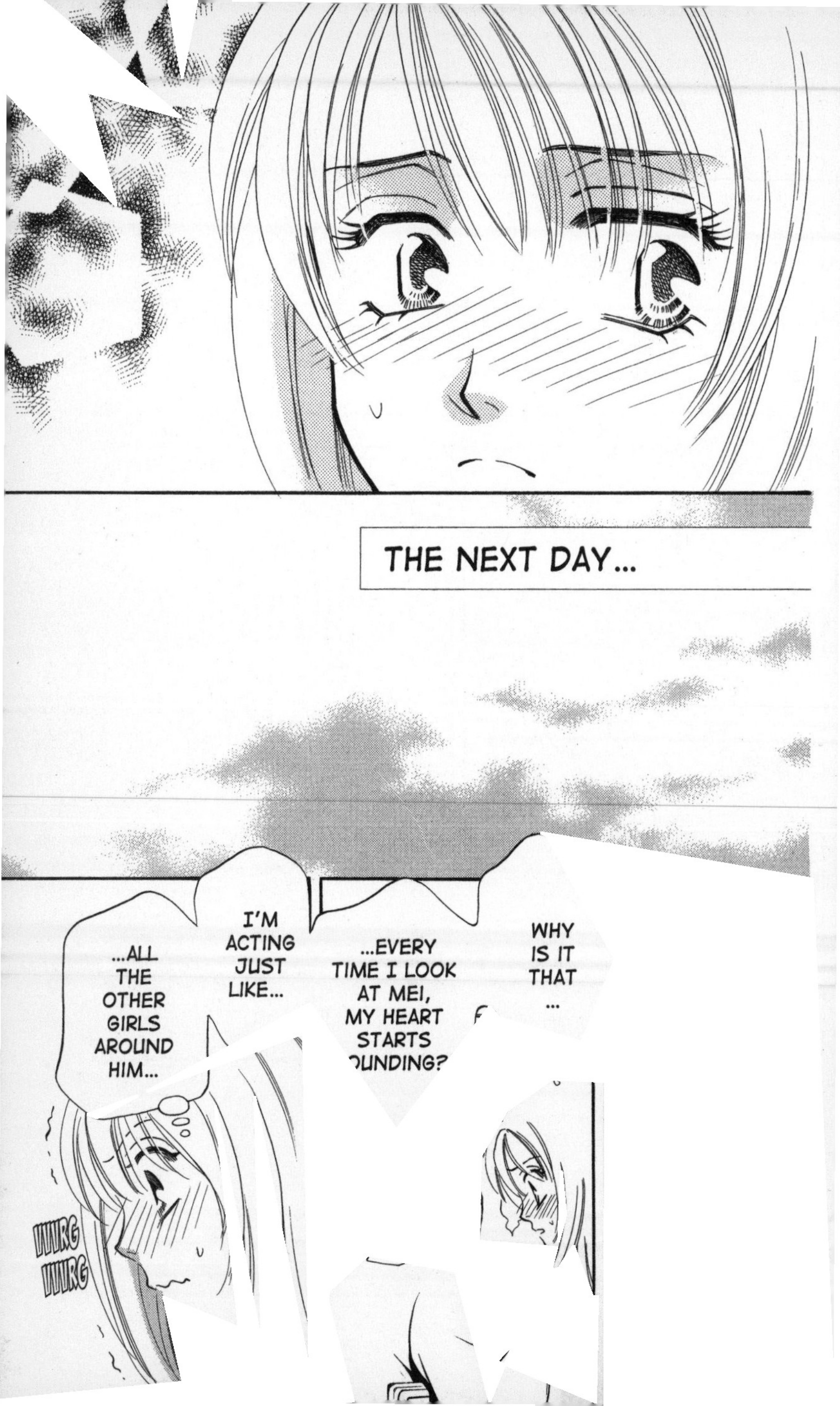
THE NEXT DAY...
WHY IS IT THAT ...
...EVERY TIME I LOOK AT MEI, MY HEART STARTS OUNDING?
I'M ACTING JUST LIKE...
...ALL THE OTHER GIRLS AROUND HIM...
WWIRG WWIRG

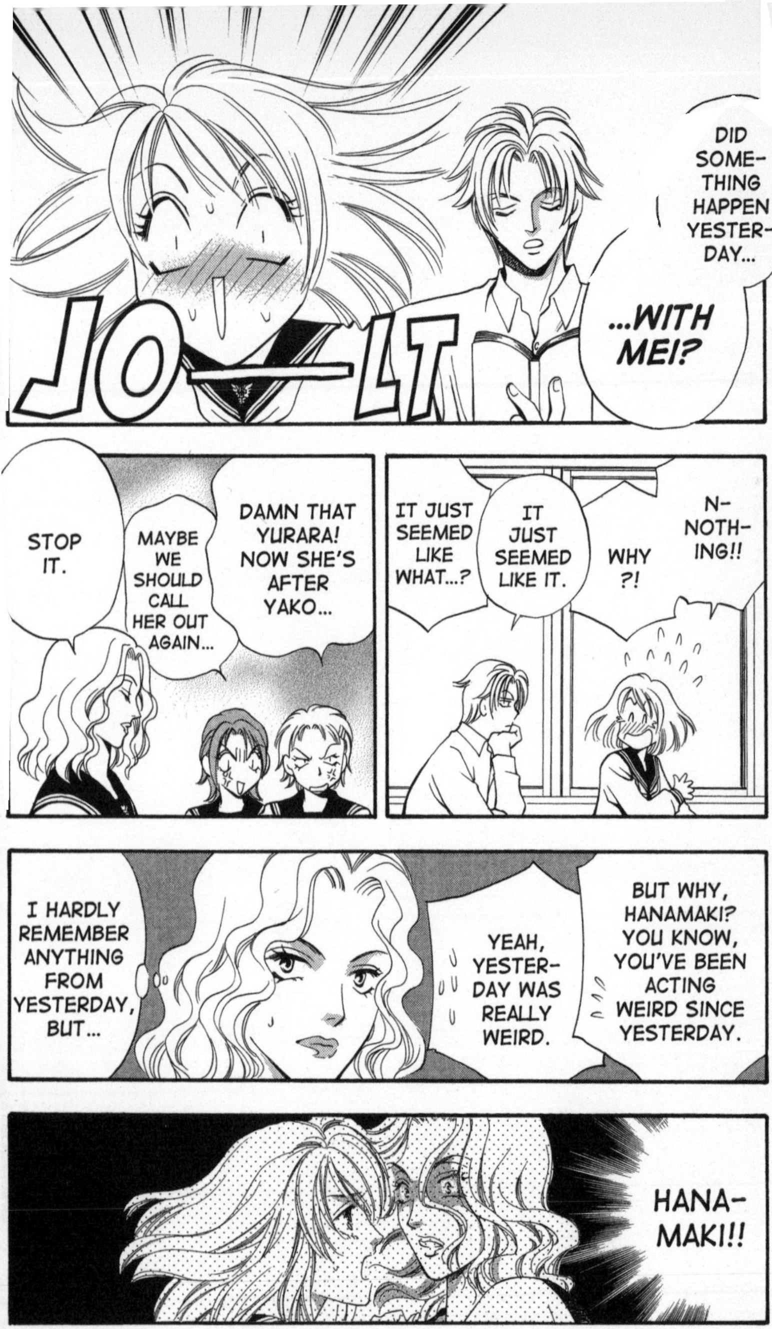
DID SOMETHING HAPPEN YESTERDAY...
...WITH MEI?
JO—LT
N-NOTHING!!
WHY?!
IT JUST SEEMED LIKE IT.
IT JUST SEEMED LIKE WHAT...?
DAMN THAT YURARA! NOW SHE'S AFTER YAKO...
MAYBE WE SHOULD CALL HER OUT AGAIN...
STOP IT.
BUT WHY, HANAMAKI? YOU KNOW, YOU'VE BEEN ACTING WEIRD SINCE YESTERDAY.
YEAH, YESTERDAY WAS REALLY WEIRD.
I HARDLY REMEMBER ANYTHING FROM YESTERDAY, BUT...
HANAMAKI!!

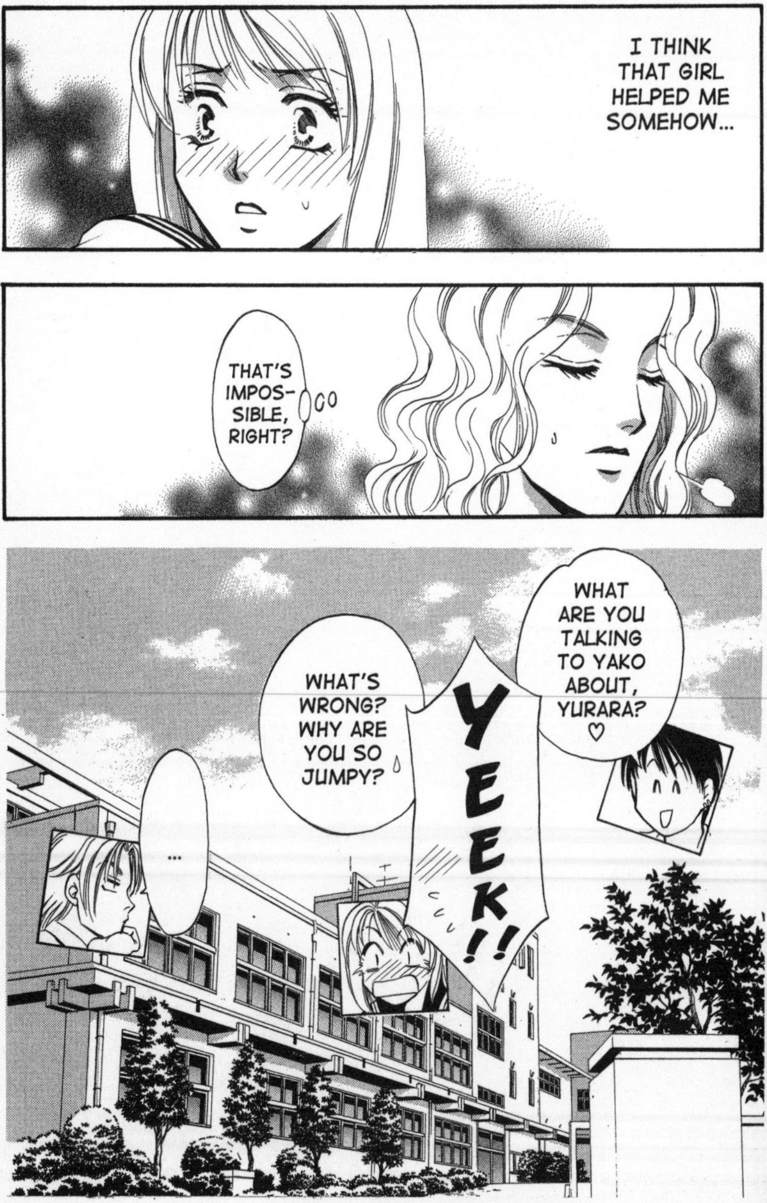
I THINK THAT GIRL HELPED ME SOMEHOW...
THAT'S IMPOSSIBLE, RIGHT?
WHAT ARE YOU TALKING TO YAKO ABOUT, YURARA? ♡
YEEK!!
WHAT'S WRONG? WHY ARE YOU SO JUMPY?
...

Chapter 5/End

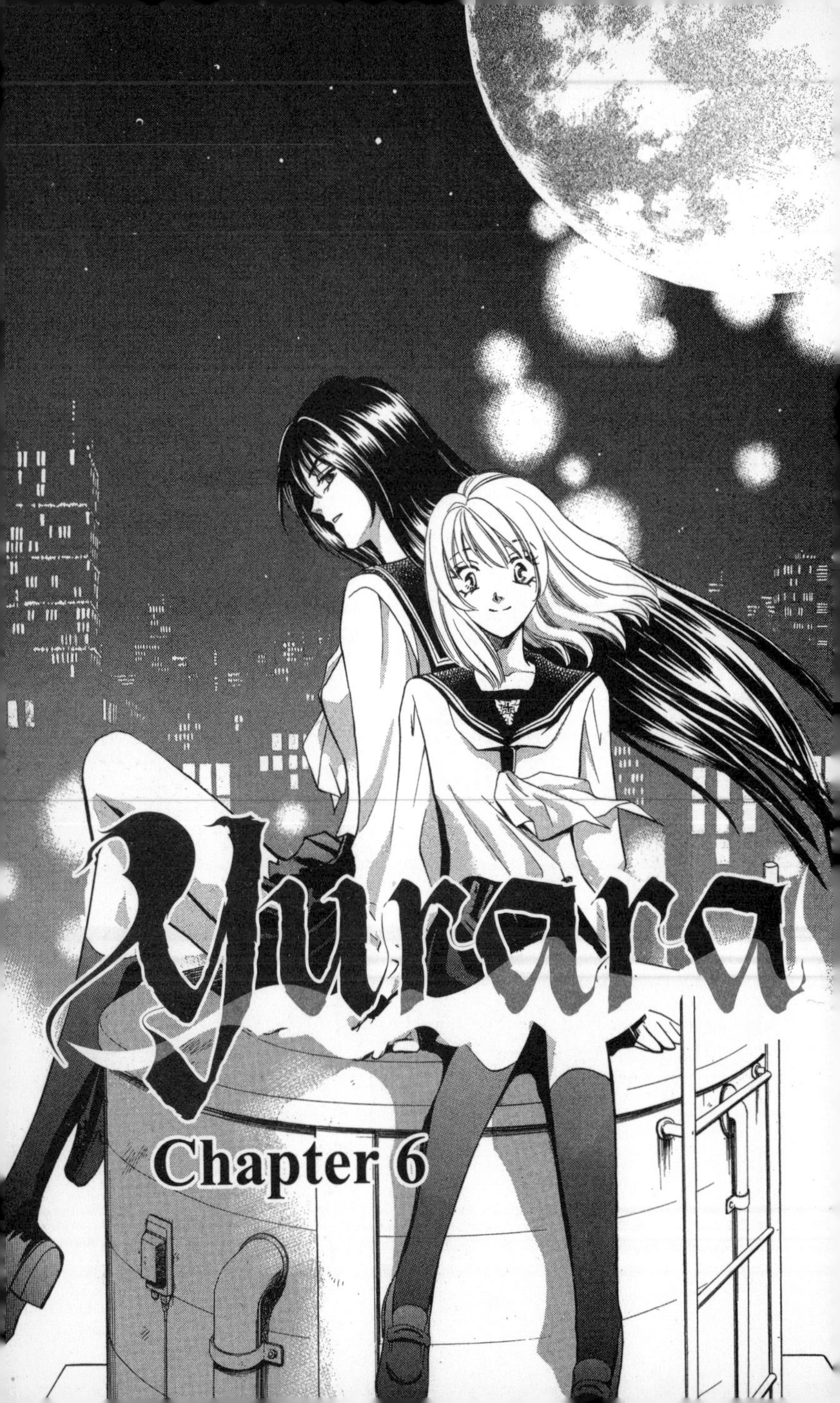
Yurara
Chapter 6

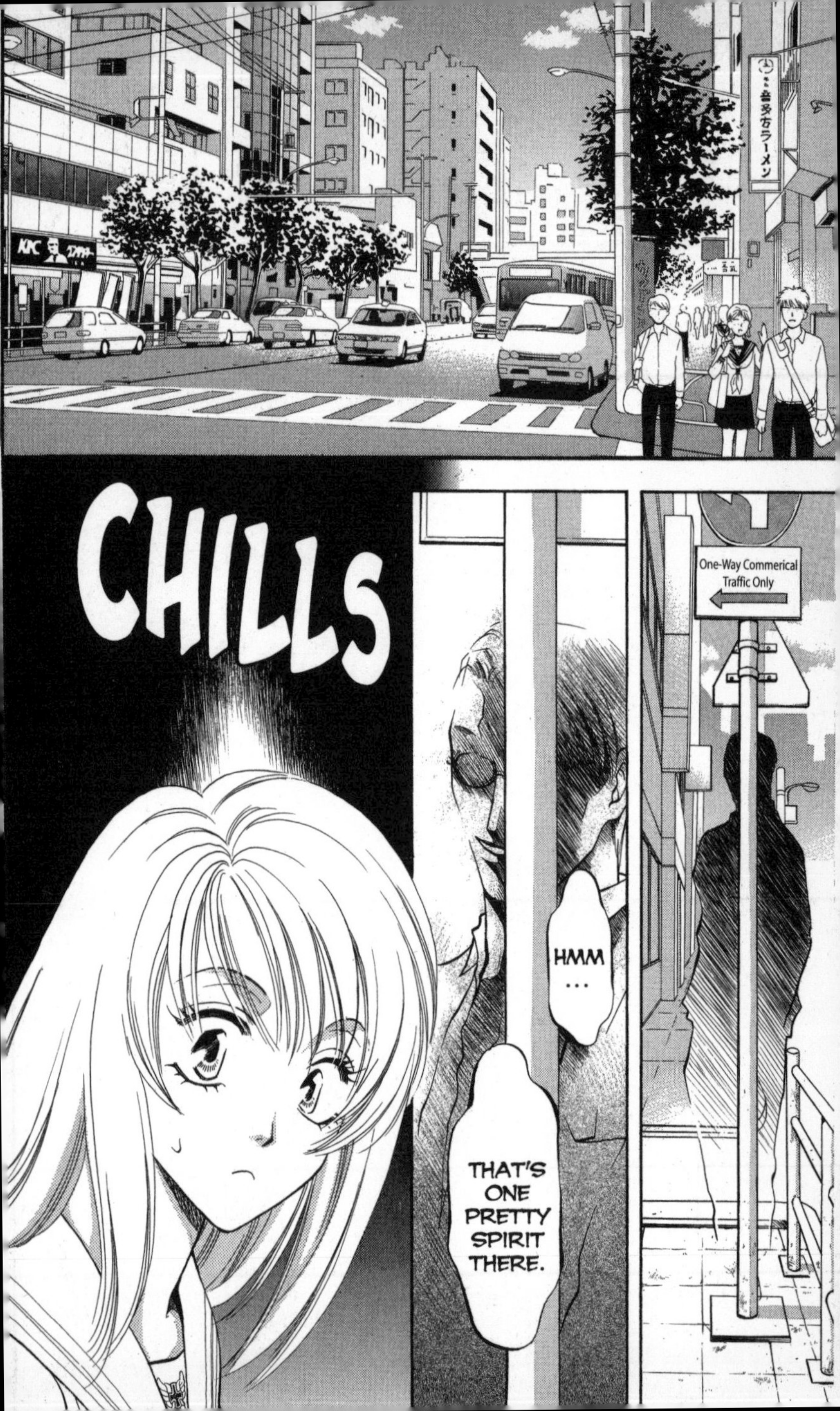
One-Way Commerical Traffic Only
HMM ...
THAT'S ONE PRETTY SPIRIT THERE.
CHILLS

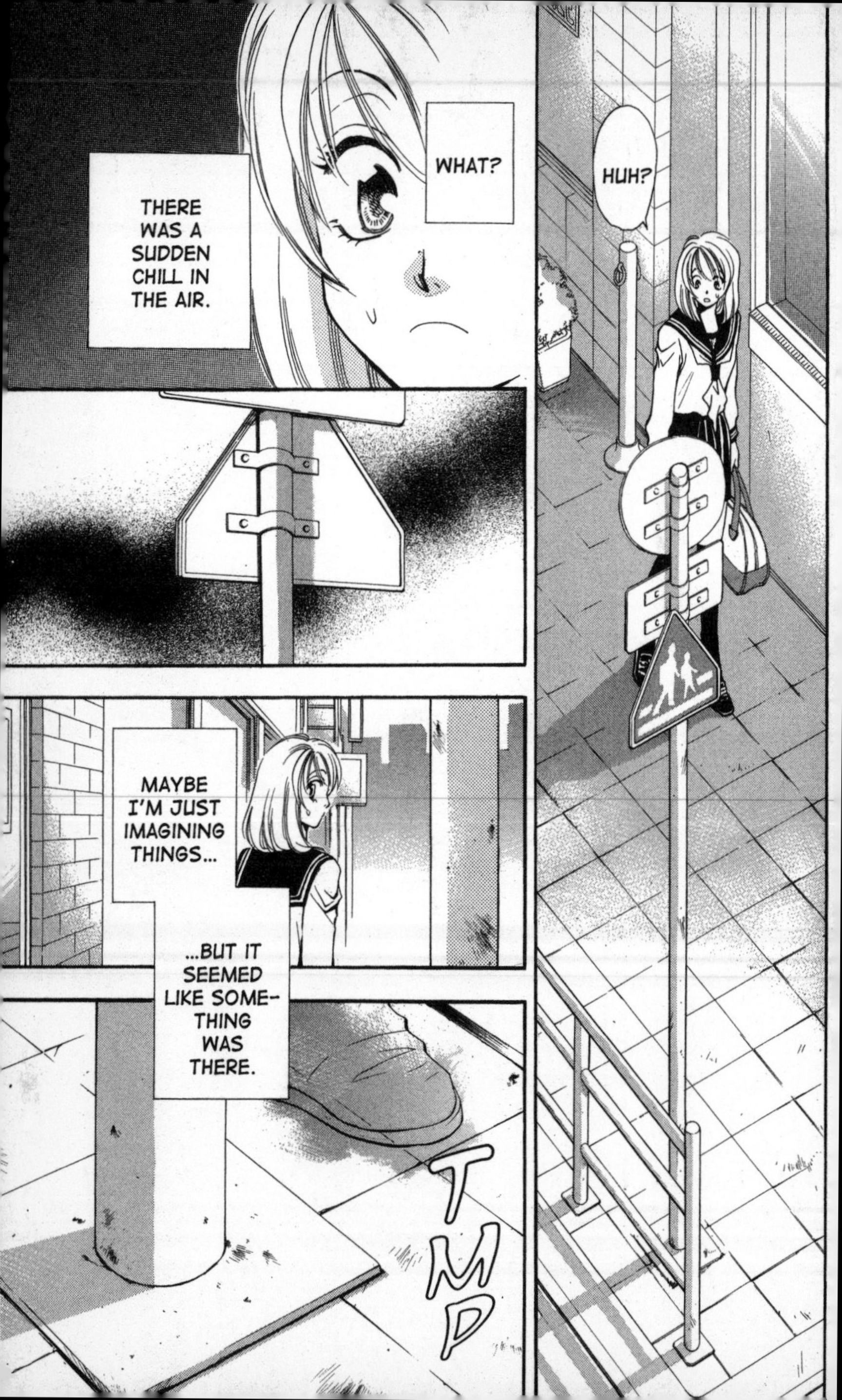
HUH?
WHAT?
THERE WAS A SUDDEN CHILL IN THE AIR.
MAYBE I'M JUST IMAGINING THINGS...
...BUT IT SEEMED LIKE SOME-THING WAS THERE.
TMP

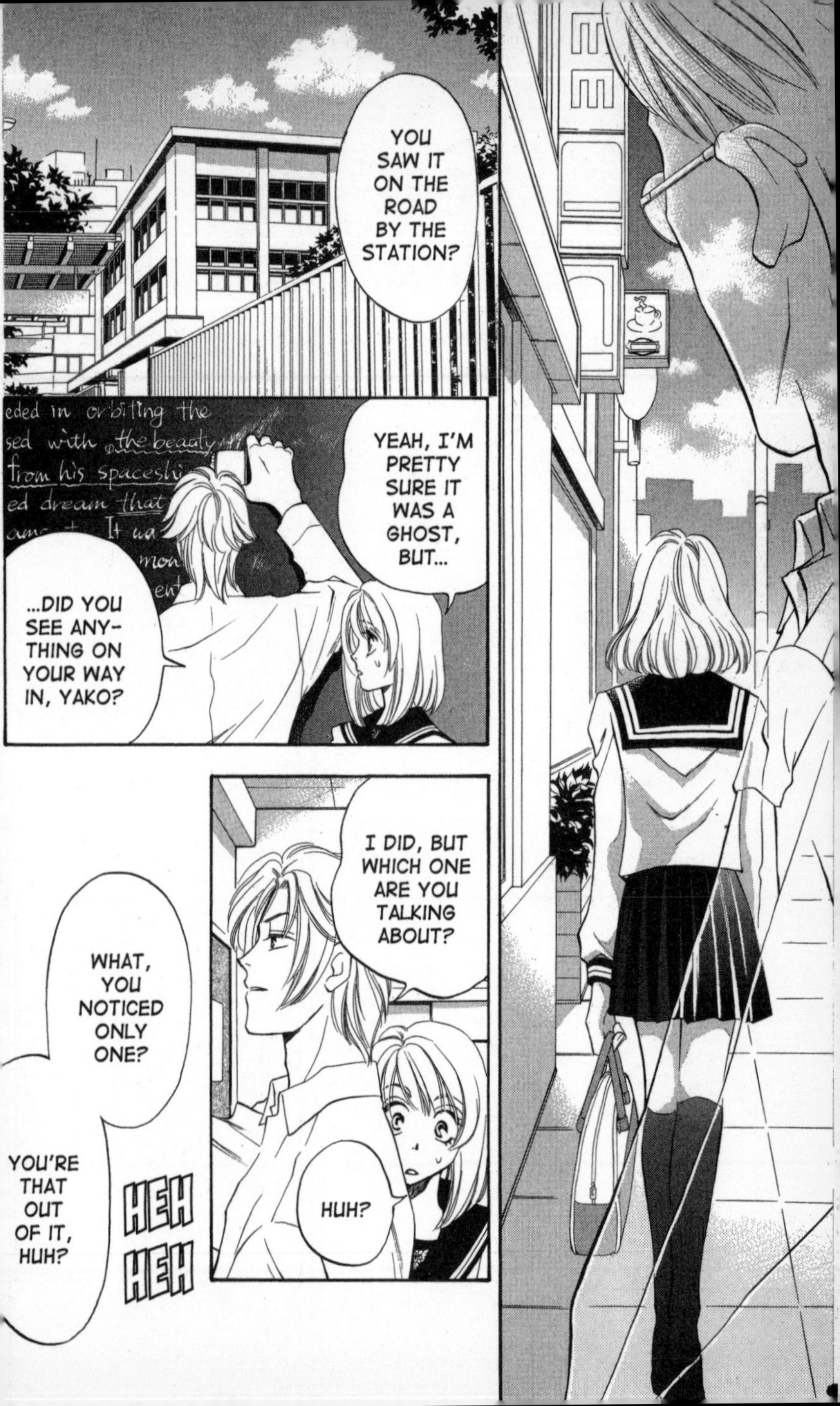
YOU SAW IT ON THE ROAD BY THE STATION?
eded in orbiting the
sed with the beauty
from his spaceshi
ed dream that
It wa
YEAH, I'M PRETTY SURE IT WAS A GHOST, BUT...
...DID YOU SEE ANY-THING ON YOUR WAY IN, YAKO?
I DID, BUT WHICH ONE ARE YOU TALKING ABOUT?
WHAT, YOU NOTICED ONLY ONE?
HUH?
YOU'RE THAT OUT OF IT, HUH?
HEH HEH

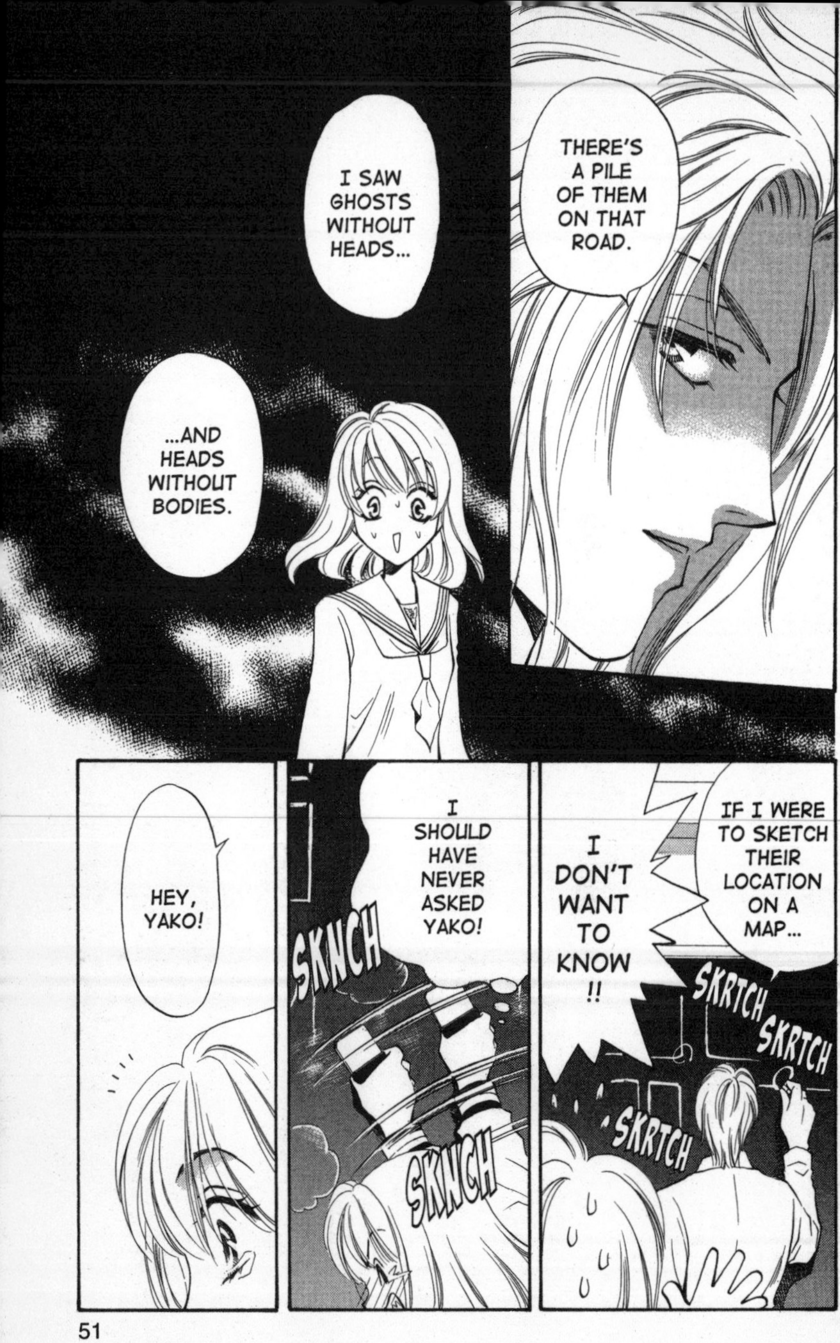
THERE'S A PILE OF THEM ON THAT ROAD.
I SAW GHOSTS WITHOUT HEADS...
...AND HEADS WITHOUT BODIES.
IF I WERE TO SKETCH THEIR LOCATION ON A MAP...
I DON'T WANT TO KNOW !!
SKRTCH
SKRTCH
SKRTCH
I SHOULD HAVE NEVER ASKED YAKO!
SKNCH
SKNCH
HEY, YAKO!

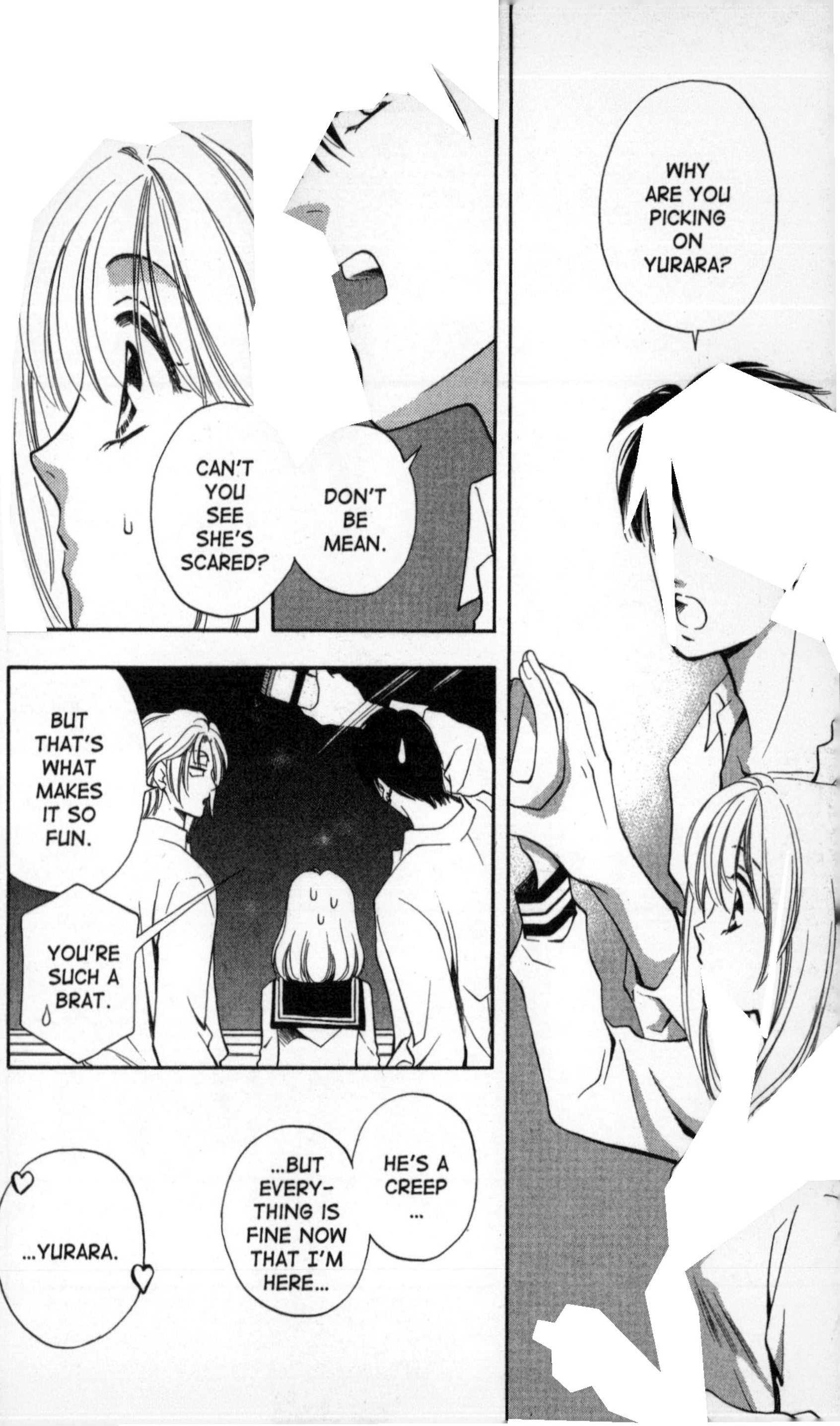
WHY ARE YOU PICKING ON YURARA?
DON'T BE MEAN.
CAN'T YOU SEE SHE'S SCARED?
BUT THAT'S WHAT MAKES IT SO FUN.
YOU'RE SUCH A BRAT.
HE'S A CREEP ...
...BUT EVERY-THING IS FINE NOW THAT I'M HERE...
...YURARA.

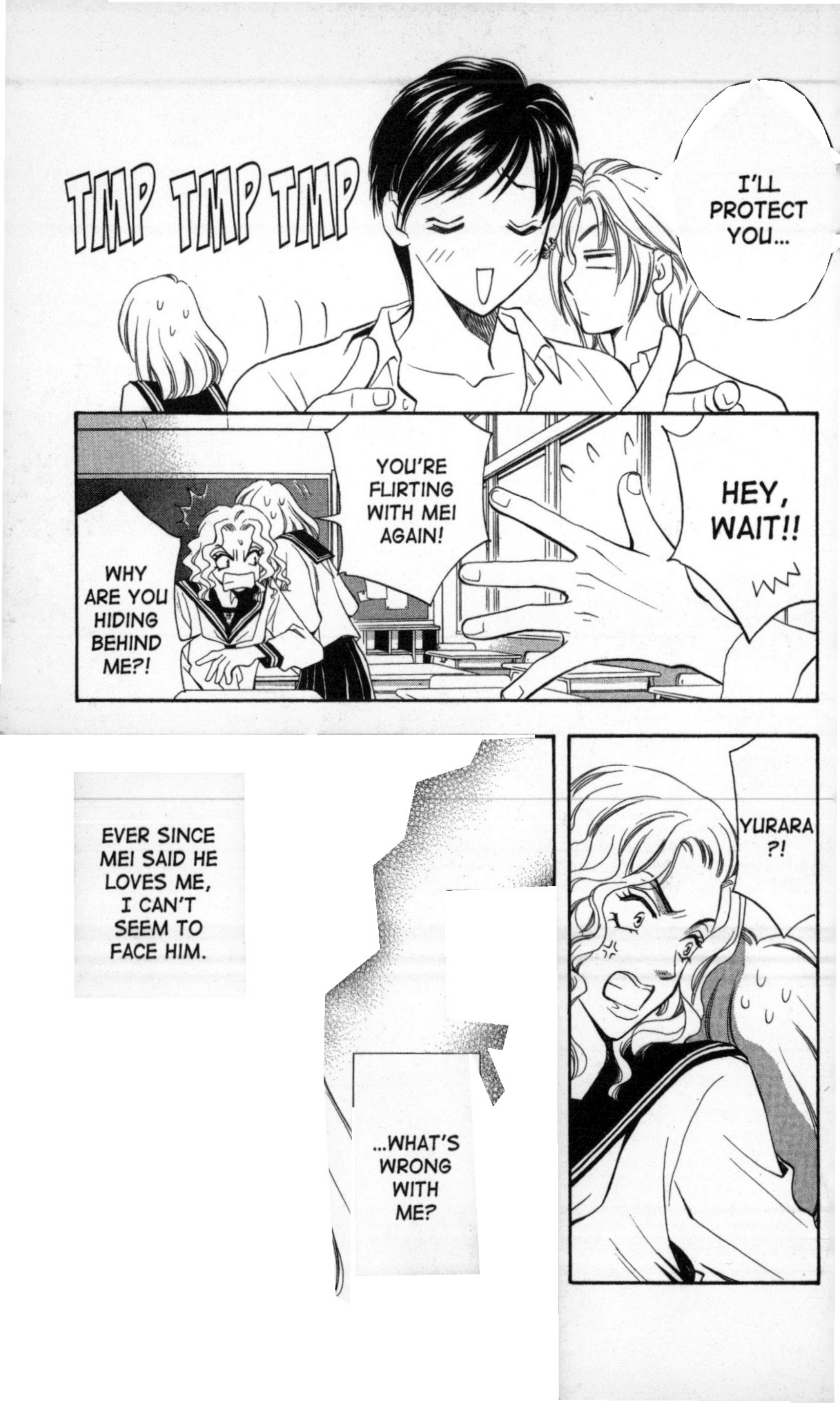
I'LL PROTECT YOU...
TMP TMP TMP
HEY, WAIT!!
YOU'RE FLIRTING WITH MEI AGAIN!
WHY ARE YOU HIDING BEHIND ME?!
YURARA ?!
EVER SINCE MEI SAID HE LOVES ME, I CAN'T SEEM TO FACE HIM.
...WHAT'S WRONG WITH ME?

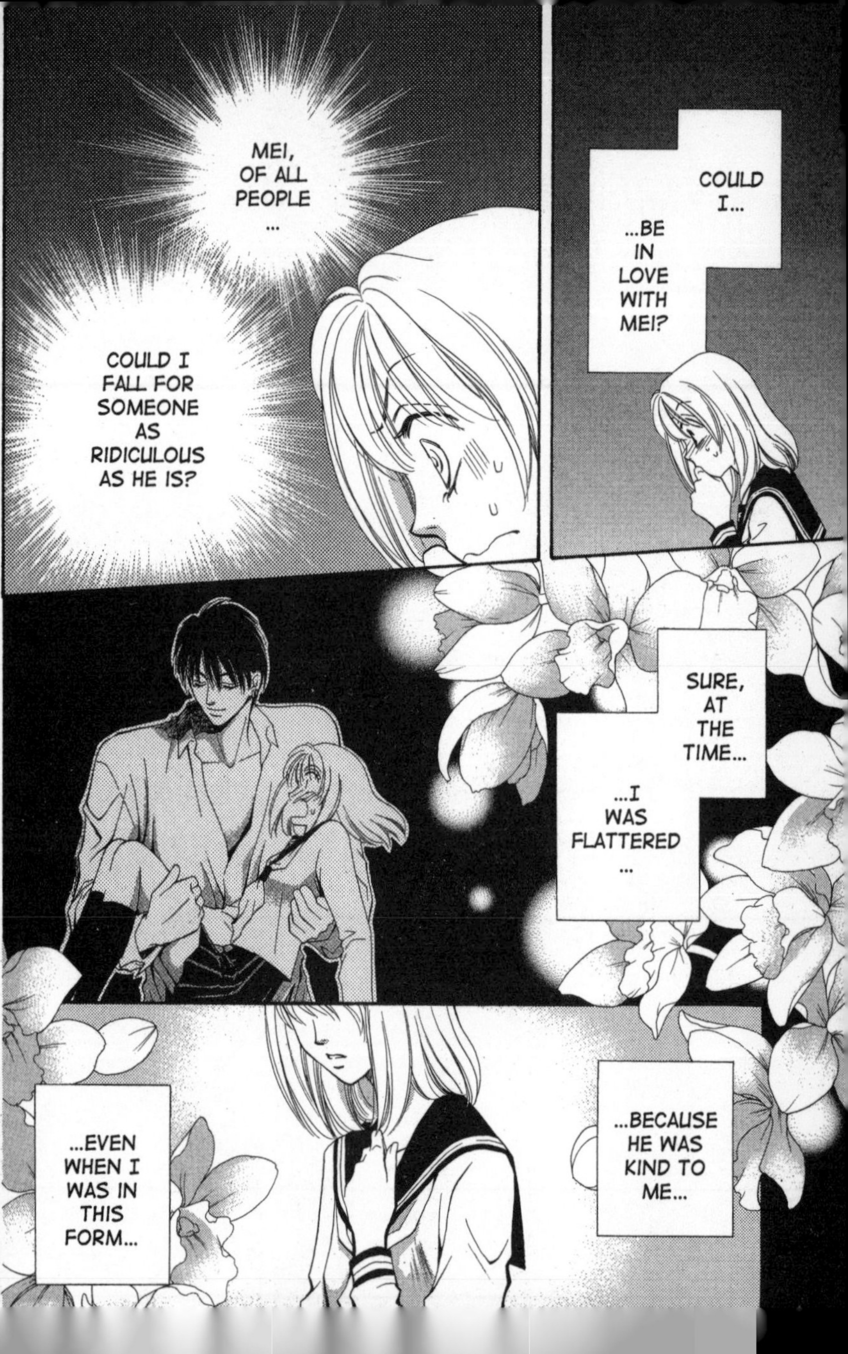
COULD I...
...BE IN LOVE WITH MEI?
MEI, OF ALL PEOPLE ...
COULD I FALL FOR SOMEONE AS RIDICULOUS AS HE IS?
SURE, AT THE TIME...
...I WAS FLATTERED ...
...BECAUSE HE WAS KIND TO ME...
...EVEN WHEN I WAS IN THIS FORM...

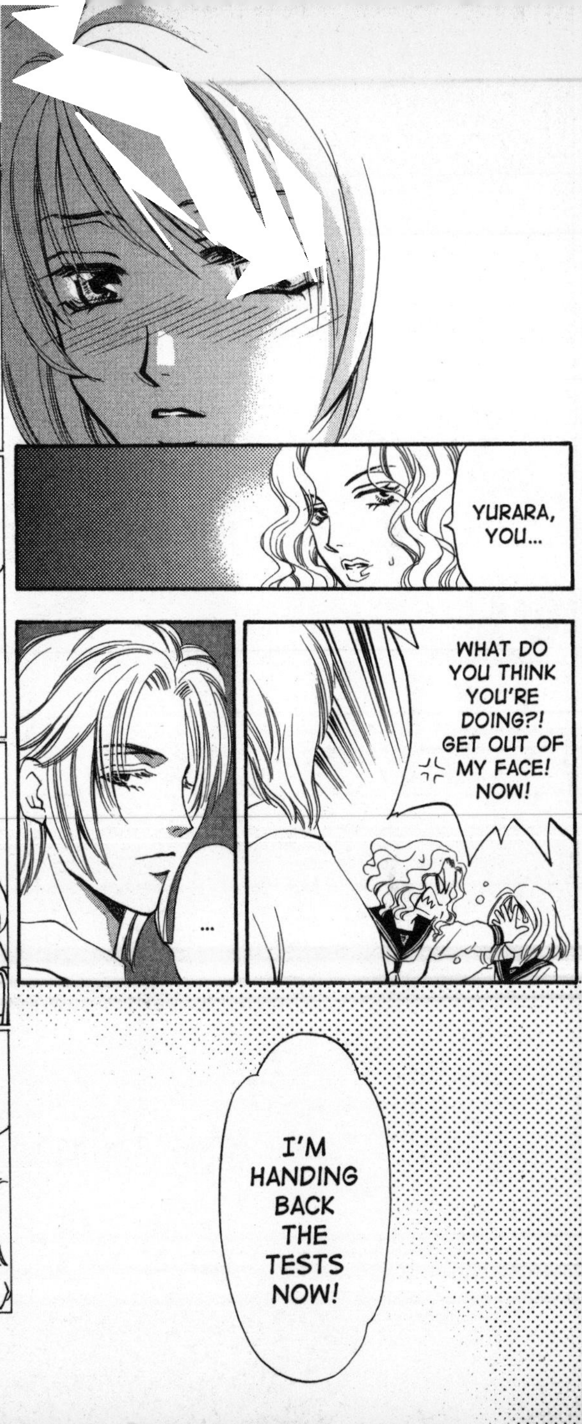
YURARA, YOU...
WHAT DO YOU THINK YOU'RE DOING?! GET OUT OF MY FACE! NOW!
...
I'M HANDING BACK THE TESTS NOW!

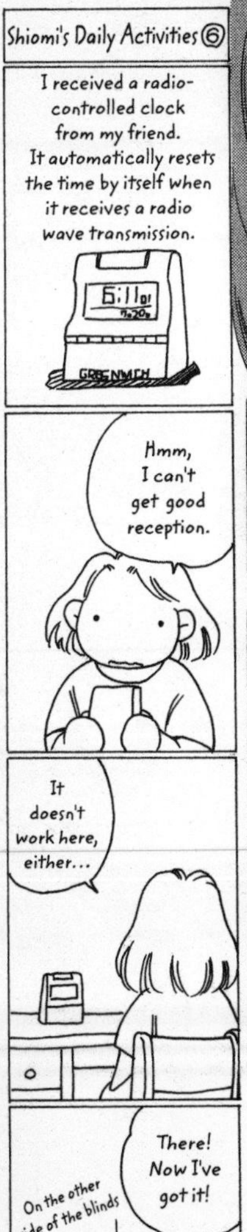
Shiomi's Daily Activities ⑥
I received a radio-controlled clock from my friend. It automatically resets the time by itself when it receives a radio wave transmission.
Hmm, I can't get good reception.
It doesn't work here, either...
There! Now I've got it!
On the other side of the blinds
What's the point in having this clock?

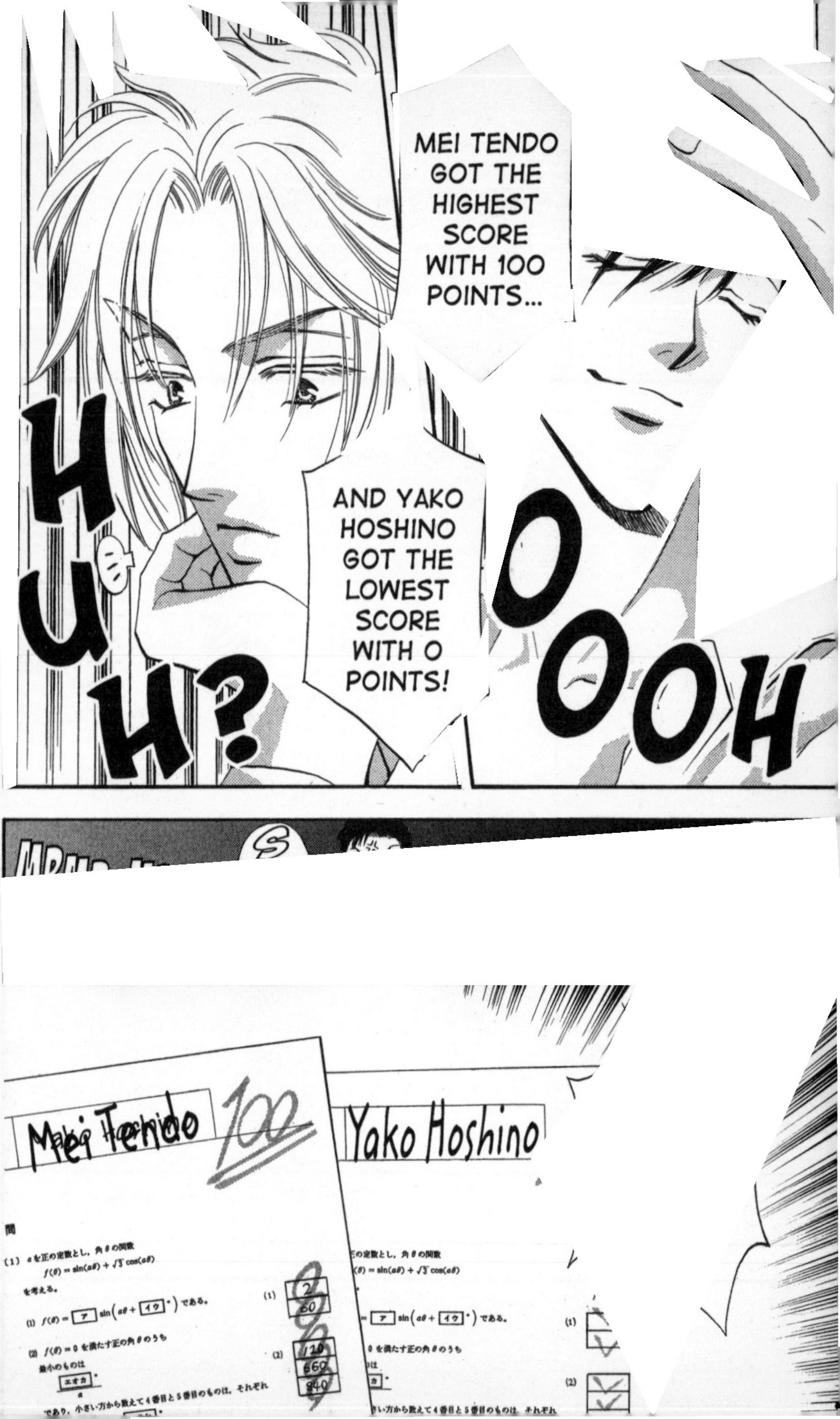
MEI TENDO GOT THE HIGHEST SCORE WITH 100 POINTS...
AND YAKO HOSHINO GOT THE LOWEST SCORE WITH 0 POINTS!
OOOH
HUH?
Yako Hoshino
Mei Tendo
100

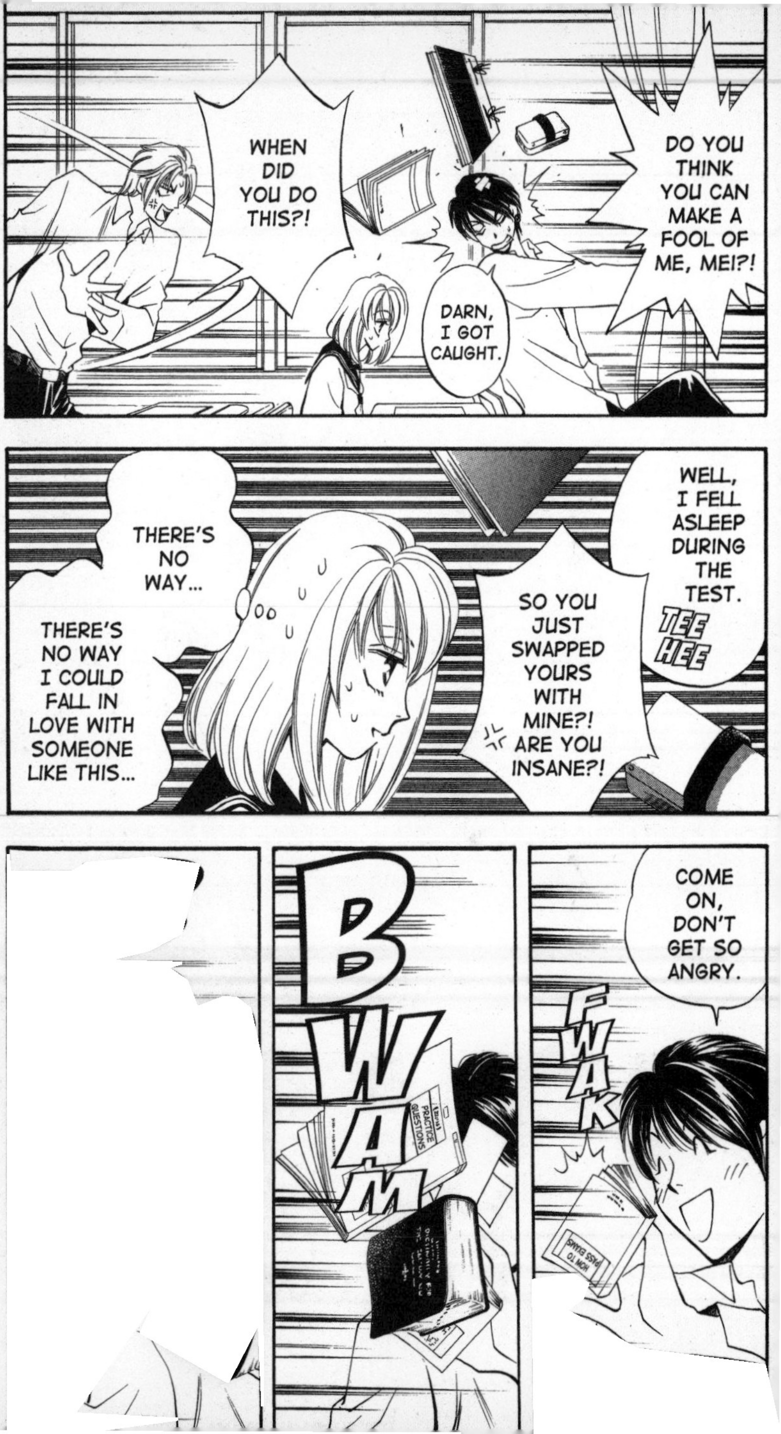

DO YOU THINK YOU CAN MAKE A FOOL OF ME, MEI?!
WHEN DID YOU DO THIS?!
DARN, I GOT CAUGHT.
WELL, I FELL ASLEEP DURING THE TEST.
TEE HEE
SO YOU JUST SWAPPED YOURS WITH MINE?! ARE YOU INSANE?!
THERE'S NO WAY...
THERE'S NO WAY I COULD FALL IN LOVE WITH SOMEONE LIKE THIS...
COME ON, DON'T GET SO ANGRY.
FWAK
HOW TO PASS EXAMS
BWAM
PRACTICE QUESTIONS

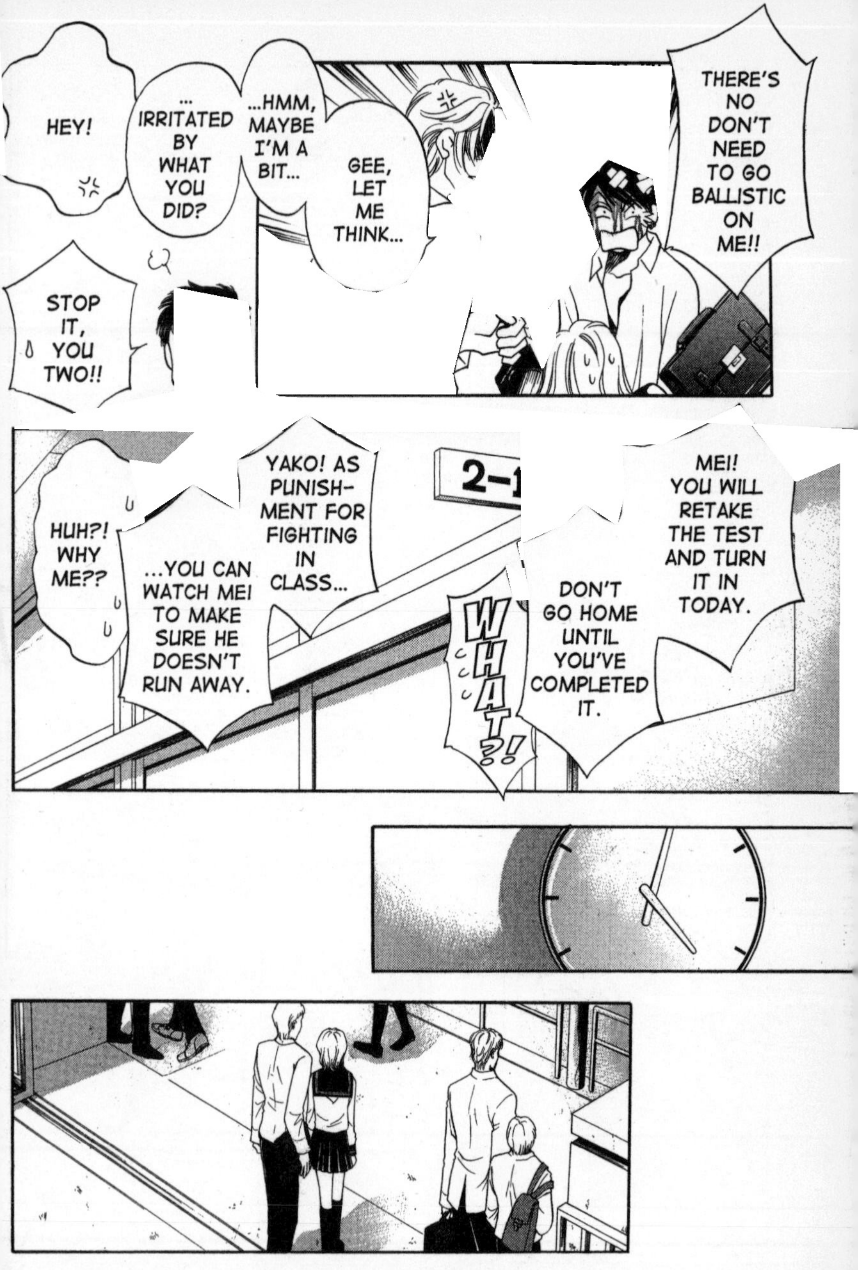
THERE'S NO DON'T NEED TO GO BALLISTIC ON ME!!
GEE, LET ME THINK...
...HMM, MAYBE I'M A BIT...
... IRRITATED BY WHAT YOU DID?
HEY!
STOP IT, YOU TWO!!
MEI! YOU WILL RETAKE THE TEST AND TURN IT IN TODAY.
DON'T GO HOME UNTIL YOU'VE COMPLETED IT.
WHAT?!
2–1
YAKO! AS PUNISH-MENT FOR FIGHTING IN CLASS...
...YOU CAN WATCH MEI TO MAKE SURE HE DOESN'T RUN AWAY.
HUH?! WHY ME??

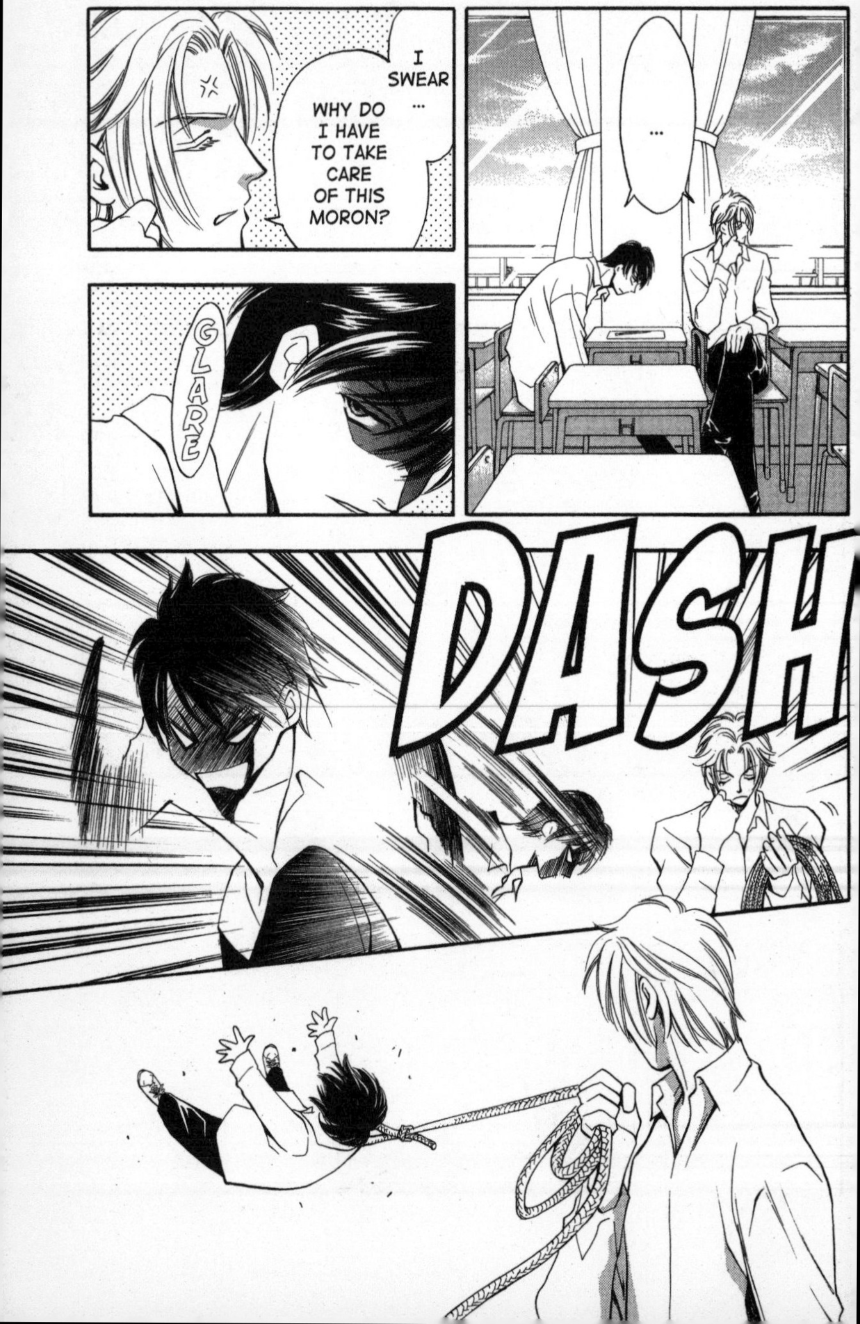
...
I SWEAR ...
WHY DO I HAVE TO TAKE CARE OF THIS MORON?
GLARE
DASH

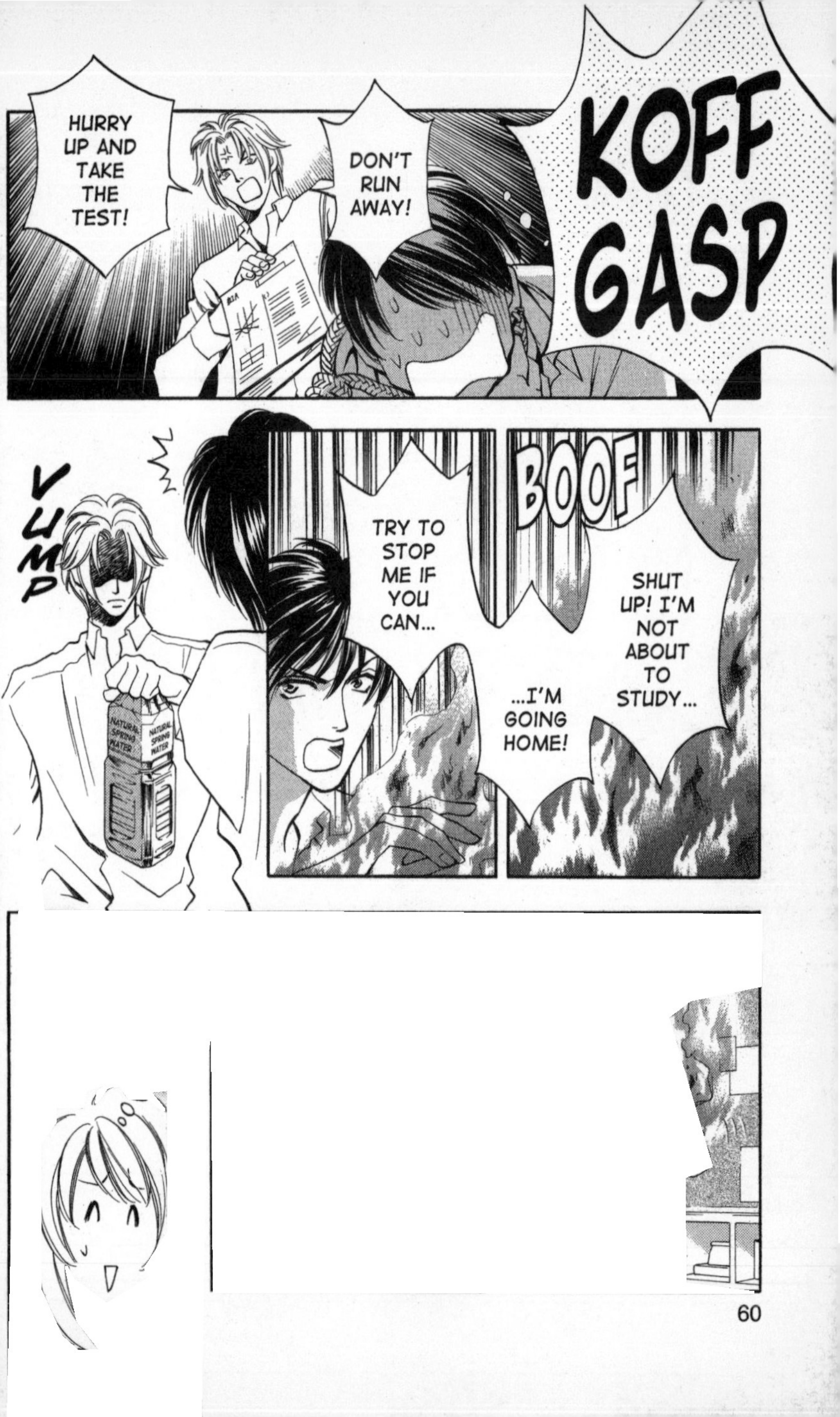
KOFF GASP
DON'T RUN AWAY!
HURRY UP AND TAKE THE TEST!
BOOF
SHUT UP! I'M NOT ABOUT TO STUDY...
...I'M GOING HOME!
TRY TO STOP ME IF YOU CAN...
VUMP
NATURAL SPRING WATER
NATURAL SPRING WATER

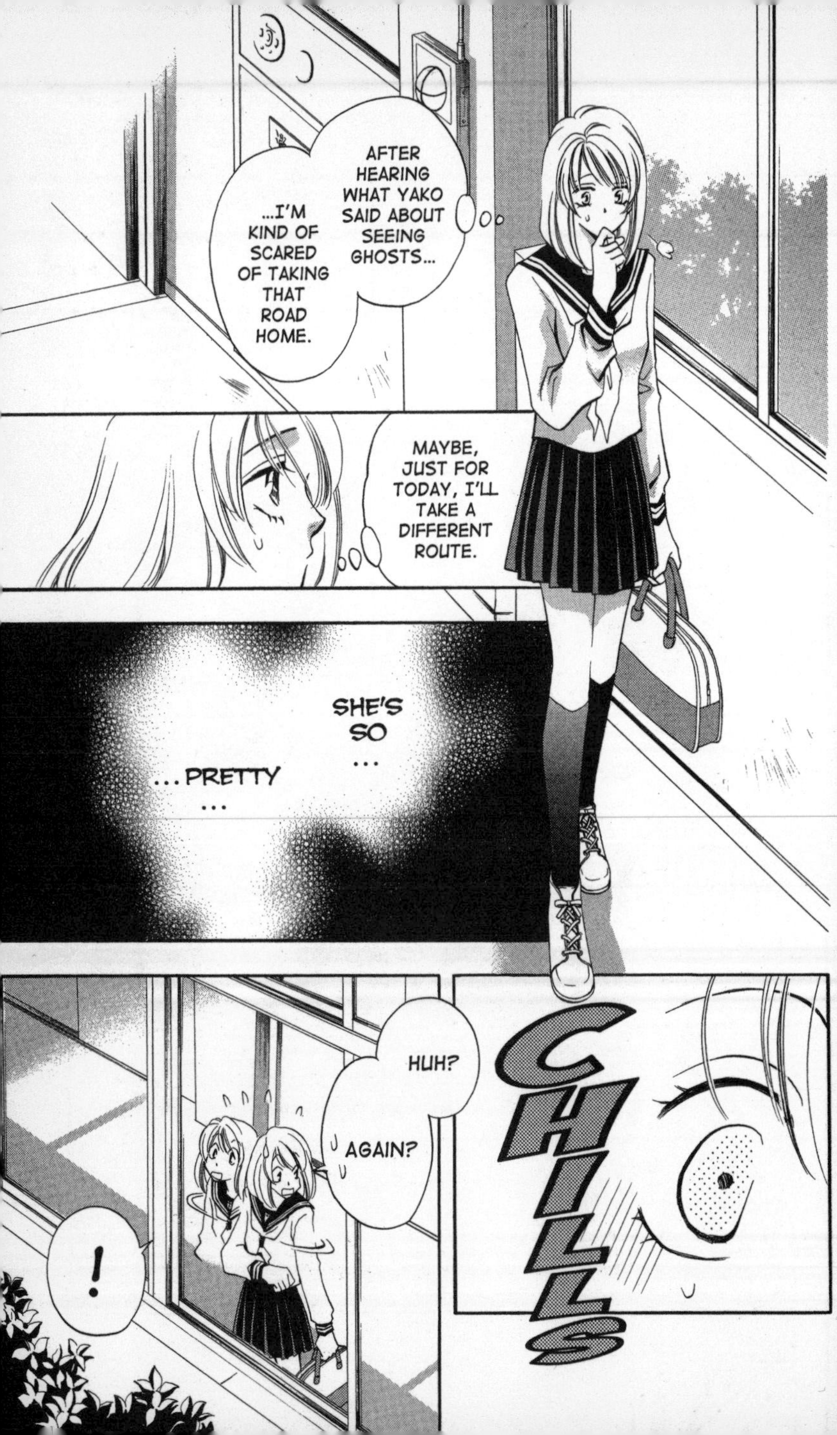
AFTER HEARING WHAT YAKO SAID ABOUT SEEING GHOSTS...
...I'M KIND OF SCARED OF TAKING THAT ROAD HOME.
MAYBE, JUST FOR TODAY, I'LL TAKE A DIFFERENT ROUTE.
SHE'S SO ...
... PRETTY ...
CHILLS
HUH?
AGAIN?
!

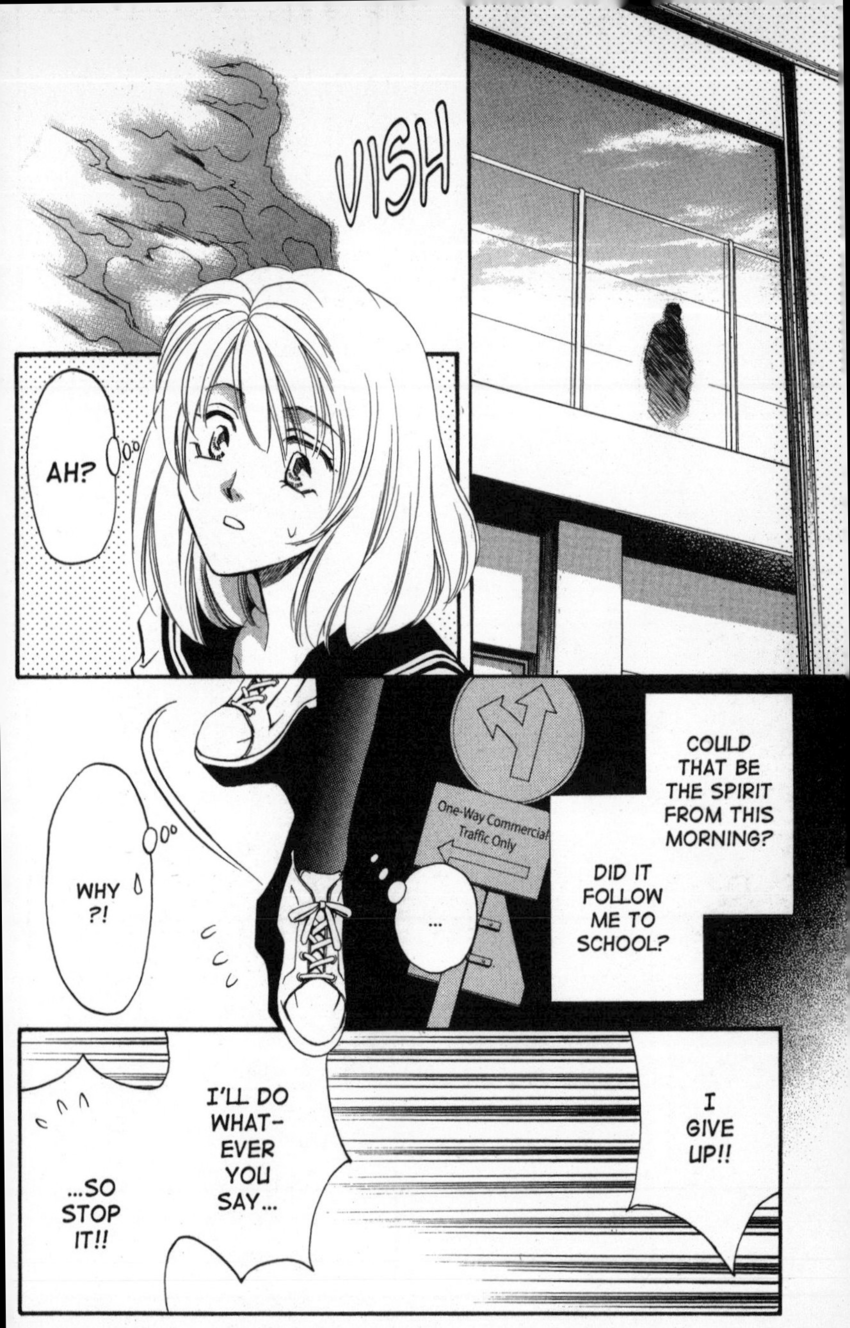
VISH
AH?
COULD THAT BE THE SPIRIT FROM THIS MORNING?
DID IT FOLLOW ME TO SCHOOL?
...
One-Way Commercial Traffic Only
WHY ?!
I GIVE UP!!
I'LL DO WHAT-EVER YOU SAY...
...SO STOP IT!!

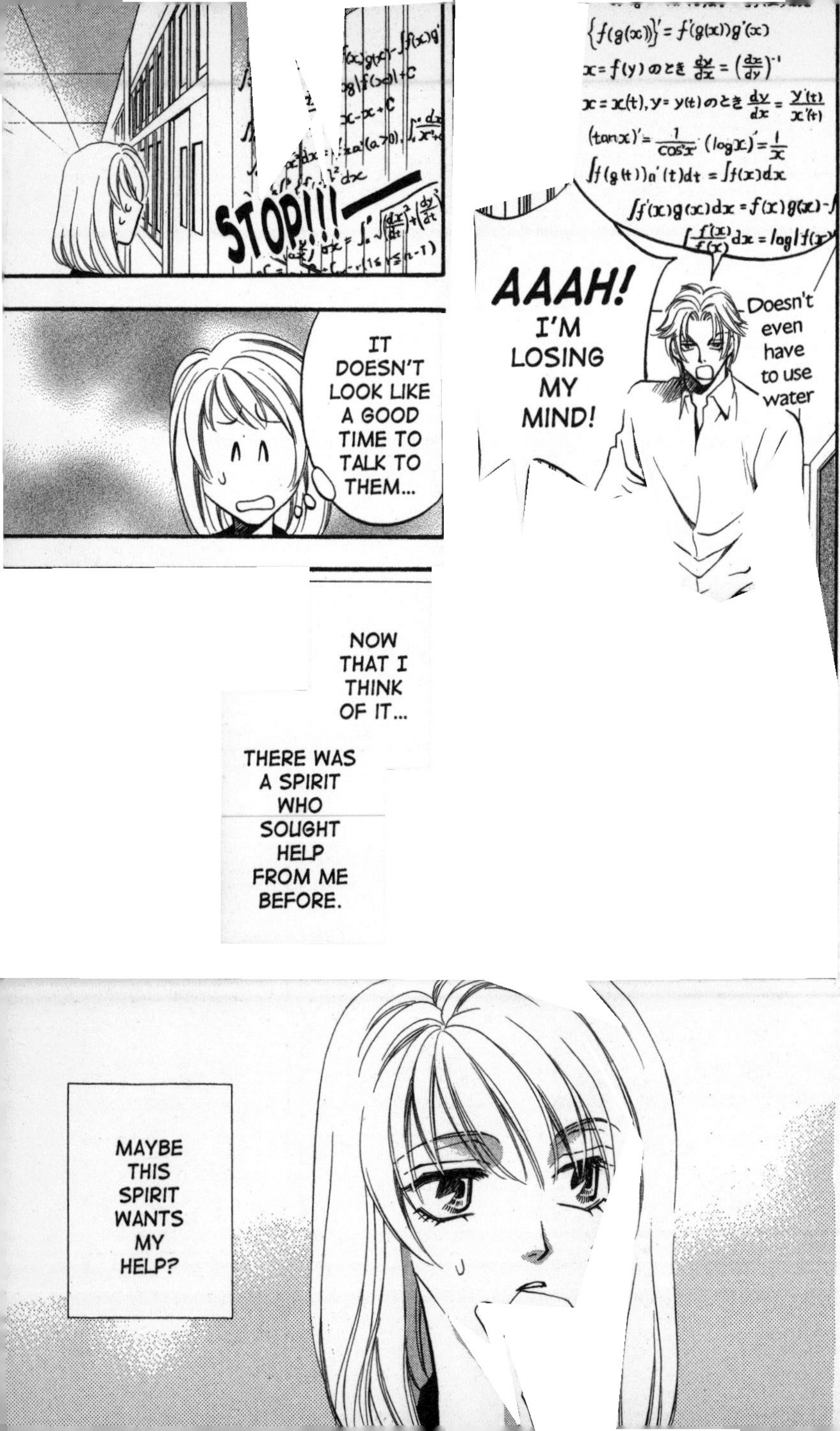
AAAH! I'M LOSING MY MIND!
Doesn't even have to use water
STOP!!!
IT DOESN'T LOOK LIKE A GOOD TIME TO TALK TO THEM...
NOW THAT I THINK OF IT...
THERE WAS A SPIRIT WHO SOUGHT HELP FROM ME BEFORE.
MAYBE THIS SPIRIT WANTS MY HELP?

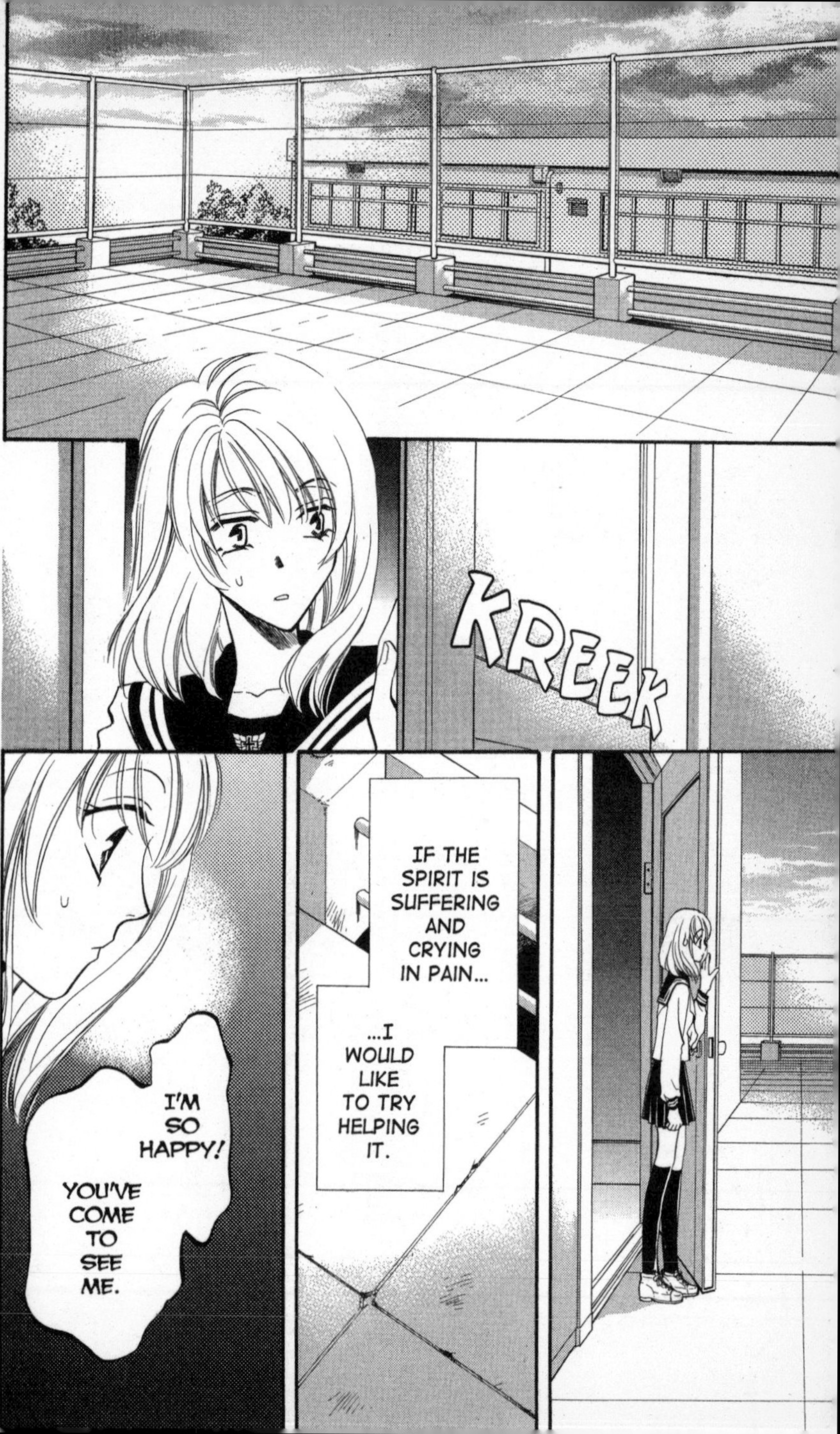
KREEK
IF THE SPIRIT IS SUFFERING AND CRYING IN PAIN...
...I WOULD LIKE TO TRY HELPING IT.
I'M SO HAPPY!
YOU'VE COME TO SEE ME.

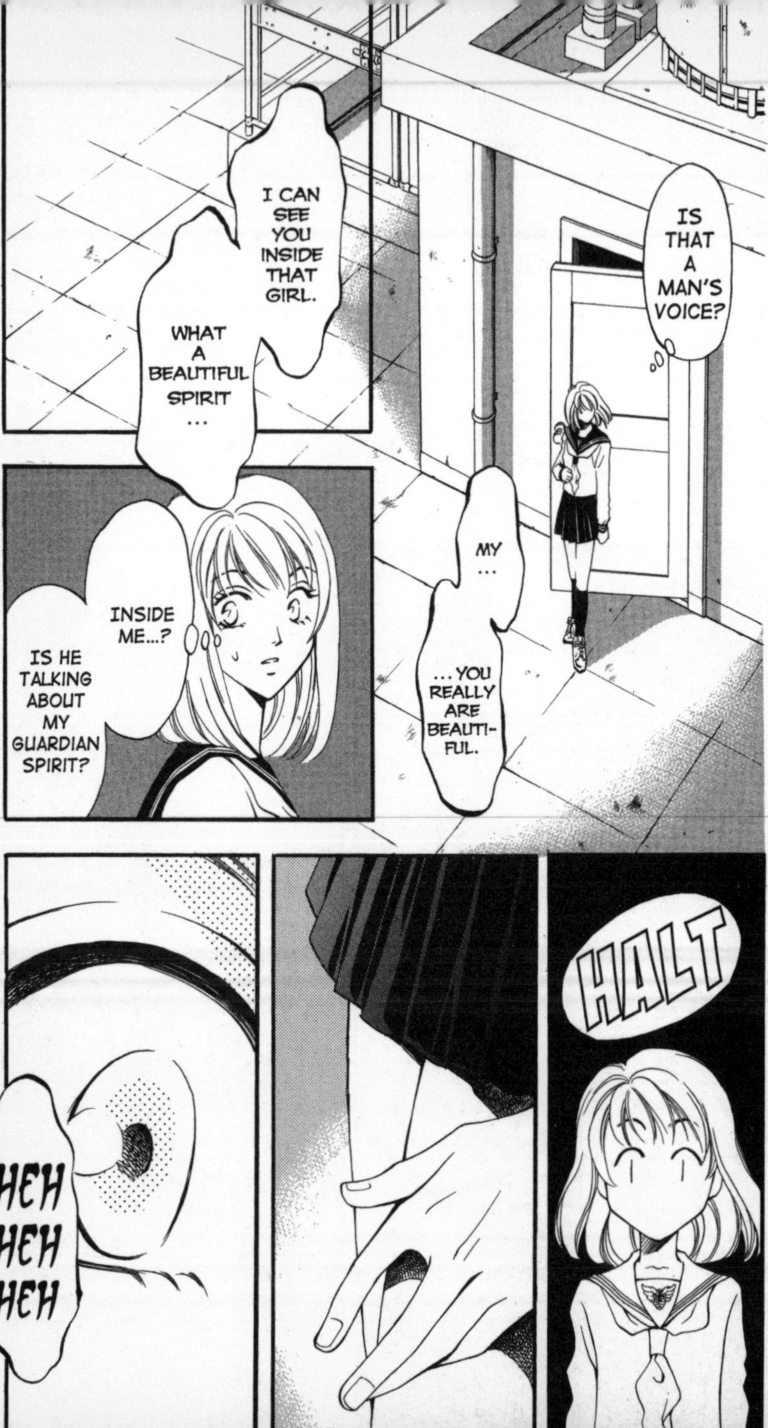
I CAN SEE YOU INSIDE THAT GIRL.
WHAT A BEAUTIFUL SPIRIT ...
IS THAT A MAN'S VOICE?
INSIDE ME...?
IS HE TALKING ABOUT MY GUARDIAN SPIRIT?
MY ...
... YOU REALLY ARE BEAUTI- FUL.
HALT
HEH HEH HEH

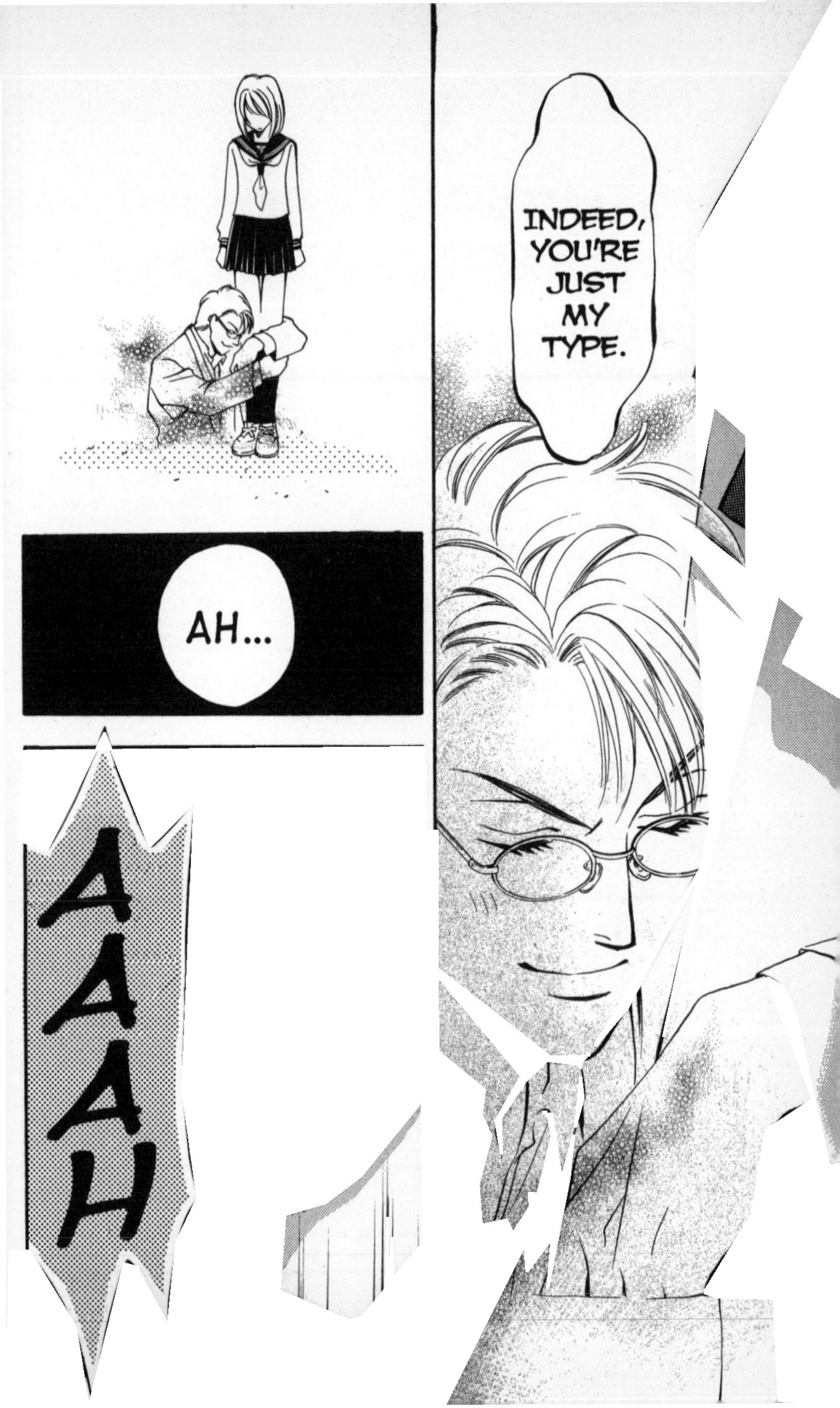
INDEED, YOU'RE JUST MY TYPE.
AH...
AAAH

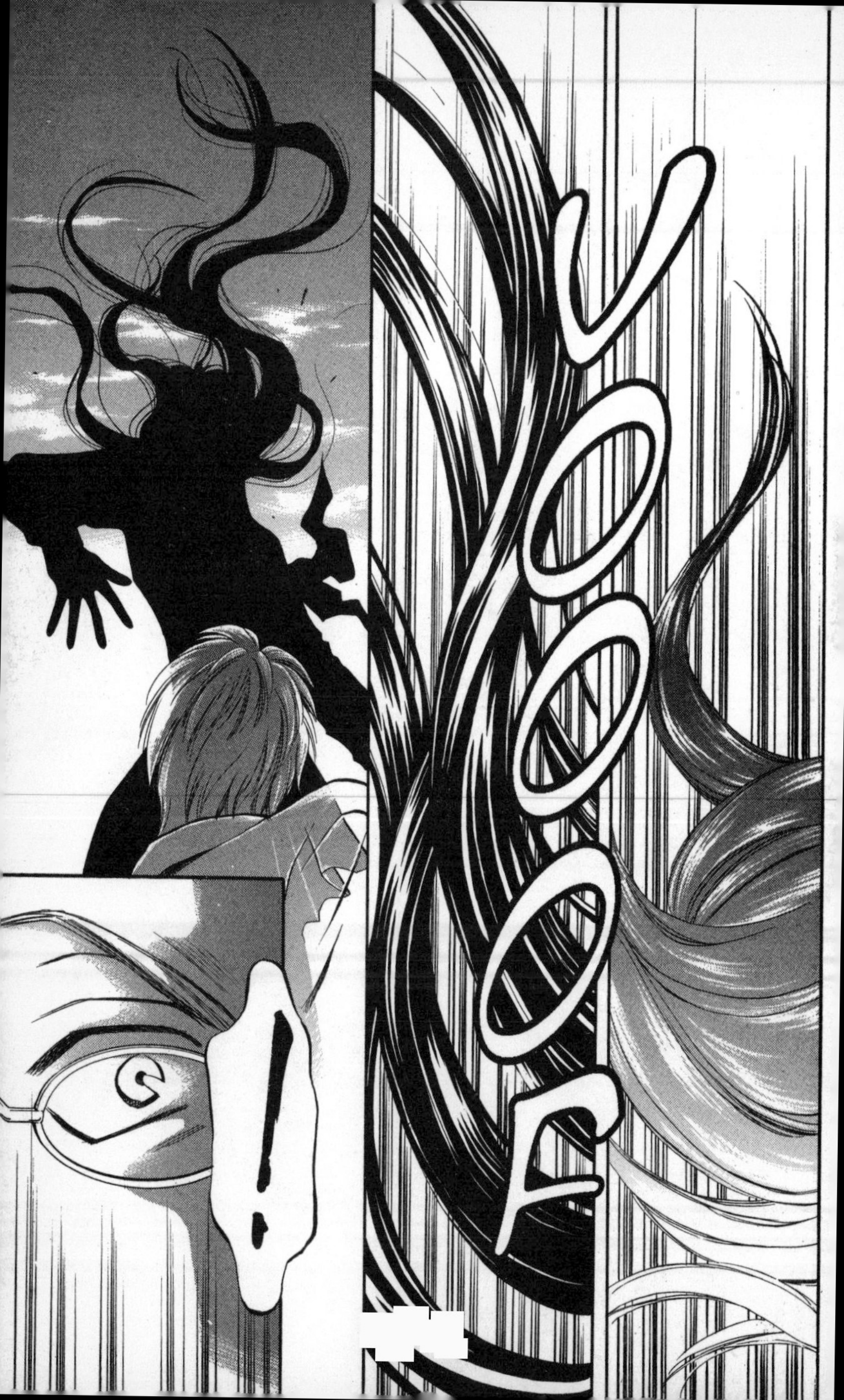
!

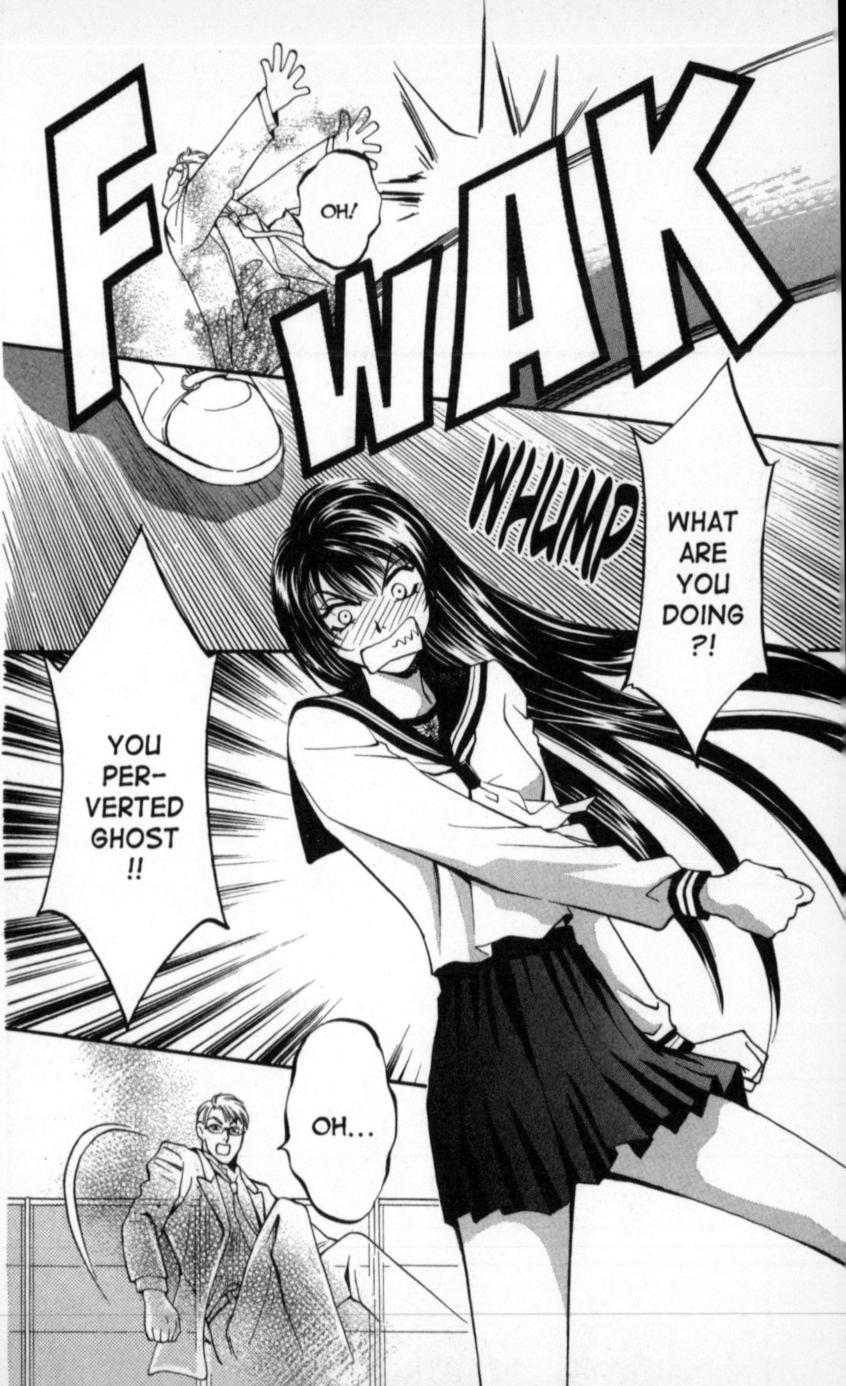
FWAK
OH!
WHUMP
WHAT ARE YOU DOING ?!
YOU PER- VERTED GHOST !!
OH...

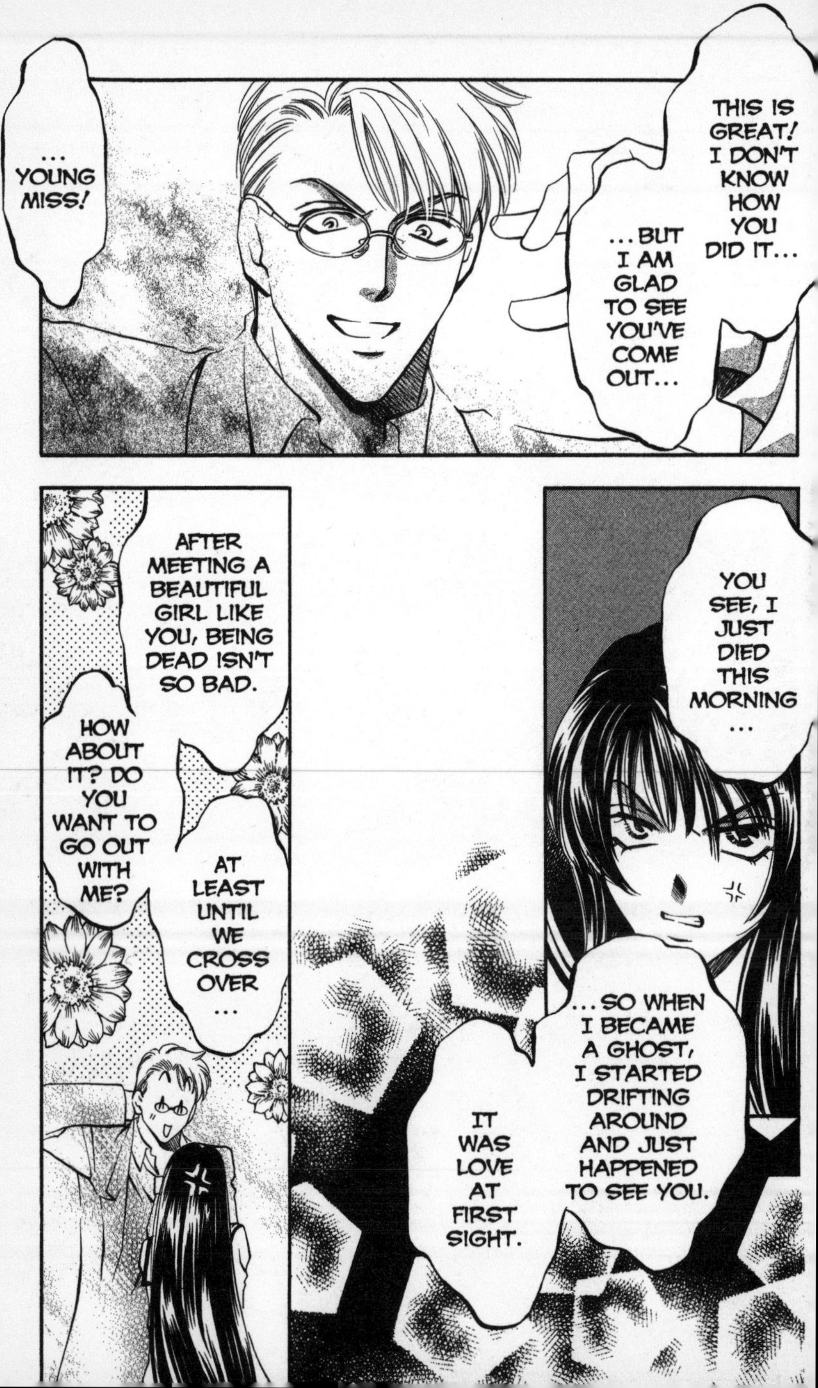
THIS IS GREAT! I DON'T KNOW HOW YOU DID IT...
...BUT I AM GLAD TO SEE YOU'VE COME OUT...
...YOUNG MISS!
YOU SEE, I JUST DIED THIS MORNING...
...SO WHEN I BECAME A GHOST, I STARTED DRIFTING AROUND AND JUST HAPPENED TO SEE YOU.
IT WAS LOVE AT FIRST SIGHT.
AFTER MEETING A BEAUTIFUL GIRL LIKE YOU, BEING DEAD ISN'T SO BAD.
HOW ABOUT IT? DO YOU WANT TO GO OUT WITH ME?
AT LEAST UNTIL WE CROSS OVER...

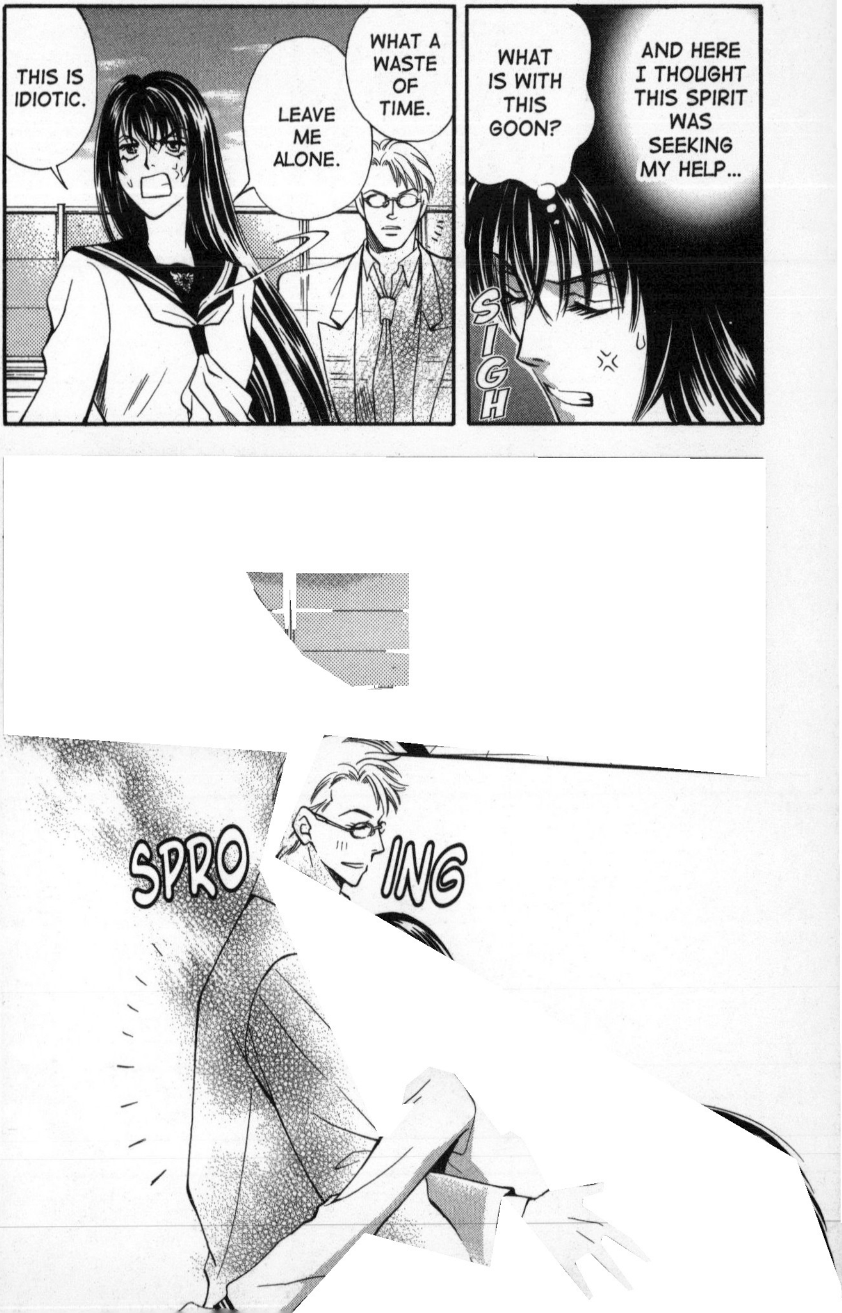
AND HERE I THOUGHT THIS SPIRIT WAS SEEKING MY HELP...
WHAT IS WITH THIS GOON?
SIGH
WHAT A WASTE OF TIME.
LEAVE ME ALONE.
THIS IS IDIOTIC.
SPRO ING

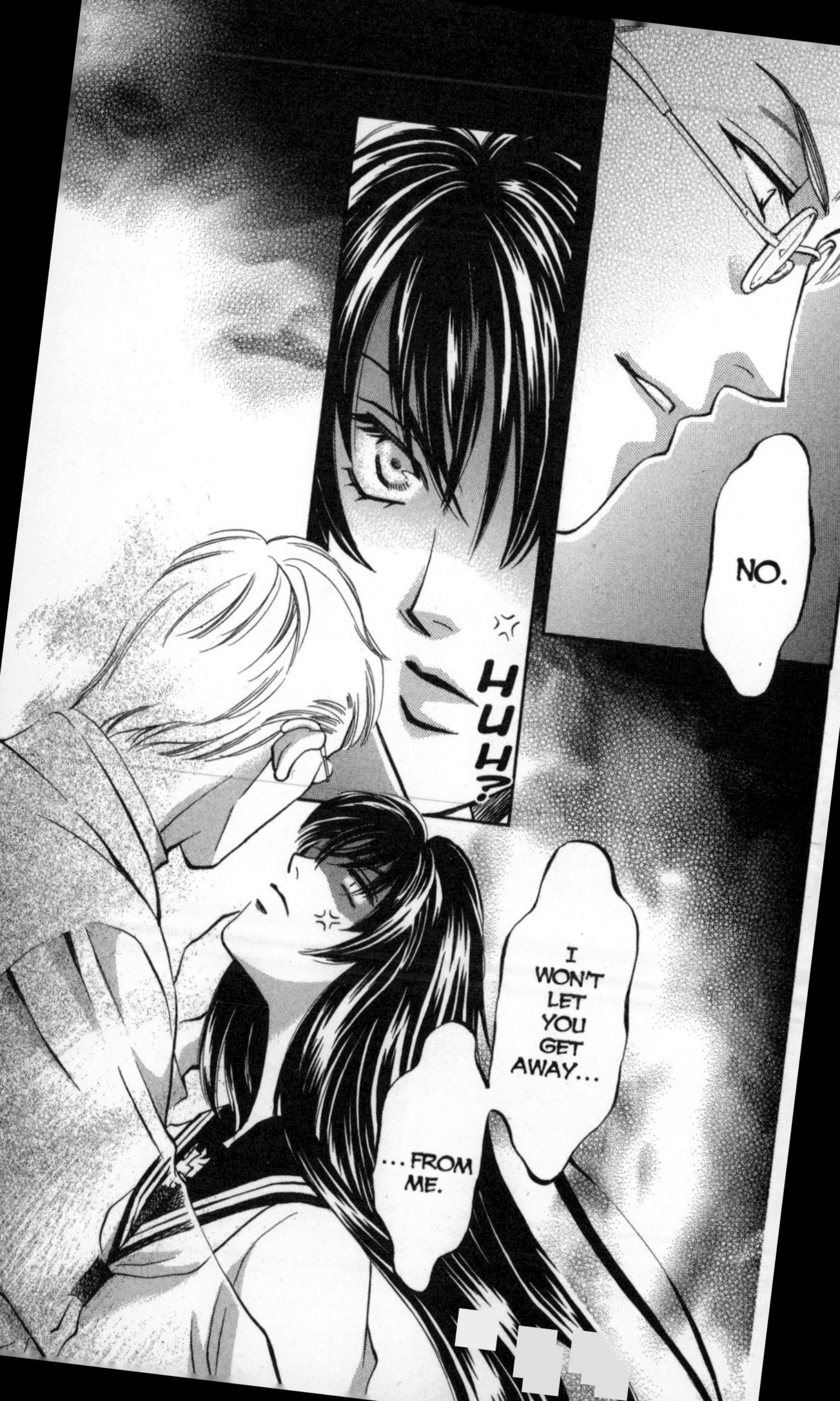
NO.
HUH?
I WON'T LET YOU GET AWAY...
...FROM ME.

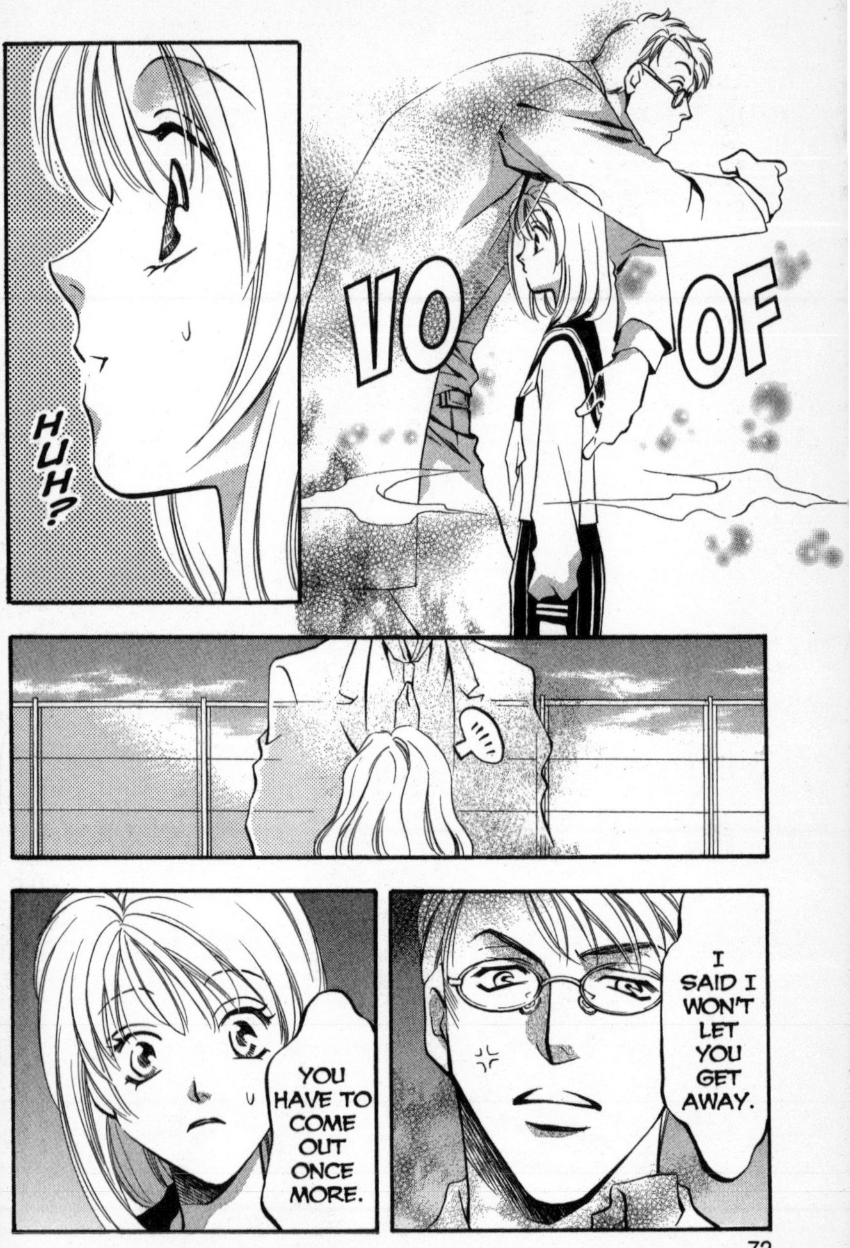
VO OF
HUH?
I SAID I WON'T LET YOU GET AWAY.
YOU HAVE TO COME OUT ONCE MORE.

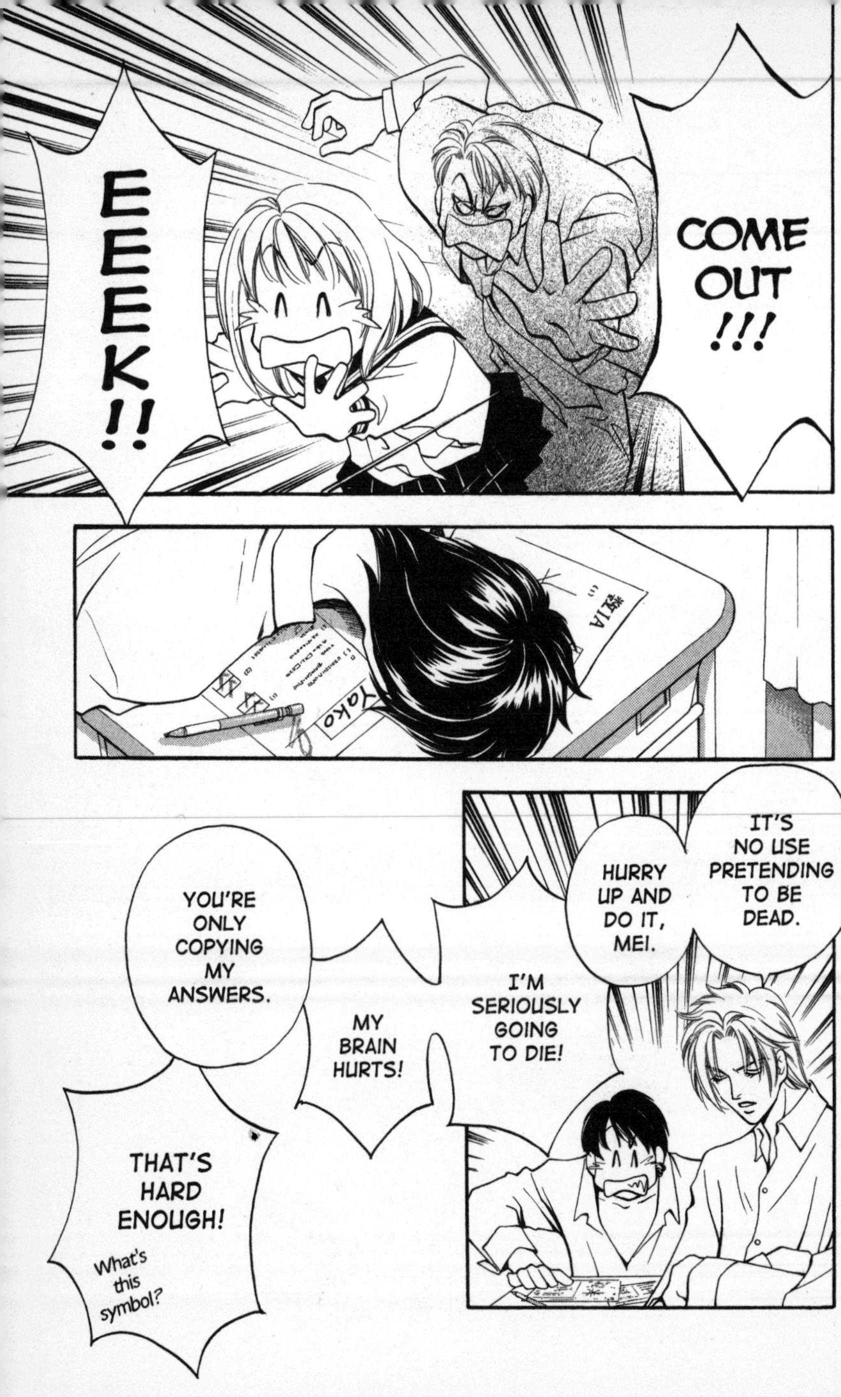
COME OUT!!!
EEEEK!!
Yako
IT'S NO USE PRETENDING TO BE DEAD.
HURRY UP AND DO IT, MEI.
I'M SERIOUSLY GOING TO DIE!
MY BRAIN HURTS!
YOU'RE ONLY COPYING MY ANSWERS.
THAT'S HARD ENOUGH!
What's this symbol?

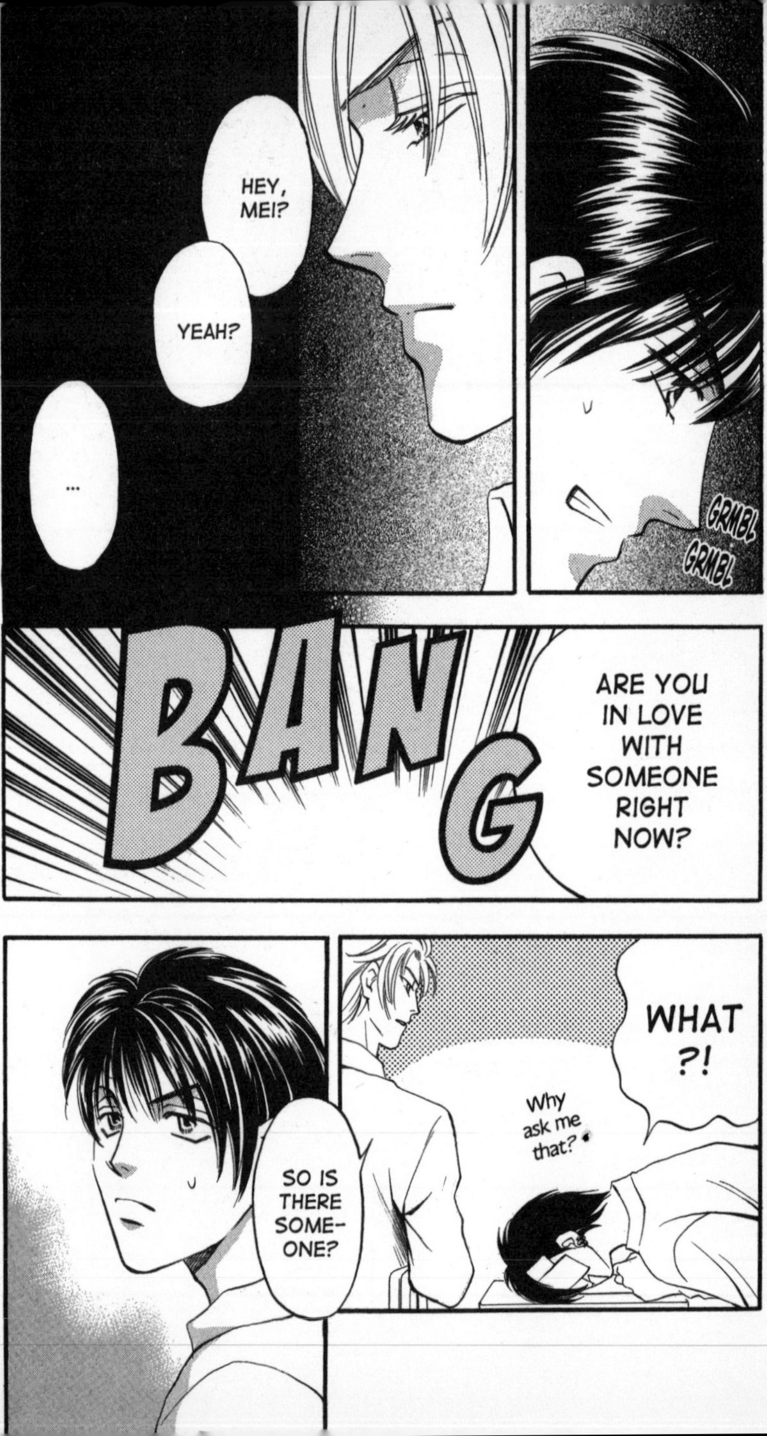
GRMBL
GRMBL
HEY, MEI?
YEAH?
...
ARE YOU IN LOVE WITH SOMEONE RIGHT NOW?
BANG
WHAT?!
Why ask me that?
SO IS THERE SOME-ONE?

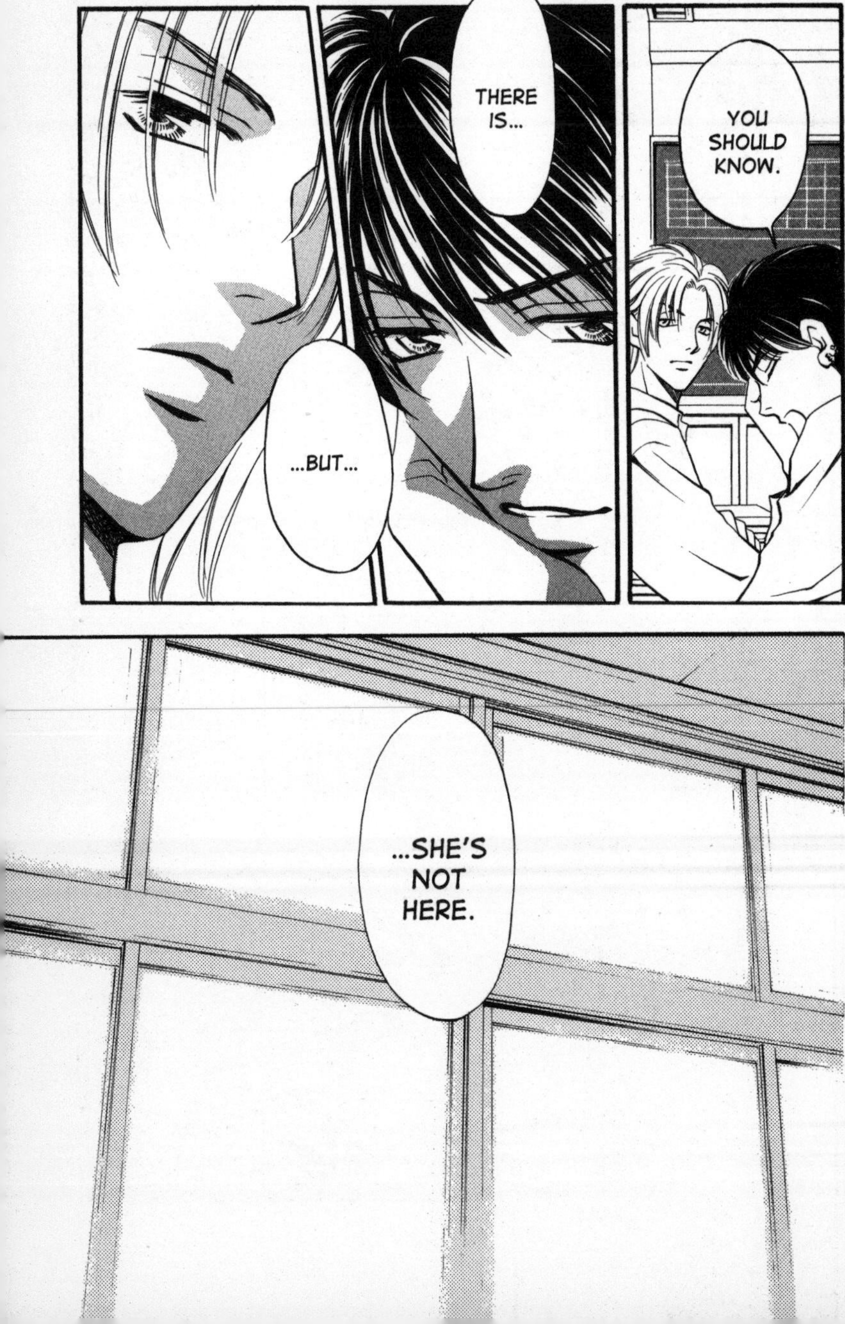
YOU SHOULD KNOW.
THERE IS...
...BUT...
...SHE'S NOT HERE.

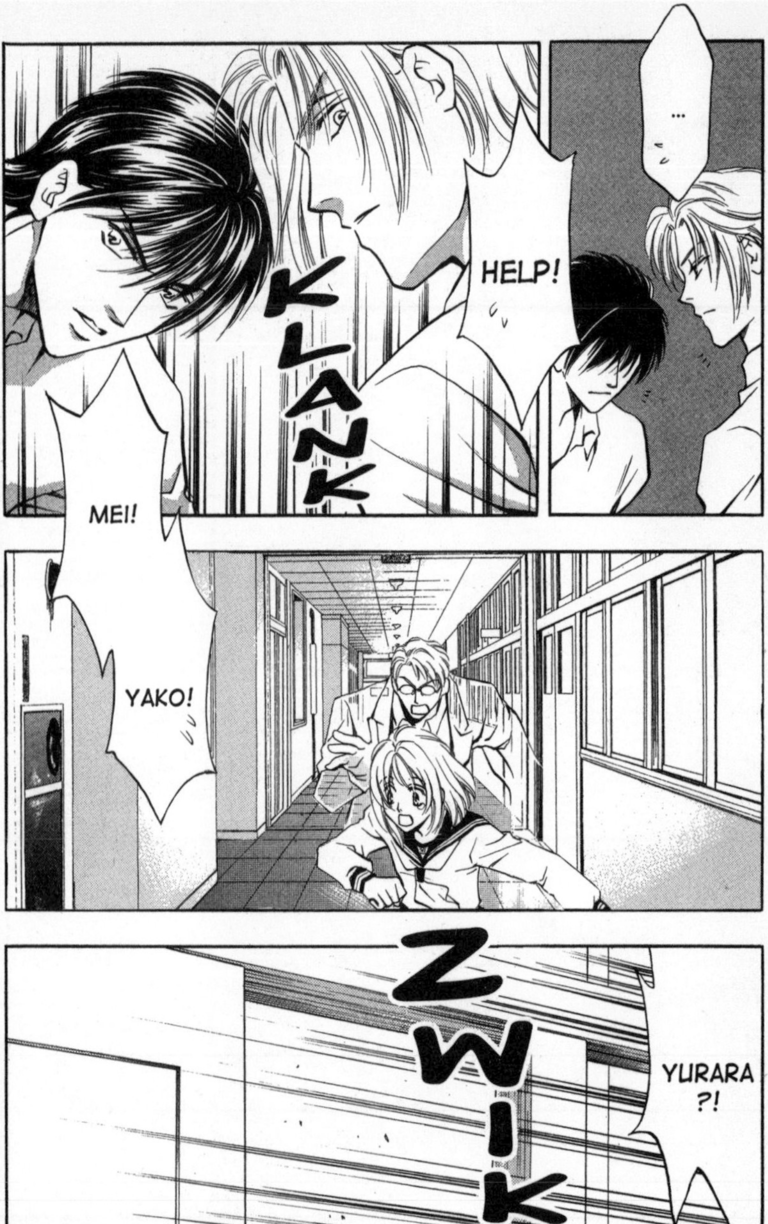
...
HELP!
KLANK
MEI!
YAKO!
ZWIK
YURARA ?!

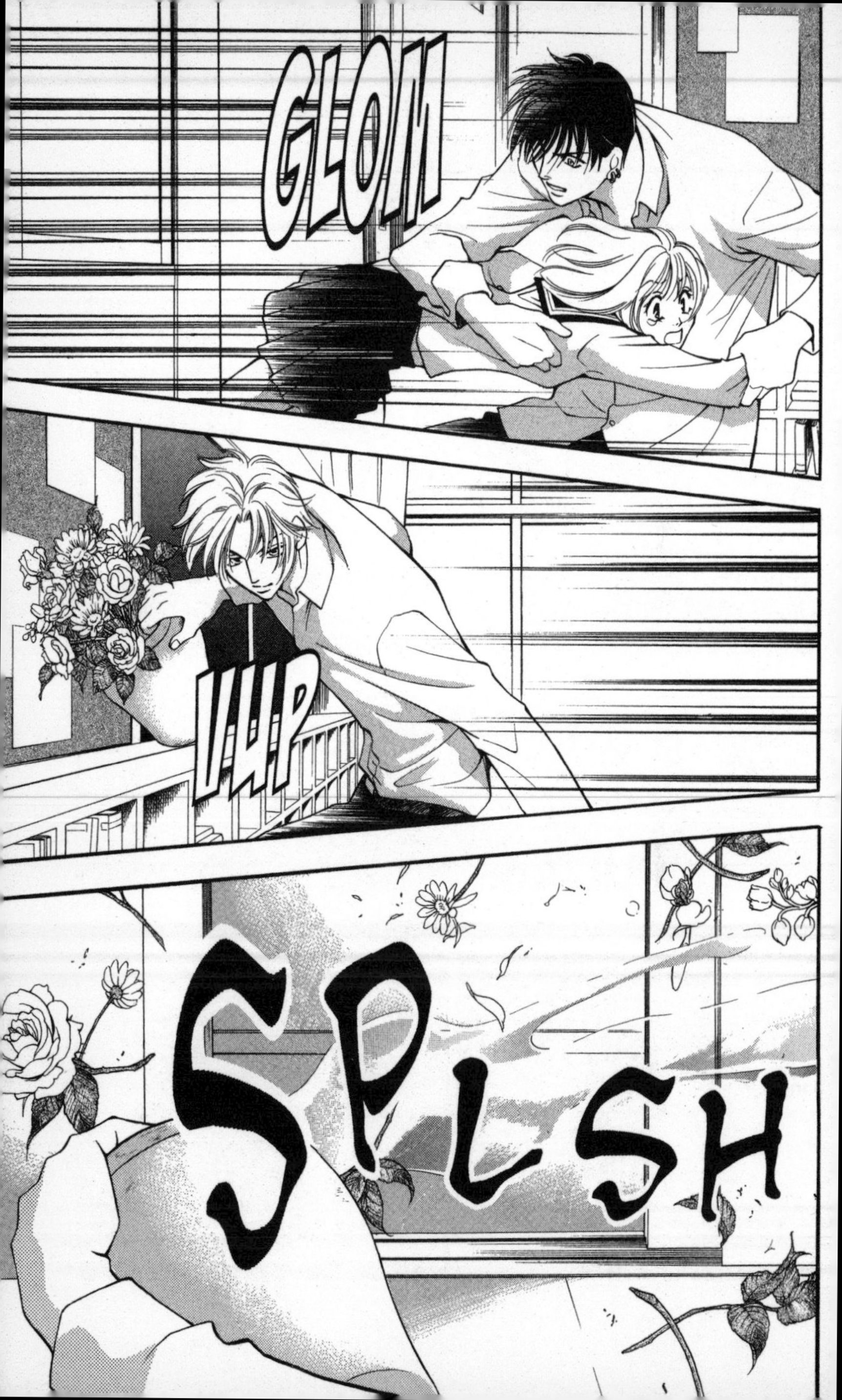
GLOM
V-U-P
SPLSH

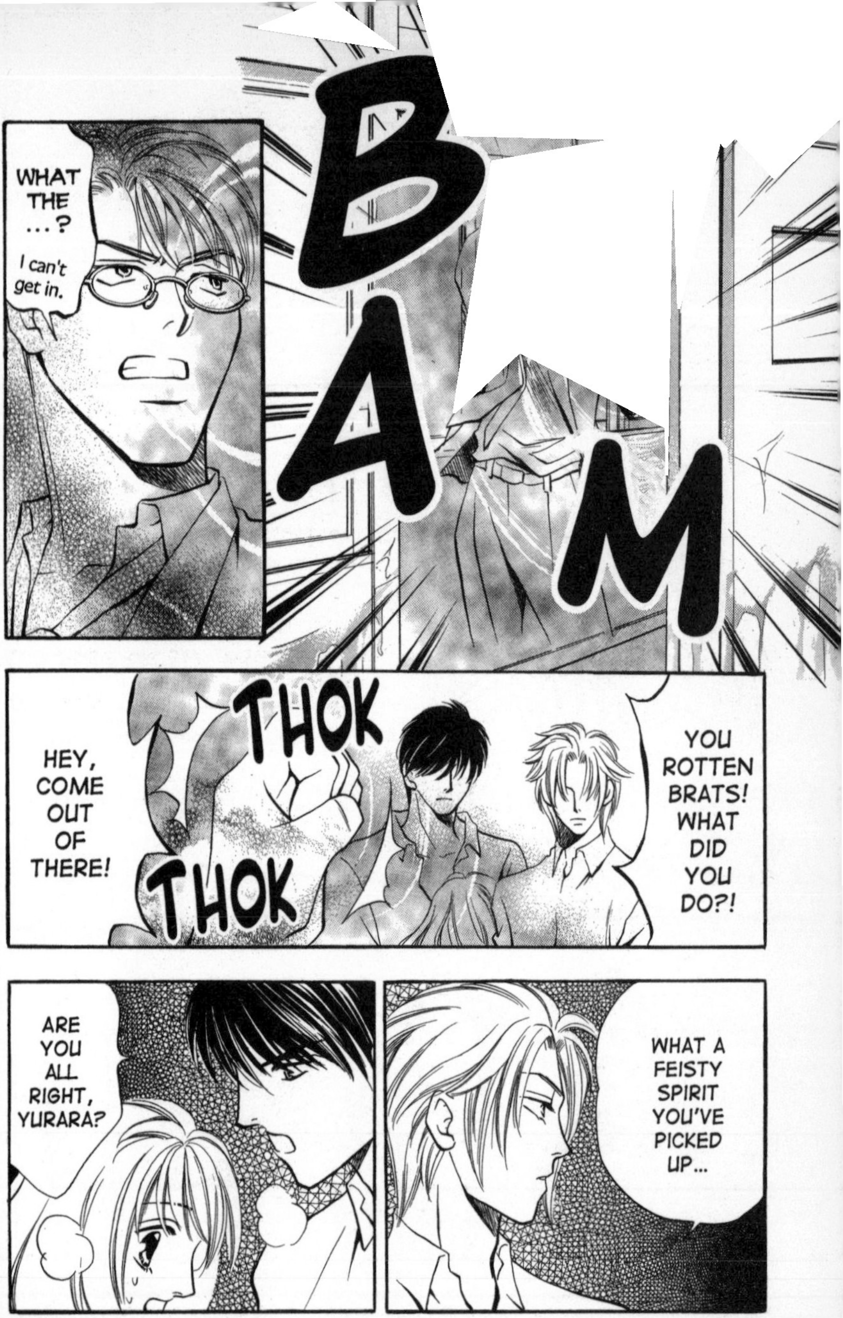
BAM
WHAT THE ...?
I can't get in.
YOU ROTTEN BRATS! WHAT DID YOU DO?!
THOK
HEY, COME OUT OF THERE!
THOK
WHAT A FEISTY SPIRIT YOU'VE PICKED UP...
ARE YOU ALL RIGHT, YURARA?

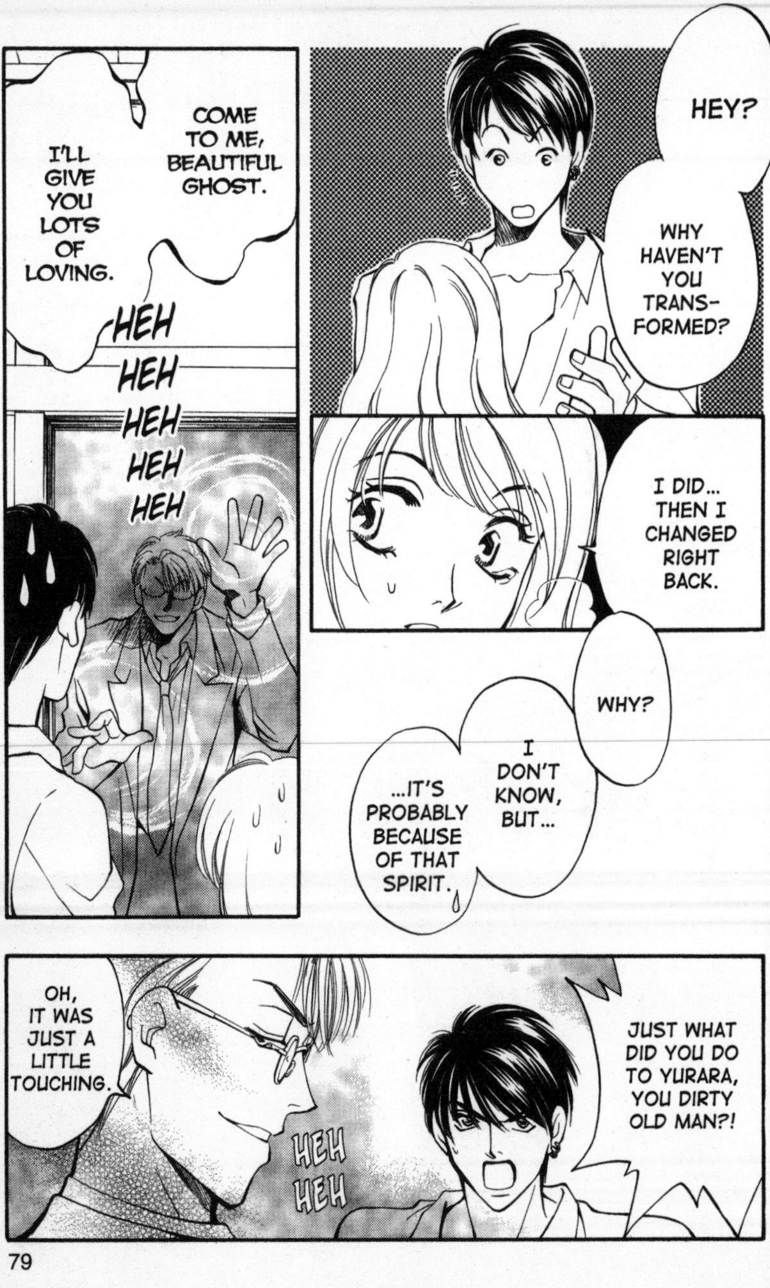
HEY?
WHY HAVEN'T YOU TRANS-FORMED?
I DID... THEN I CHANGED RIGHT BACK.
WHY?
I DON'T KNOW, BUT...
...IT'S PROBABLY BECAUSE OF THAT SPIRIT.
COME TO ME, BEAUTIFUL GHOST.
I'LL GIVE YOU LOTS OF LOVING.
HEH HEH HEH HEH HEH
JUST WHAT DID YOU DO TO YURARA, YOU DIRTY OLD MAN?!
OH, IT WAS JUST A LITTLE TOUCHING.
HEH HEH

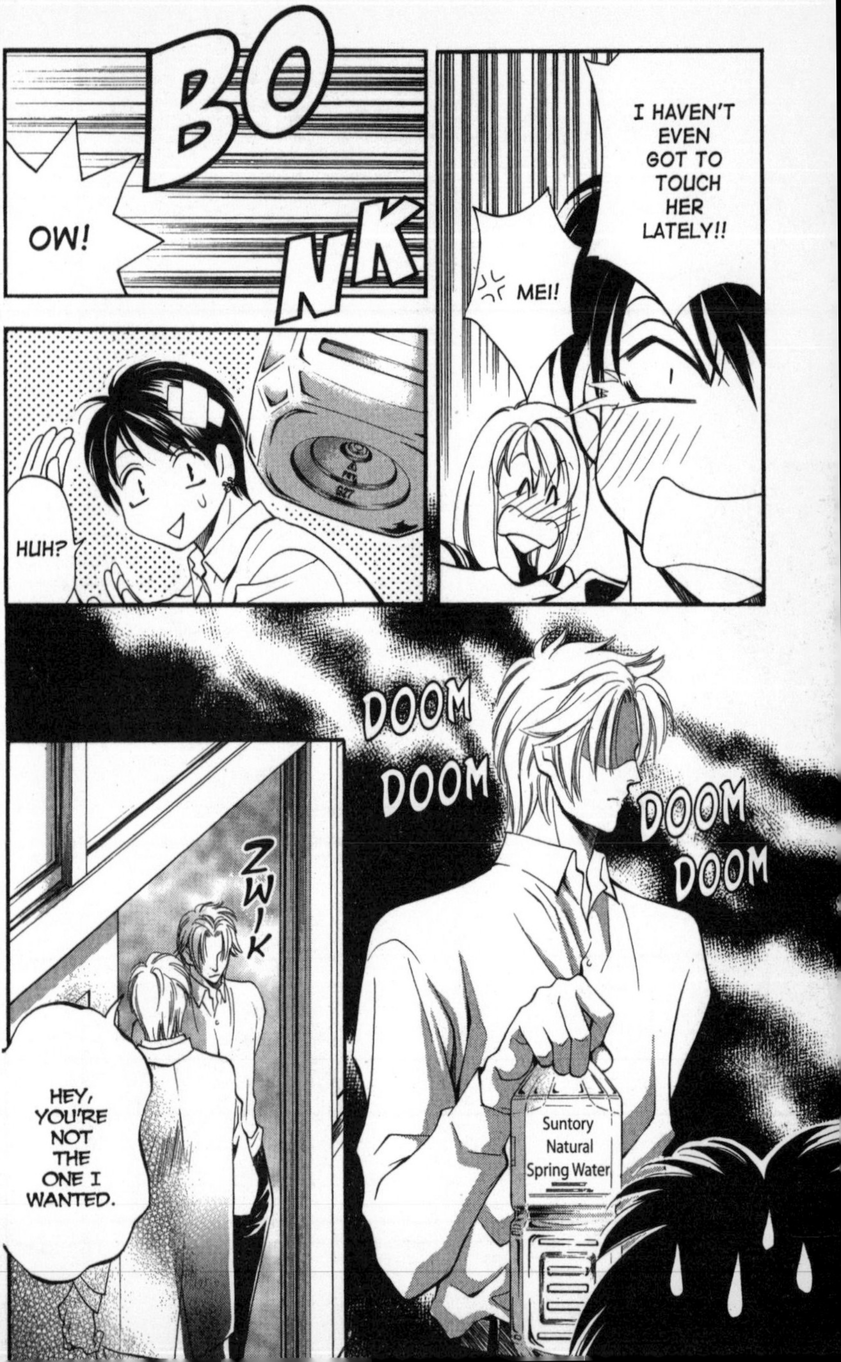
I HAVEN'T EVEN GOT TO TOUCH HER LATELY!!
MEI!
BONK
OW!
HUH?
DOOM DOOM
DOOM DOOM
Suntory Natural Spring Water
ZWIK
HEY, YOU'RE NOT THE ONE I WANTED.

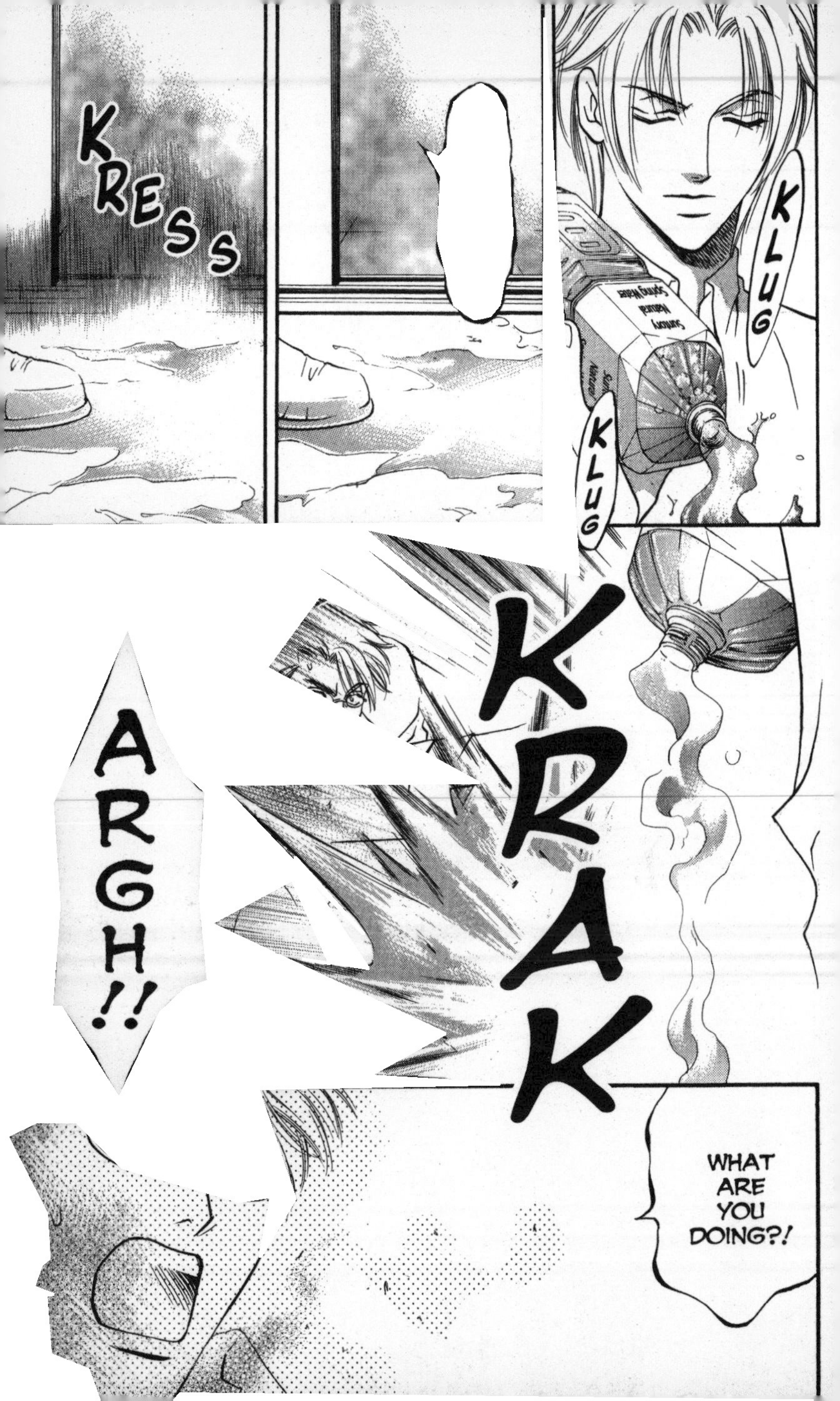
KLUG
Suntory Natural Spring Water
KLUG
KRESS
KRAK
ARGH!!
WHAT ARE YOU DOING?!

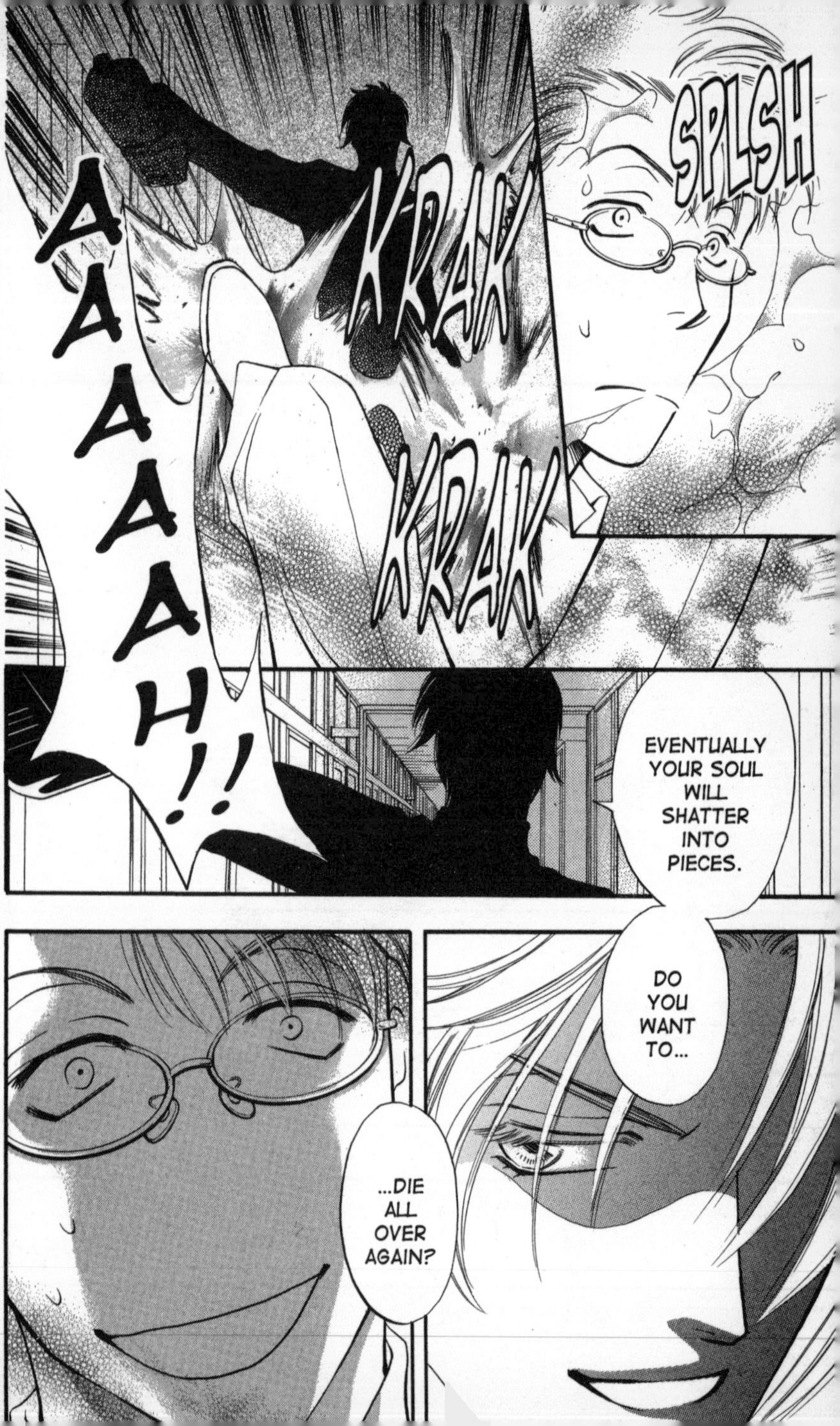
SPLSH
KRAK
KRAK
AAAAAAH!!
EVENTUALLY YOUR SOUL WILL SHATTER INTO PIECES.
DO YOU WANT TO...
...DIE ALL OVER AGAIN?

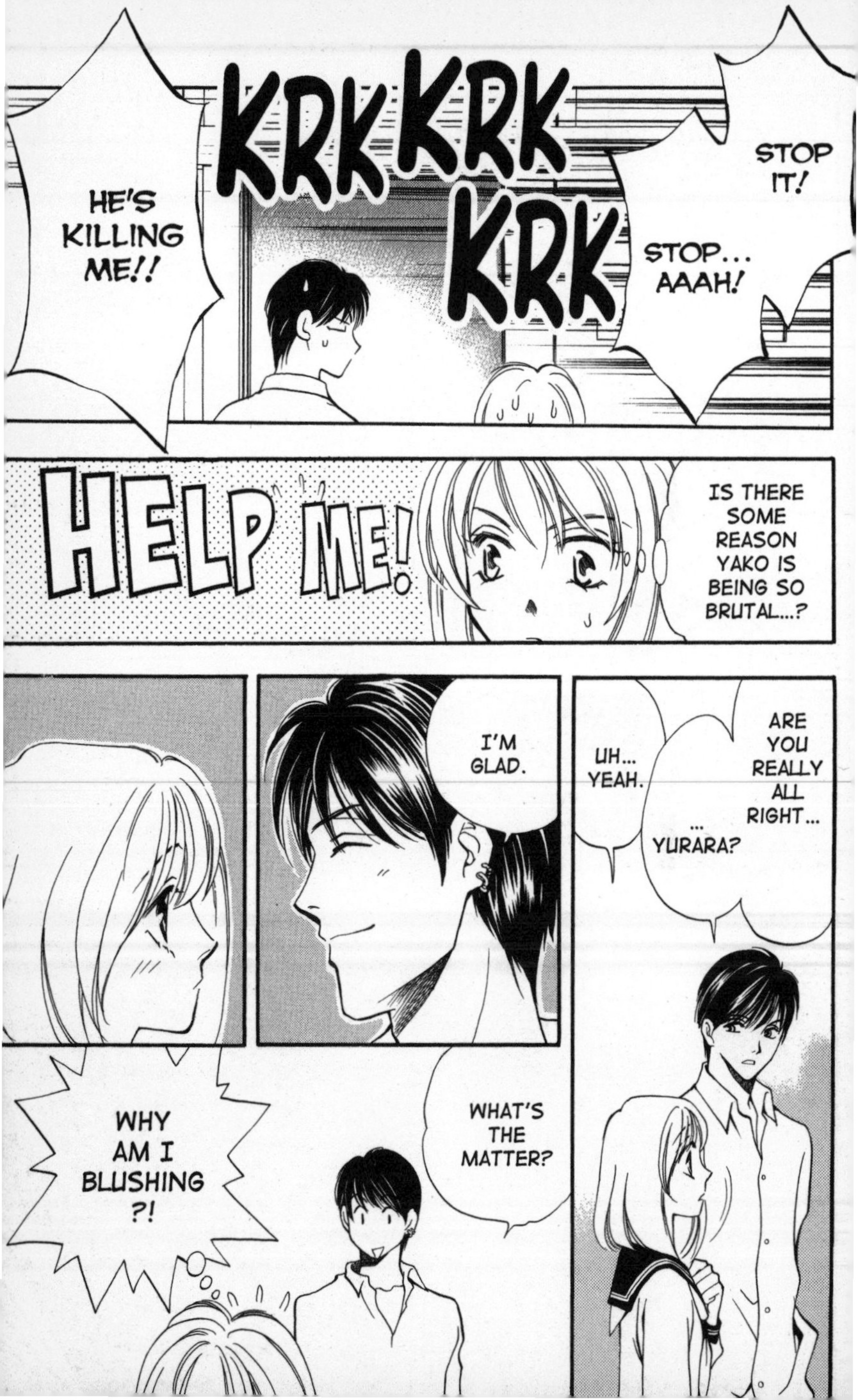

STOP IT!
STOP... AAAH!
KRK KRK KRK
HE'S KILLING ME!!
IS THERE SOME REASON YAKO IS BEING SO BRUTAL...?
HELP ME!
ARE YOU REALLY ALL RIGHT...
...YURARA?
UH... YEAH.
I'M GLAD.
WHAT'S THE MATTER?
WHY AM I BLUSHING?!

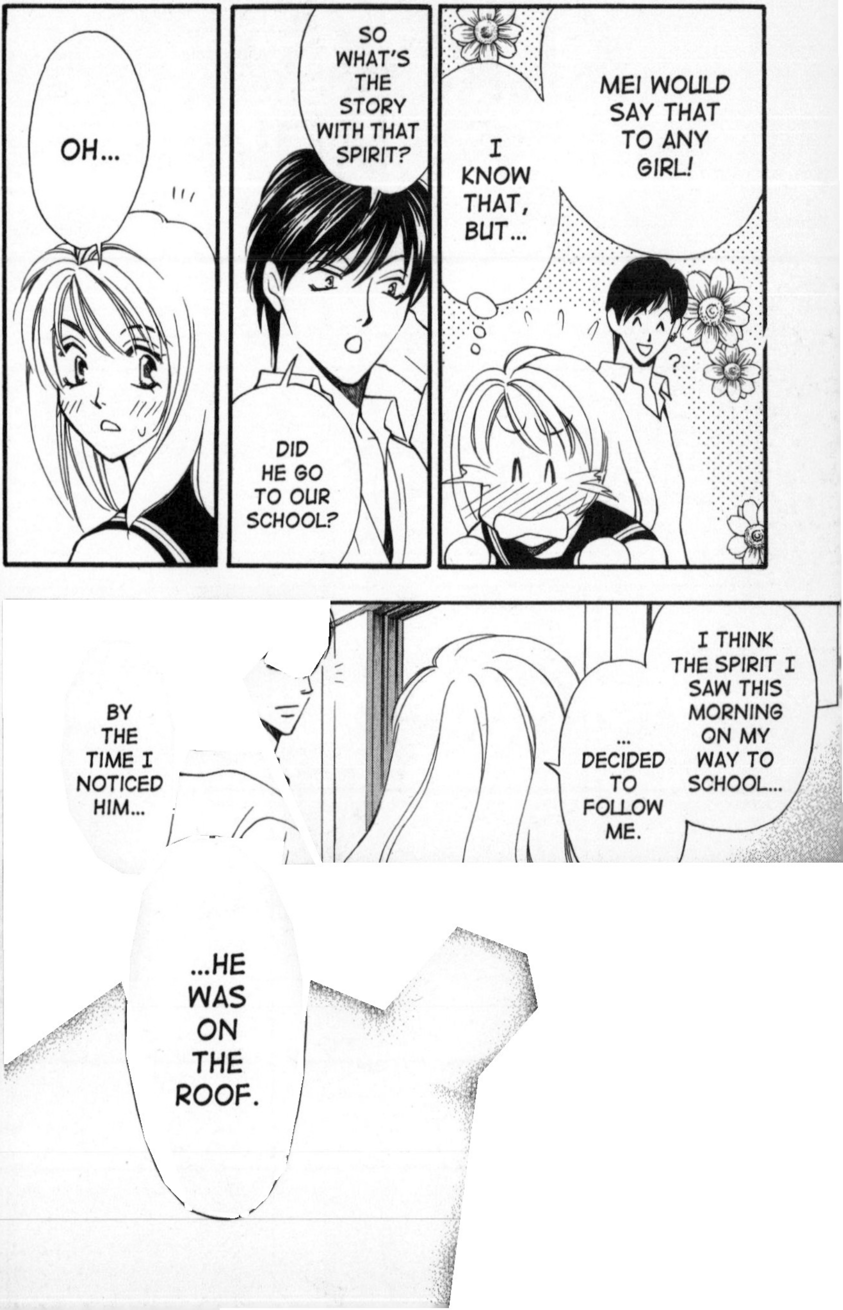
MEI WOULD SAY THAT TO ANY GIRL!
I KNOW THAT, BUT...
SO WHAT'S THE STORY WITH THAT SPIRIT?
DID HE GO TO OUR SCHOOL?
OH...
I THINK THE SPIRIT I SAW THIS MORNING ON MY WAY TO SCHOOL...
...DECIDED TO FOLLOW ME.
BY THE TIME I NOTICED HIM...
...HE WAS ON THE ROOF.

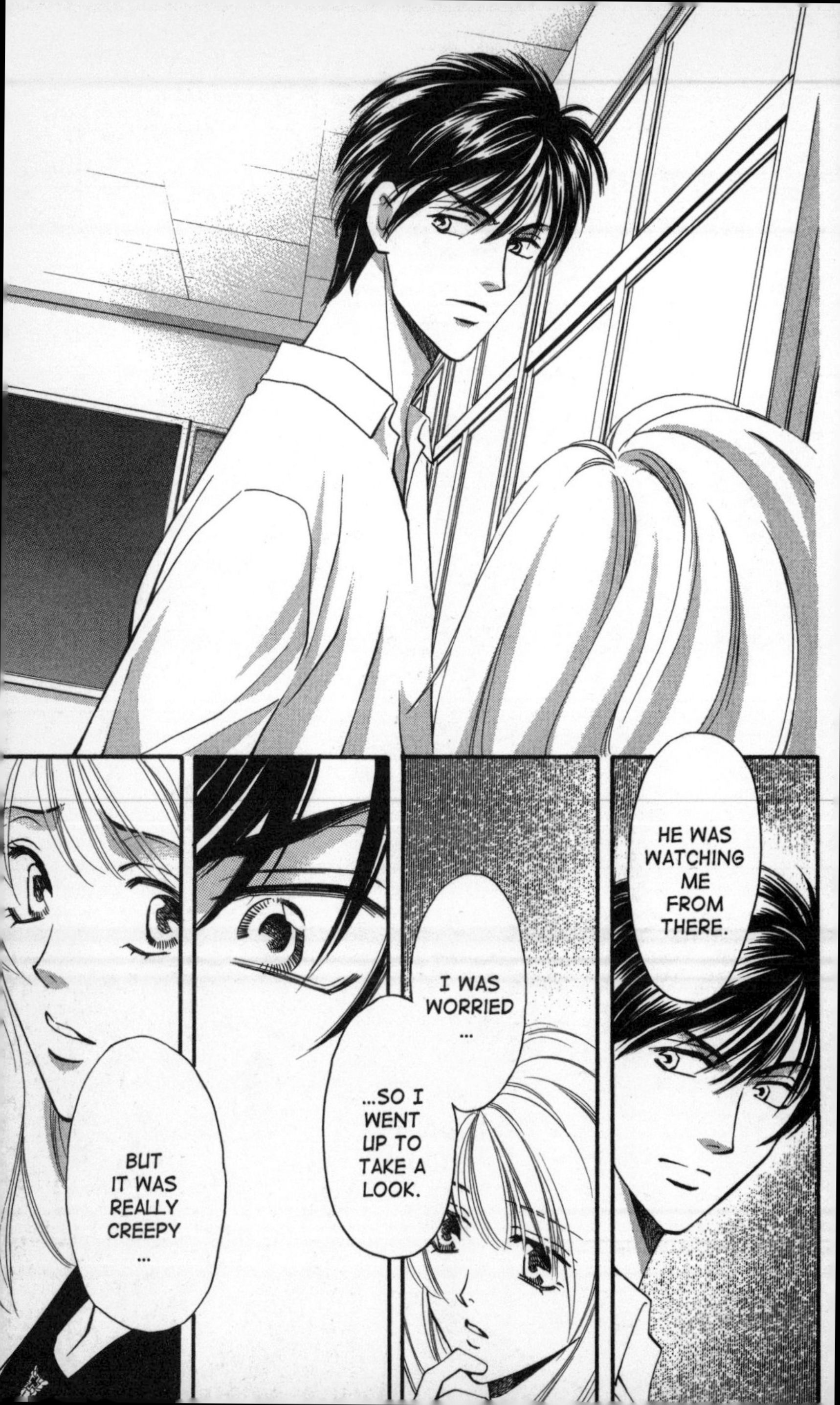
HE WAS WATCHING ME FROM THERE.
I WAS WORRIED ...
...SO I WENT UP TO TAKE A LOOK.
BUT IT WAS REALLY CREEPY ...

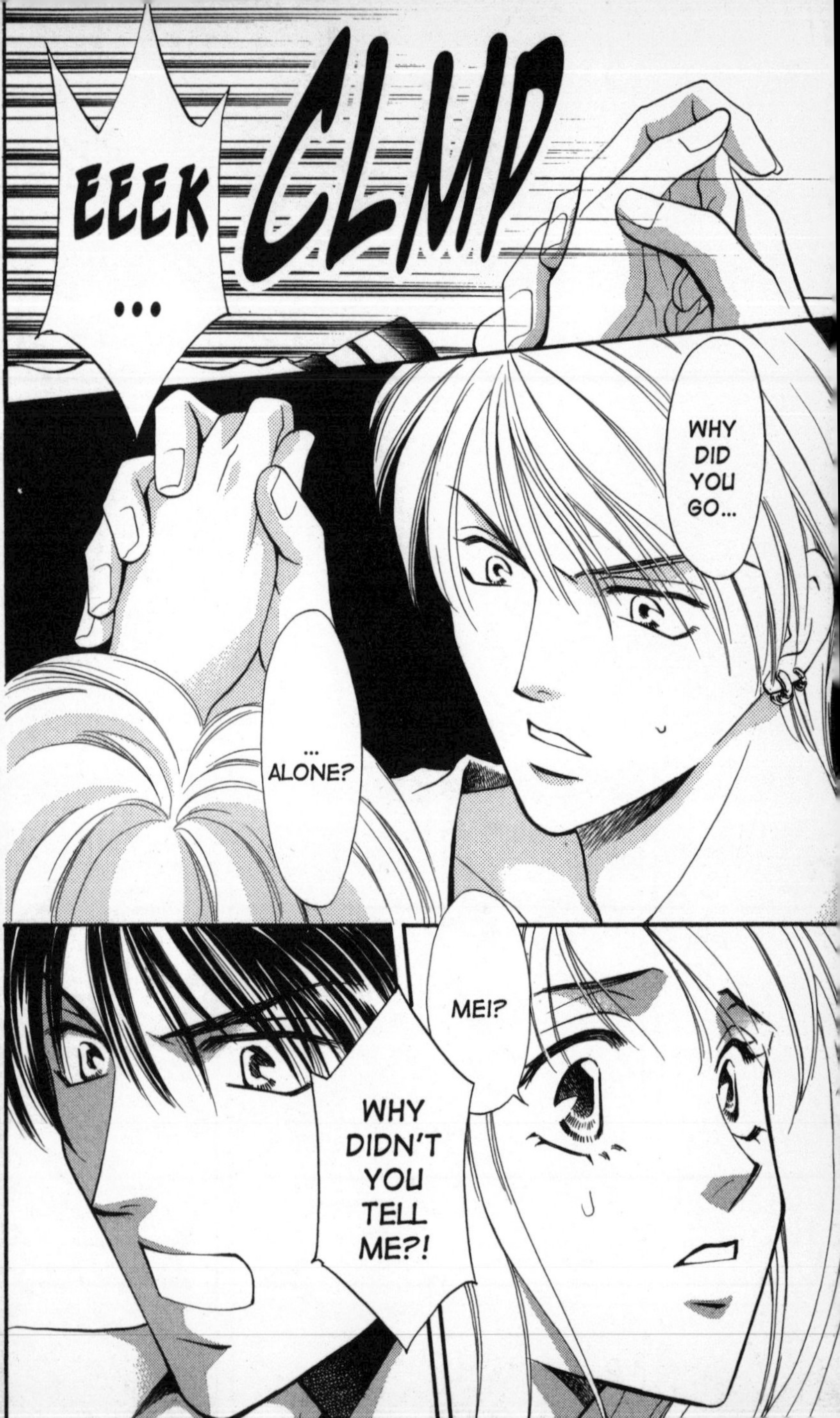
CLMP
EEEK
...
WHY DID YOU GO...
... ALONE?
MEI?
WHY DIDN'T YOU TELL ME?!

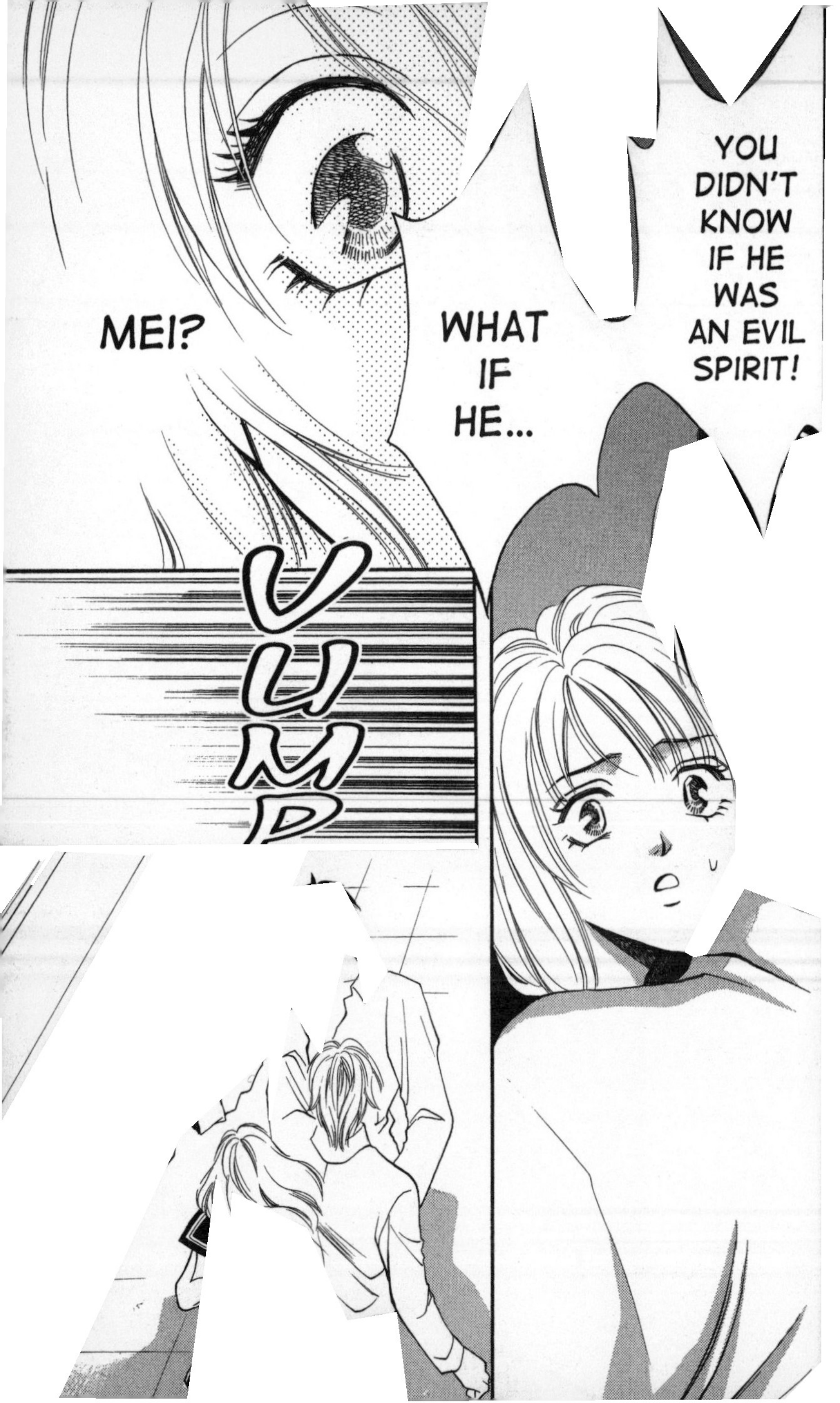
YOU DIDN'T KNOW IF HE WAS AN EVIL SPIRIT!
WHAT IF HE...
MEI?

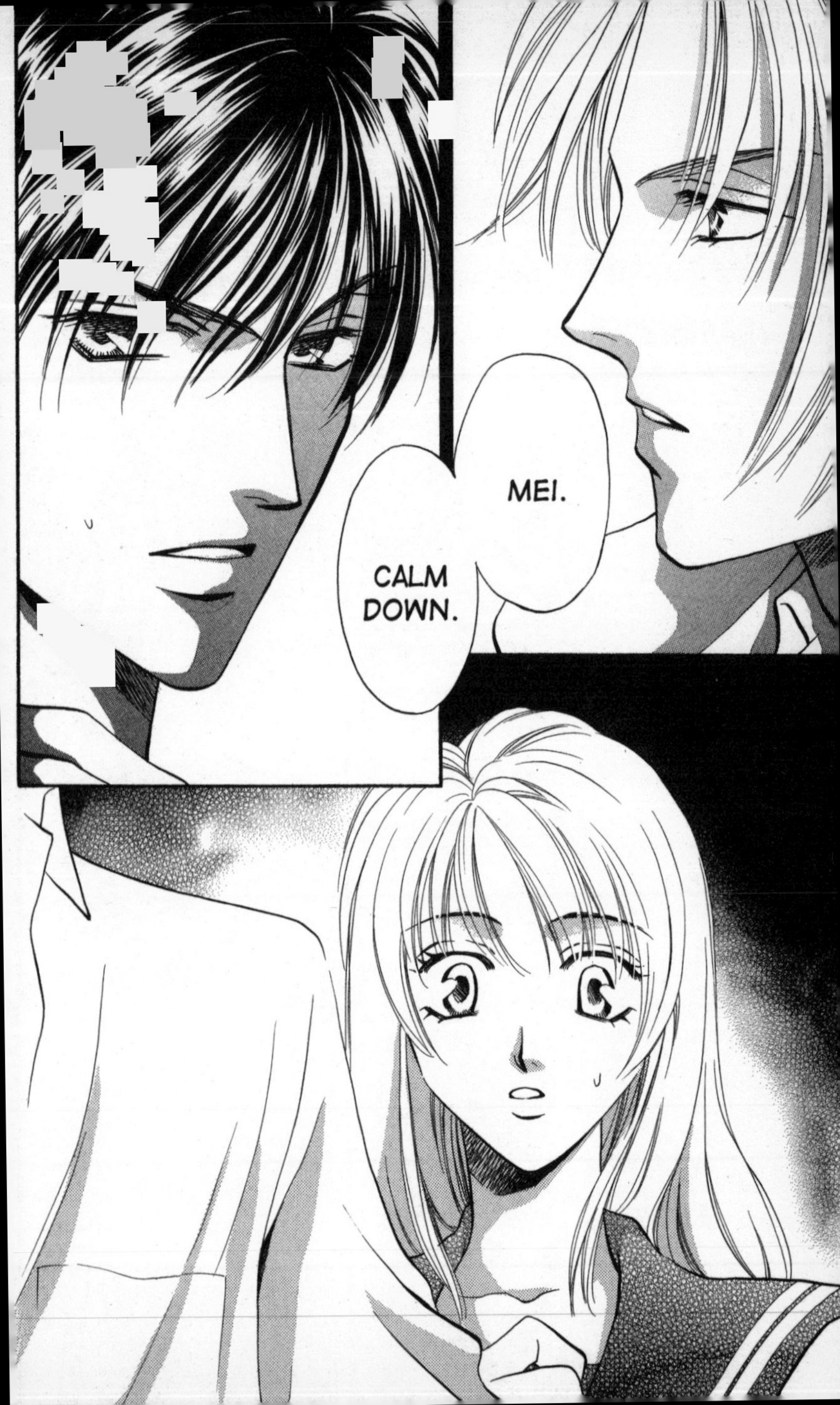
MEI.
CALM DOWN.

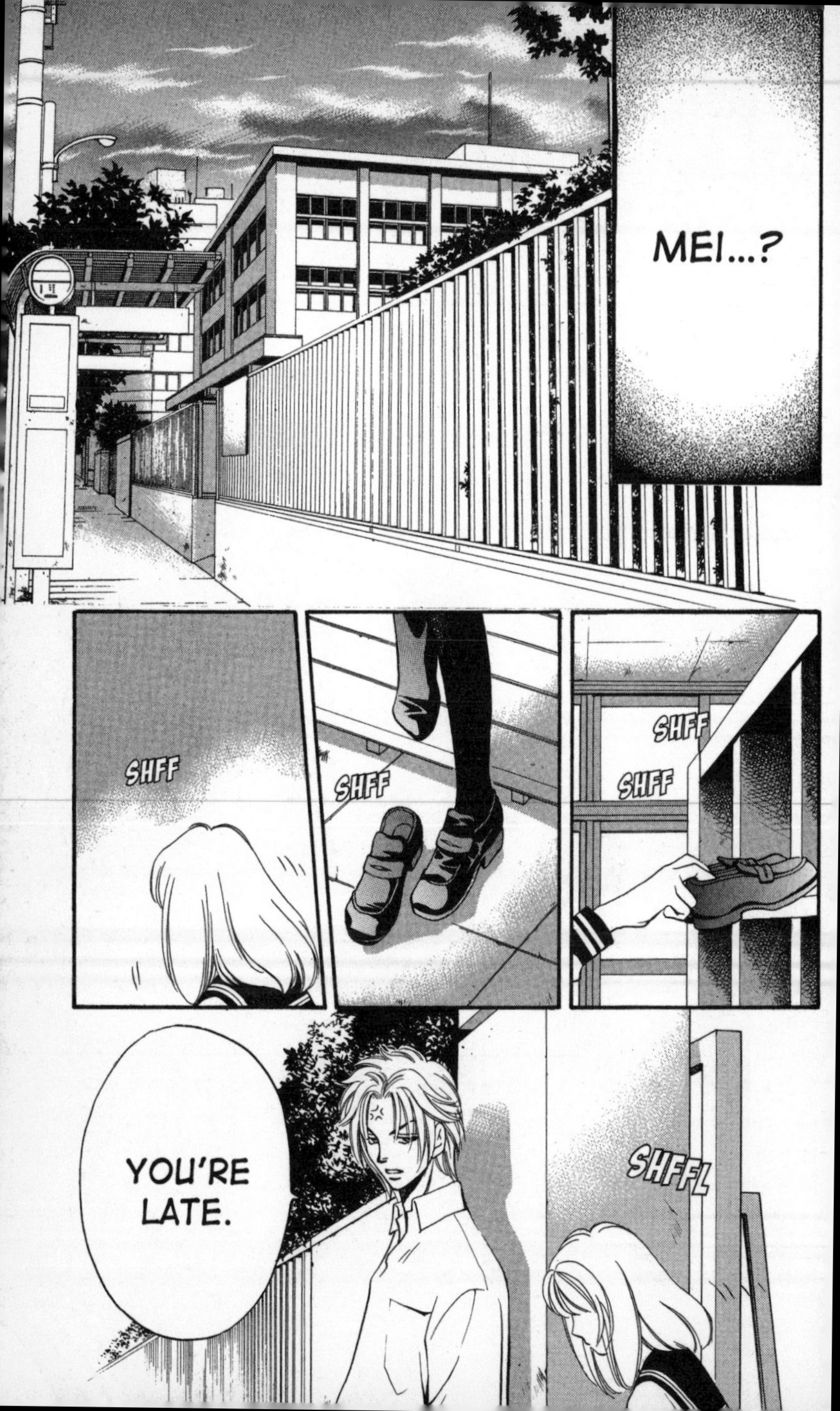
MEI...?
SHFF
SHFF
SHFF
SHFF
SHFFL
YOU'RE LATE.

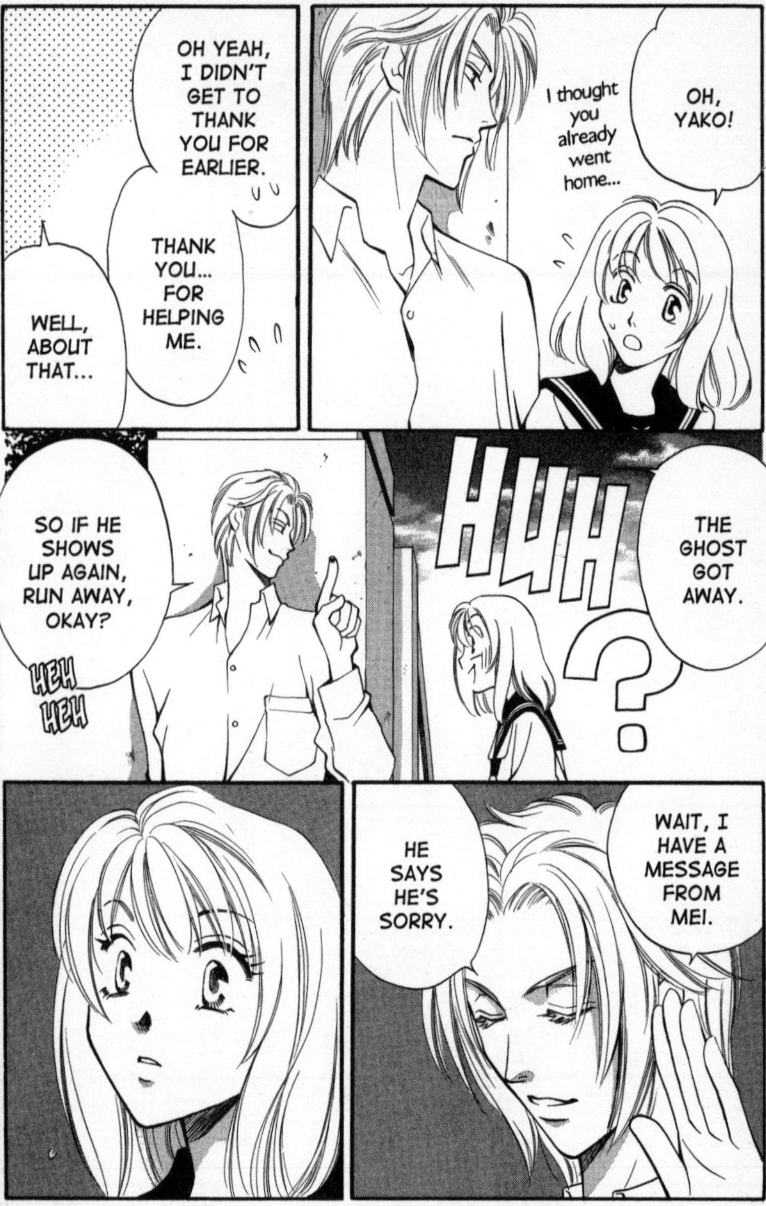
OH, YAKO!
I thought you already went home...
OH YEAH, I DIDN'T GET TO THANK YOU FOR EARLIER.
THANK YOU... FOR HELPING ME.
WELL, ABOUT THAT...
THE GHOST GOT AWAY.
HUH
?
SO IF HE SHOWS UP AGAIN, RUN AWAY, OKAY?
HEH HEH
WAIT, I HAVE A MESSAGE FROM MEI.
HE SAYS HE'S SORRY.

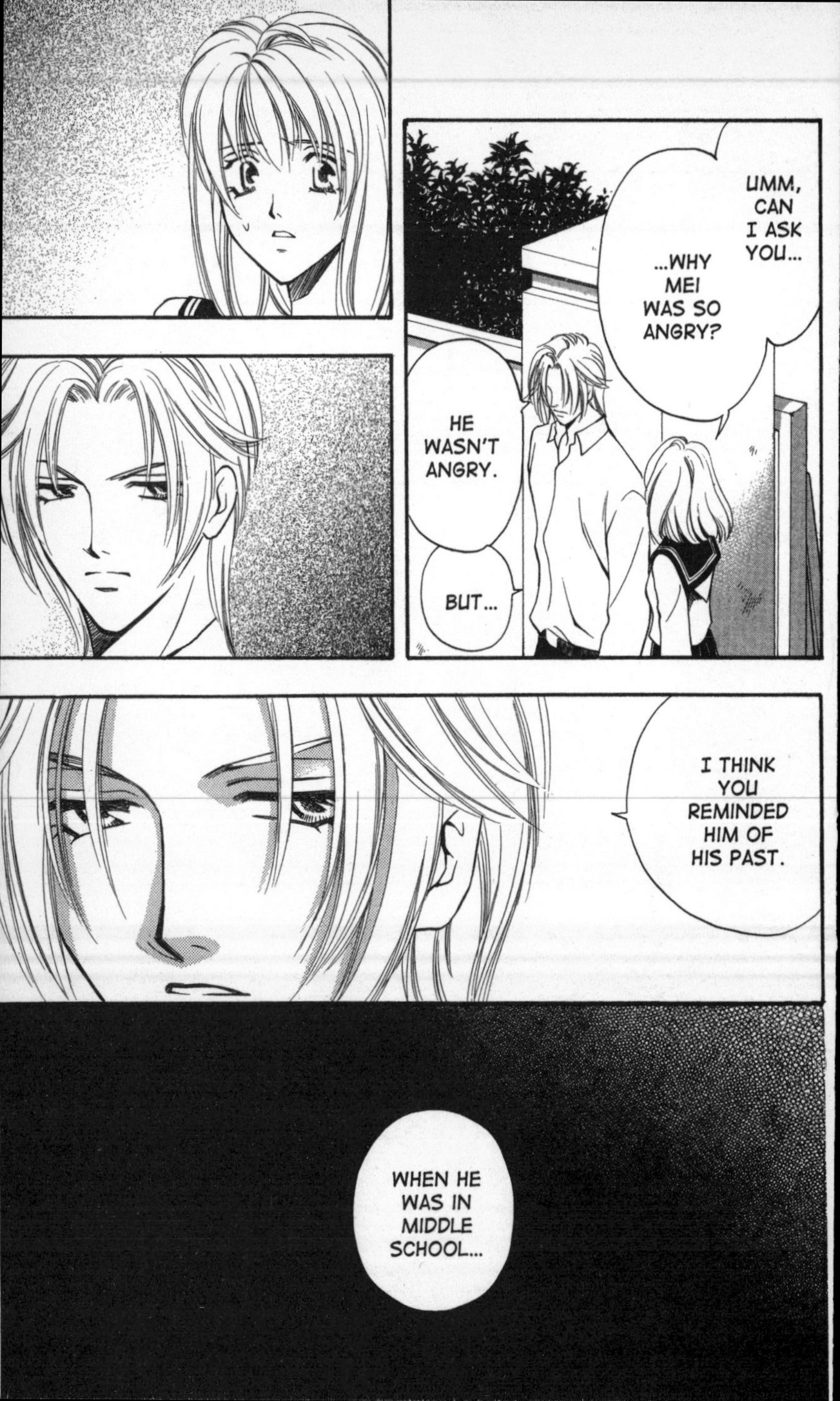
UMM, CAN I ASK YOU...
...WHY MEI WAS SO ANGRY?
HE WASN'T ANGRY.
BUT...
I THINK YOU REMINDED HIM OF HIS PAST.
WHEN HE WAS IN MIDDLE SCHOOL...

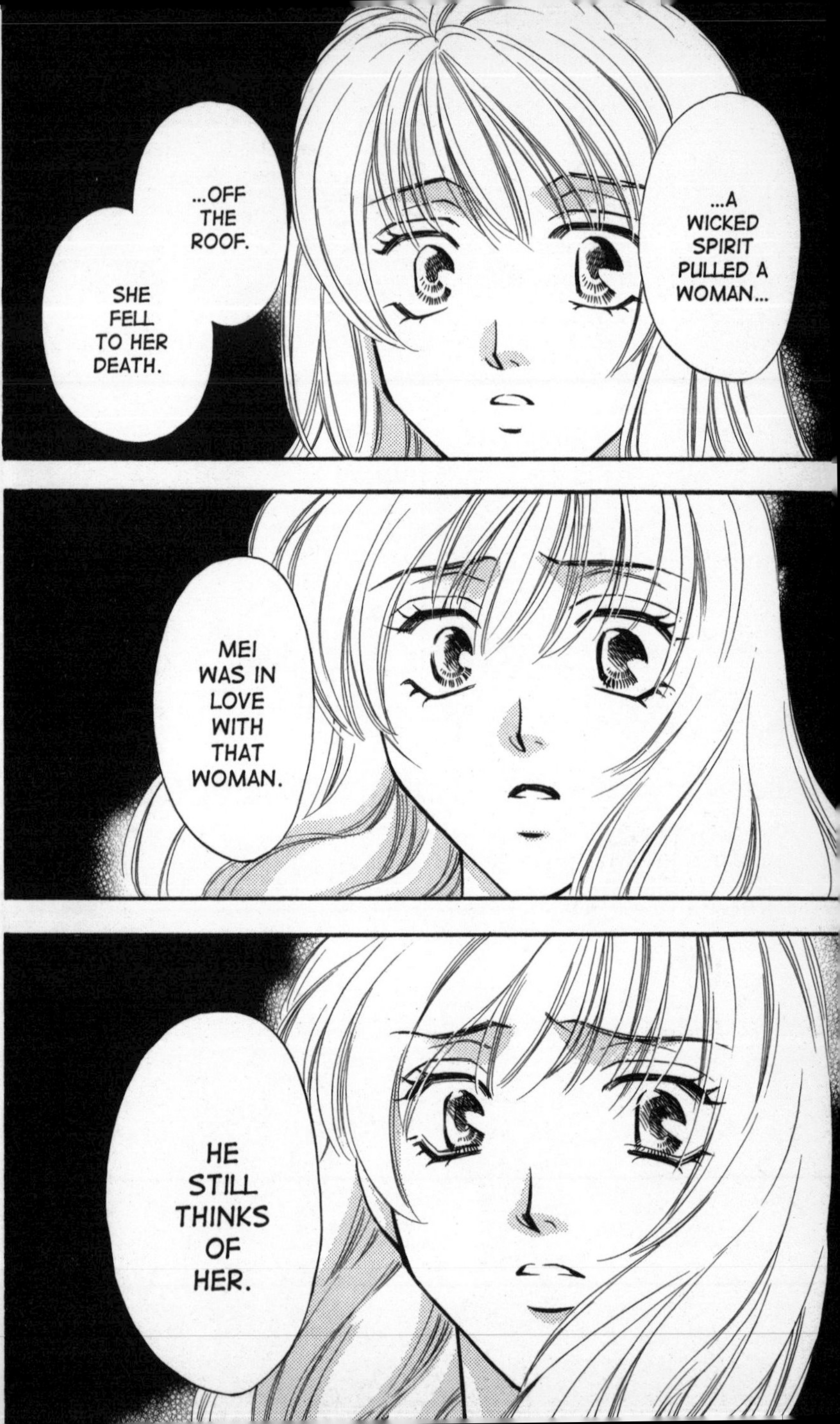
...A WICKED SPIRIT PULLED A WOMAN...
...OFF THE ROOF.
SHE FELL TO HER DEATH.
MEI WAS IN LOVE WITH THAT WOMAN.
HE STILL THINKS OF HER.

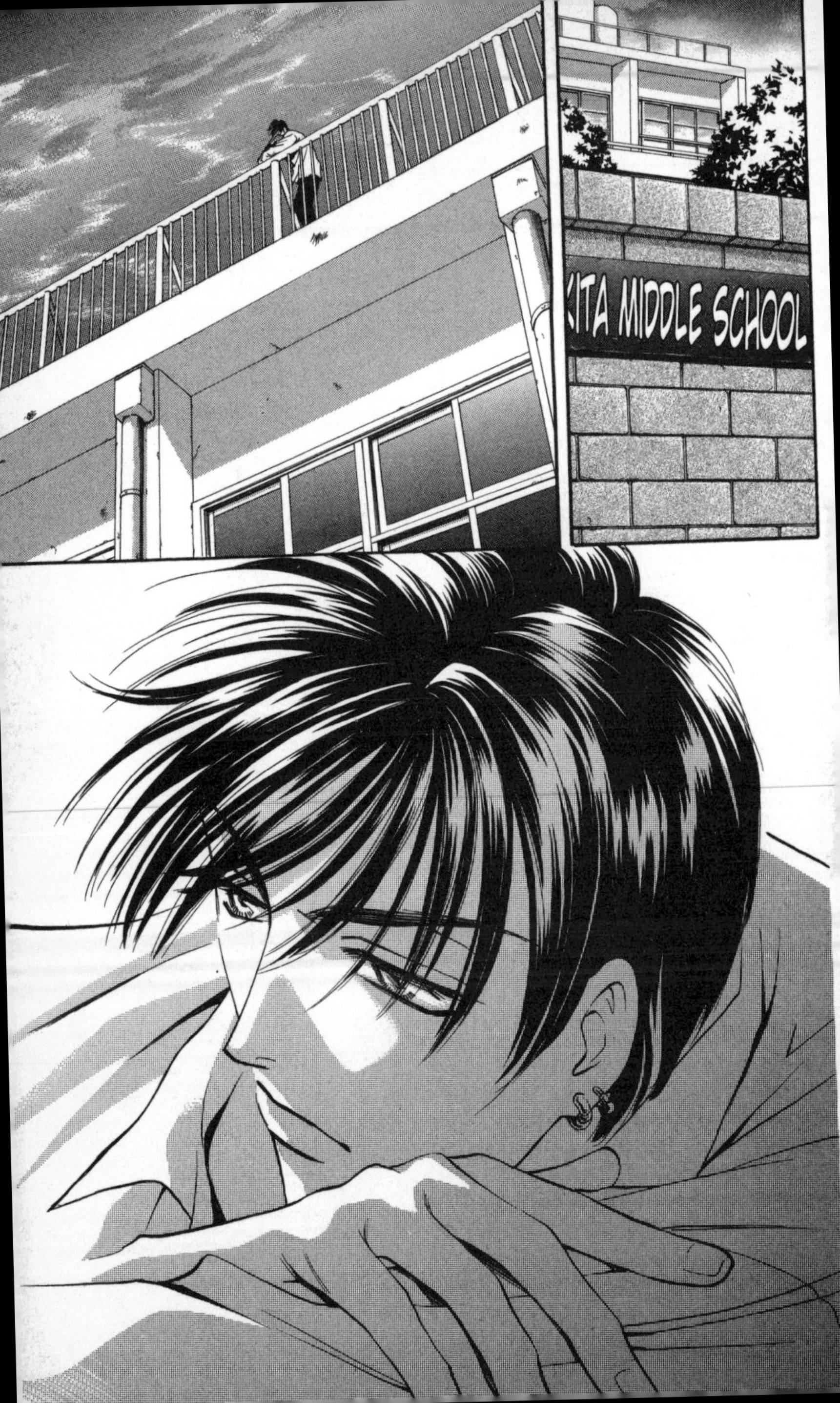
KITA MIDDLE SCHOOL

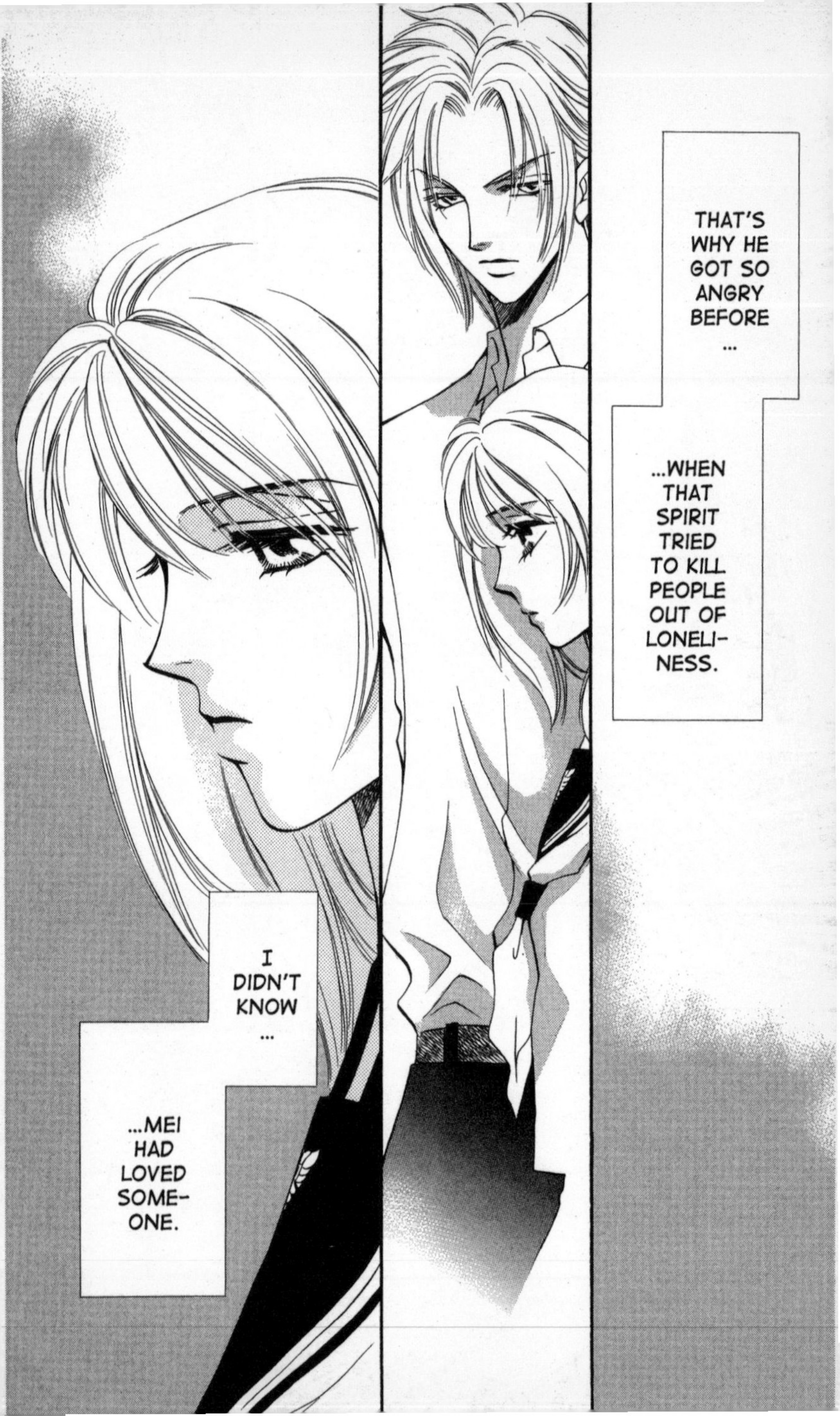
THAT'S WHY HE GOT SO ANGRY BEFORE ...
...WHEN THAT SPIRIT TRIED TO KILL PEOPLE OUT OF LONELI-NESS.
I DIDN'T KNOW ...
...MEI HAD LOVED SOME-ONE.

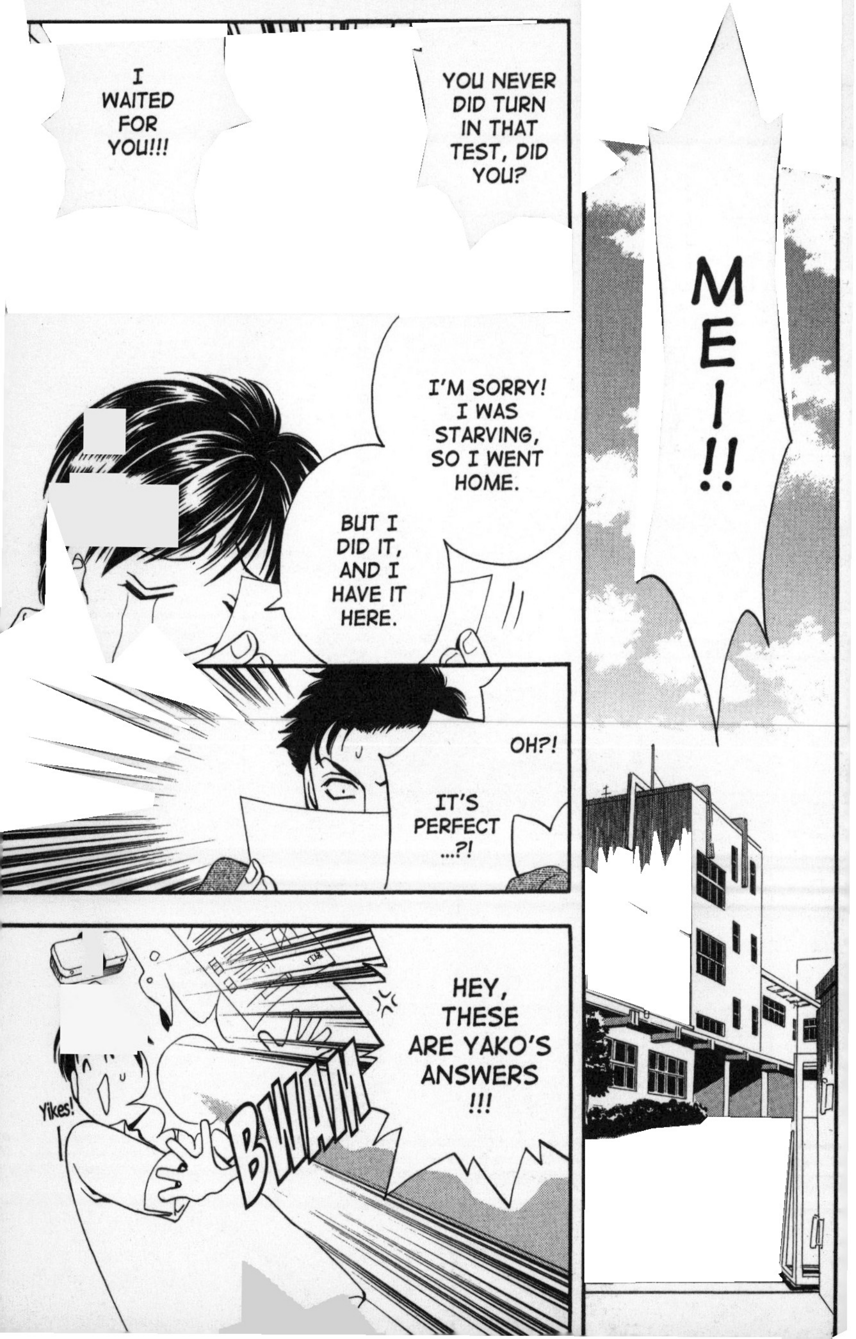
MEI!!
YOU NEVER DID TURN IN THAT TEST, DID YOU?
I WAITED FOR YOU!!!
I'M SORRY! I WAS STARVING, SO I WENT HOME.
BUT I DID IT, AND I HAVE IT HERE.
OH?!
IT'S PERFECT ...?!
HEY, THESE ARE YAKO'S ANSWERS !!!
BWAM
Yikes!

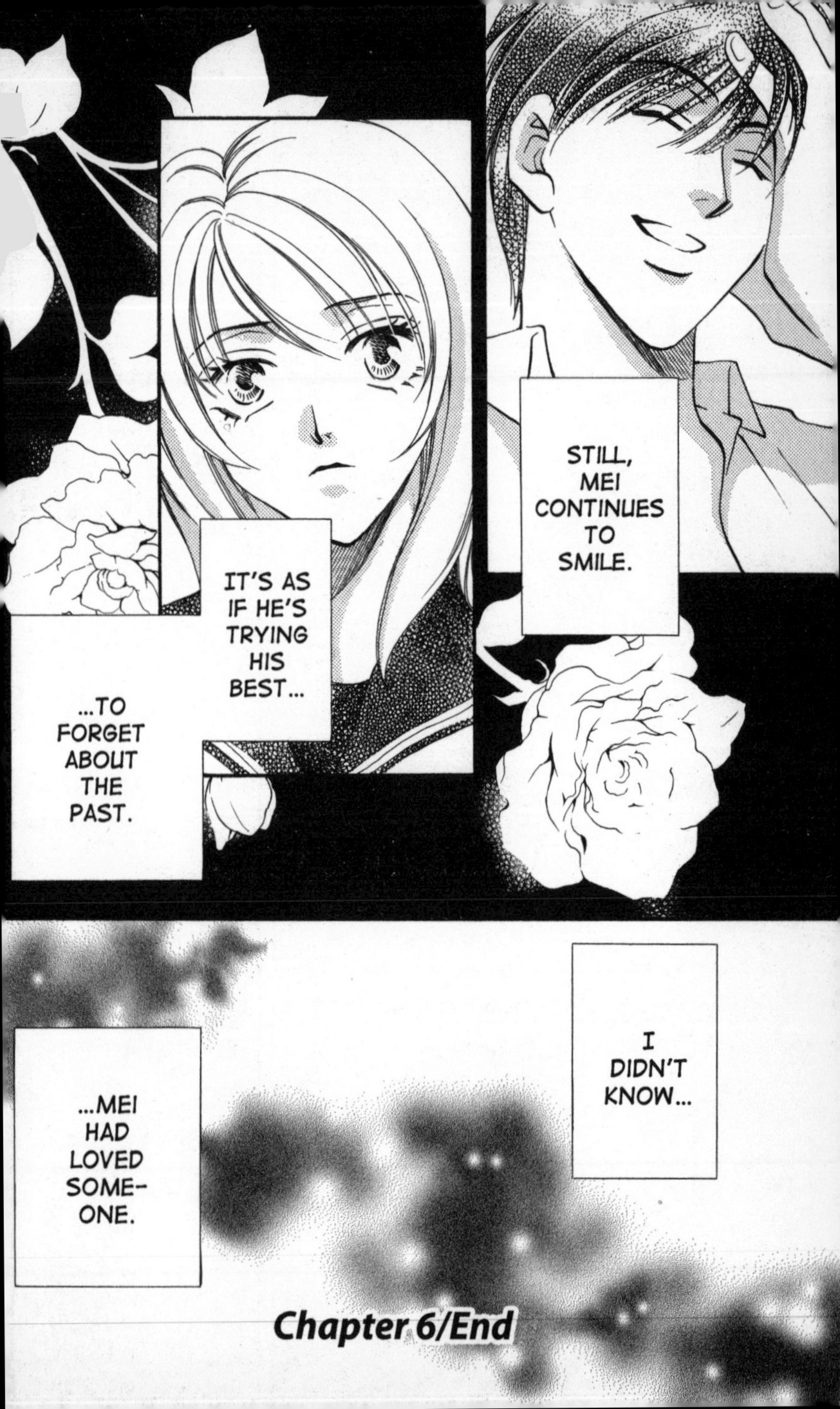
STILL, MEI CONTINUES TO SMILE.
IT'S AS IF HE'S TRYING HIS BEST...
...TO FORGET ABOUT THE PAST.
I DIDN'T KNOW...
...MEI HAD LOVED SOME-ONE.
Chapter 6/End

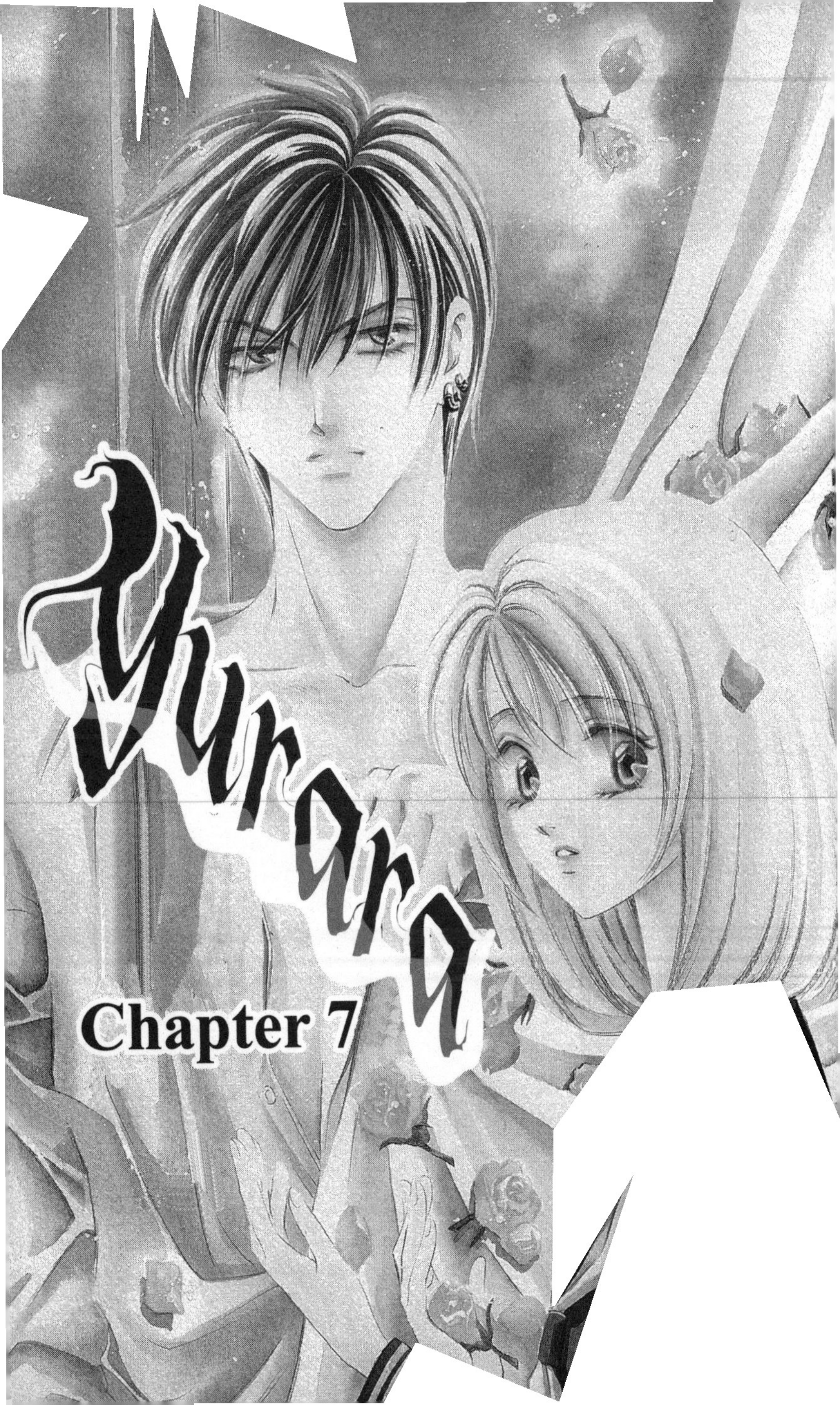
Yurara
Chapter 7

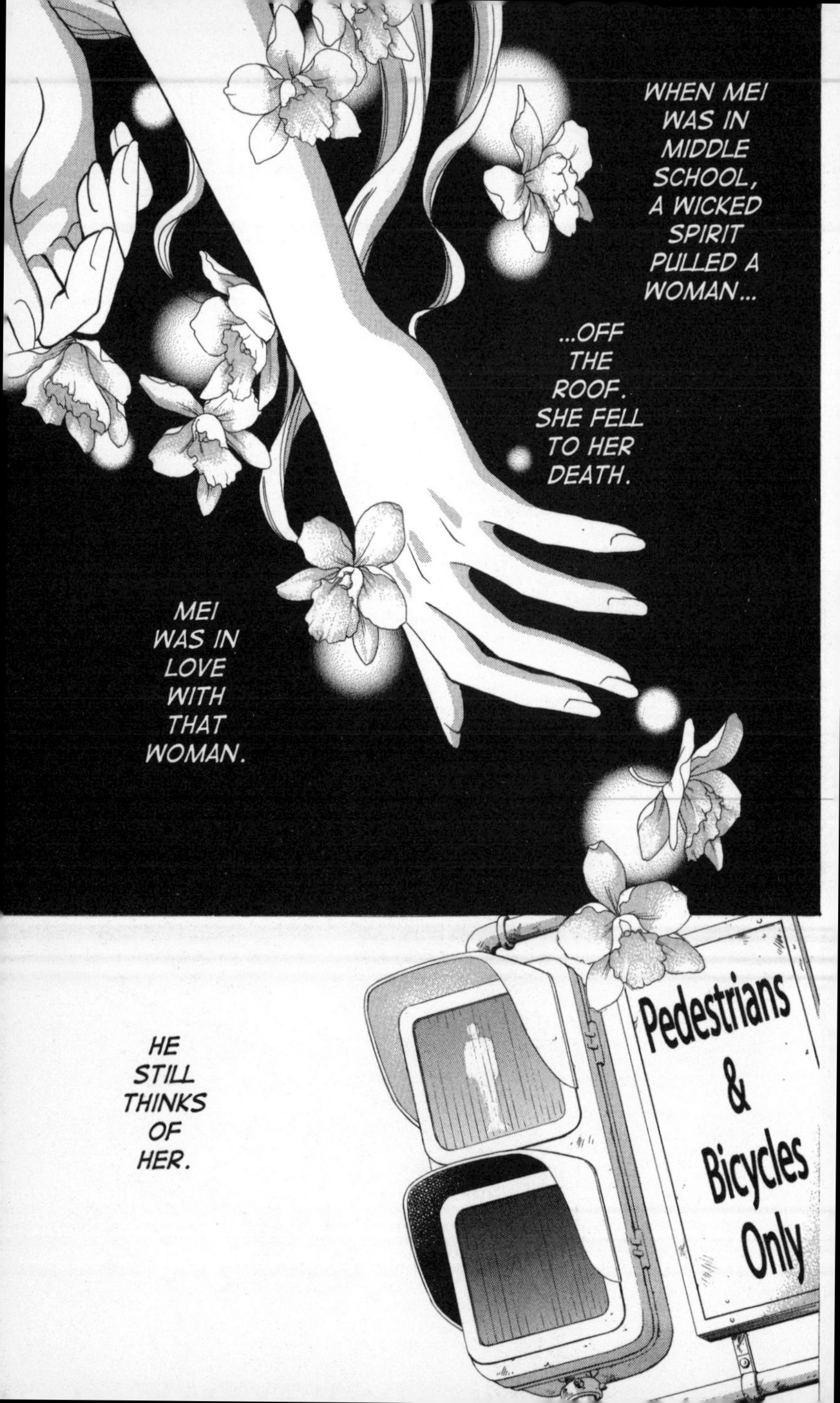
WHEN MEI WAS IN MIDDLE SCHOOL, A WICKED SPIRIT PULLED A WOMAN...
...OFF THE ROOF. SHE FELL TO HER DEATH.
MEI WAS IN LOVE WITH THAT WOMAN.
Pedestrians & Bicycles Only
HE STILL THINKS OF HER.

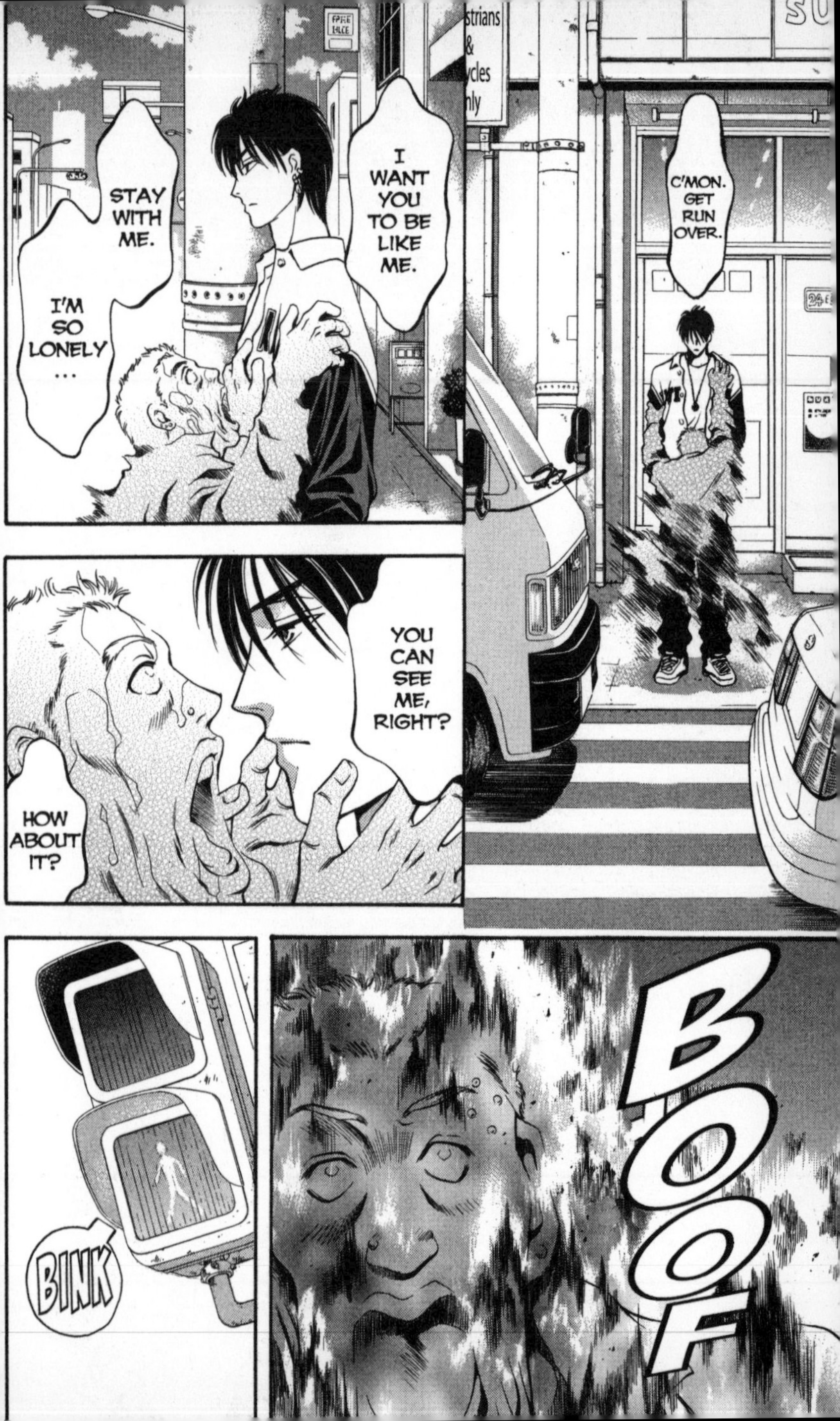
C'MON. GET RUN OVER.
I WANT YOU TO BE LIKE ME.
STAY WITH ME.
I'M SO LONELY ...
YOU CAN SEE ME, RIGHT?
HOW ABOUT IT?
BOOF
BINK

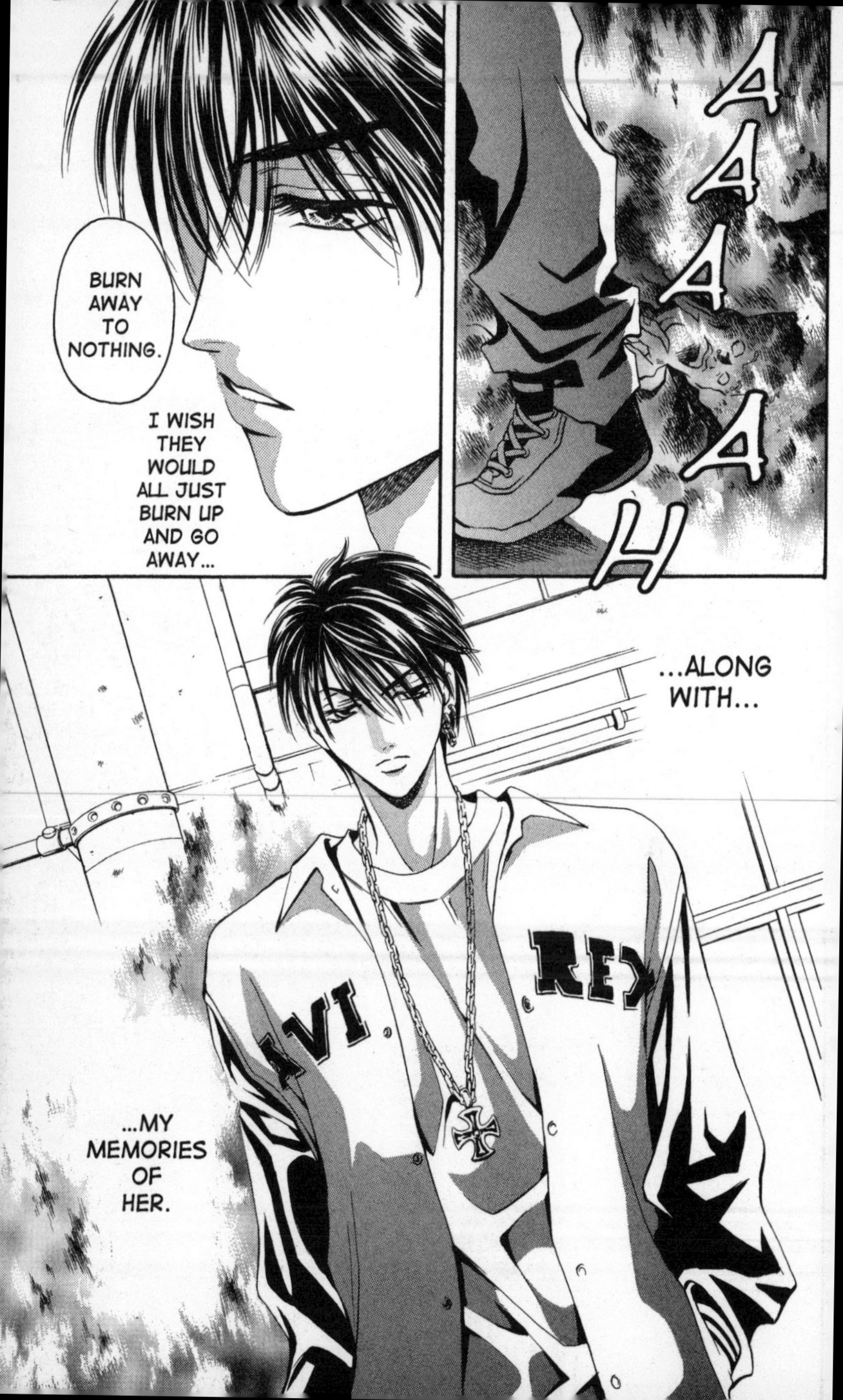
AAAAH
BURN AWAY TO NOTHING.
I WISH THEY WOULD ALL JUST BURN UP AND GO AWAY...
...ALONG WITH...
...MY MEMORIES OF HER.

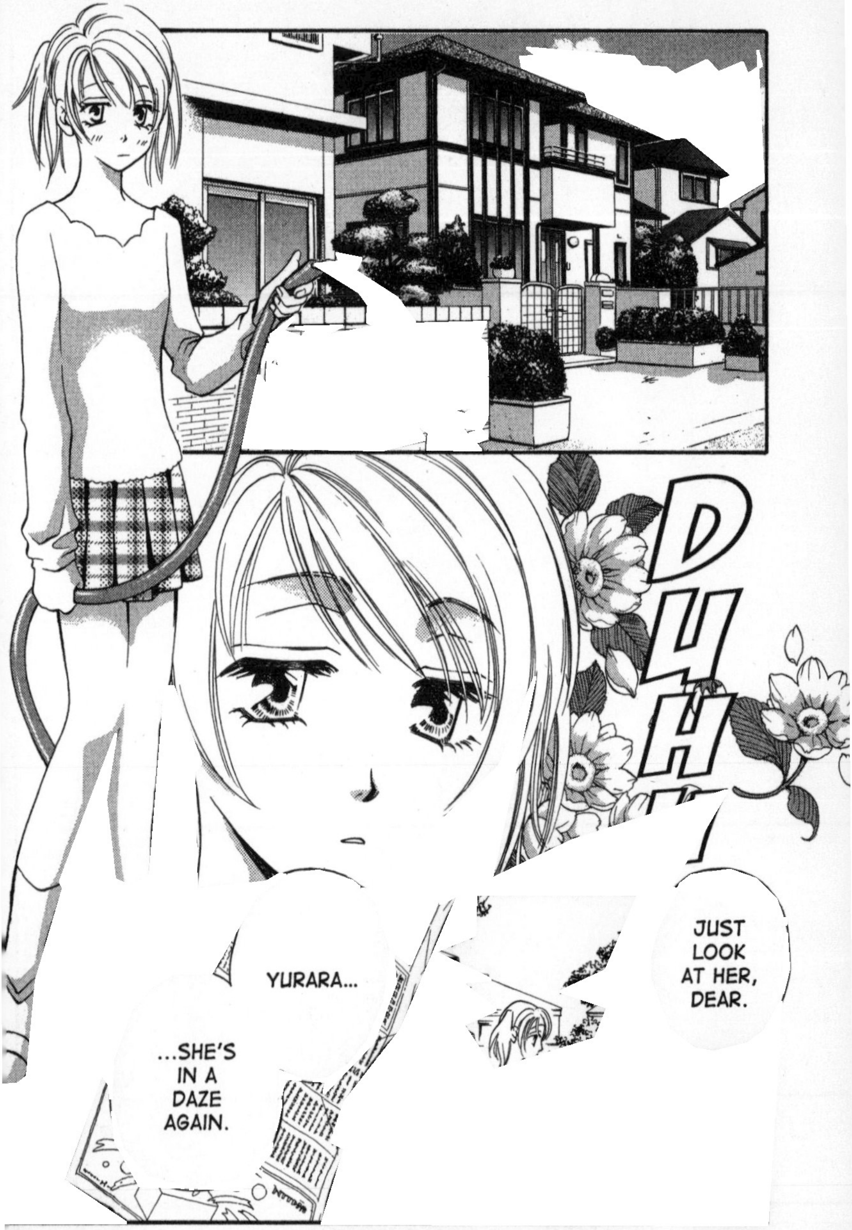
DUH
JUST LOOK AT HER, DEAR.
YURARA...
...SHE'S IN A DAZE AGAIN.

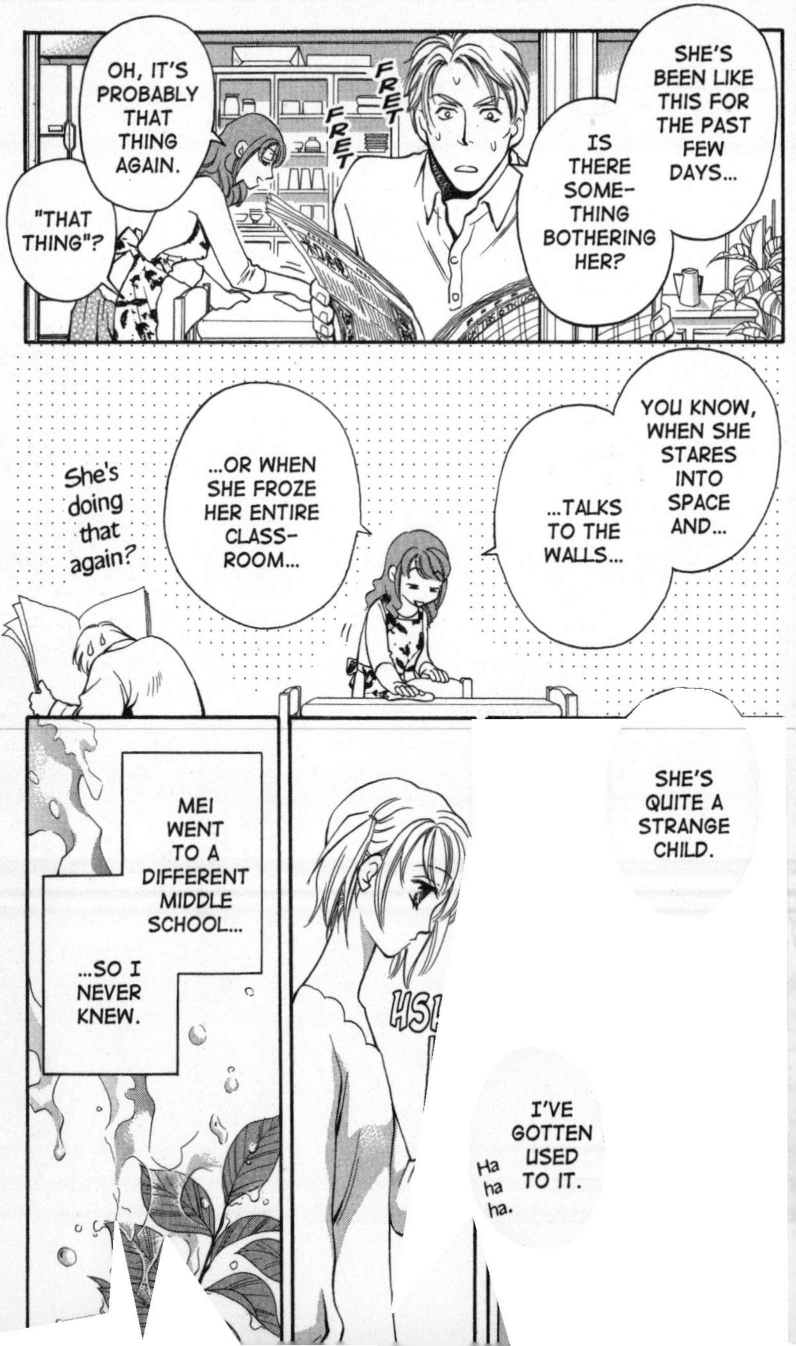
SHE'S BEEN LIKE THIS FOR THE PAST FEW DAYS...
IS THERE SOMETHING BOTHERING HER?
FRET FRET
OH, IT'S PROBABLY THAT THING AGAIN.
"THAT THING"?
YOU KNOW, WHEN SHE STARES INTO SPACE AND...
...TALKS TO THE WALLS...
...OR WHEN SHE FROZE HER ENTIRE CLASSROOM...
She's doing that again?
SHE'S QUITE A STRANGE CHILD.
I'VE GOTTEN USED TO IT.
Ha ha ha.
MEI WENT TO A DIFFERENT MIDDLE SCHOOL...
...SO I NEVER KNEW.

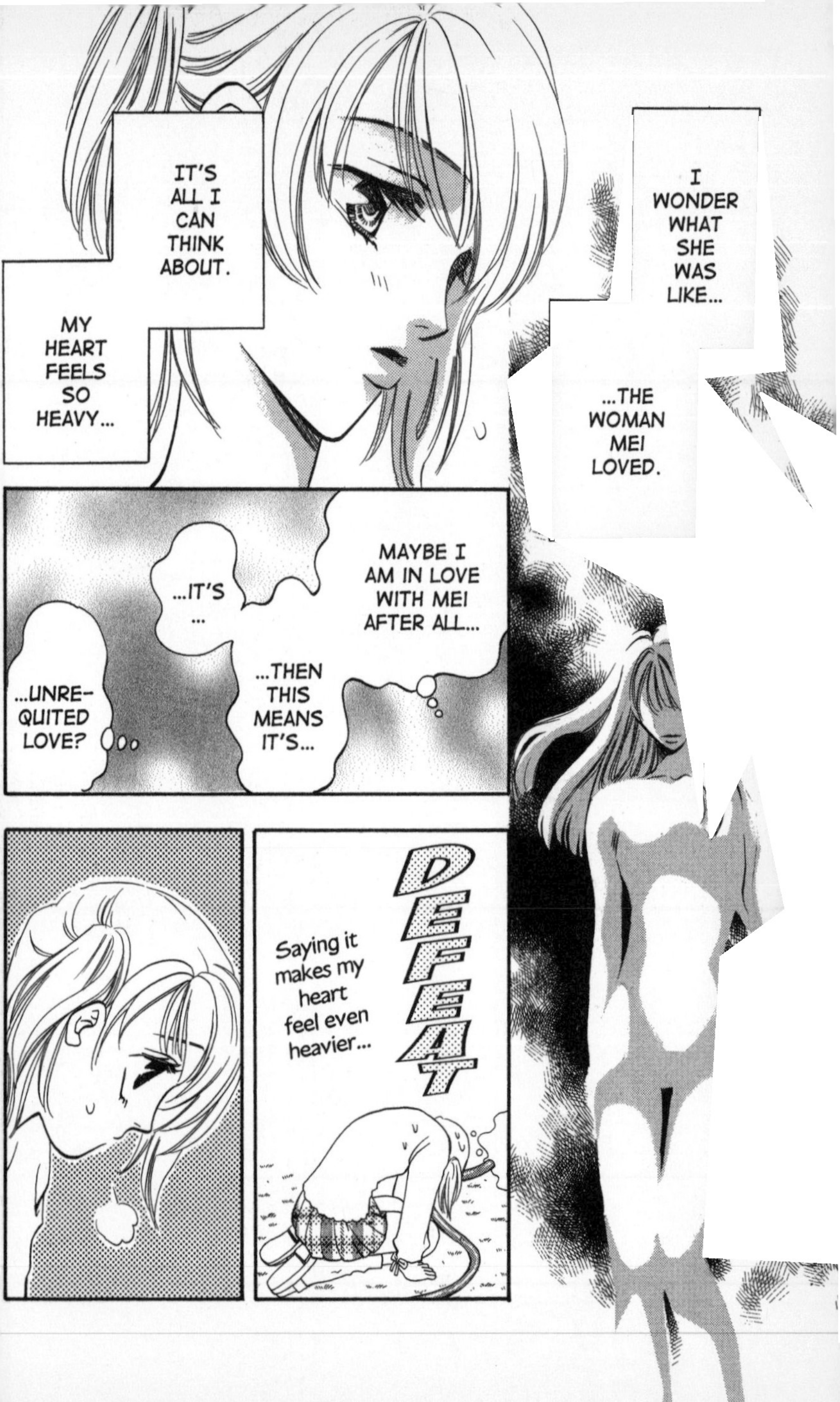
I WONDER WHAT SHE WAS LIKE...
...THE WOMAN MEI LOVED.
IT'S ALL I CAN THINK ABOUT.
MY HEART FEELS SO HEAVY...
MAYBE I AM IN LOVE WITH MEI AFTER ALL...
...IT'S ...
...THEN THIS MEANS IT'S...
...UNRE-QUITED LOVE?
DEFEAT
Saying it makes my heart feel even heavier...

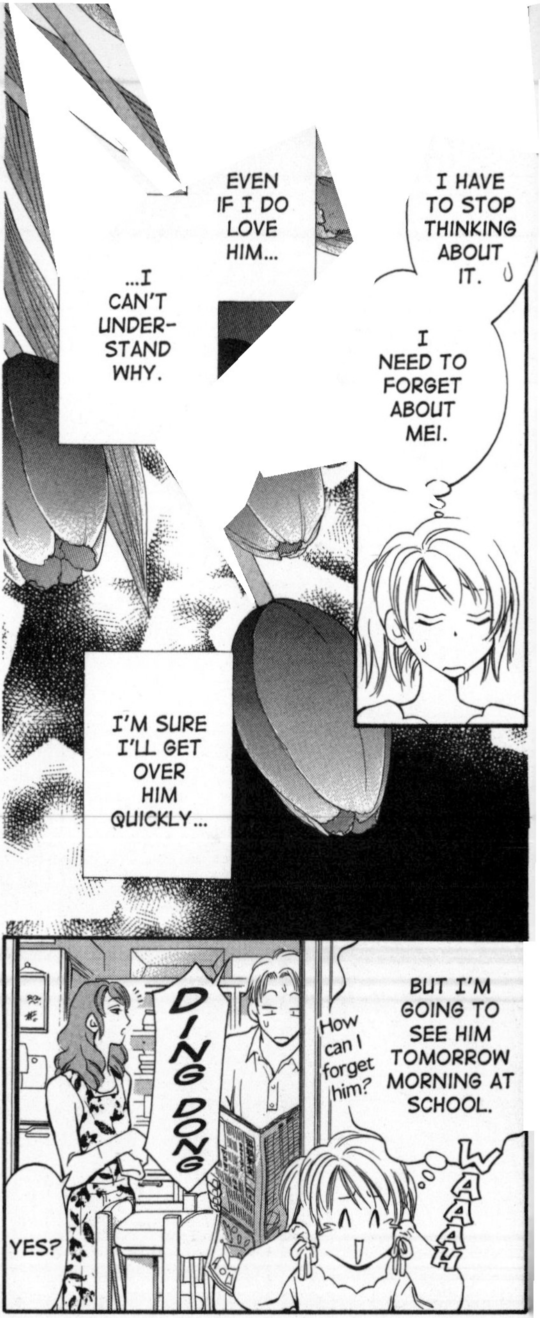
I HAVE TO STOP THINKING ABOUT IT.
I NEED TO FORGET ABOUT MEI.
EVEN IF I DO LOVE HIM...
...I CAN'T UNDER-STAND WHY.
I'M SURE I'LL GET OVER HIM QUICKLY...
BUT I'M GOING TO SEE HIM TOMORROW MORNING AT SCHOOL.
How can I forget him?
WAAAH
DING DONG
YES?

Shiomi's Daily Activities 7

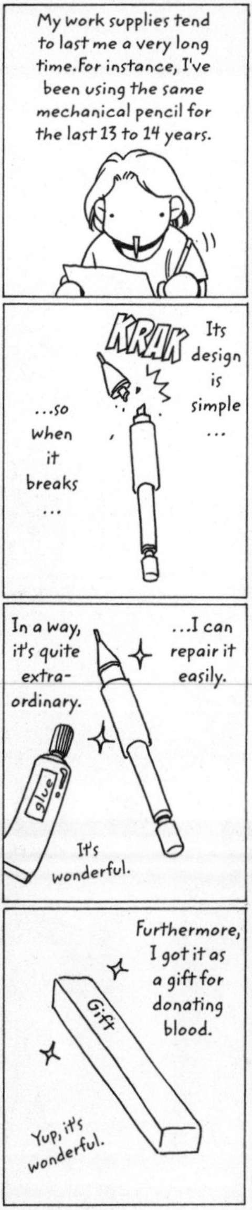
My work supplies tend to last me a very long time. For instance, I've been using the same mechanical pencil for the last 13 to 14 years.
Its design is simple...
KRAK
...so when it breaks...
In a way, it's quite extra-ordinary.
...I can repair it easily.
glue
It's wonderful.
Furthermore, I got it as a gift for donating blood.
Gift
Yup, it's wonderful.

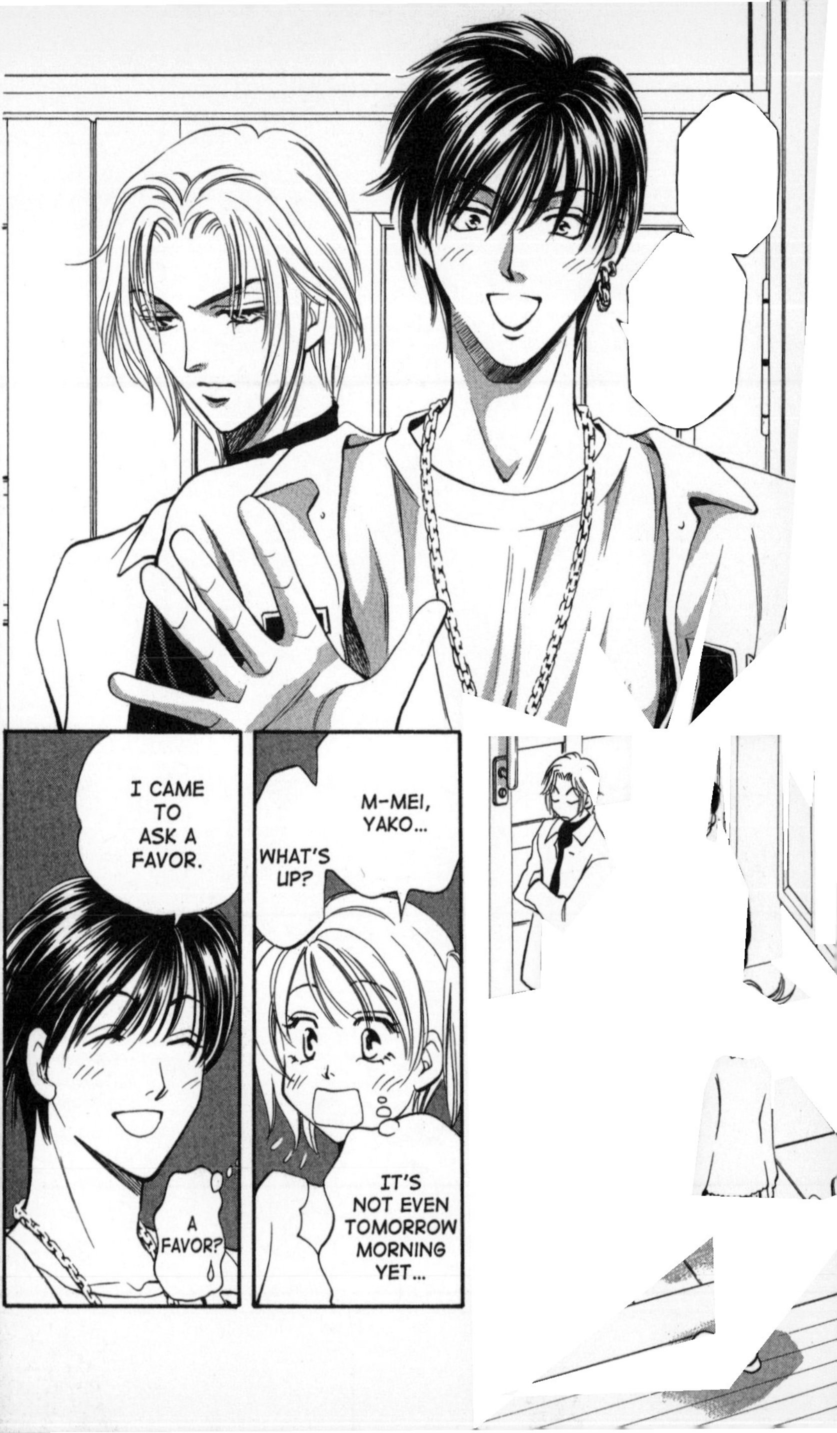
M-MEI, YAKO...
WHAT'S UP?
IT'S NOT EVEN TOMORROW MORNING YET...
I CAME TO ASK A FAVOR.
A FAVOR?

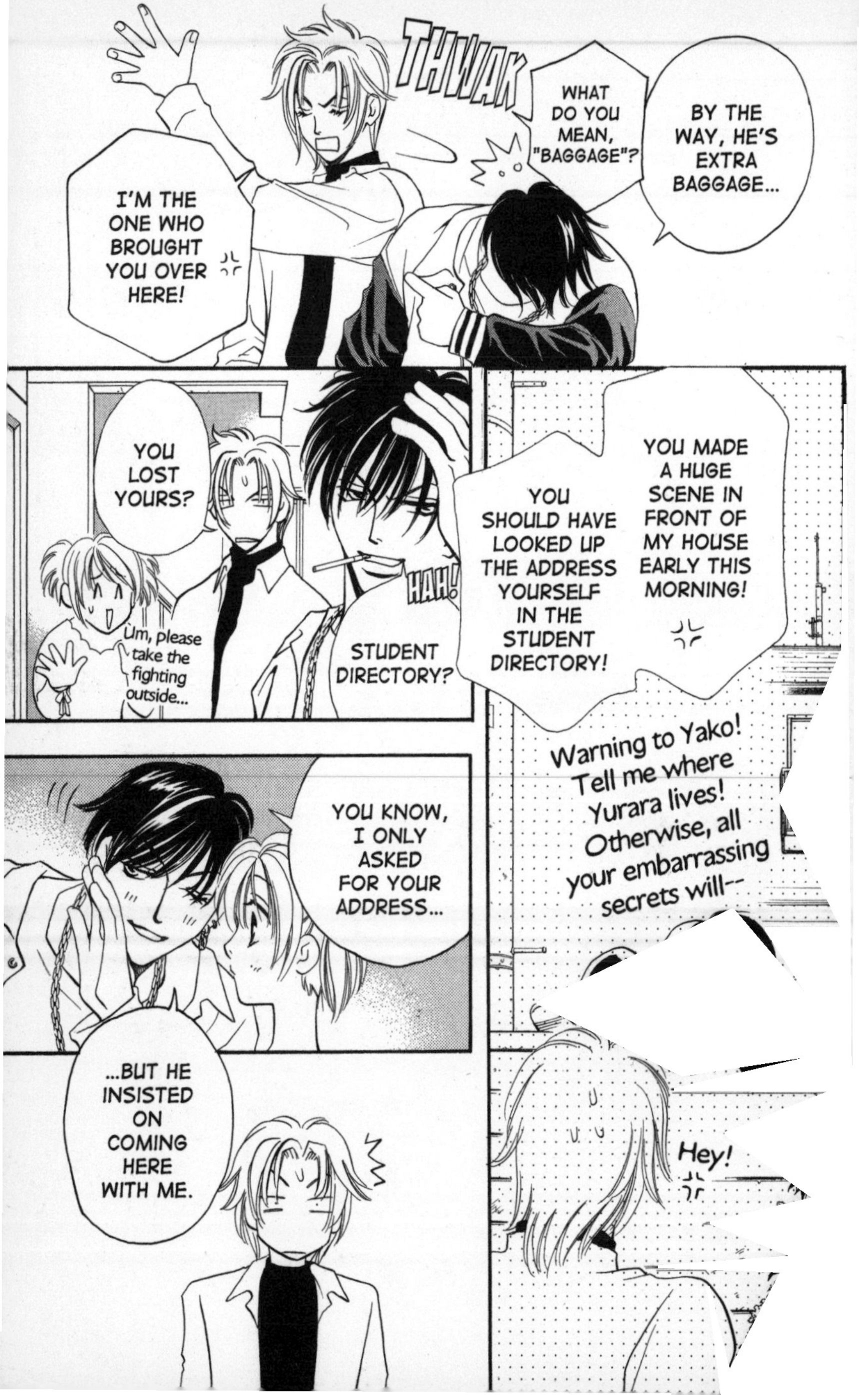
BY THE WAY, HE'S EXTRA BAGGAGE...
THWAK
WHAT DO YOU MEAN, "BAGGAGE"?
I'M THE ONE WHO BROUGHT YOU OVER HERE!
YOU MADE A HUGE SCENE IN FRONT OF MY HOUSE EARLY THIS MORNING!
YOU SHOULD HAVE LOOKED UP THE ADDRESS YOURSELF IN THE STUDENT DIRECTORY!
Warning to Yako! Tell me where Yurara lives! Otherwise, all your embarrassing secrets will--
Hey!
HAH!
STUDENT DIRECTORY?
YOU LOST YOURS?
Um, please take the fighting outside...
YOU KNOW, I ONLY ASKED FOR YOUR ADDRESS...
...BUT HE INSISTED ON COMING HERE WITH ME.

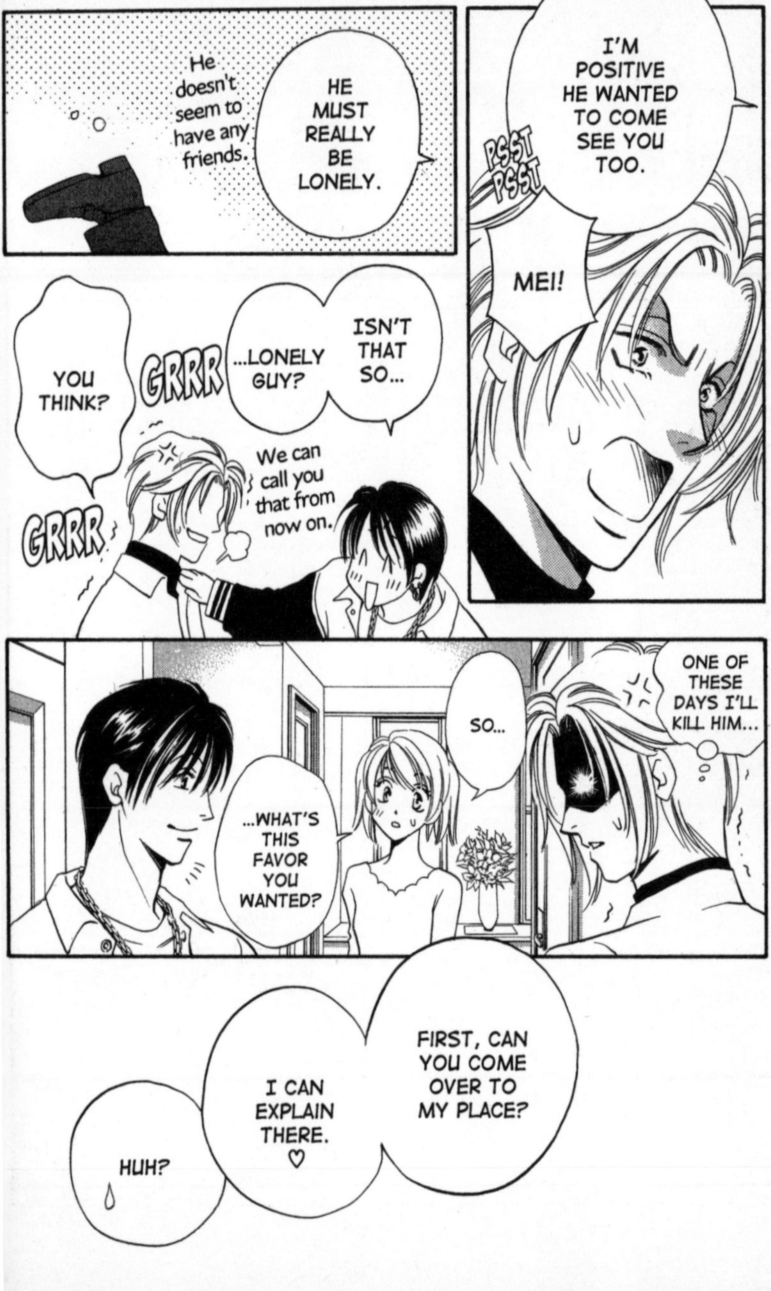

I'M POSITIVE HE WANTED TO COME SEE YOU TOO.
PSST PSST
MEI!
HE MUST REALLY BE LONELY.
He doesn't seem to have any friends.
ISN'T THAT SO...
...LONELY GUY?
GRRR
YOU THINK?
We can call you that from now on.
GRRR
ONE OF THESE DAYS I'LL KILL HIM...
SO...
...WHAT'S THIS FAVOR YOU WANTED?
FIRST, CAN YOU COME OVER TO MY PLACE?
I CAN EXPLAIN THERE. ♡
HUH?

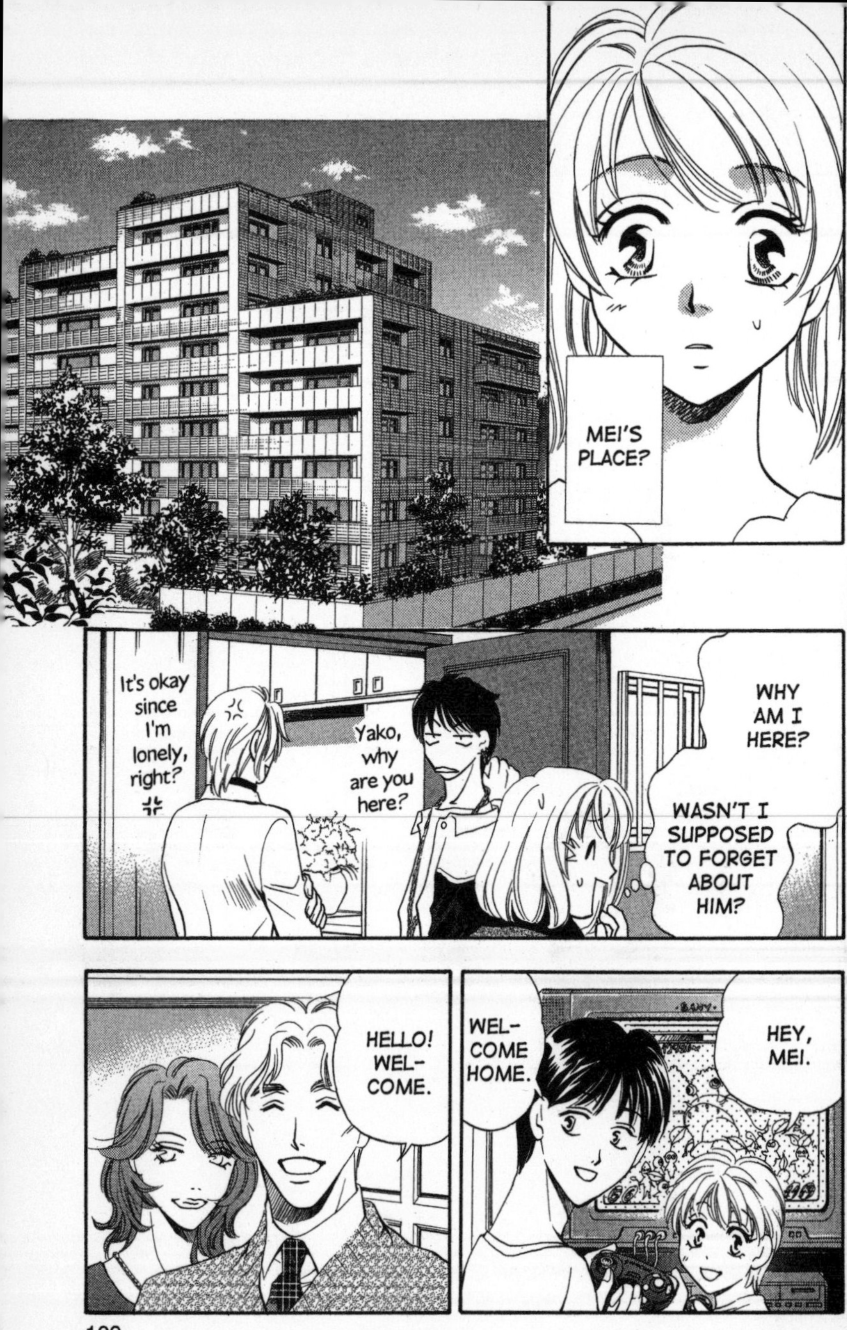
MEI'S PLACE?
WHY AM I HERE?
WASN'T I SUPPOSED TO FORGET ABOUT HIM?
Yako, why are you here?
It's okay since I'm lonely, right?
HEY, MEI.
WEL-COME HOME.
HELLO! WEL-COME.

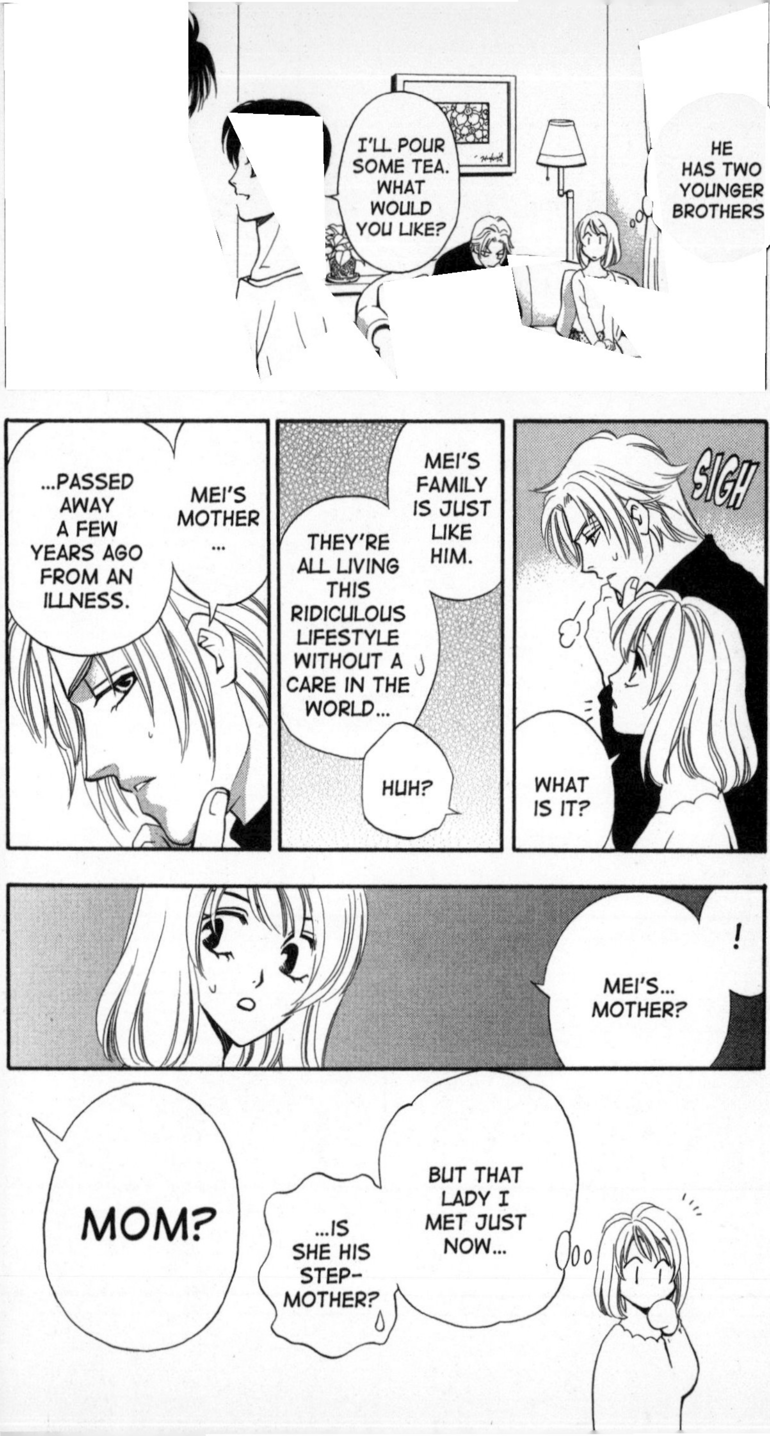
HE HAS TWO YOUNGER BROTHERS
I'LL POUR SOME TEA. WHAT WOULD YOU LIKE?
SIGH
WHAT IS IT?
MEI'S FAMILY IS JUST LIKE HIM.
THEY'RE ALL LIVING THIS RIDICULOUS LIFESTYLE WITHOUT A CARE IN THE WORLD...
HUH?
MEI'S MOTHER ...
...PASSED AWAY A FEW YEARS AGO FROM AN ILLNESS.
!
MEI'S... MOTHER?
BUT THAT LADY I MET JUST NOW...
...IS SHE HIS STEP-MOTHER?
MOM?

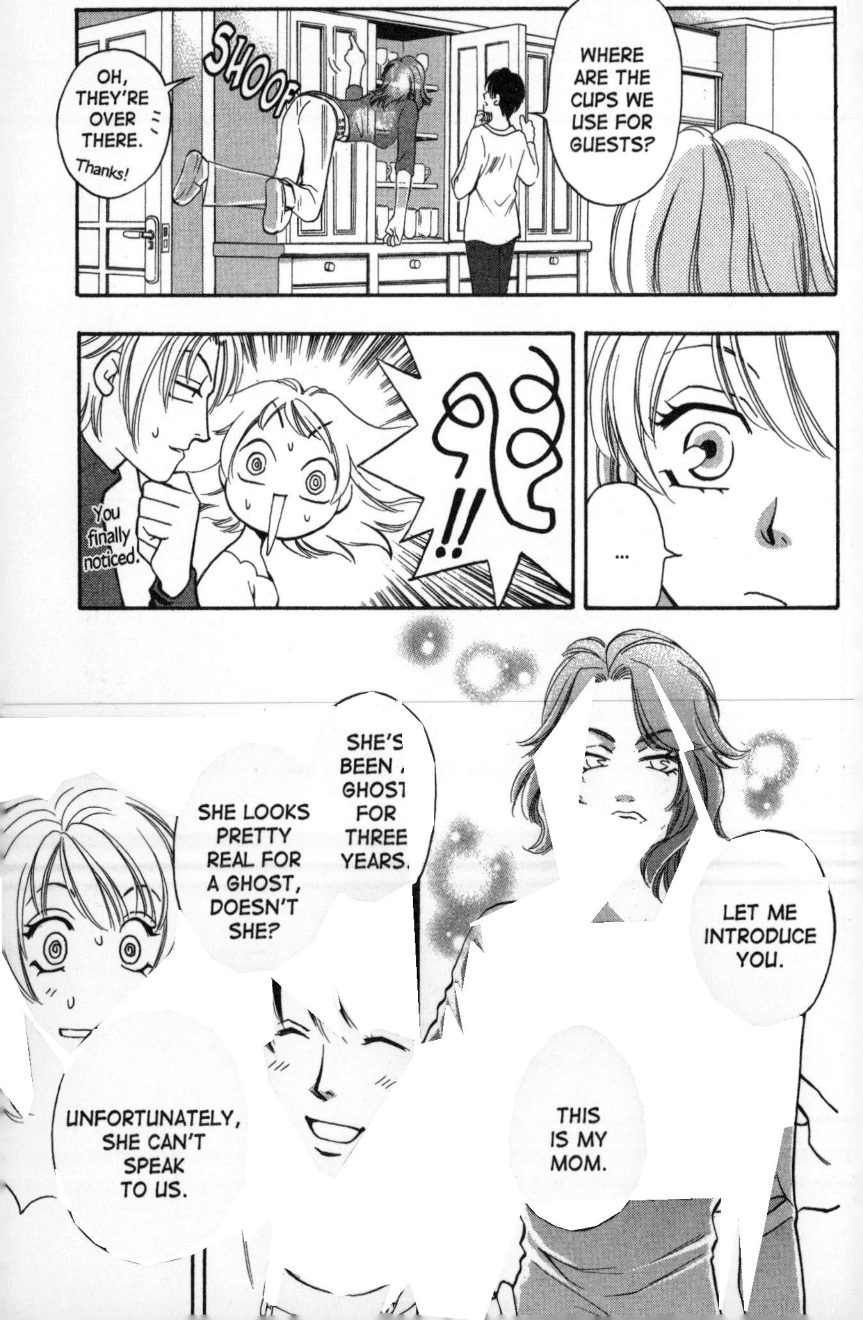
WHERE ARE THE CUPS WE USE FOR GUESTS?
SHOOF
OH, THEY'RE OVER THERE.
Thanks!
...
!!
You finally noticed.
LET ME INTRODUCE YOU.
THIS IS MY MOM.
SHE'S BEEN GHOST FOR THREE YEARS.
SHE LOOKS PRETTY REAL FOR A GHOST, DOESN'T SHE?
UNFORTUNATELY, SHE CAN'T SPEAK TO US.

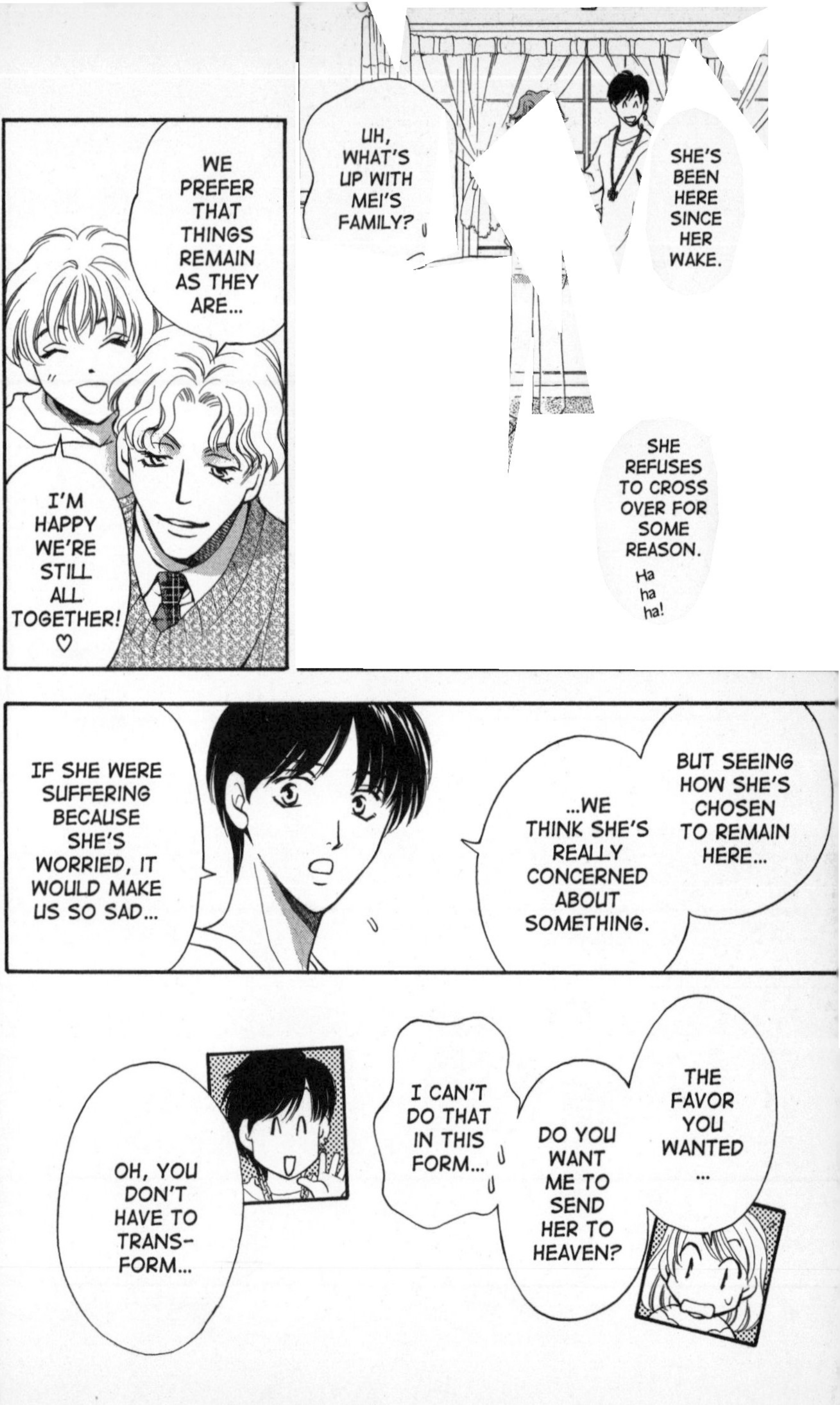
UH, WHAT'S UP WITH MEI'S FAMILY?
SHE'S BEEN HERE SINCE HER WAKE.
SHE REFUSES TO CROSS OVER FOR SOME REASON.
Ha ha ha!
WE PREFER THAT THINGS REMAIN AS THEY ARE...
I'M HAPPY WE'RE STILL ALL TOGETHER! ♡
BUT SEEING HOW SHE'S CHOSEN TO REMAIN HERE...
...WE THINK SHE'S REALLY CONCERNED ABOUT SOMETHING.
IF SHE WERE SUFFERING BECAUSE SHE'S WORRIED, IT WOULD MAKE US SO SAD...
THE FAVOR YOU WANTED ...
DO YOU WANT ME TO SEND HER TO HEAVEN?
I CAN'T DO THAT IN THIS FORM...
OH, YOU DON'T HAVE TO TRANS-FORM...

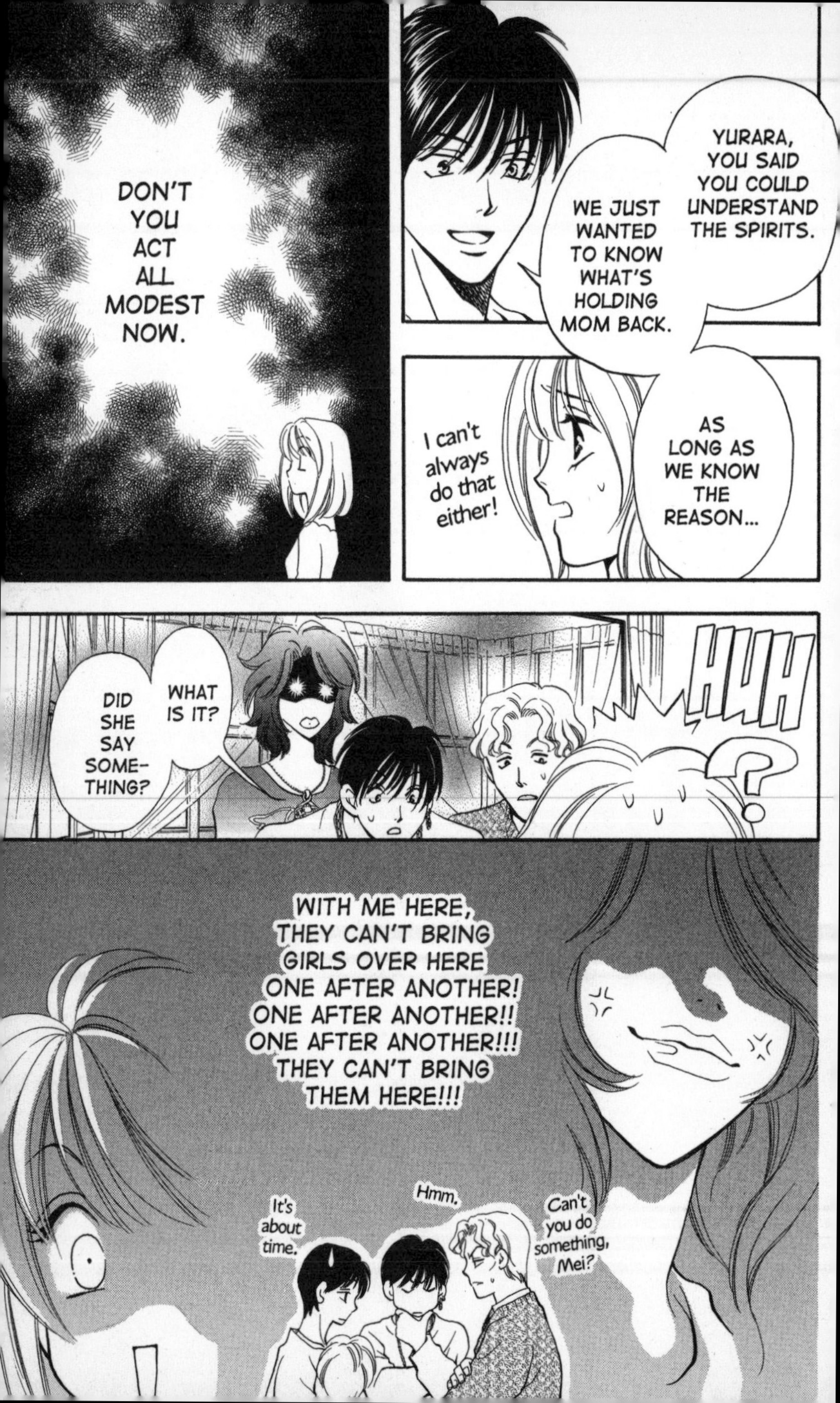

YURARA, YOU SAID YOU COULD UNDERSTAND THE SPIRITS.
WE JUST WANTED TO KNOW WHAT'S HOLDING MOM BACK.
AS LONG AS WE KNOW THE REASON...
I can't always do that either!
DON'T YOU ACT ALL MODEST NOW.
HUH
WHAT IS IT?
DID SHE SAY SOME-THING?
WITH ME HERE, THEY CAN'T BRING GIRLS OVER HERE ONE AFTER ANOTHER! ONE AFTER ANOTHER!! ONE AFTER ANOTHER!!! THEY CAN'T BRING THEM HERE!!!
Can't you do something, Mei?
Hmm.
It's about time.

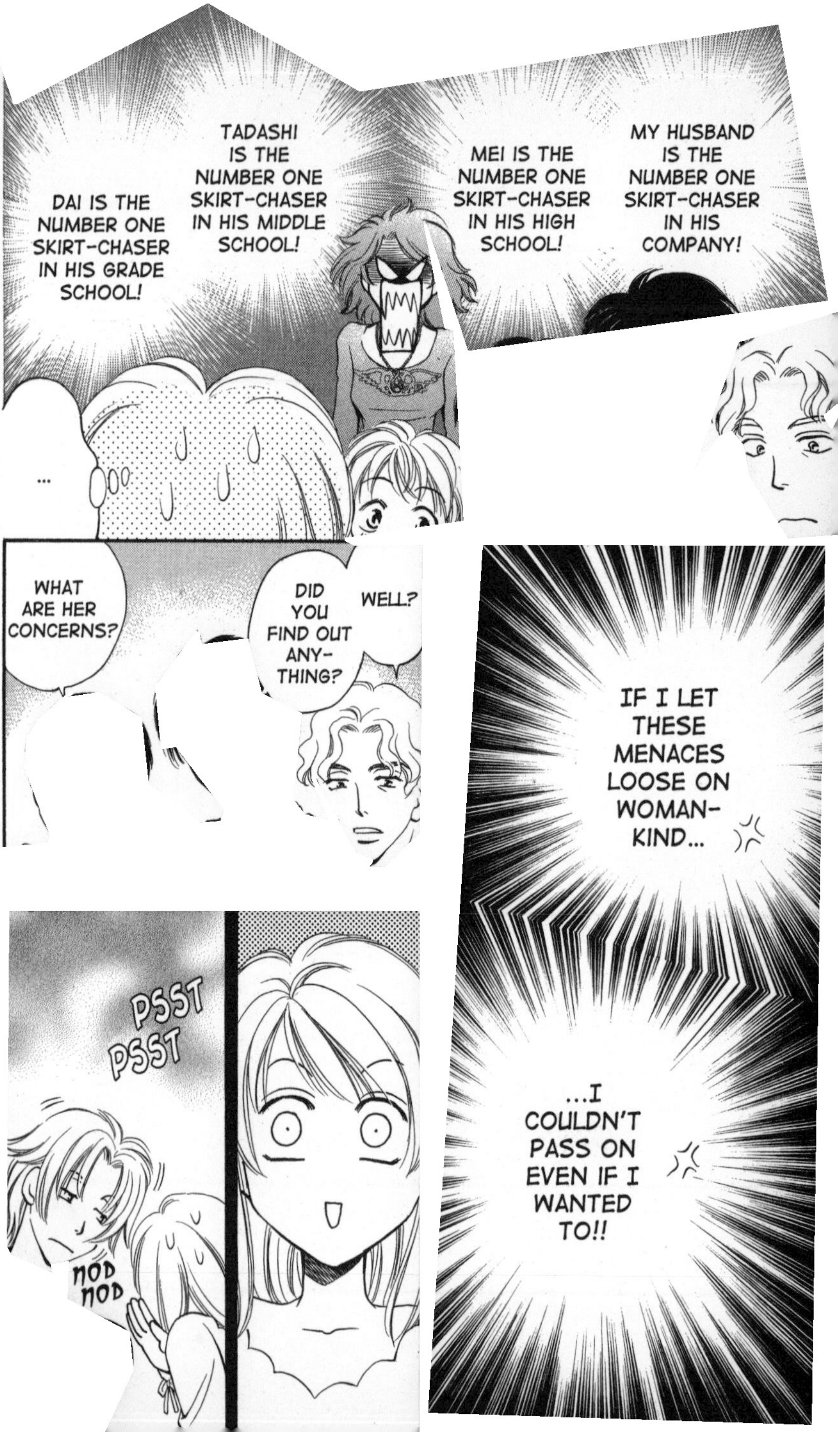
MY HUSBAND IS THE NUMBER ONE SKIRT-CHASER IN HIS COMPANY!
MEI IS THE NUMBER ONE SKIRT-CHASER IN HIS HIGH SCHOOL!
TADASHI IS THE NUMBER ONE SKIRT-CHASER IN HIS MIDDLE SCHOOL!
DAI IS THE NUMBER ONE SKIRT-CHASER IN HIS GRADE SCHOOL!
...
IF I LET THESE MENACES LOOSE ON WOMAN-KIND...
...I COULDN'T PASS ON EVEN IF I WANTED TO!!
WELL?
DID YOU FIND OUT ANY-THING?
WHAT ARE HER CONCERNS?
PSST PSST
NOD NOD

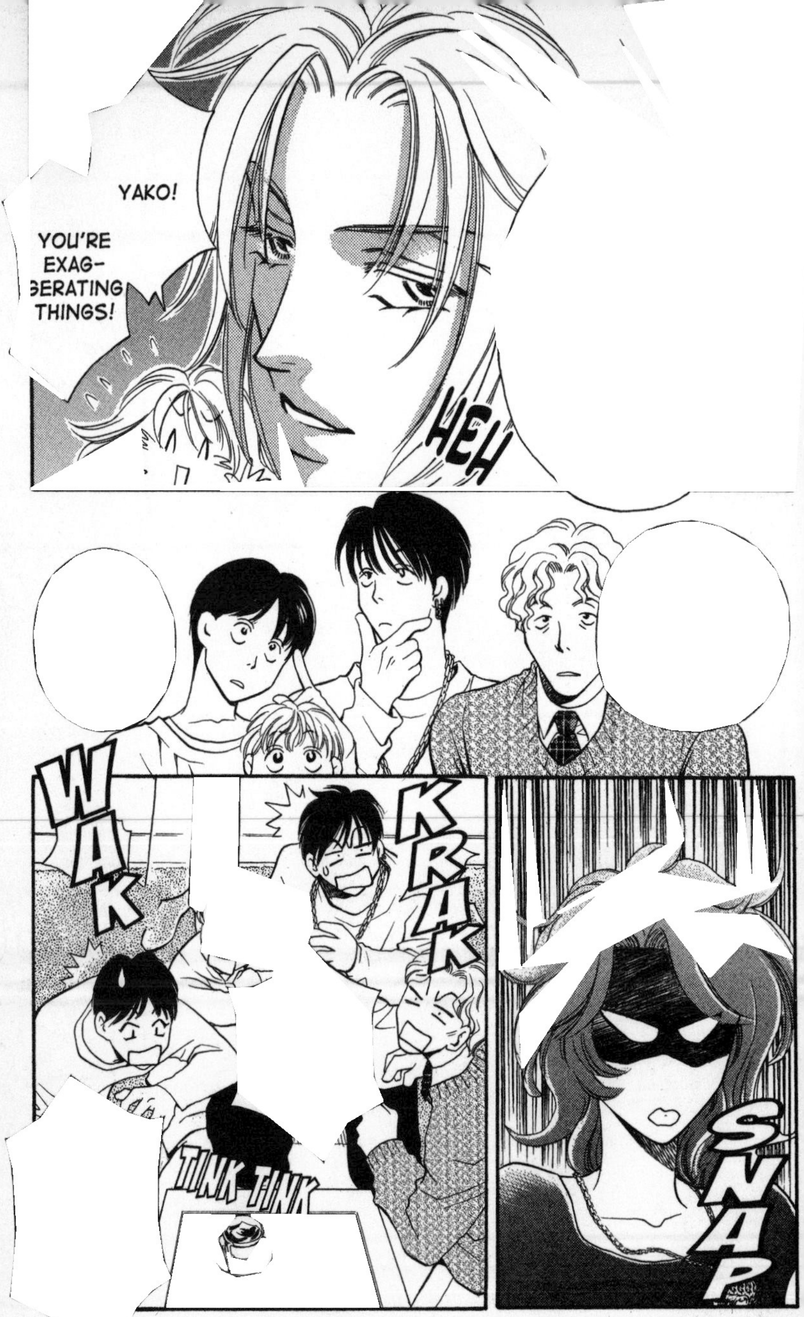
YAKO!
YOU'RE EXAG-GERATING THINGS!
HEH
SNAP
KRAK
WAK
TINK TINK

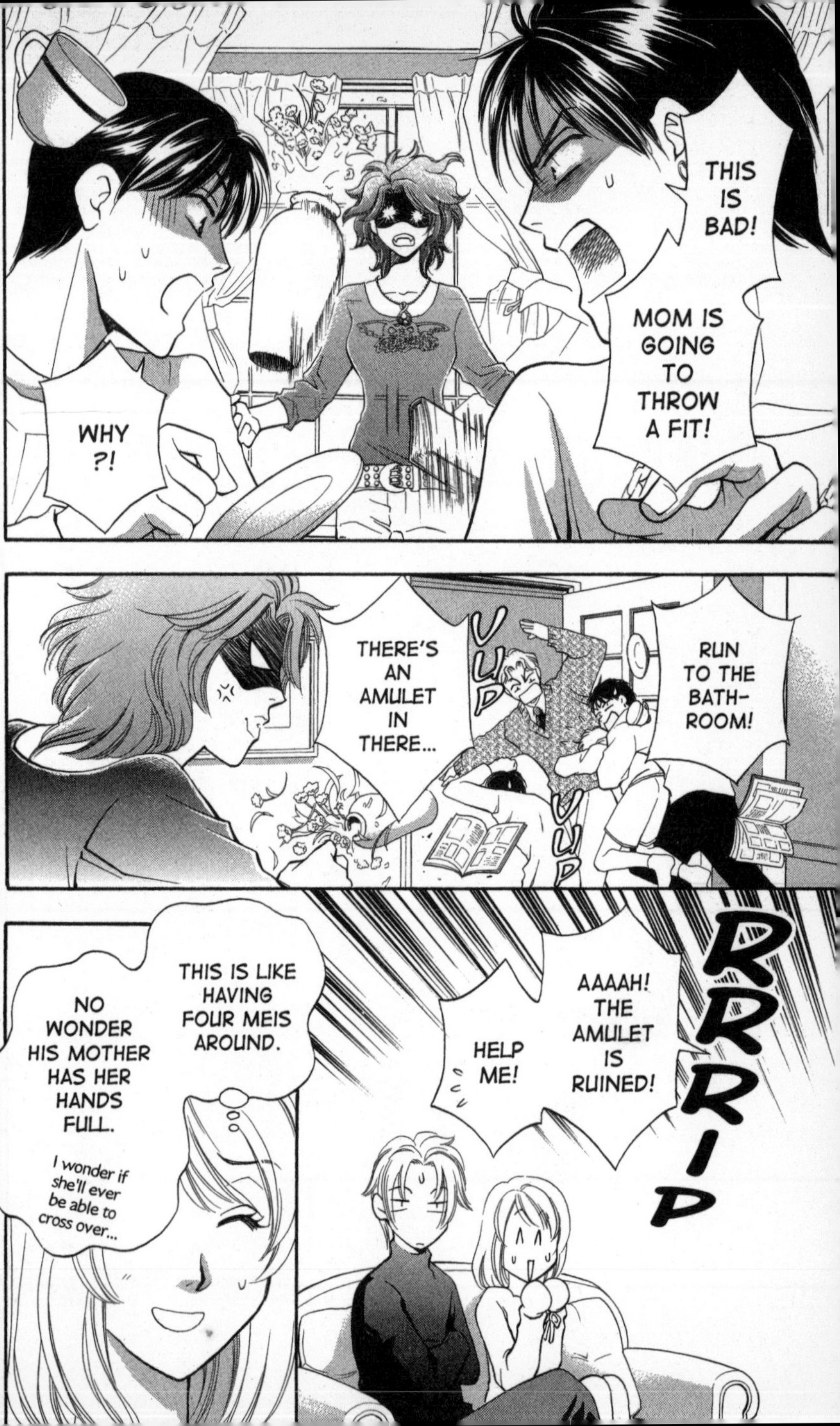
THIS IS BAD!
MOM IS GOING TO THROW A FIT!
WHY?!
RUN TO THE BATH-ROOM!
VUD
VUD
THERE'S AN AMULET IN THERE...
RRRIP
AAAAH! THE AMULET IS RUINED!
HELP ME!
THIS IS LIKE HAVING FOUR MEIS AROUND.
NO WONDER HIS MOTHER HAS HER HANDS FULL.
I wonder if she'll ever be able to cross over...

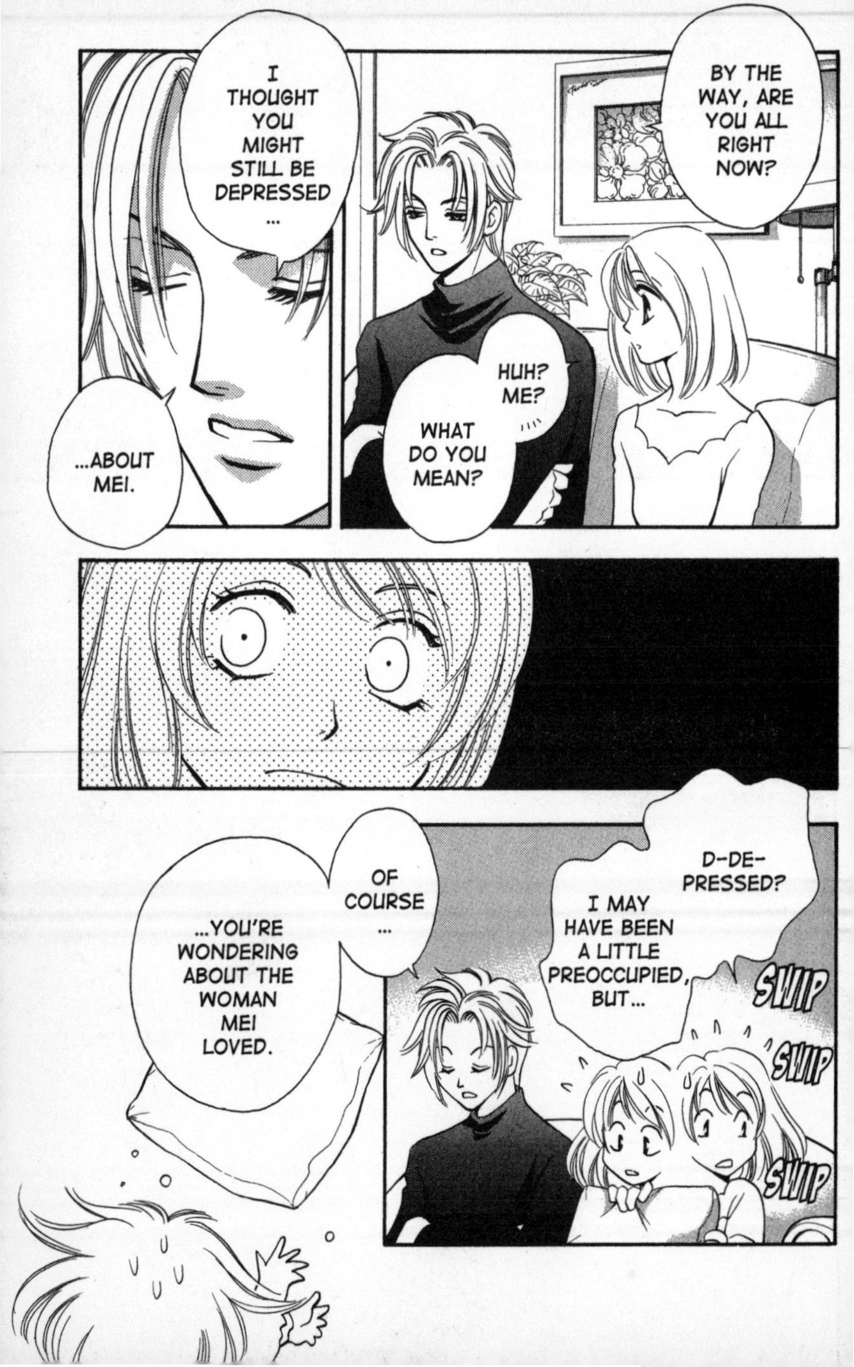
BY THE WAY, ARE YOU ALL RIGHT NOW?
HUH? ME?
WHAT DO YOU MEAN?
I THOUGHT YOU MIGHT STILL BE DEPRESSED ...
...ABOUT MEI.
D-DE-PRESSED?
I MAY HAVE BEEN A LITTLE PREOCCUPIED, BUT...
SWIP
SWIP
SWIP
OF COURSE ...
...YOU'RE WONDERING ABOUT THE WOMAN MEI LOVED.

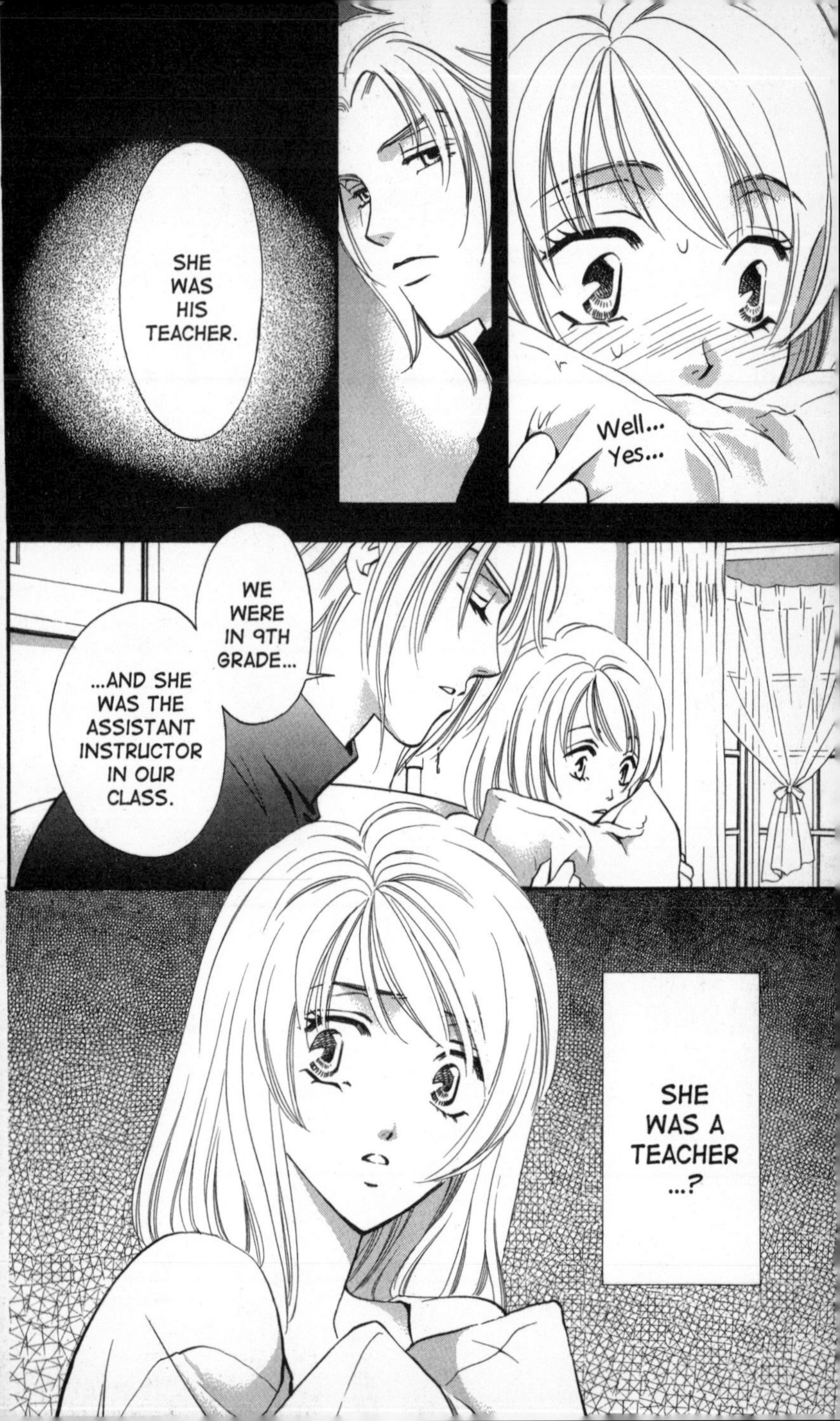
Well... Yes...
SHE WAS HIS TEACHER.
WE WERE IN 9TH GRADE...
...AND SHE WAS THE ASSISTANT INSTRUCTOR IN OUR CLASS.
SHE WAS A TEACHER ...?

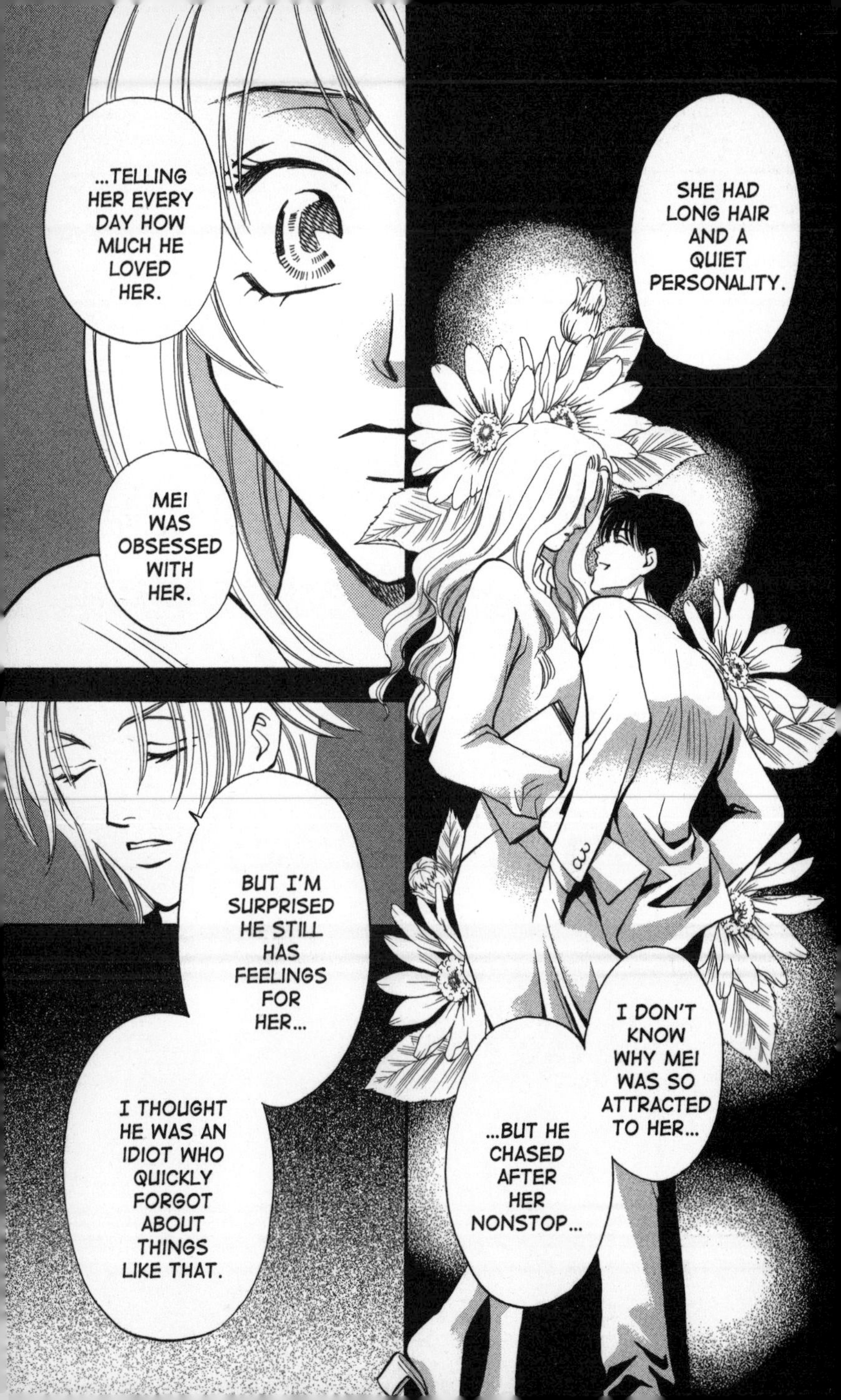
SHE HAD LONG HAIR AND A QUIET PERSONALITY.
I DON'T KNOW WHY MEI WAS SO ATTRACTED TO HER...
...BUT HE CHASED AFTER HER NONSTOP...
...TELLING HER EVERY DAY HOW MUCH HE LOVED HER.
MEI WAS OBSESSED WITH HER.
BUT I'M SURPRISED HE STILL HAS FEELINGS FOR HER...
I THOUGHT HE WAS AN IDIOT WHO QUICKLY FORGOT ABOUT THINGS LIKE THAT.

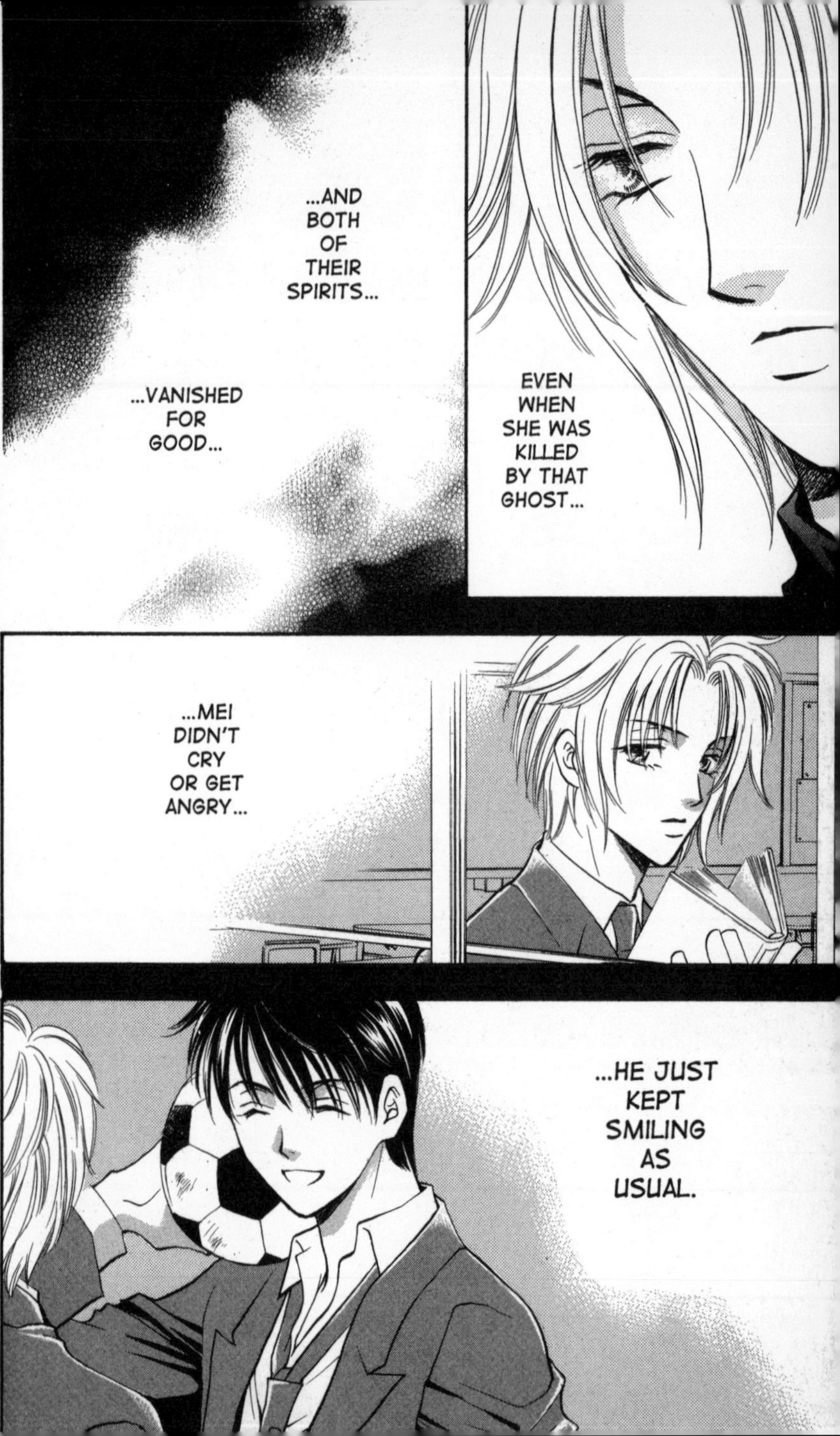
EVEN WHEN SHE WAS KILLED BY THAT GHOST...
...AND BOTH OF THEIR SPIRITS...
...VANISHED FOR GOOD...
...MEI DIDN'T CRY OR GET ANGRY...
...HE JUST KEPT SMILING AS USUAL.

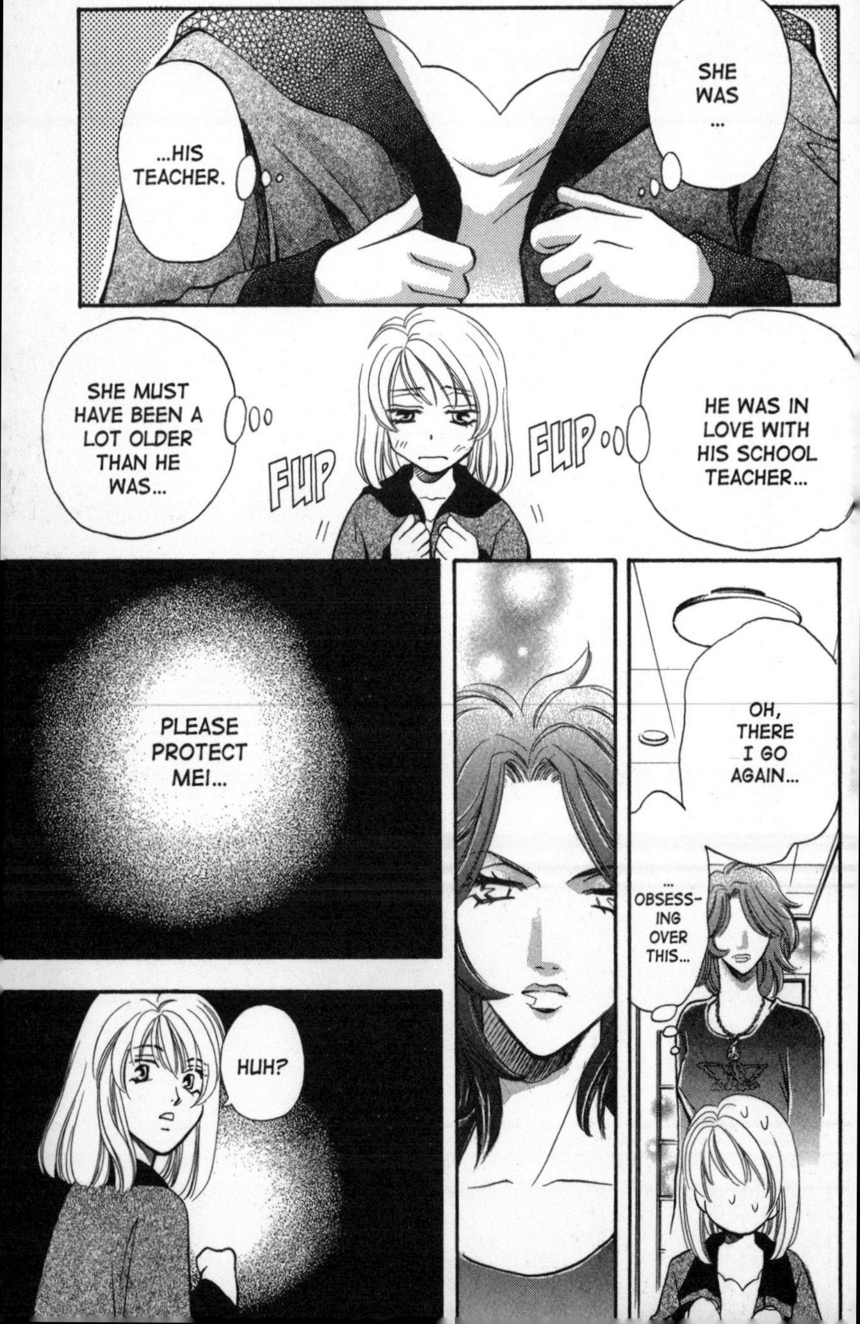
SHE WAS ...
...HIS TEACHER.
HE WAS IN LOVE WITH HIS SCHOOL TEACHER...
FUP
FUP
SHE MUST HAVE BEEN A LOT OLDER THAN HE WAS...
OH, THERE I GO AGAIN...
... OBSESS-ING OVER THIS...
PLEASE PROTECT MEI...
HUH?

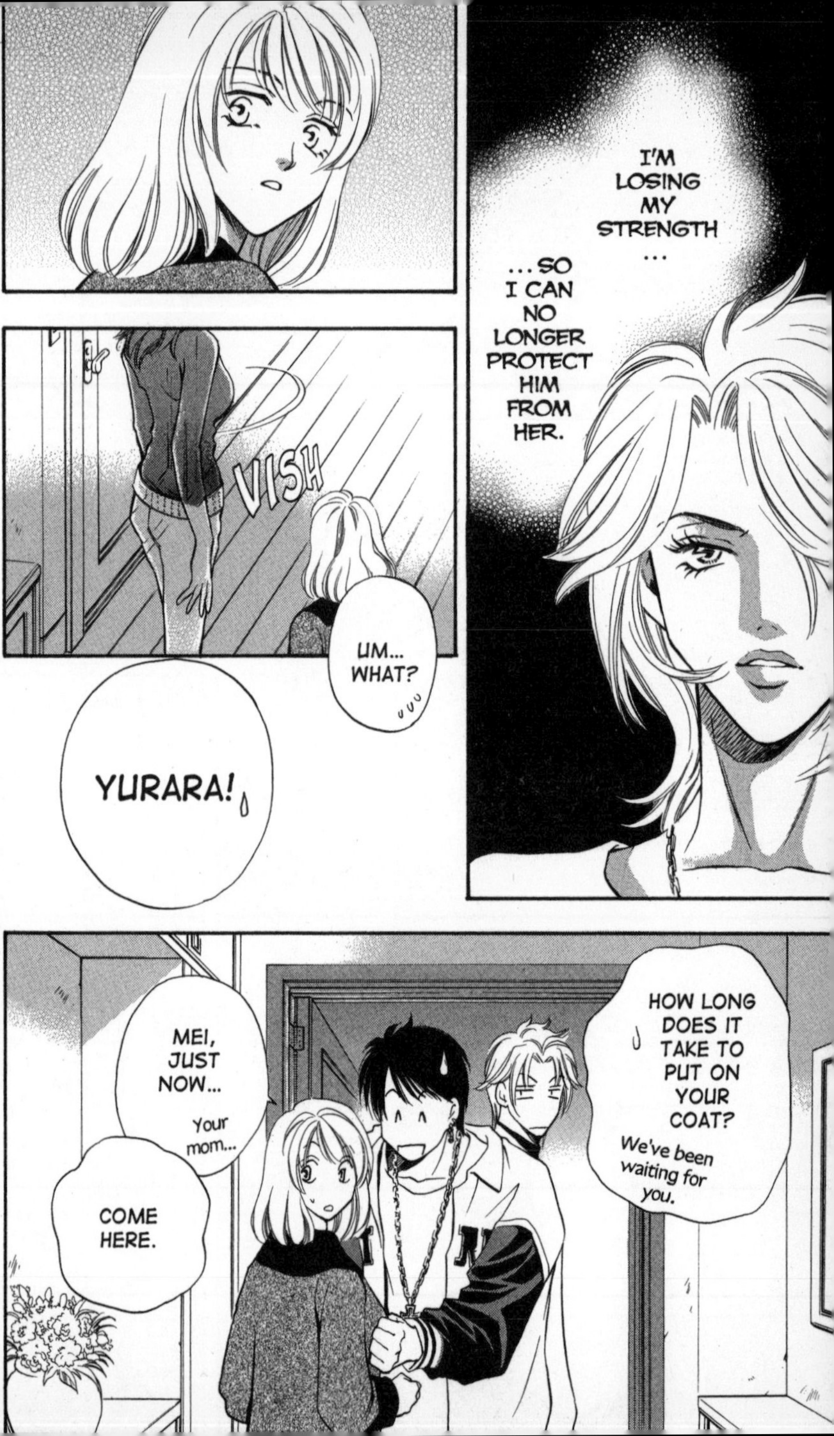
I'M LOSING MY STRENGTH...
...SO I CAN NO LONGER PROTECT HIM FROM HER.
VISH
UM... WHAT?
YURARA!
HOW LONG DOES IT TAKE TO PUT ON YOUR COAT?
We've been waiting for you.
MEI, JUST NOW...
Your mom...
COME HERE.

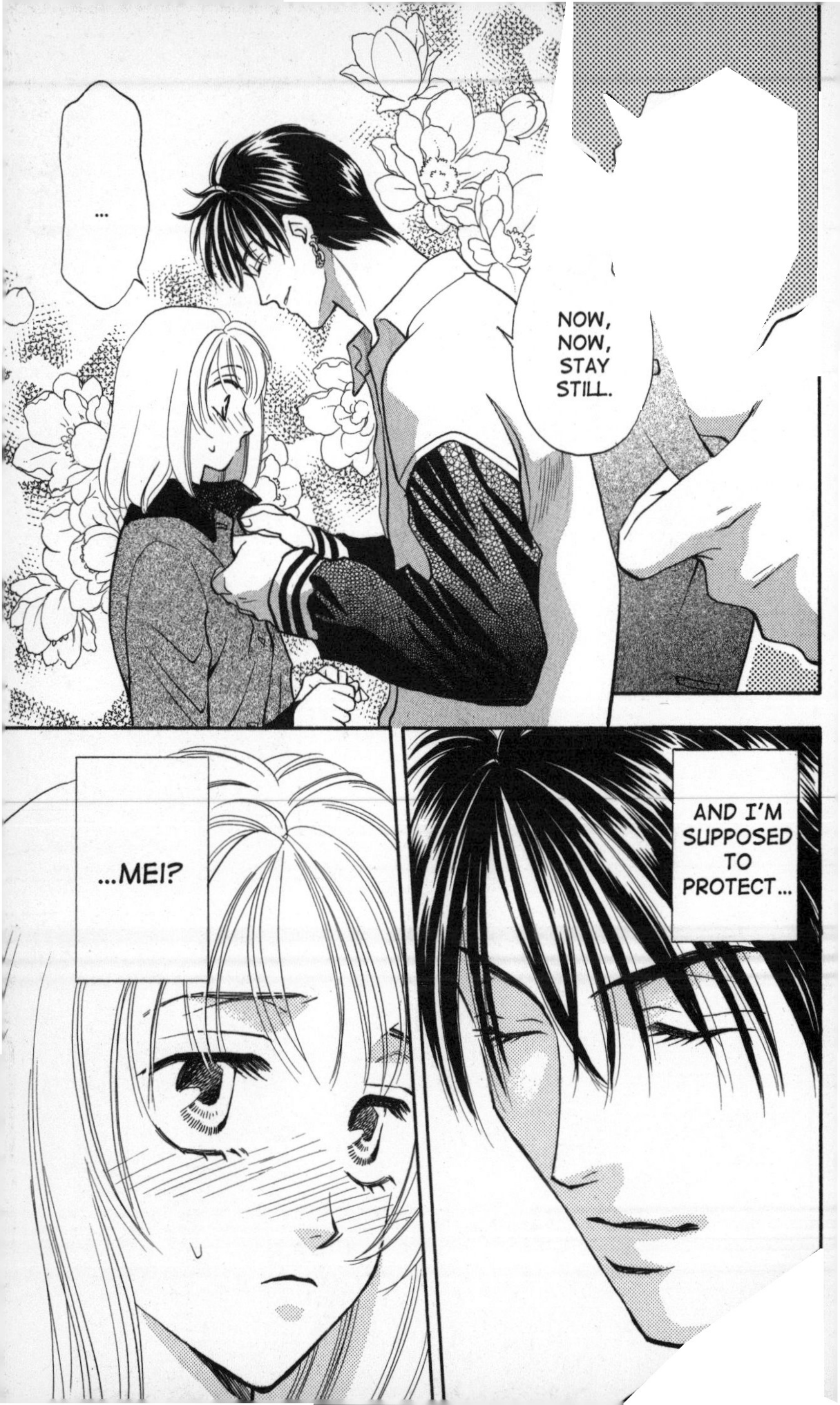
NOW, NOW, STAY STILL.
...
AND I'M SUPPOSED TO PROTECT...
...MEI?

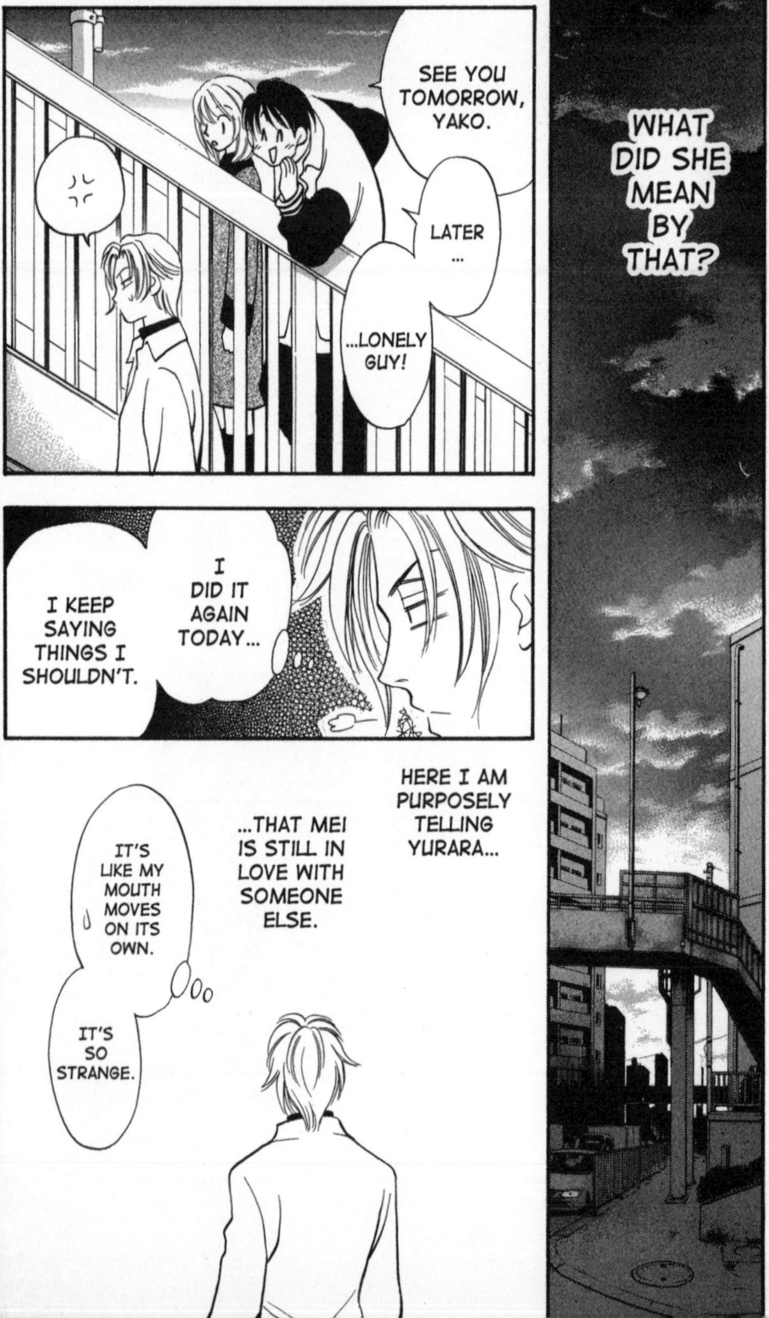
WHAT DID SHE MEAN BY THAT?
SEE YOU TOMORROW, YAKO.
LATER...
...LONELY GUY!
I DID IT AGAIN TODAY...
I KEEP SAYING THINGS I SHOULDN'T.
HERE I AM PURPOSELY TELLING YURARA...
...THAT MEI IS STILL IN LOVE WITH SOMEONE ELSE.
IT'S LIKE MY MOUTH MOVES ON ITS OWN.
IT'S SO STRANGE.

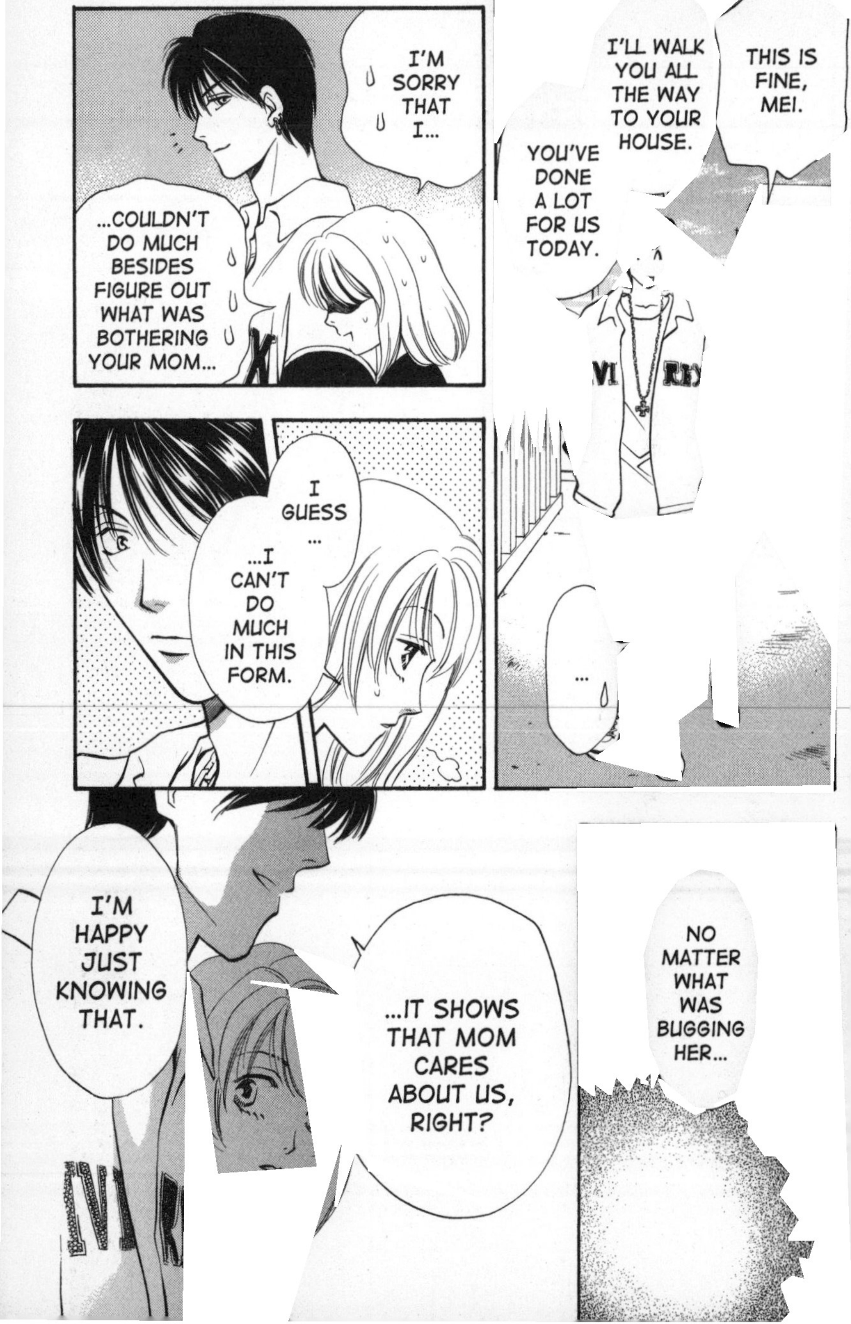
THIS IS FINE, MEI.
I'LL WALK YOU ALL THE WAY TO YOUR HOUSE.
YOU'VE DONE A LOT FOR US TODAY.
...
I'M SORRY THAT I...
...COULDN'T DO MUCH BESIDES FIGURE OUT WHAT WAS BOTHERING YOUR MOM...
I GUESS...
...I CAN'T DO MUCH IN THIS FORM.
NO MATTER WHAT WAS BUGGING HER...
...IT SHOWS THAT MOM CARES ABOUT US, RIGHT?
I'M HAPPY JUST KNOWING THAT.

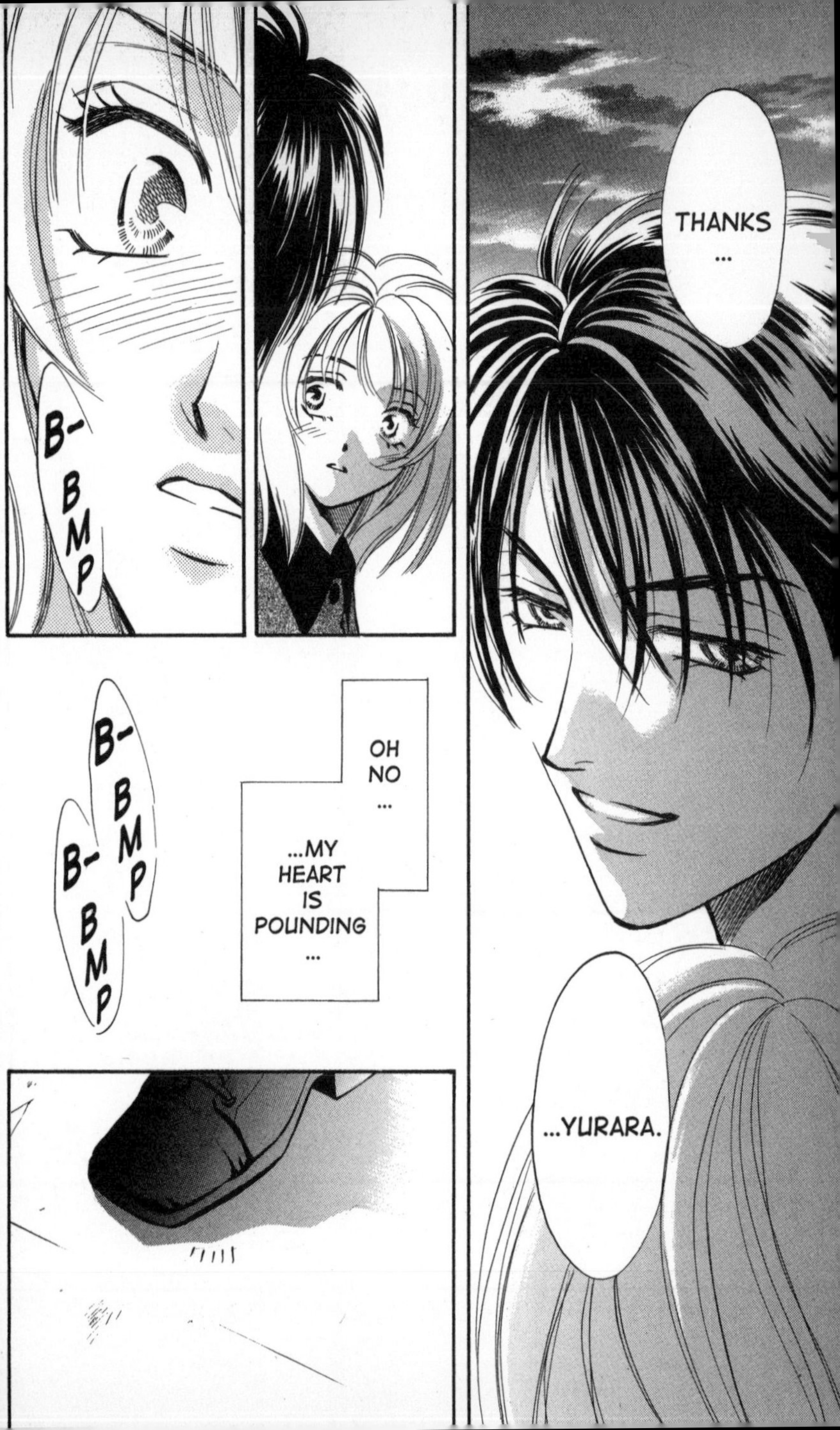
THANKS ...
...YURARA.
B-BMP
OH NO ...
...MY HEART IS POUNDING ...
B-BMP
B-BMP

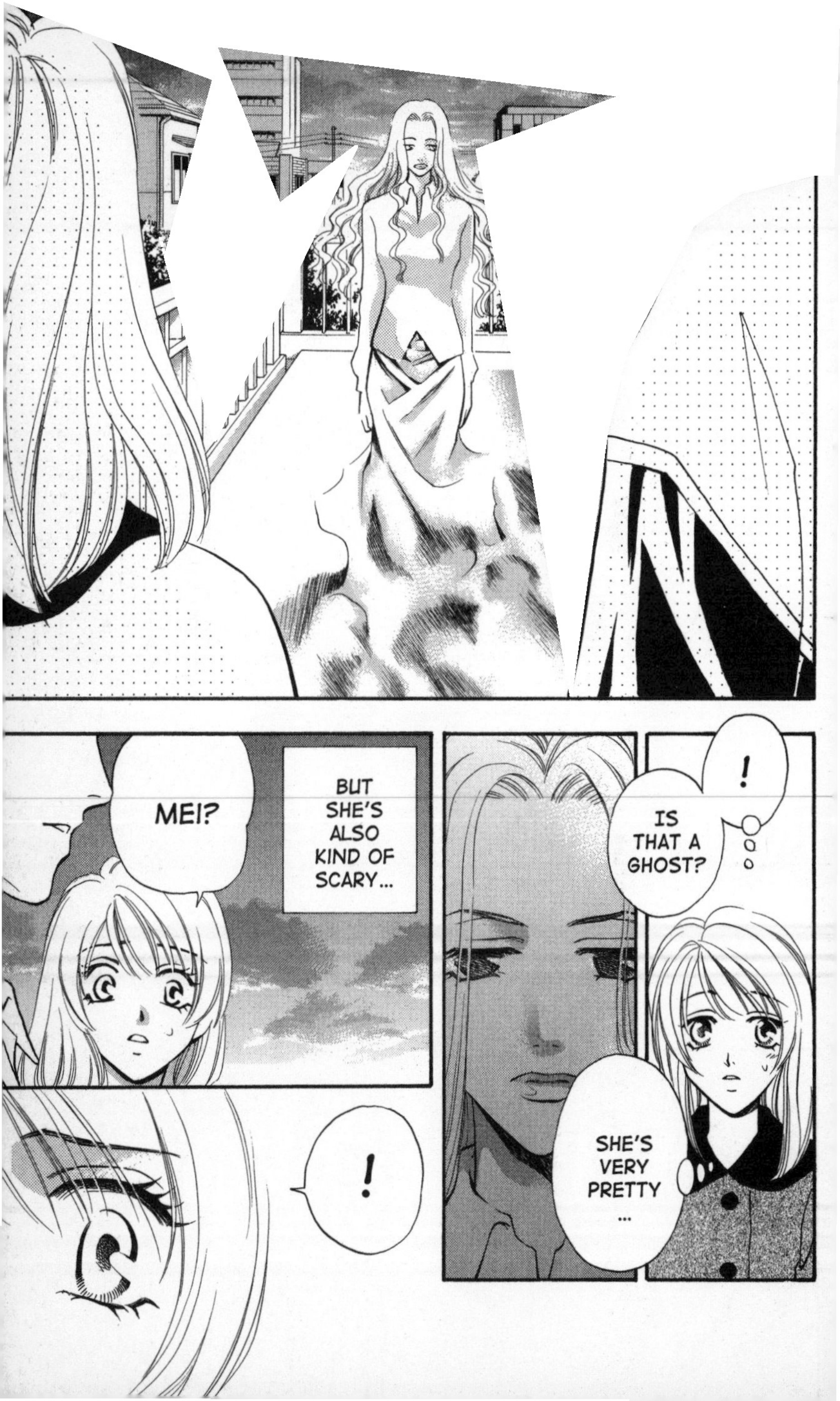
!
IS THAT A GHOST?
SHE'S VERY PRETTY ...
BUT SHE'S ALSO KIND OF SCARY...
MEI?
!

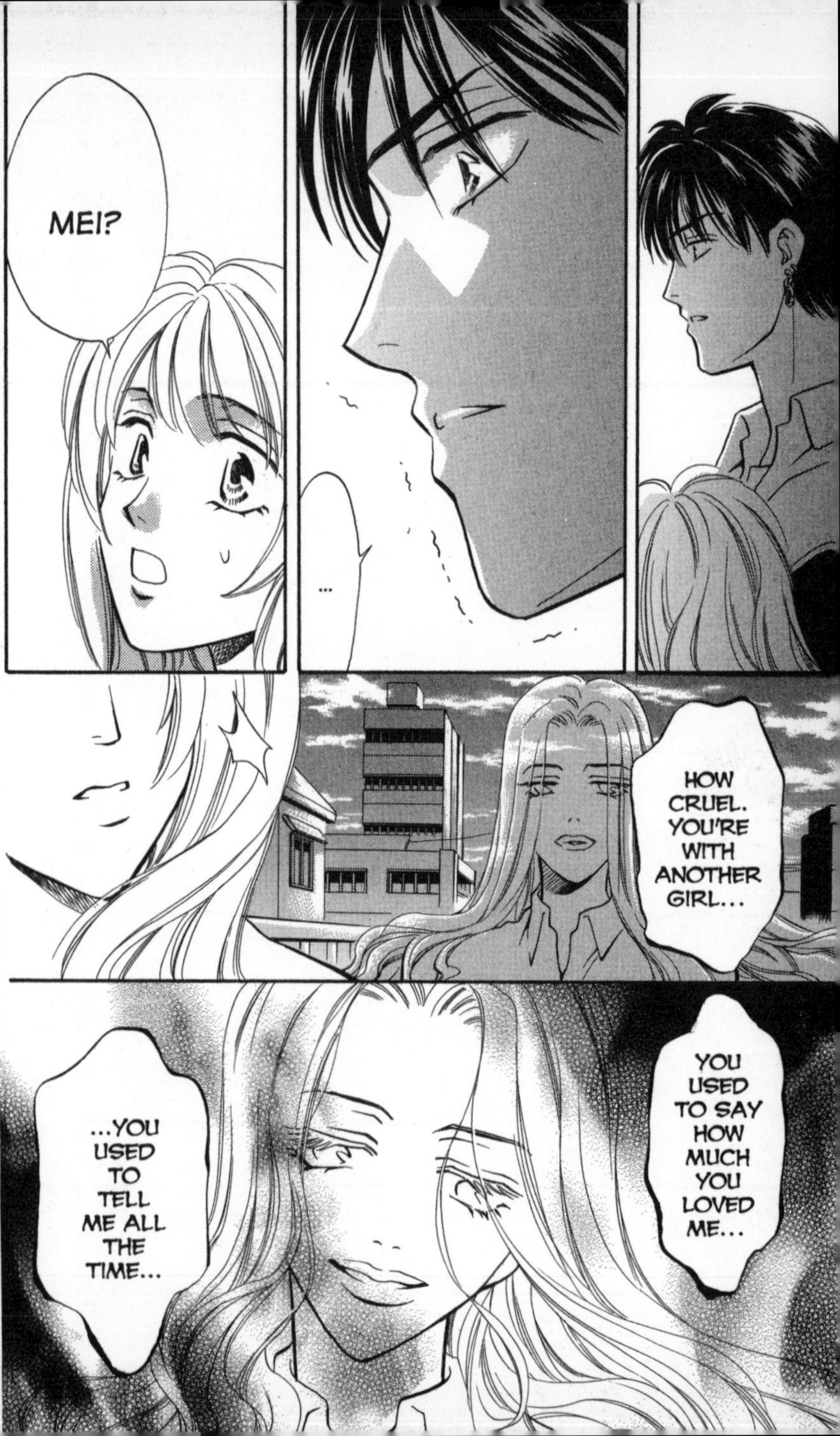
...
MEI?
HOW CRUEL. YOU'RE WITH ANOTHER GIRL...
YOU USED TO SAY HOW MUCH YOU LOVED ME...
...YOU USED TO TELL ME ALL THE TIME...

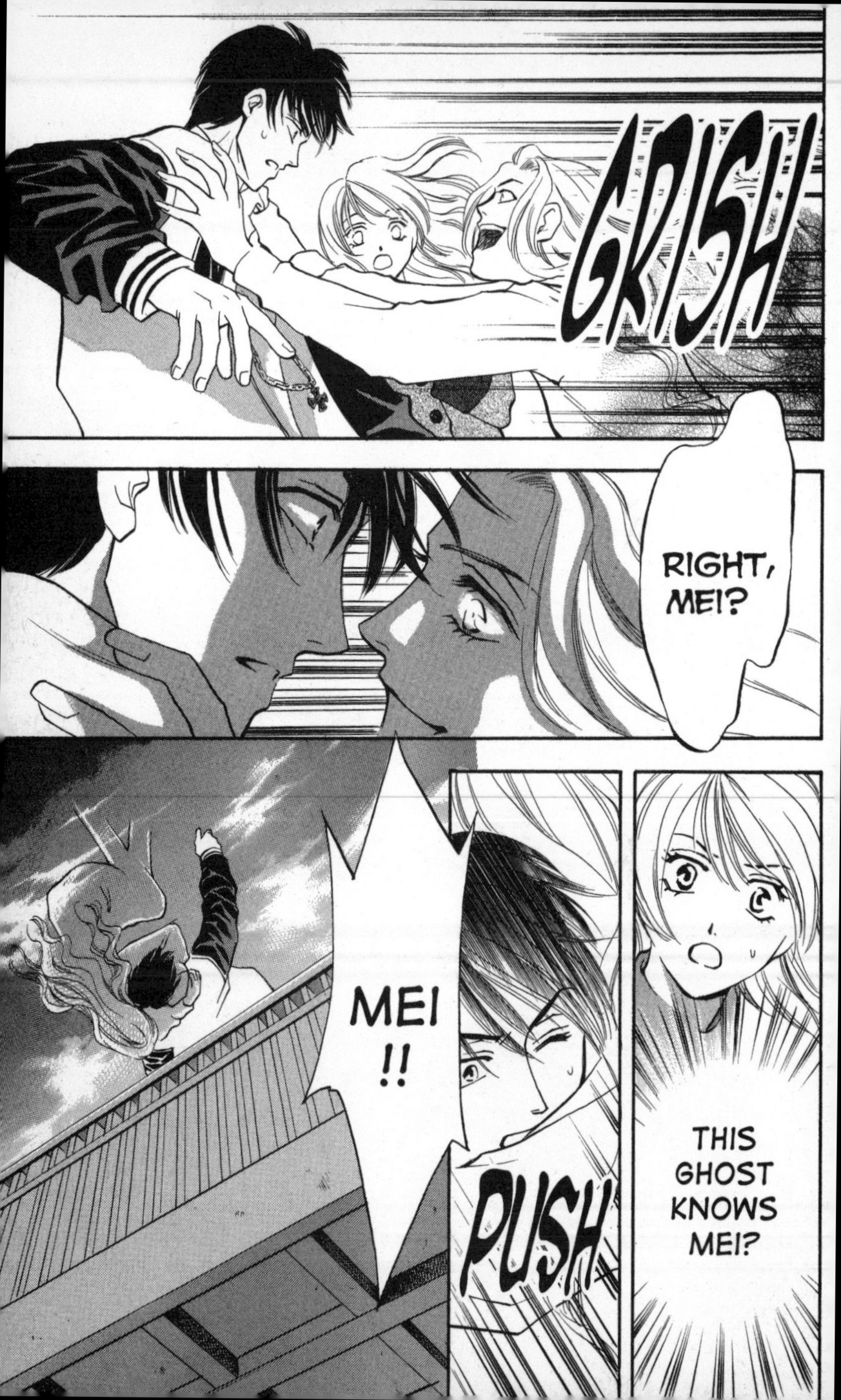
GRISH
RIGHT, MEI?
THIS GHOST KNOWS MEI?
PUSH
MEI !!

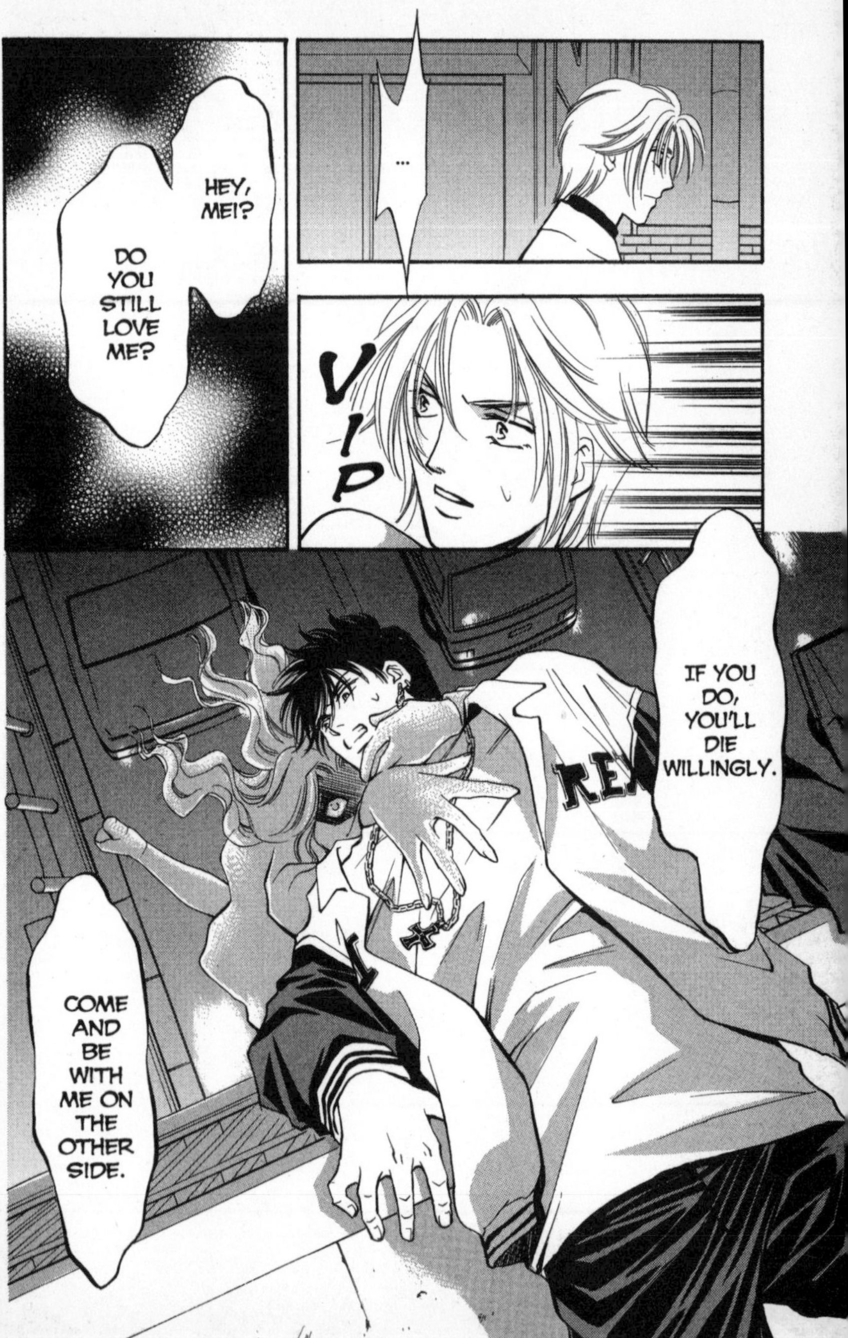
...
VIP
HEY, MEI?
DO YOU STILL LOVE ME?
IF YOU DO, YOU'LL DIE WILLINGLY.
COME AND BE WITH ME ON THE OTHER SIDE.

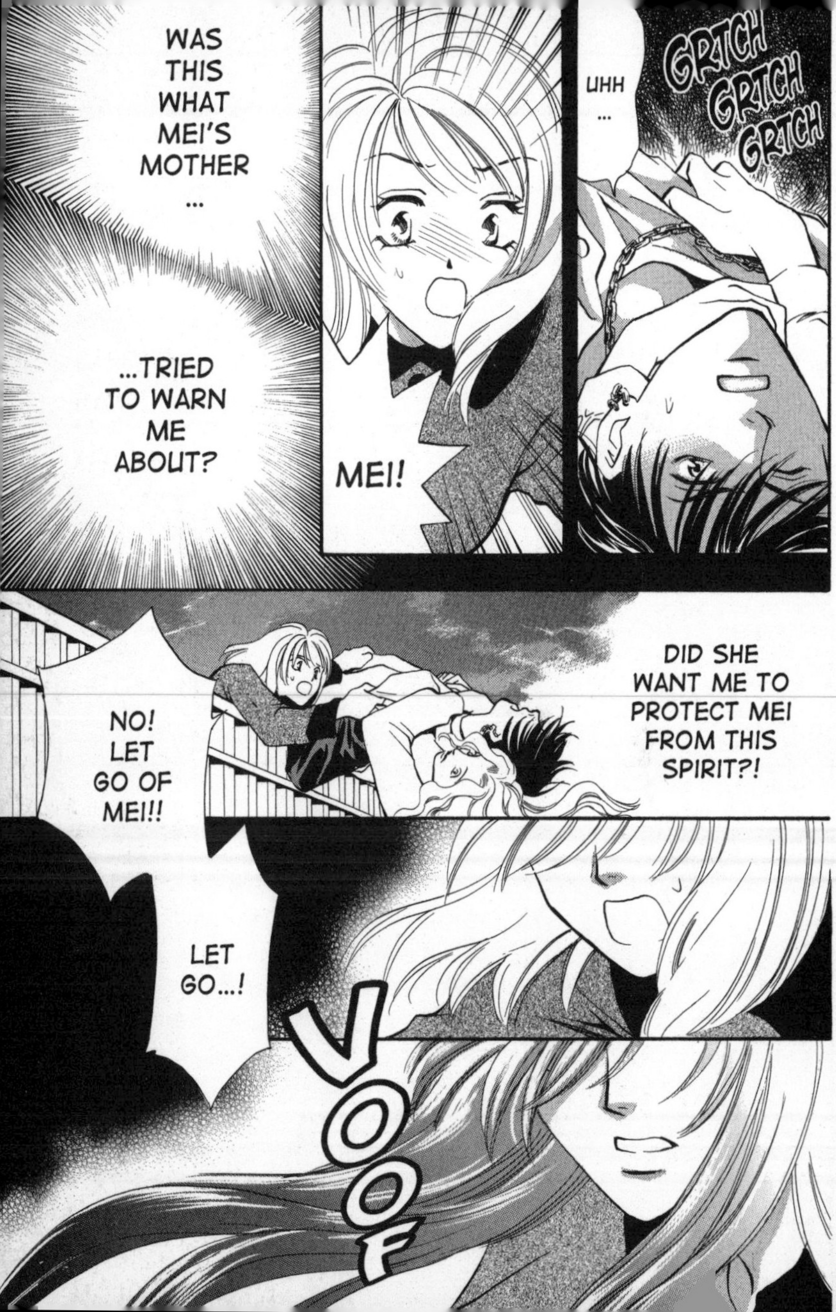
GRTCH GRTCH GRTCH
UHH ...
MEI!
WAS THIS WHAT MEI'S MOTHER ...
...TRIED TO WARN ME ABOUT?
DID SHE WANT ME TO PROTECT MEI FROM THIS SPIRIT?!
NO! LET GO OF MEI!!
LET GO...!
VOOF

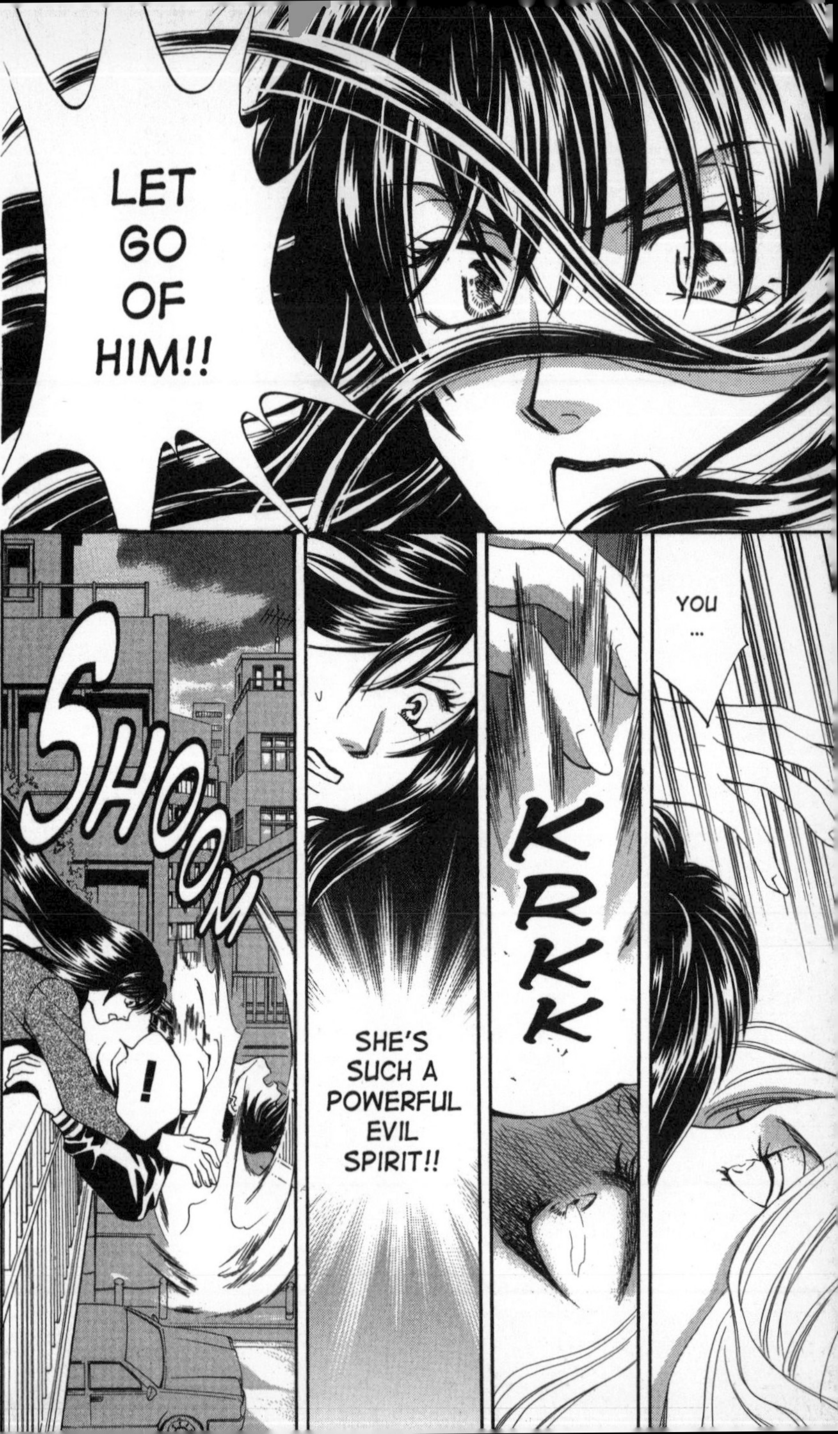
LET GO OF HIM!!
YOU...
KRKK
SHE'S SUCH A POWERFUL EVIL SPIRIT!!
SHOOM
!

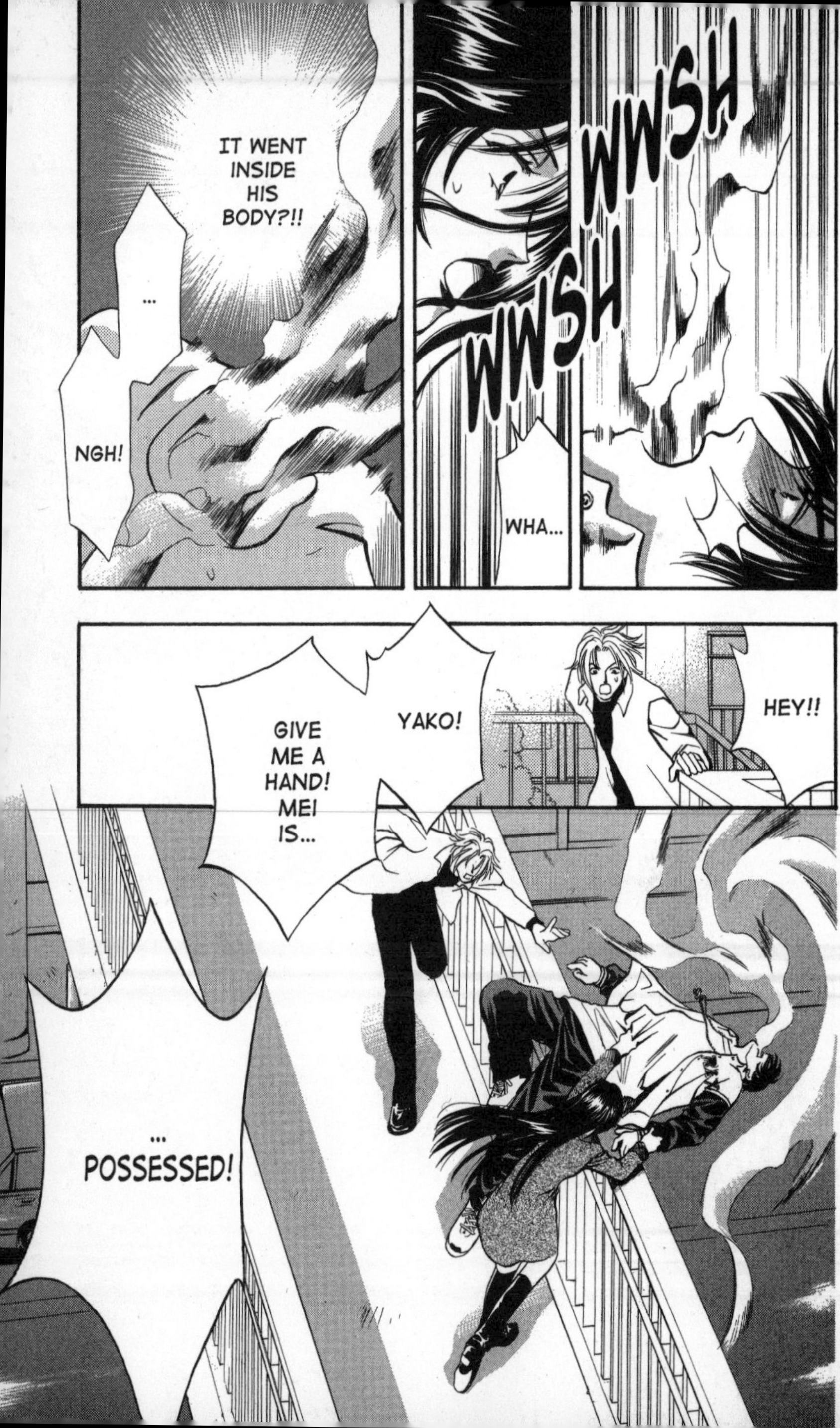
WWSH
WWSH
WHA...
IT WENT INSIDE HIS BODY?!!
...
NGH!
HEY!!
YAKO!
GIVE ME A HAND! MEI IS...
... POSSESSED!

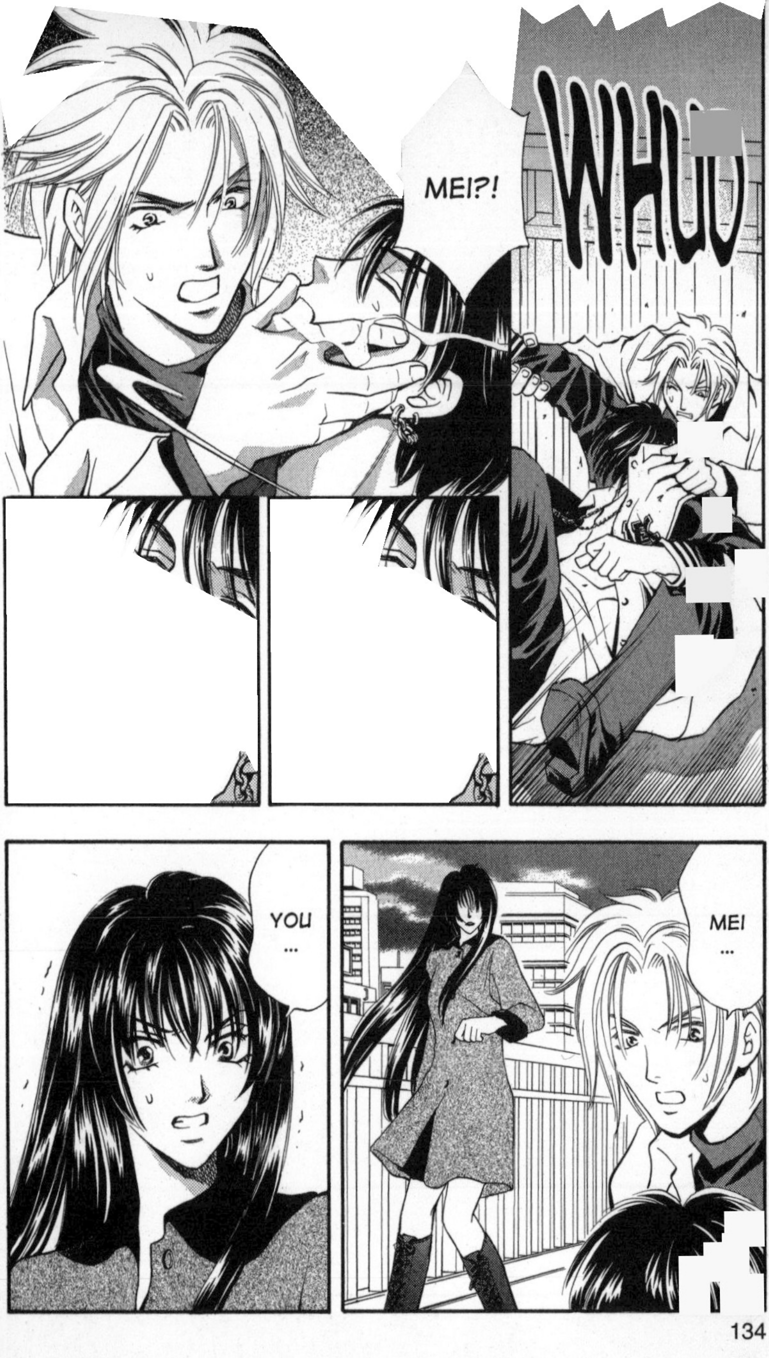
WHU
MEI?!
MEI ...
YOU ...

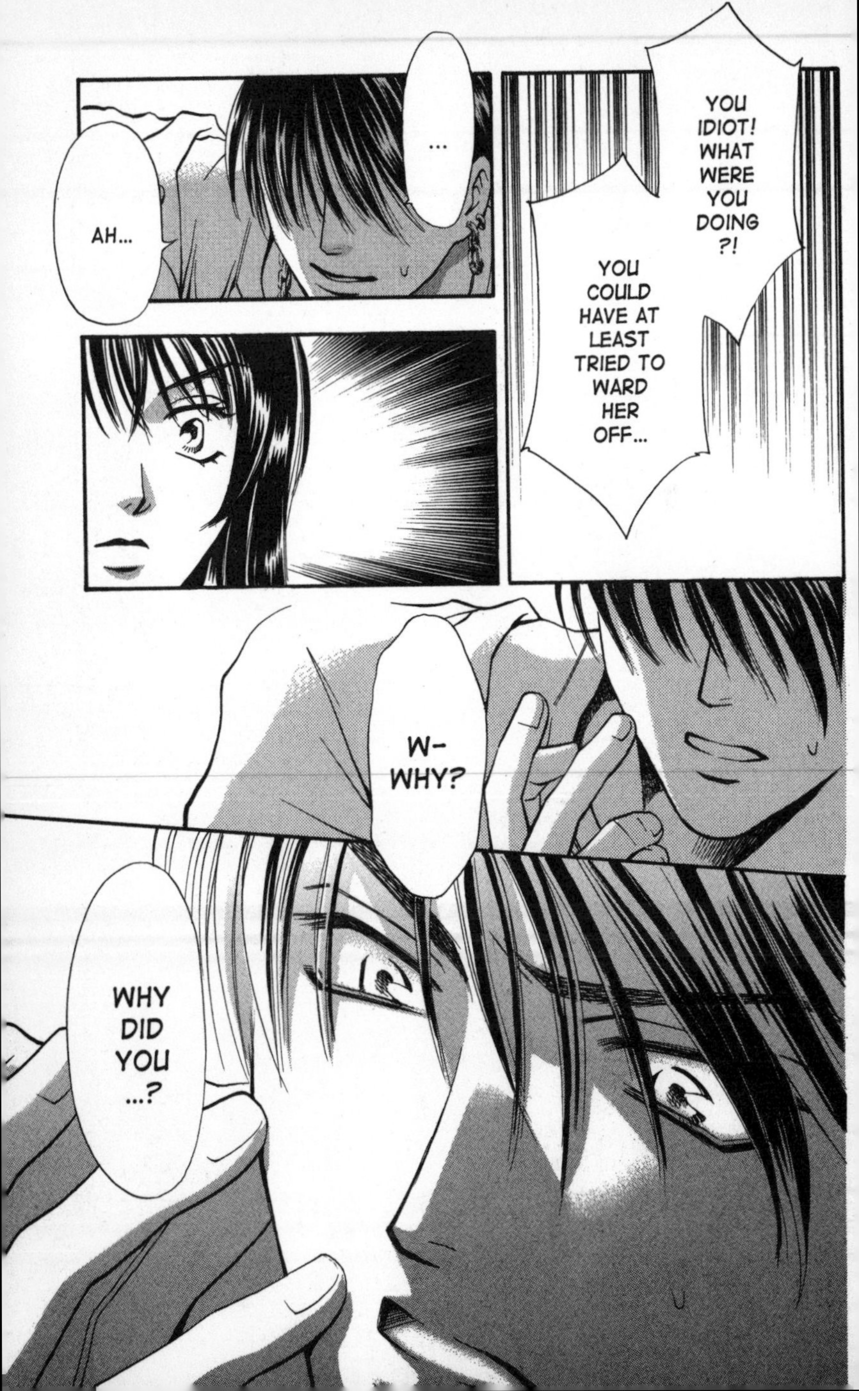

YOU IDIOT! WHAT WERE YOU DOING ?!
YOU COULD HAVE AT LEAST TRIED TO WARD HER OFF...
...
AH...
W-WHY?
WHY DID YOU ...?

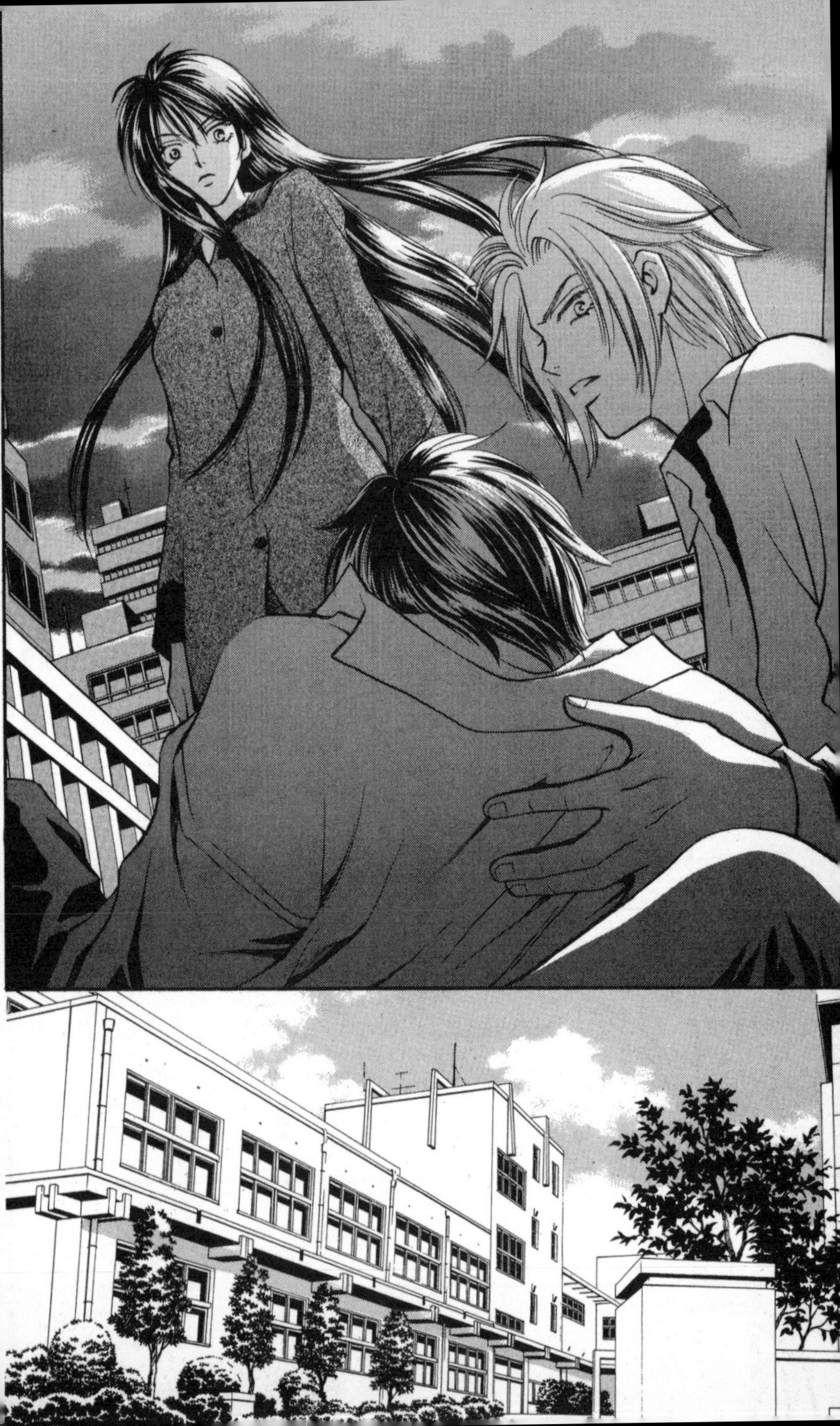

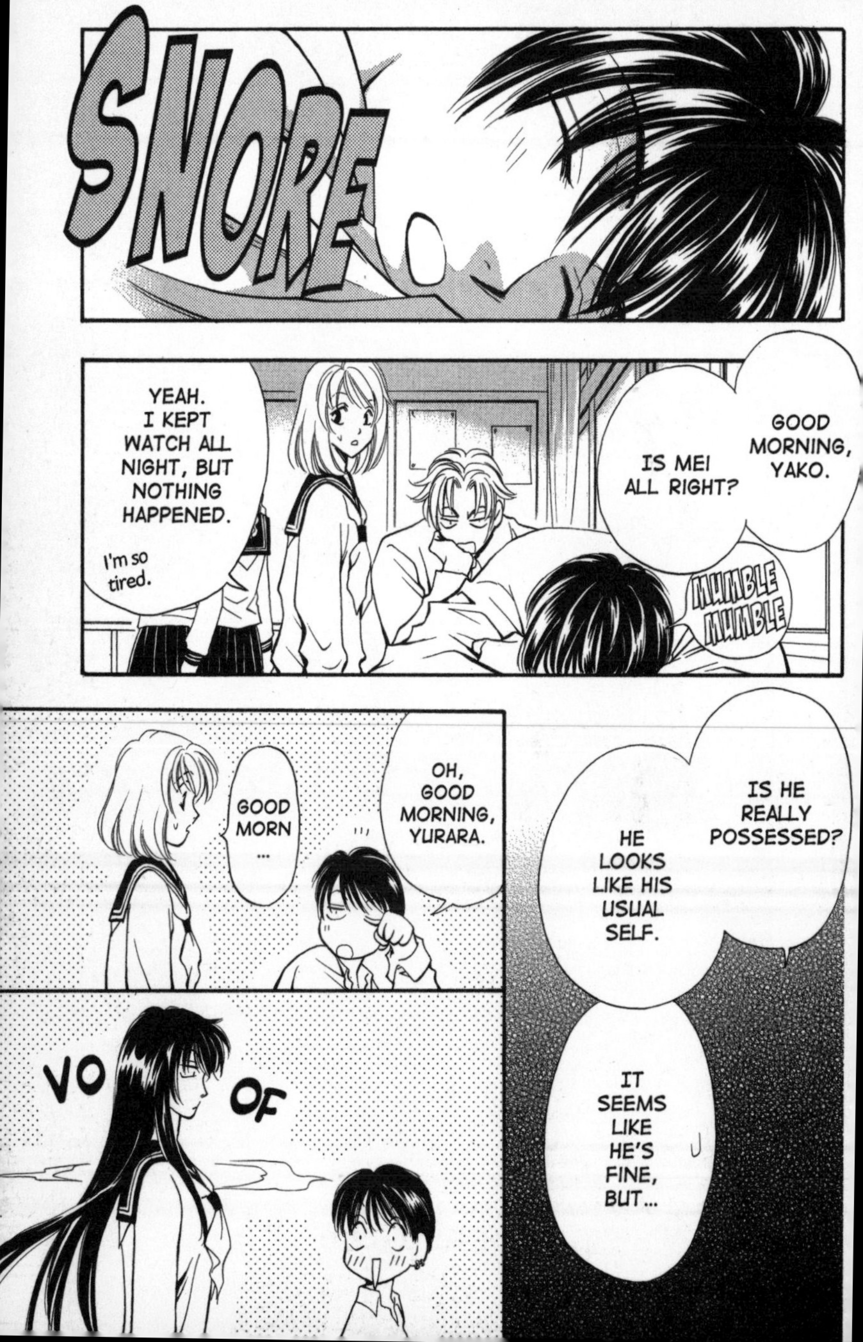
SNORE
GOOD MORNING, YAKO.
IS MEI ALL RIGHT?
MUMBLE MUMBLE
YEAH. I KEPT WATCH ALL NIGHT, BUT NOTHING HAPPENED.
I'm so tired.
IS HE REALLY POSSESSED?
HE LOOKS LIKE HIS USUAL SELF.
IT SEEMS LIKE HE'S FINE, BUT...
OH, GOOD MORNING, YURARA.
GOOD MORN...
VO OF

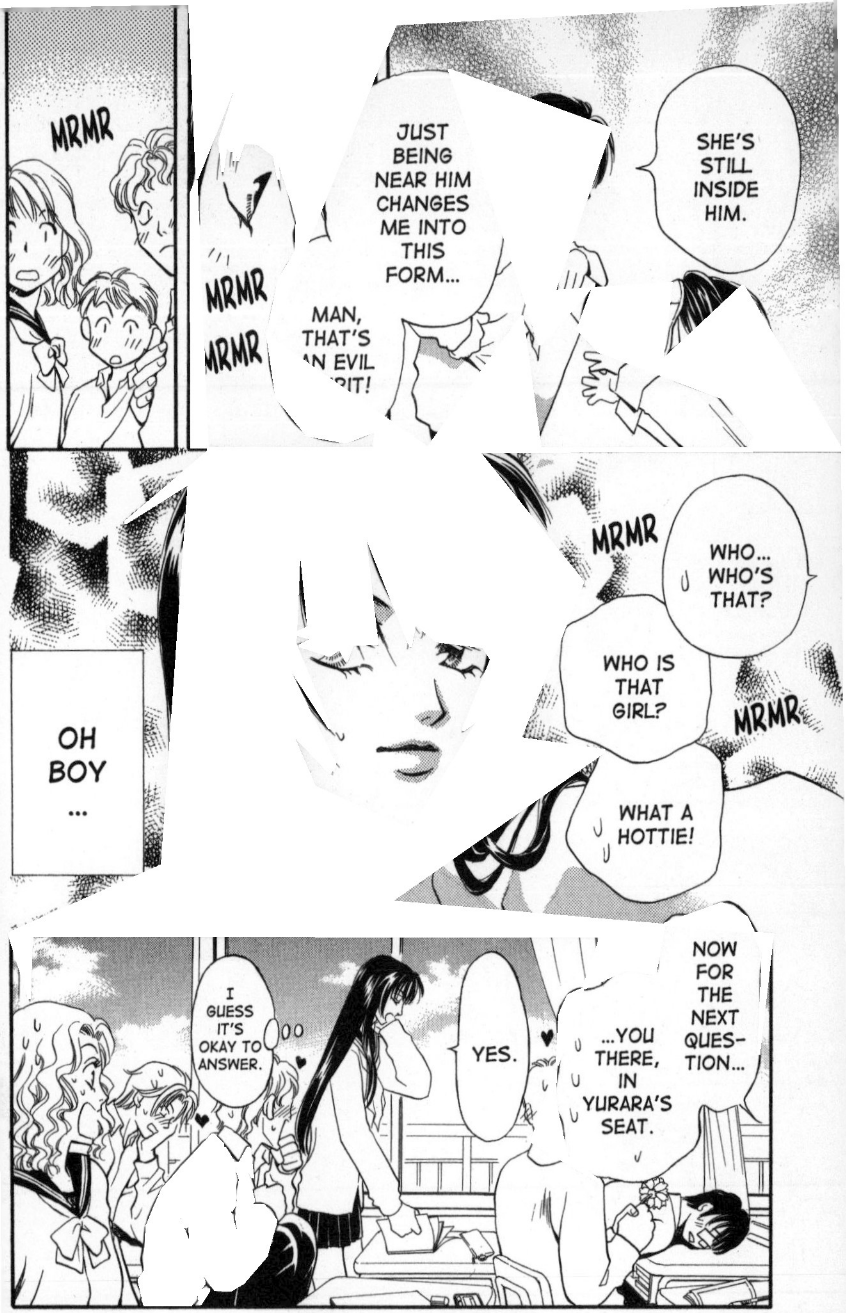
SHE'S STILL INSIDE HIM.
JUST BEING NEAR HIM CHANGES ME INTO THIS FORM...
MAN, THAT'S AN EVIL
MRMR
MRMR
MRMR
MRMR
WHO... WHO'S THAT?
WHO IS THAT GIRL?
MRMR
WHAT A HOTTIE!
OH BOY ...
NOW FOR THE NEXT QUES-TION...
...YOU THERE, IN YURARA'S SEAT.
YES.
I GUESS IT'S OKAY TO ANSWER.

Chapter 7/End

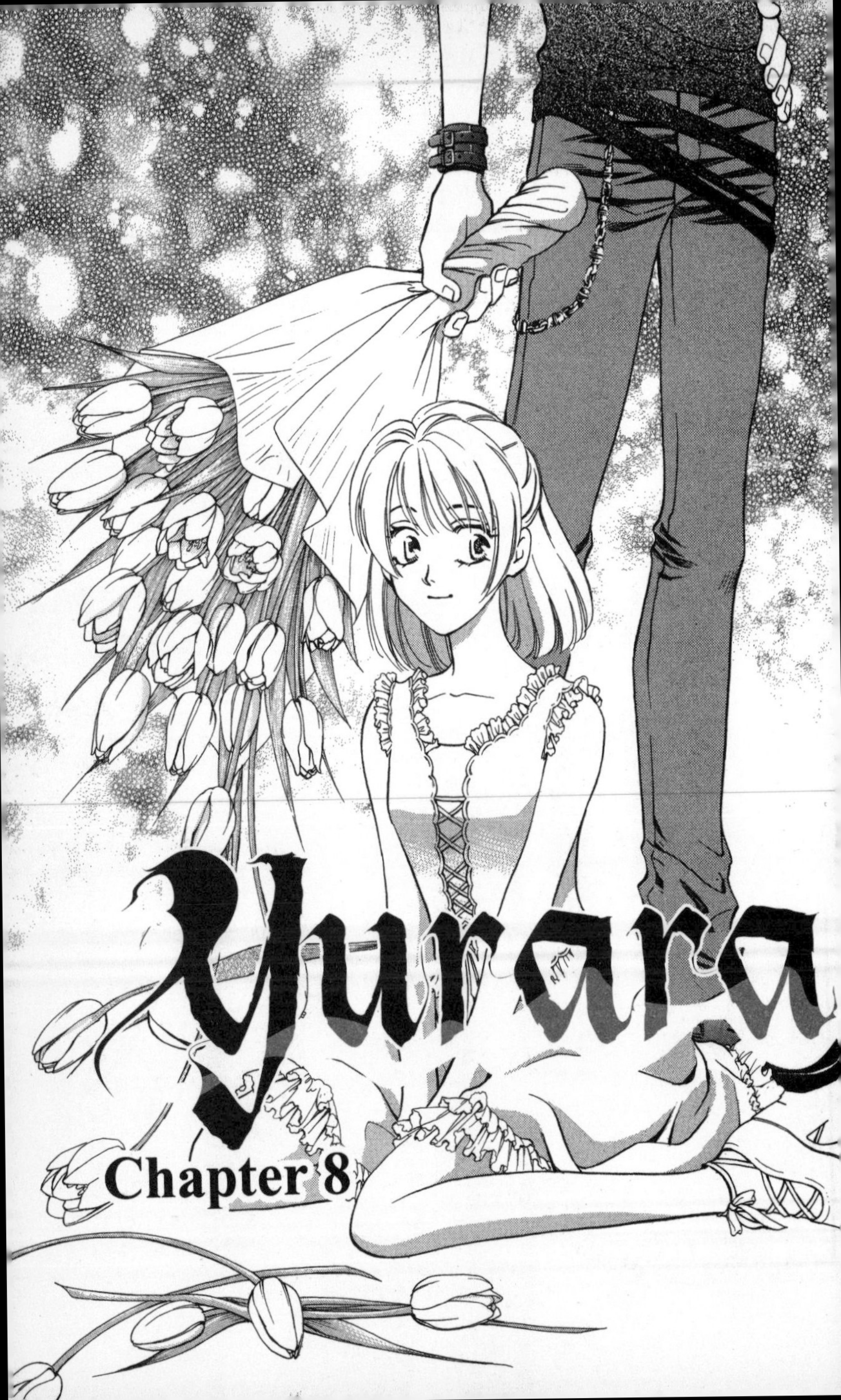
Yurara
Chapter 8

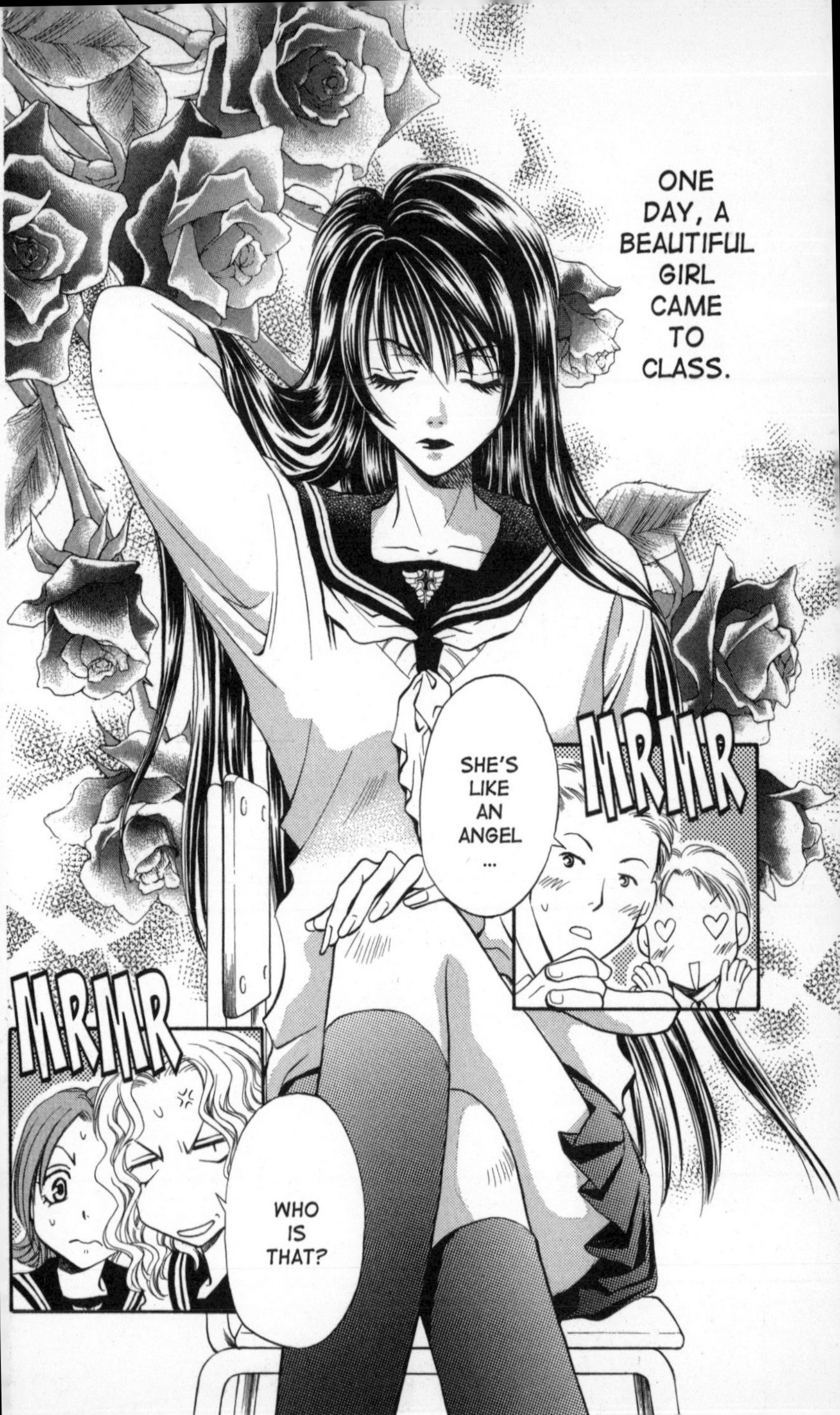
ONE DAY, A BEAUTIFUL GIRL CAME TO CLASS.
MRMR
SHE'S LIKE AN ANGEL ...
MRMR
WHO IS THAT?

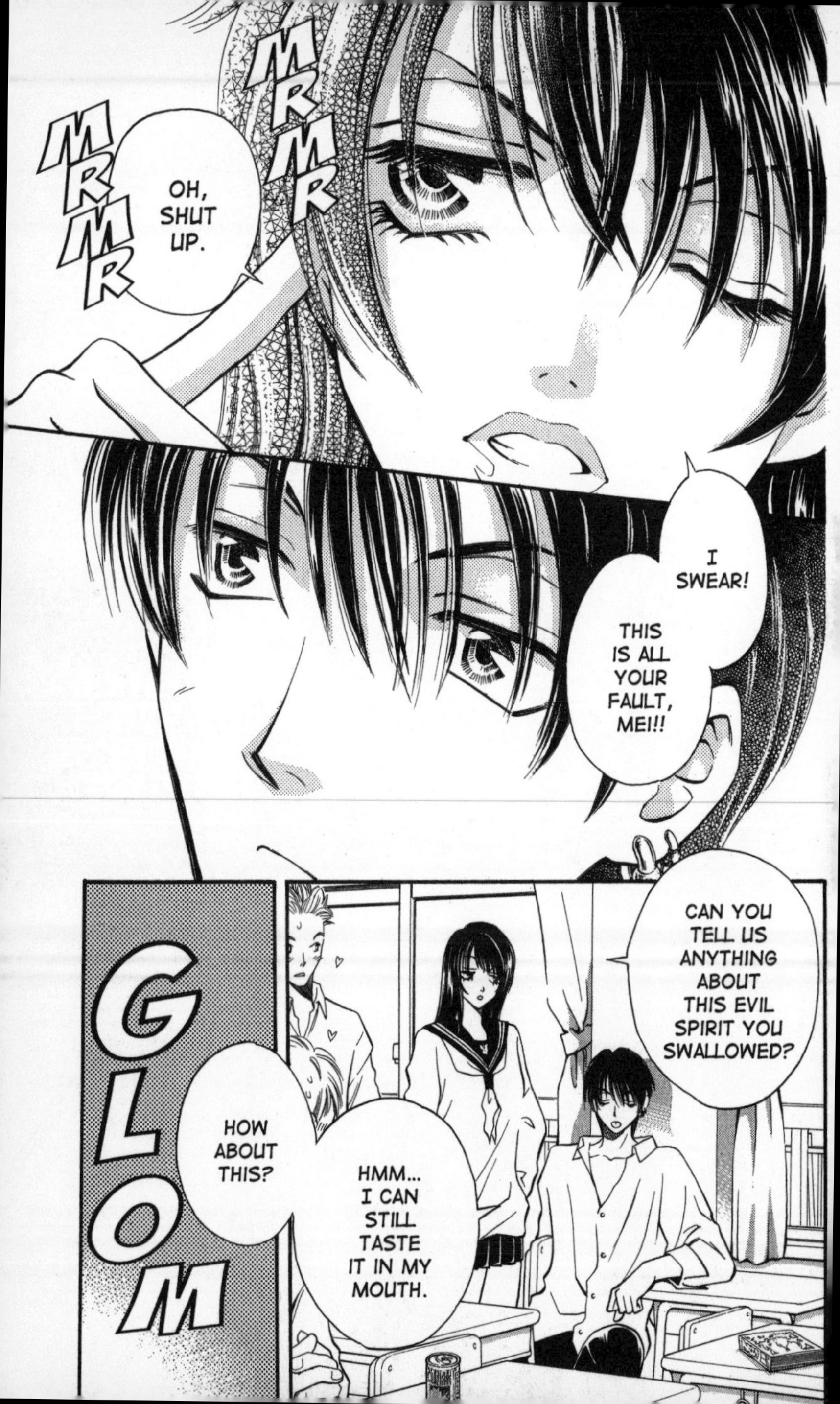
MRMR
OH, SHUT UP.
MRMR
I SWEAR!
THIS IS ALL YOUR FAULT, MEI!!
CAN YOU TELL US ANYTHING ABOUT THIS EVIL SPIRIT YOU SWALLOWED?
HOW ABOUT THIS?
HMM... I CAN STILL TASTE IT IN MY MOUTH.
GLOM

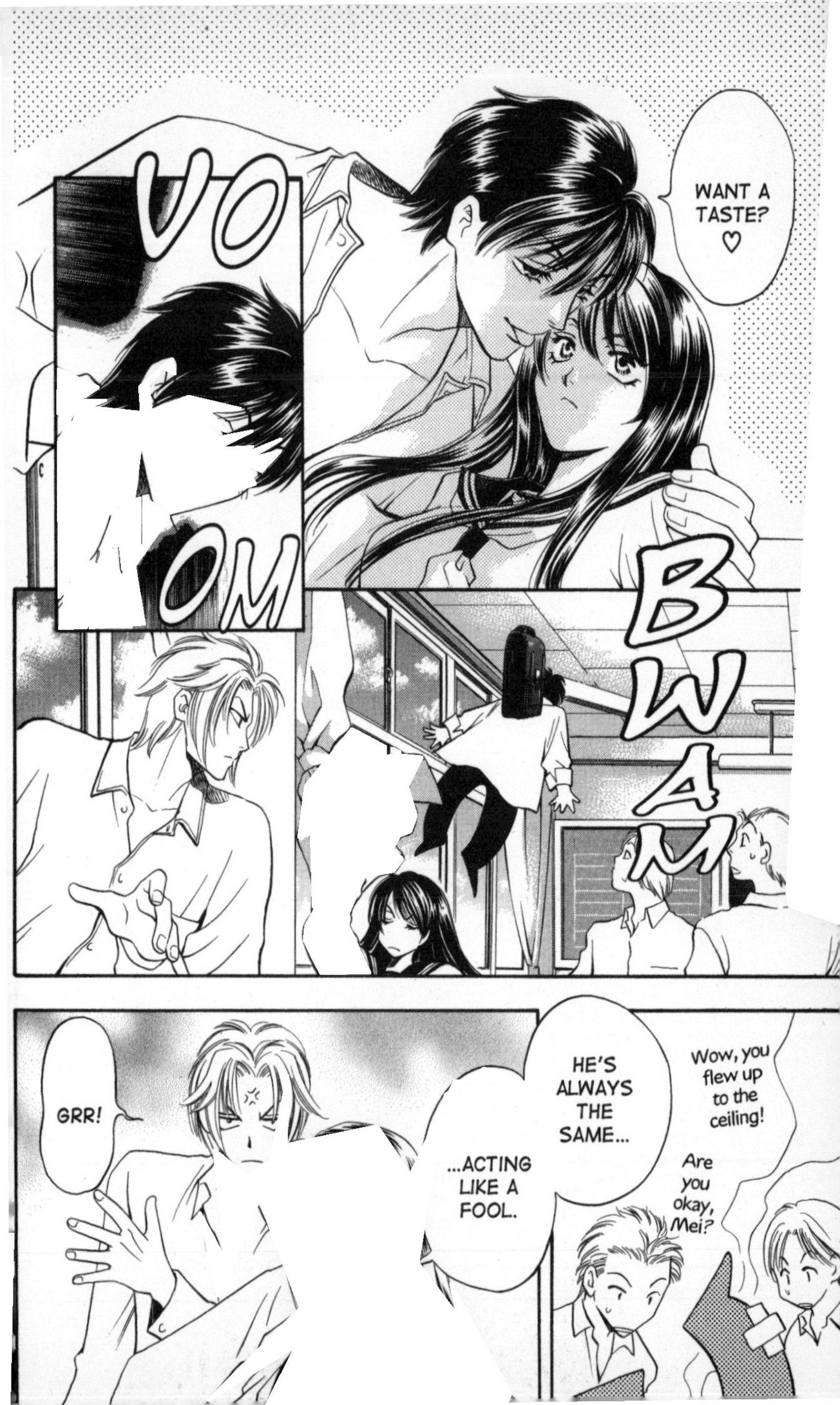
WANT A TASTE? ♡
VO
OM
BWAM
Wow, you flew up to the ceiling!
Are you okay, Mei?
HE'S ALWAYS THE SAME...
...ACTING LIKE A FOOL.
GRR!

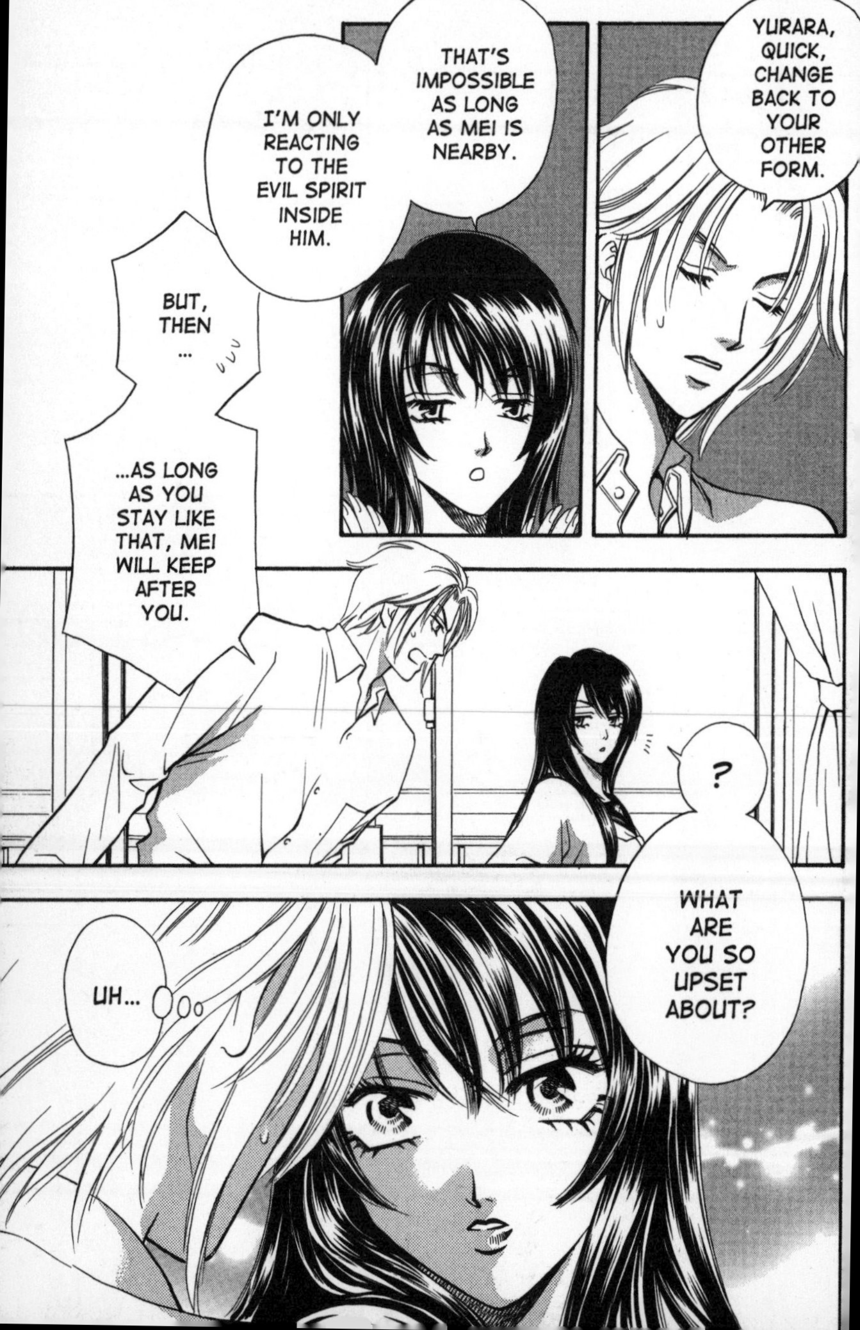
YURARA, QUICK, CHANGE BACK TO YOUR OTHER FORM.
THAT'S IMPOSSIBLE AS LONG AS MEI IS NEARBY.
I'M ONLY REACTING TO THE EVIL SPIRIT INSIDE HIM.
BUT, THEN ...
...AS LONG AS YOU STAY LIKE THAT, MEI WILL KEEP AFTER YOU.
?
WHAT ARE YOU SO UPSET ABOUT?
UH...

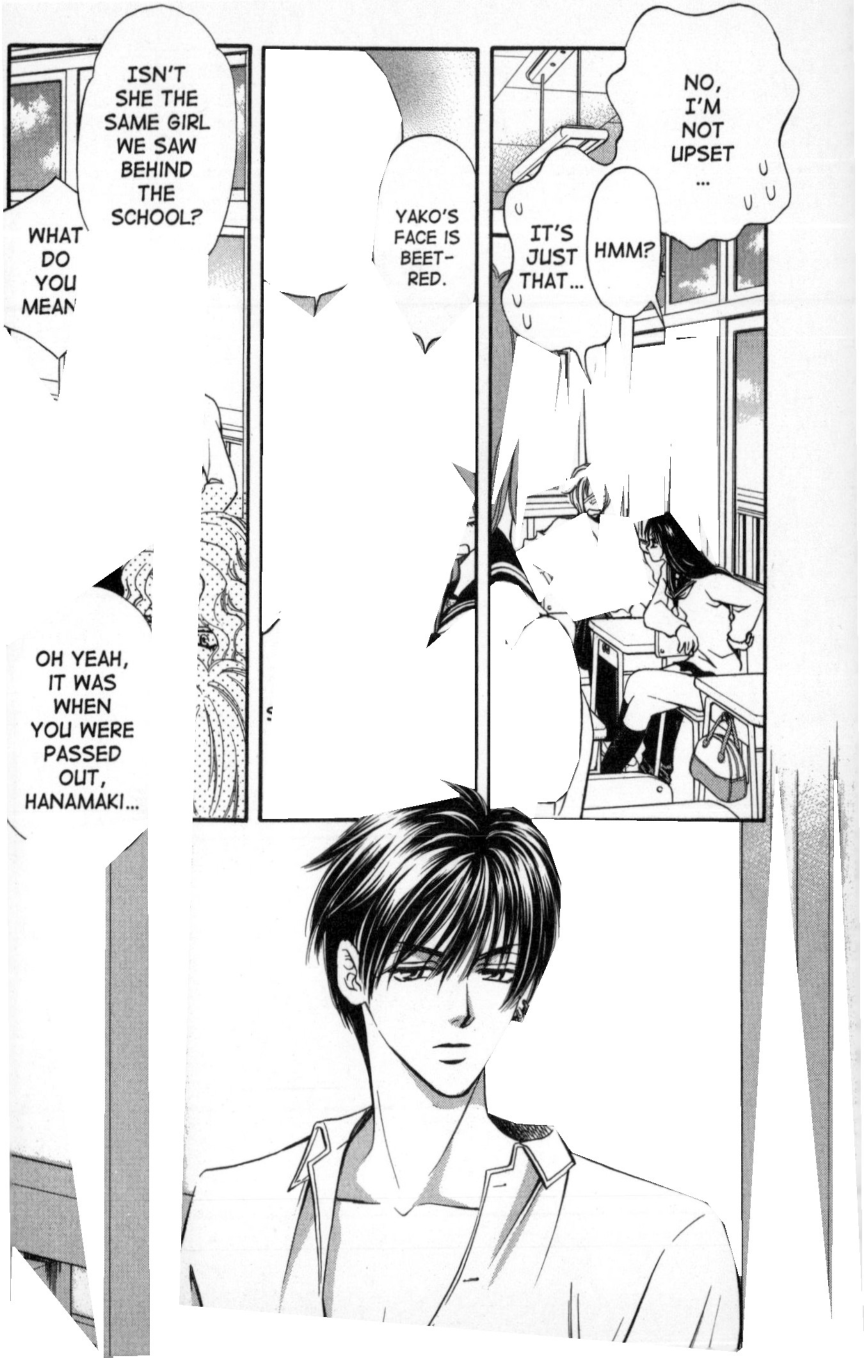
NO, I'M NOT UPSET ...
HMM?
IT'S JUST THAT...
YAKO'S FACE IS BEET-RED.
ISN'T SHE THE SAME GIRL WE SAW BEHIND THE SCHOOL?
WHAT DO YOU MEAN
OH YEAH, IT WAS WHEN YOU WERE PASSED OUT, HANAMAKI...

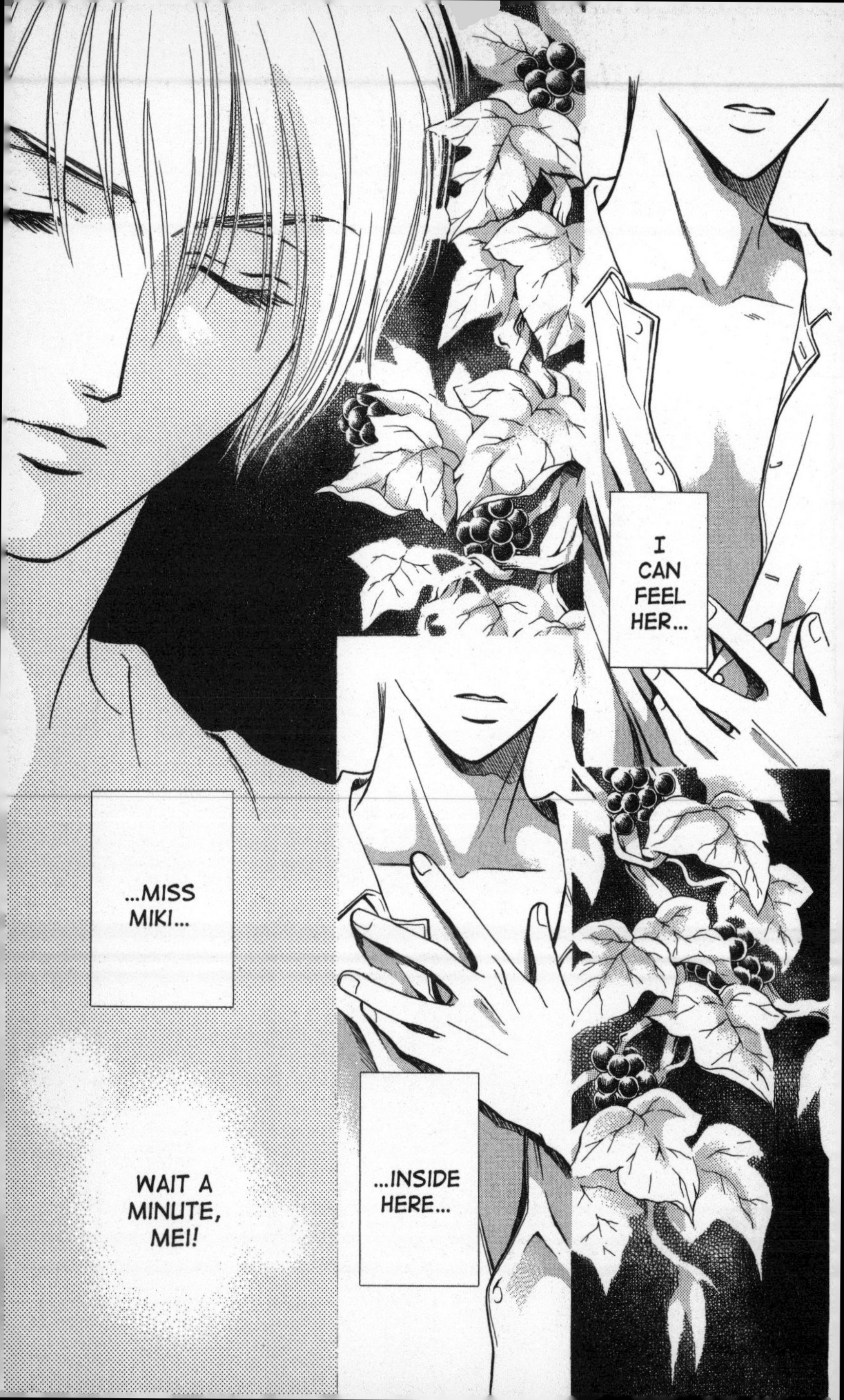
I CAN FEEL HER...
...INSIDE HERE...
...MISS MIKI...
WAIT A MINUTE, MEI!

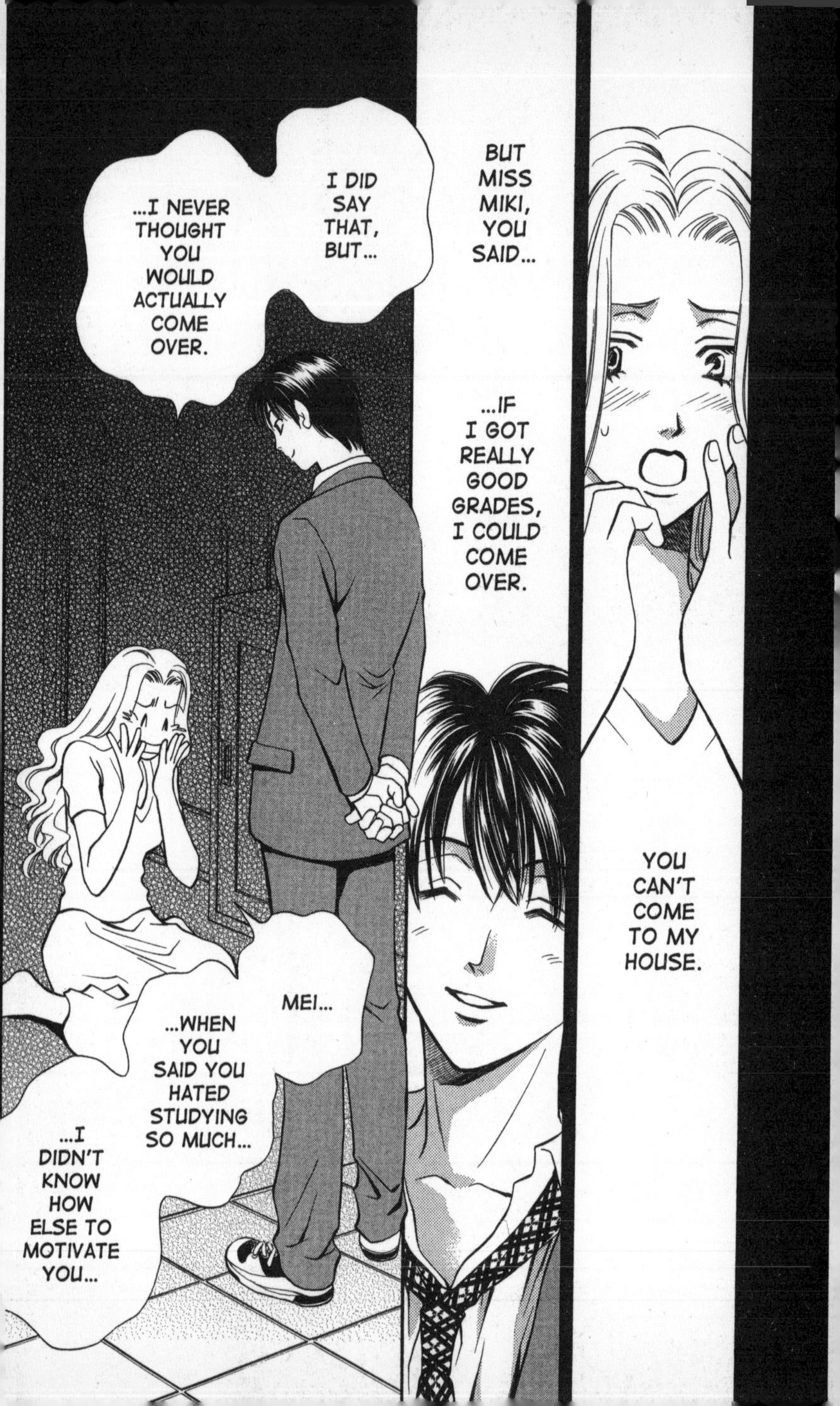
YOU CAN'T COME TO MY HOUSE.
BUT MISS MIKI, YOU SAID...
...IF I GOT REALLY GOOD GRADES, I COULD COME OVER.
I DID SAY THAT, BUT...
...I NEVER THOUGHT YOU WOULD ACTUALLY COME OVER.
MEI...
...WHEN YOU SAID YOU HATED STUDYING SO MUCH...
...I DIDN'T KNOW HOW ELSE TO MOTIVATE YOU...

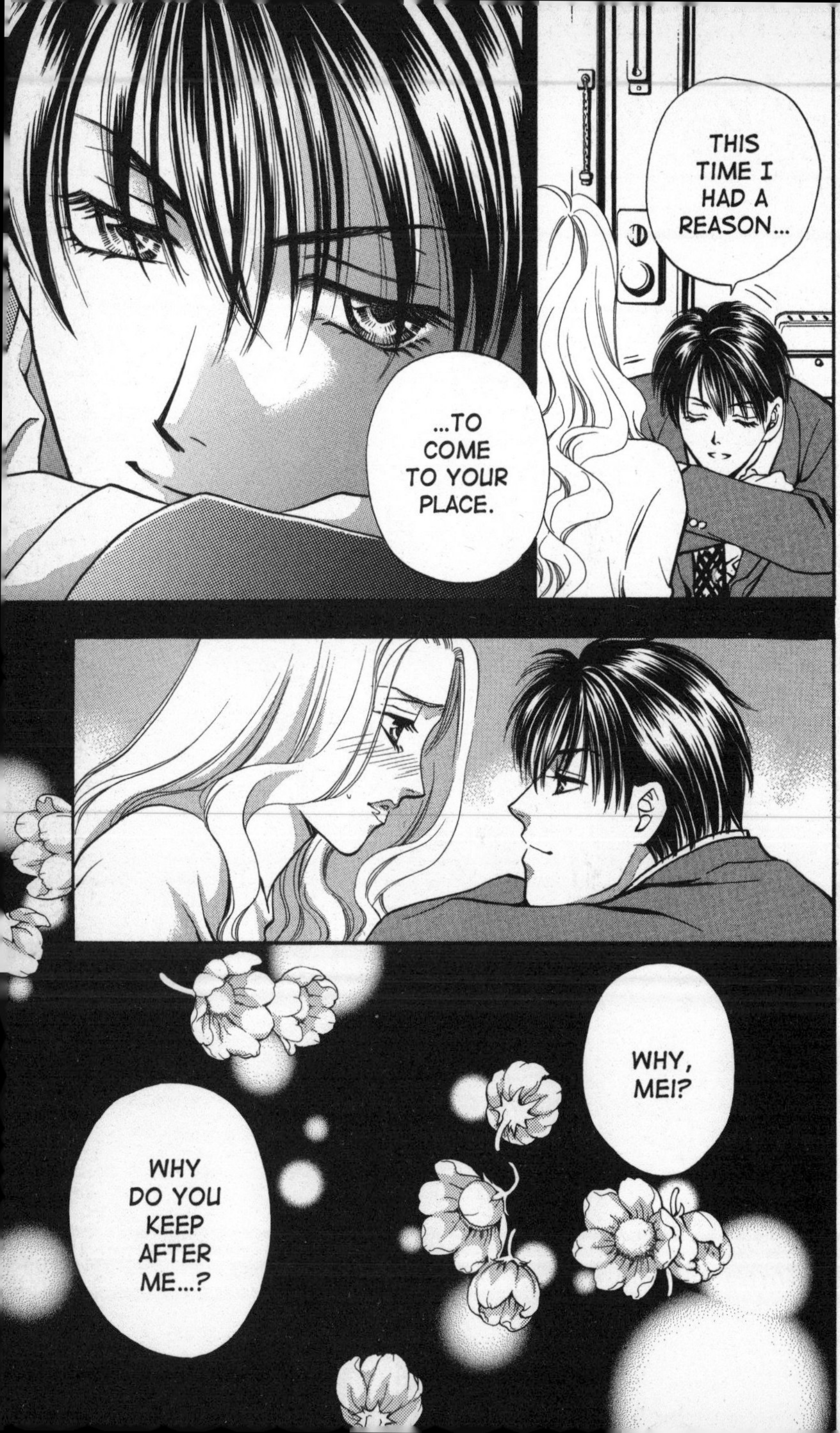
THIS TIME I HAD A REASON...
...TO COME TO YOUR PLACE.
WHY, MEI?
WHY DO YOU KEEP AFTER ME...?

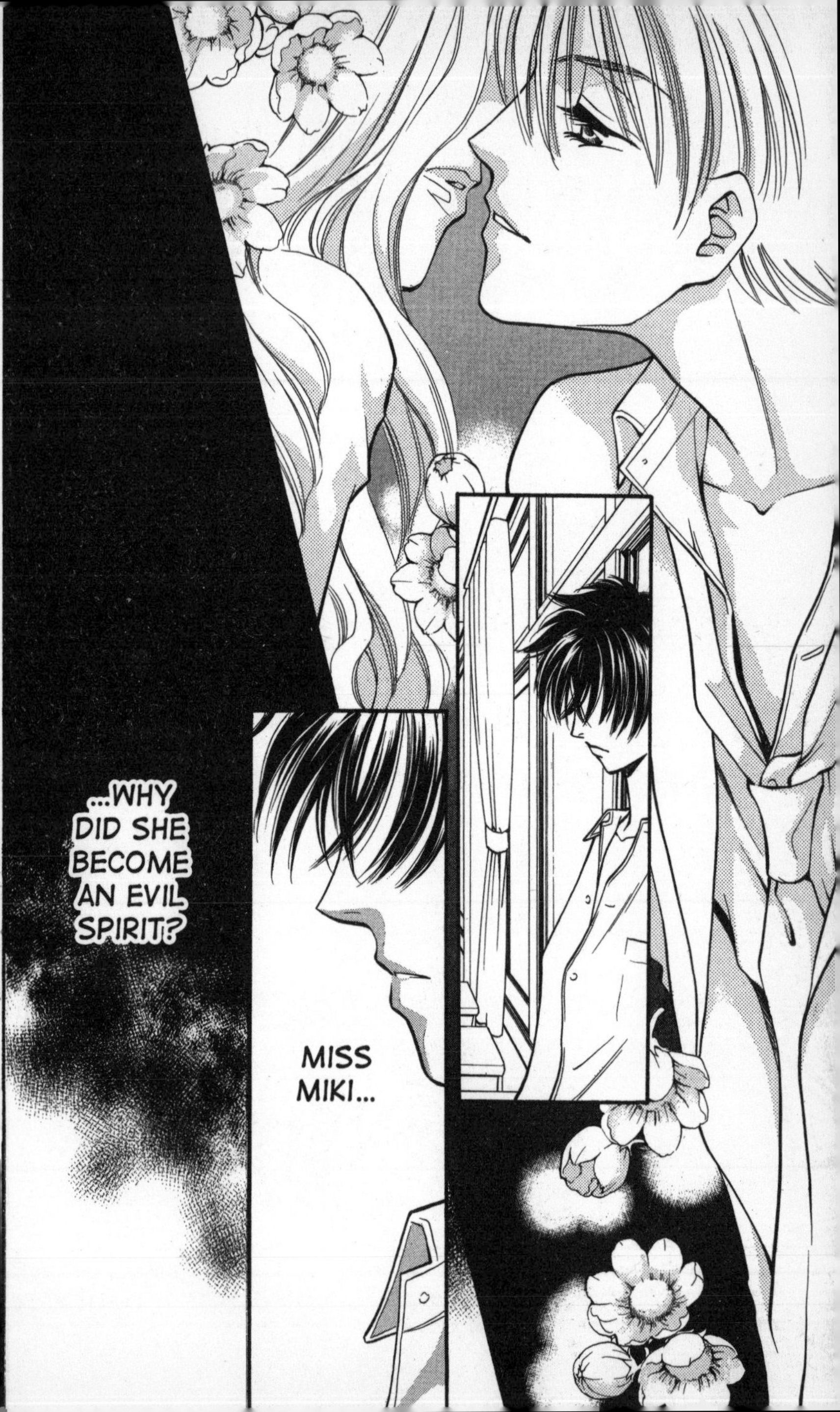
MISS MIKI...
...WHY DID SHE BECOME AN EVIL SPIRIT?

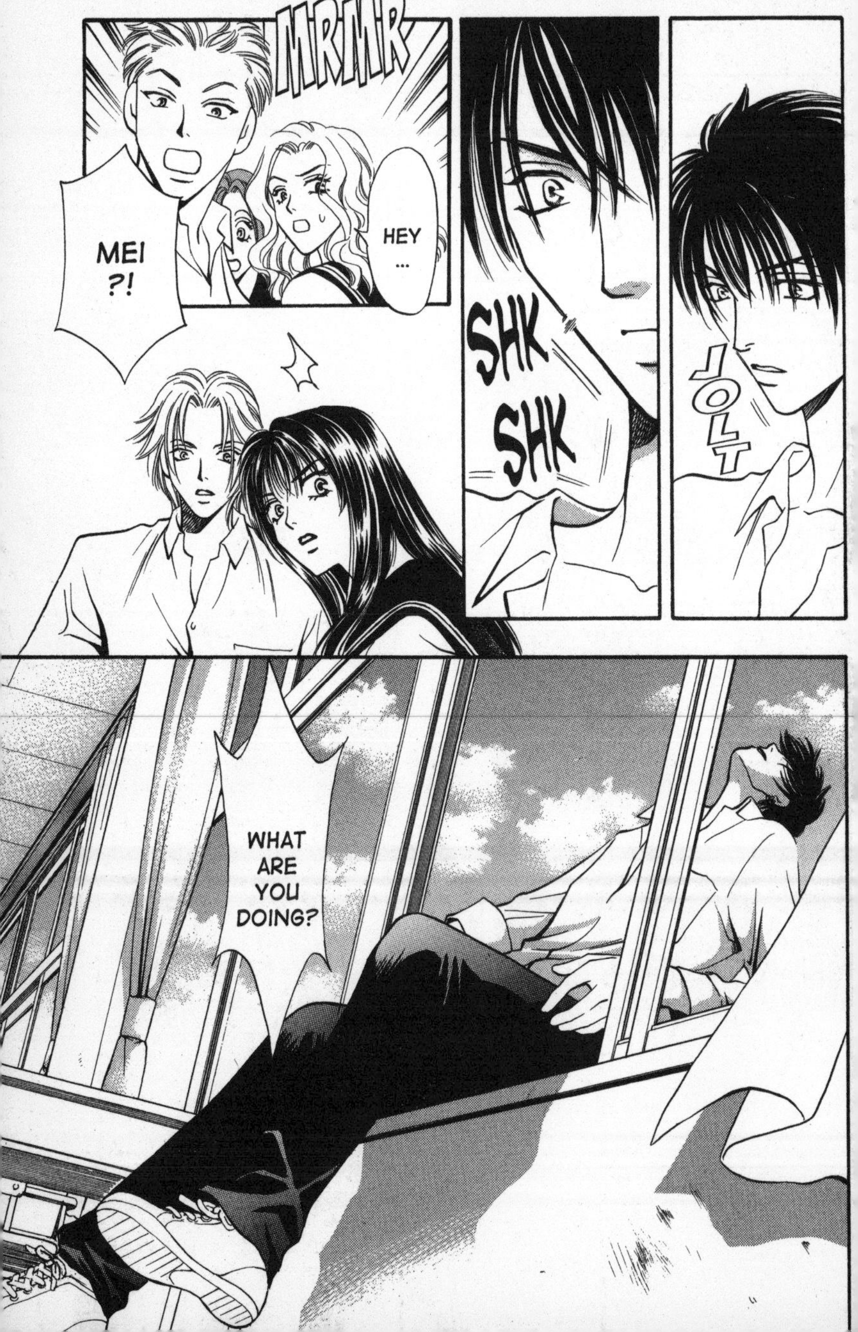
JOLT
SHK SHK
MRMR
HEY ...
MEI ?!
WHAT ARE YOU DOING?

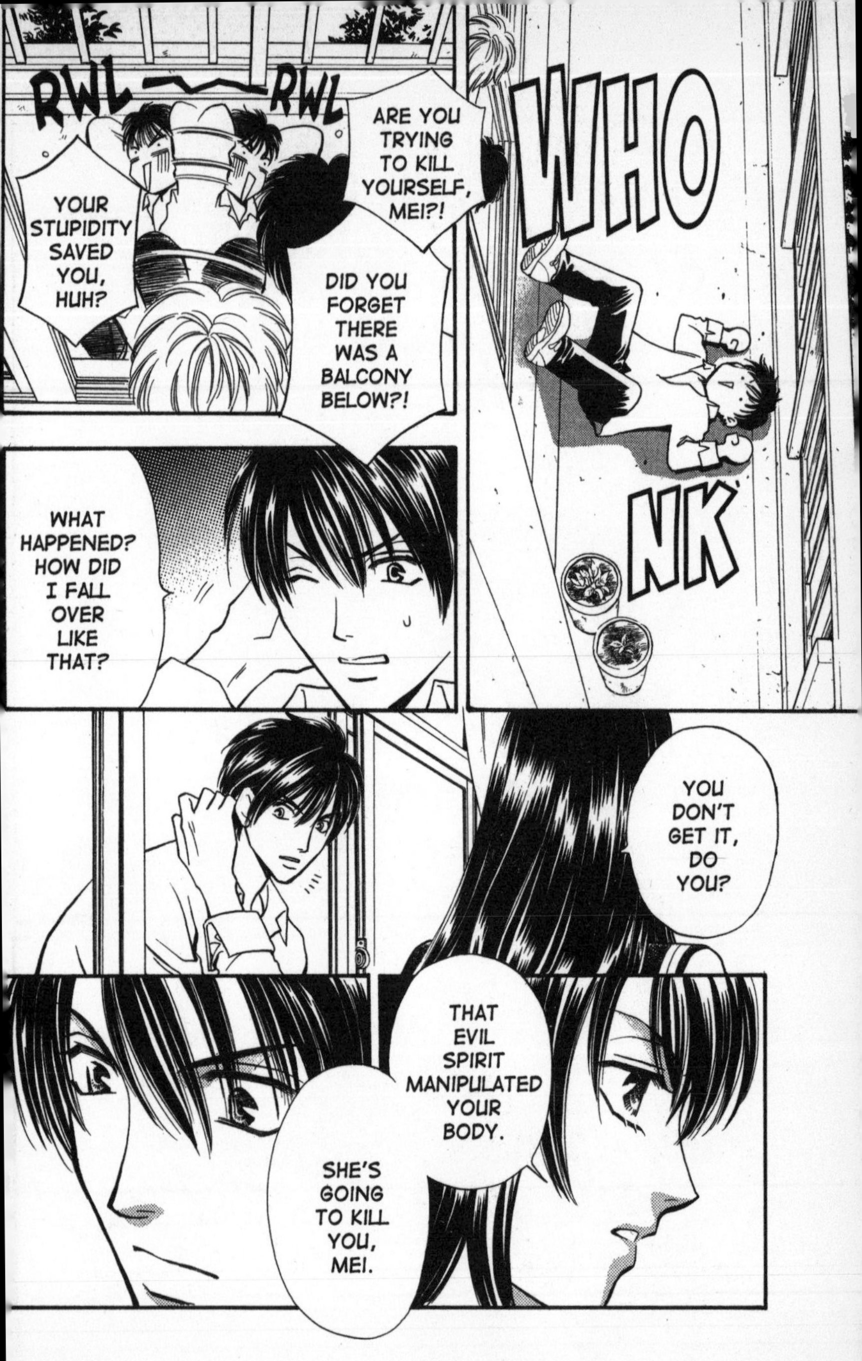
WHO
NK
ARE YOU TRYING TO KILL YOURSELF, MEI?!
RWL — RWL
DID YOU FORGET THERE WAS A BALCONY BELOW?!
YOUR STUPIDITY SAVED YOU, HUH?
WHAT HAPPENED? HOW DID I FALL OVER LIKE THAT?
YOU DON'T GET IT, DO YOU?
THAT EVIL SPIRIT MANIPULATED YOUR BODY.
SHE'S GOING TO KILL YOU, MEI.

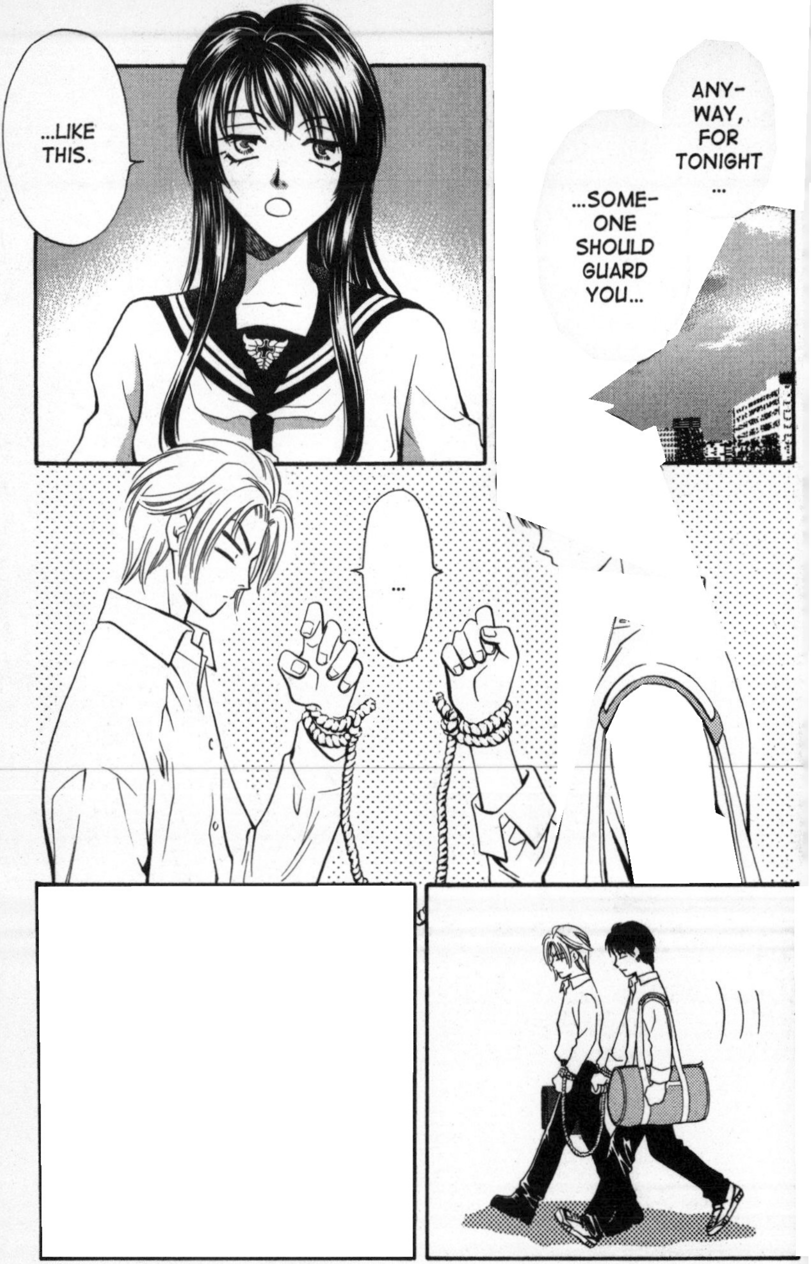
ANY-WAY, FOR TONIGHT...
...SOME-ONE SHOULD GUARD YOU...
...LIKE THIS.
...

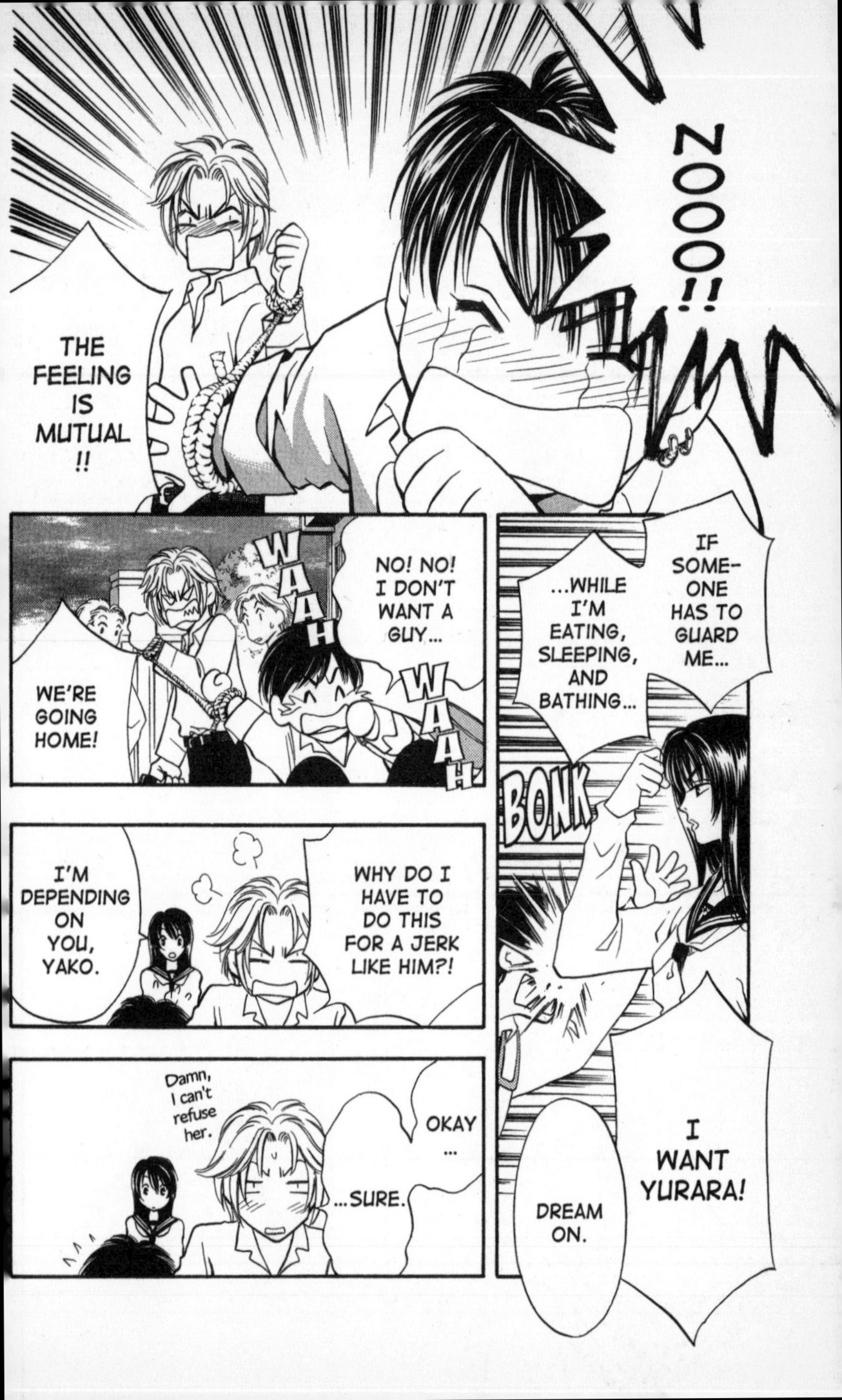
NOOOO!!
THE FEELING IS MUTUAL!!
IF SOME-ONE HAS TO GUARD ME...
...WHILE I'M EATING, SLEEPING, AND BATHING...
I WANT YURARA!
BONK
DREAM ON.
NO! NO! I DON'T WANT A GUY...
WAAH
WAAH
WE'RE GOING HOME!
WHY DO I HAVE TO DO THIS FOR A JERK LIKE HIM?!
I'M DEPENDING ON YOU, YAKO.
OKAY...
...SURE.
Damn, I can't refuse her.

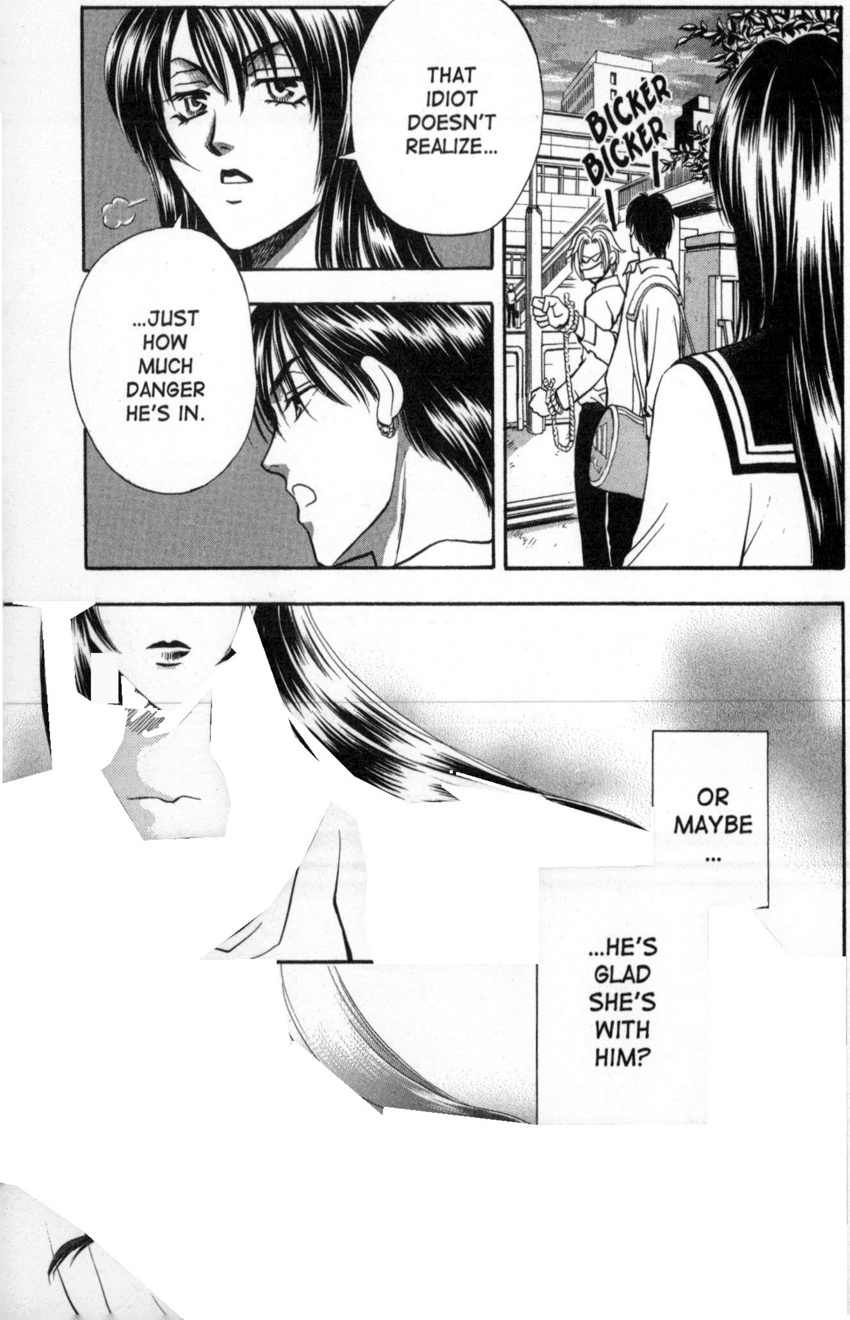
BICKER BICKER
THAT IDIOT DOESN'T REALIZE...
...JUST HOW MUCH DANGER HE'S IN.
OR MAYBE ...
...HE'S GLAD SHE'S WITH HIM?

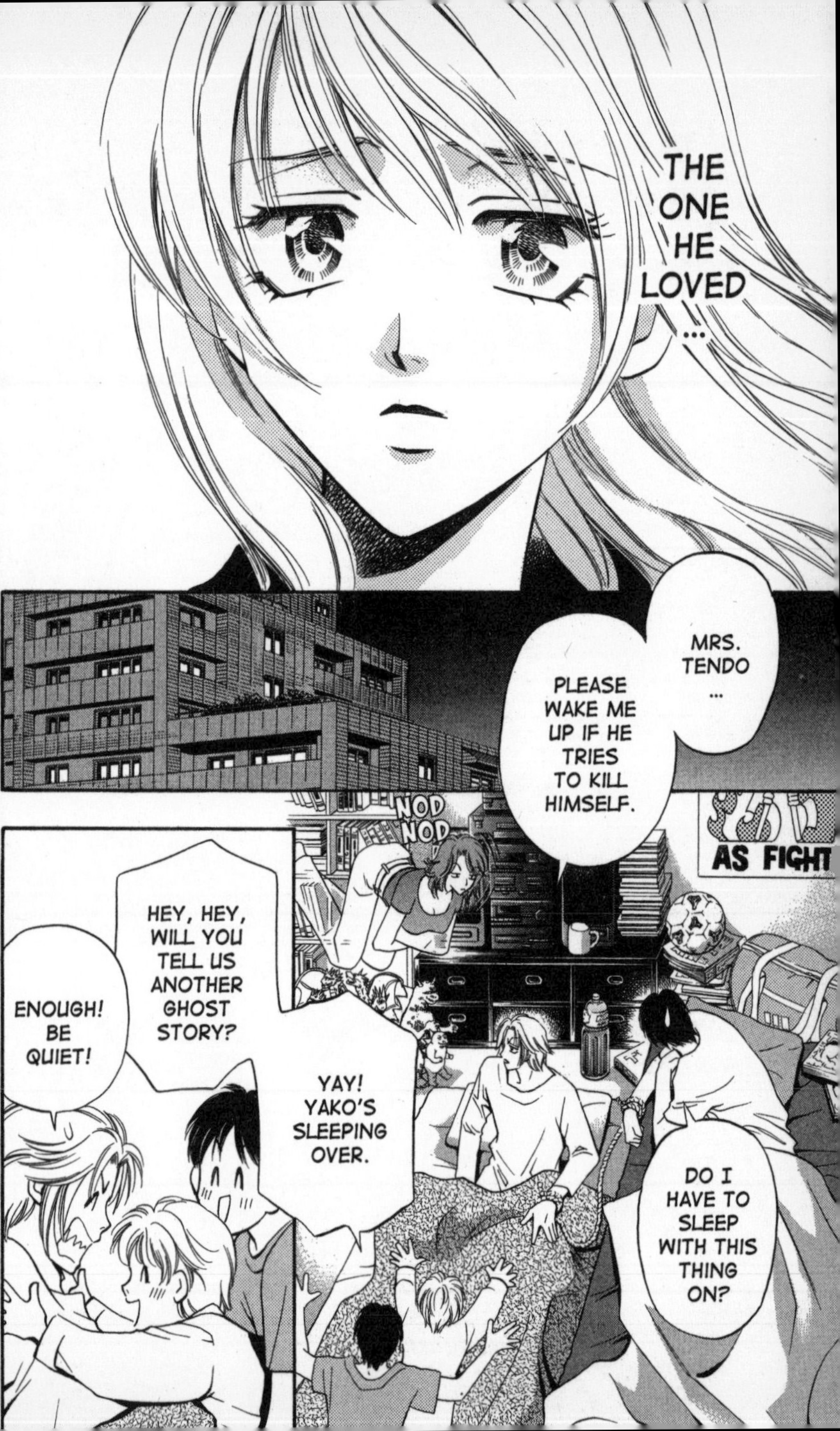
THE ONE HE LOVED ...
MRS. TENDO ...
PLEASE WAKE ME UP IF HE TRIES TO KILL HIMSELF.
AS FIGHT
NOD NOD
HEY, HEY, WILL YOU TELL US ANOTHER GHOST STORY?
YAY! YAKO'S SLEEPING OVER.
DO I HAVE TO SLEEP WITH THIS THING ON?
ENOUGH! BE QUIET!

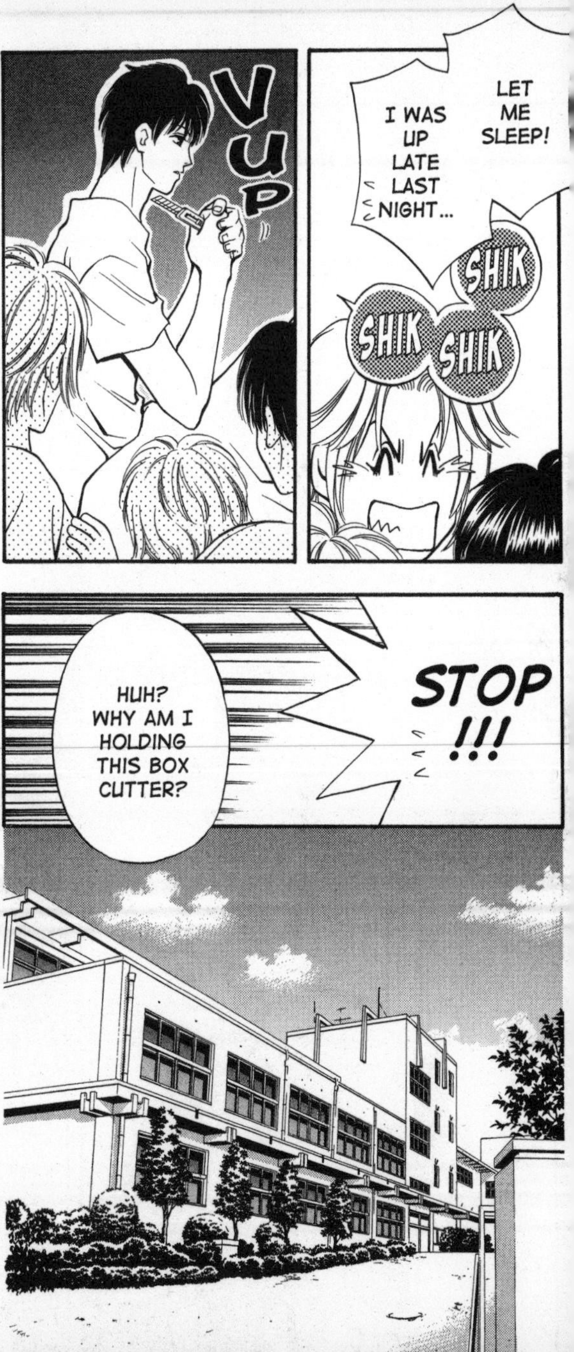
LET ME SLEEP!
I WAS UP LATE LAST NIGHT...
SHIK
SHIK
SHIK
VUP
STOP!!!
HUH? WHY AM I HOLDING THIS BOX CUTTER?

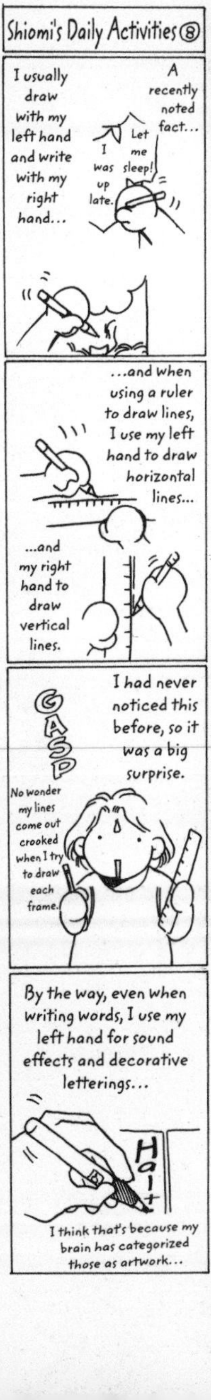
Shiomi's Daily Activities 8
A recently noted fact...
I usually draw with my left hand and write with my right hand...
Let me sleep!
I was up late.
...and when using a ruler to draw lines, I use my left hand to draw horizontal lines...
...and my right hand to draw vertical lines.
I had never noticed this before, so it was a big surprise.
GASP
No wonder my lines come out crooked when I try to draw each frame.
By the way, even when writing words, I use my left hand for sound effects and decorative letterings...
Halt
I think that's because my brain has categorized those as artwork...

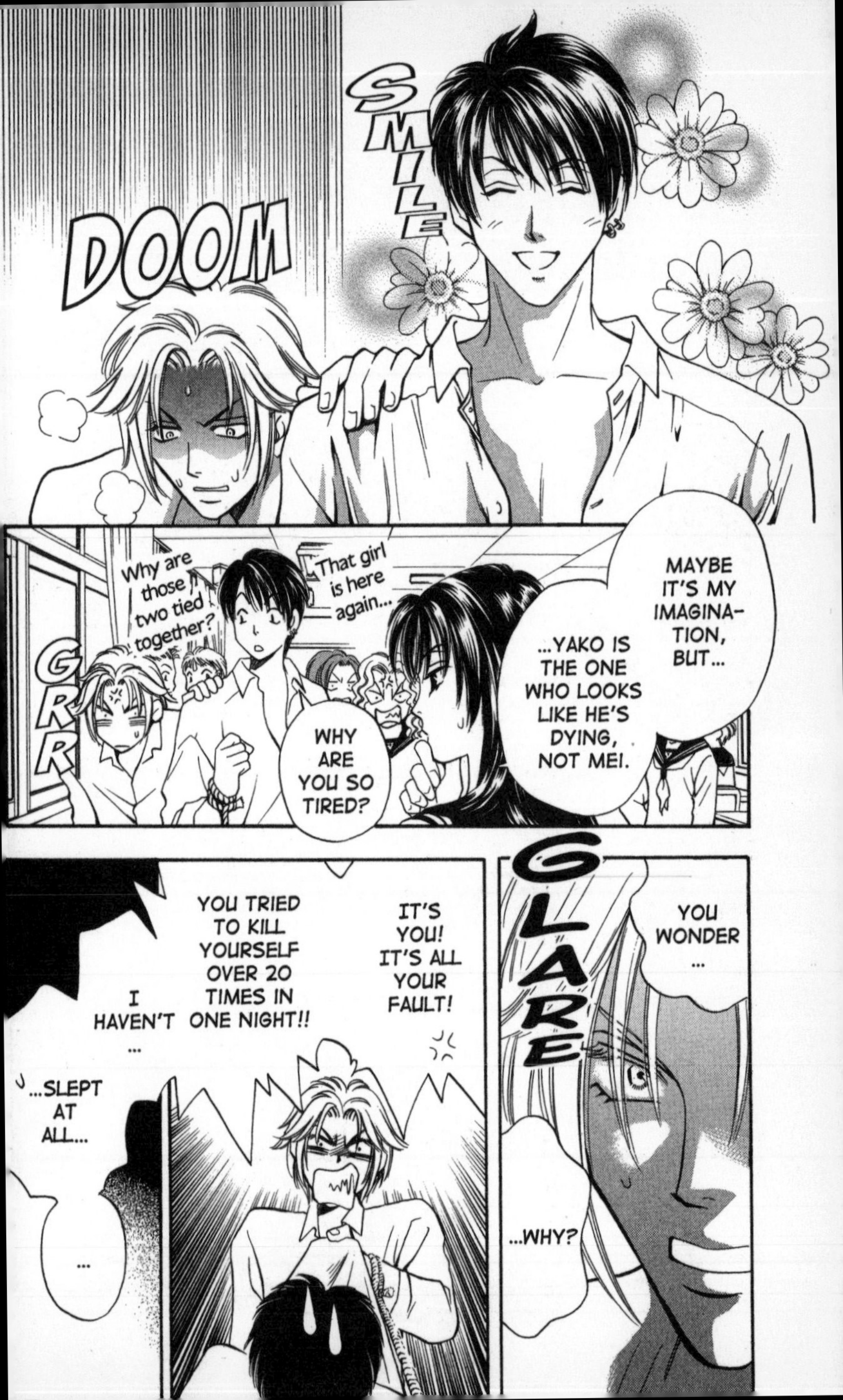
SMILE
DOOM
MAYBE IT'S MY IMAGINATION, BUT...
...YAKO IS THE ONE WHO LOOKS LIKE HE'S DYING, NOT ME!.
That girl is here again...
Why are those two tied together?
WHY ARE YOU SO TIRED?
GRR
GLARE
YOU WONDER...
...WHY?
IT'S YOU! IT'S ALL YOUR FAULT!
YOU TRIED TO KILL YOURSELF OVER 20 TIMES IN ONE NIGHT!!
I HAVEN'T...
...SLEPT AT ALL...
...

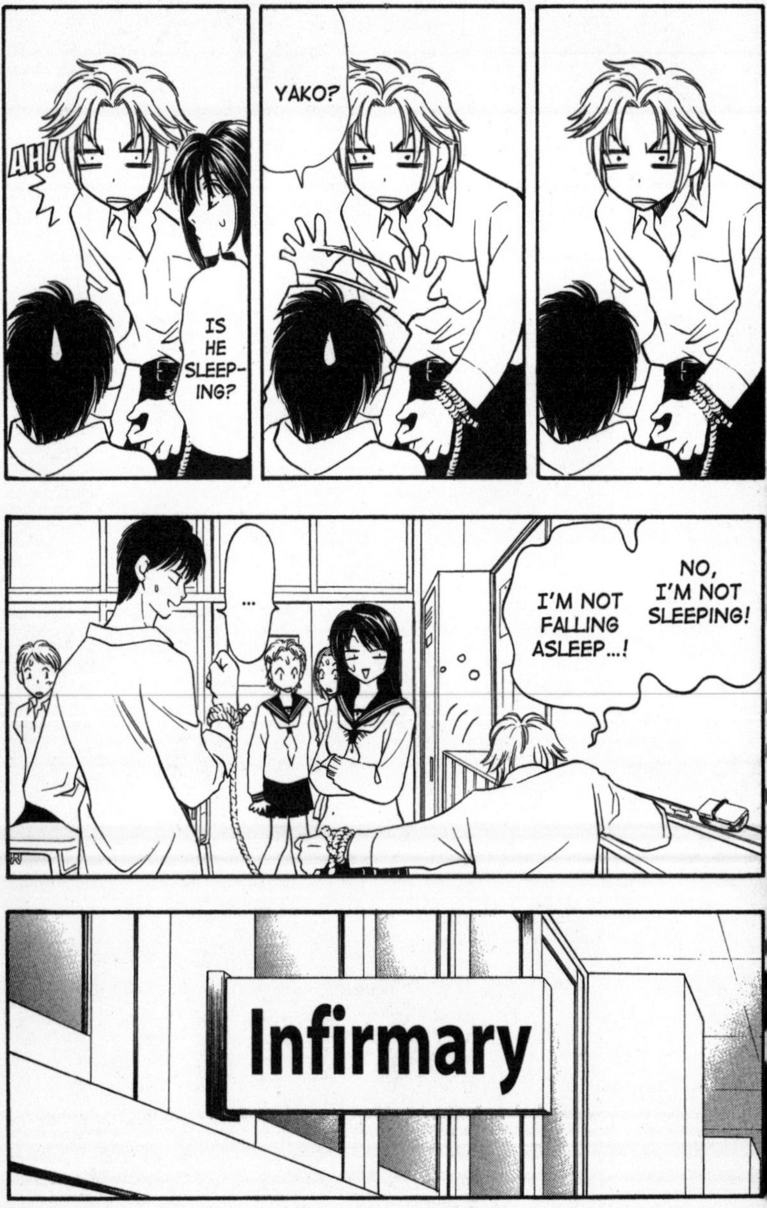
YAKO?
AH!
IS HE SLEEPING?
NO, I'M NOT SLEEPING!
I'M NOT FALLING ASLEEP...!
...
Infirmary

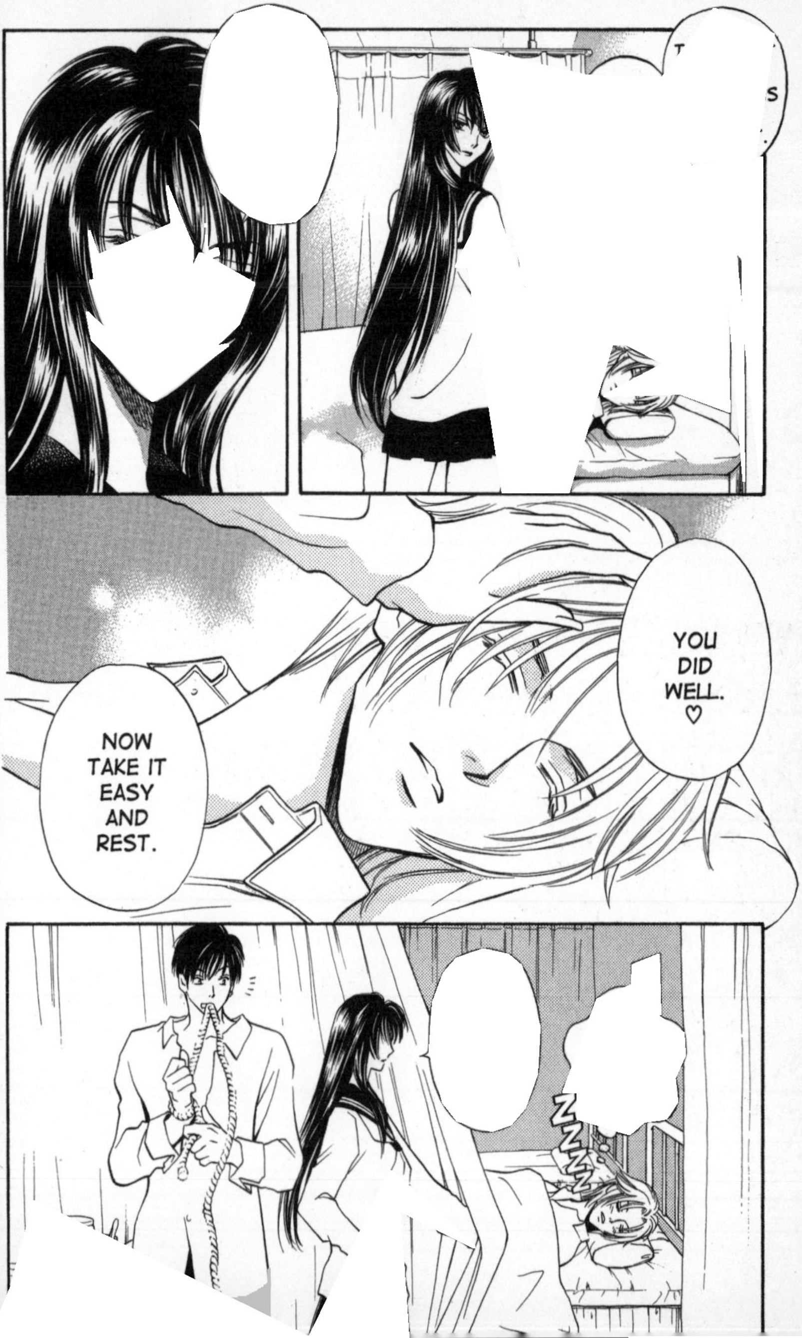
YOU DID WELL. ♡
NOW TAKE IT EASY AND REST.
ZZZZ

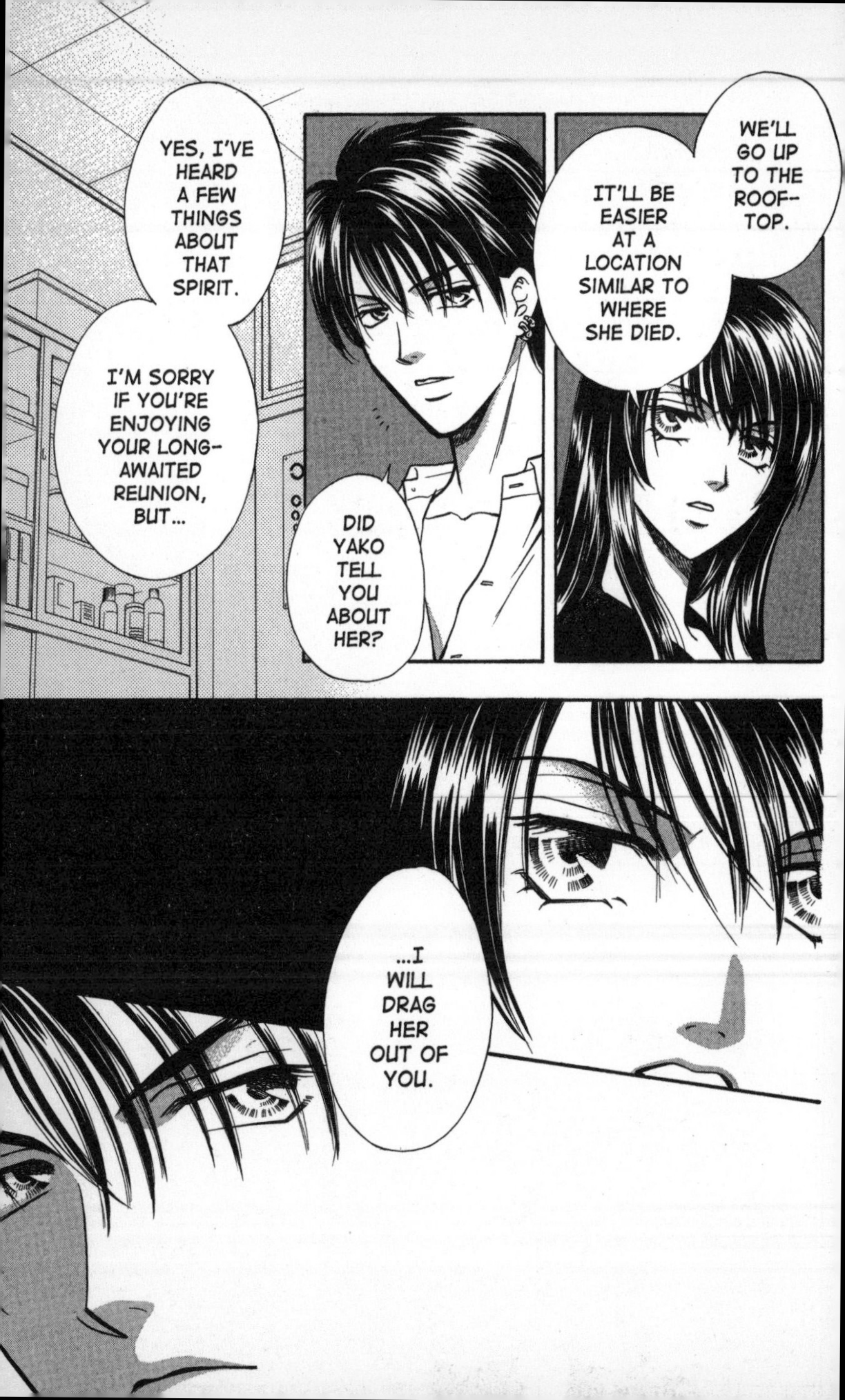

WE'LL GO UP TO THE ROOF-TOP.
IT'LL BE EASIER AT A LOCATION SIMILAR TO WHERE SHE DIED.
DID YAKO TELL YOU ABOUT HER?
YES, I'VE HEARD A FEW THINGS ABOUT THAT SPIRIT.
I'M SORRY IF YOU'RE ENJOYING YOUR LONG-AWAITED REUNION, BUT...
...I WILL DRAG HER OUT OF YOU.

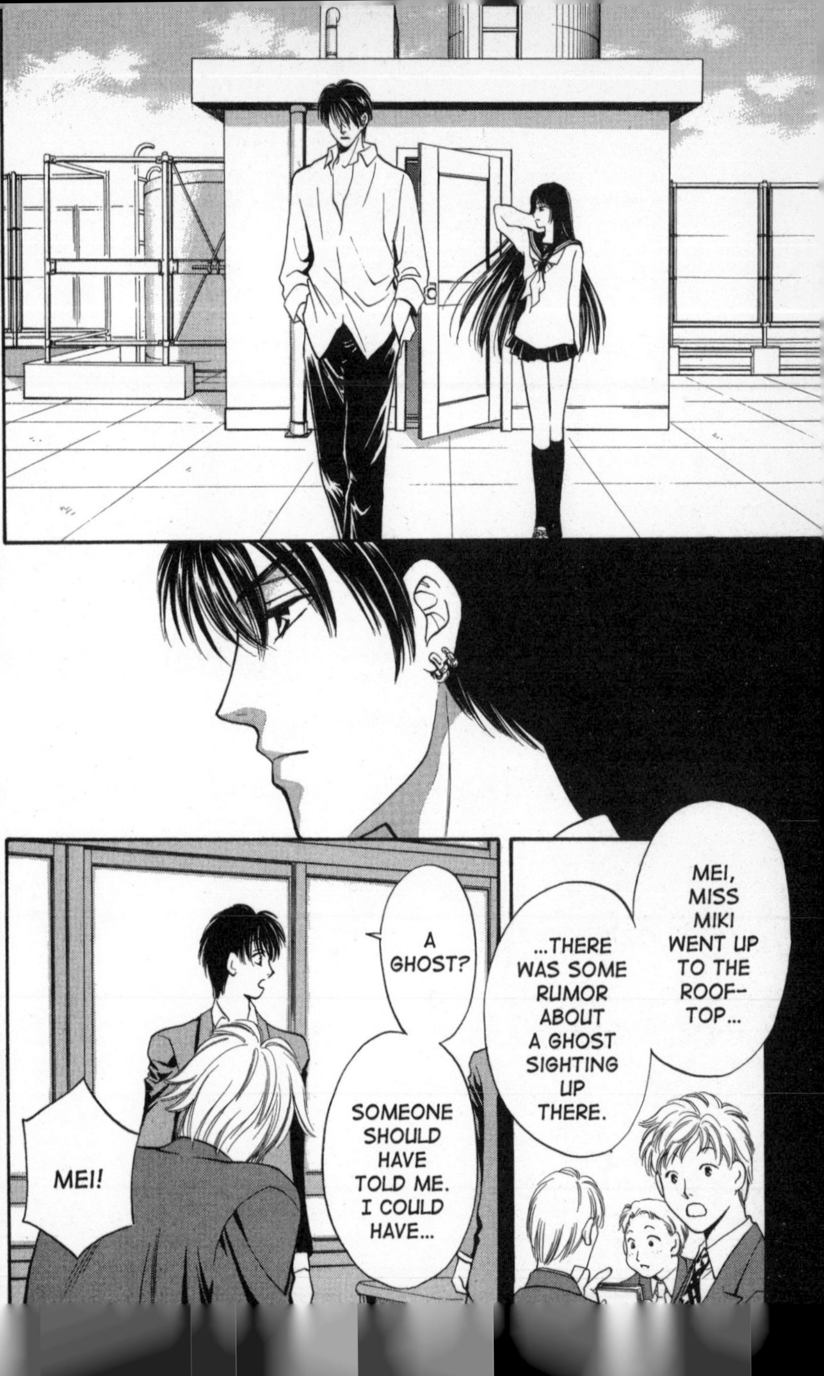
MEI, MISS MIKI WENT UP TO THE ROOF-TOP...
...THERE WAS SOME RUMOR ABOUT A GHOST SIGHTING UP THERE.
A GHOST?
SOMEONE SHOULD HAVE TOLD ME. I COULD HAVE...
MEI!

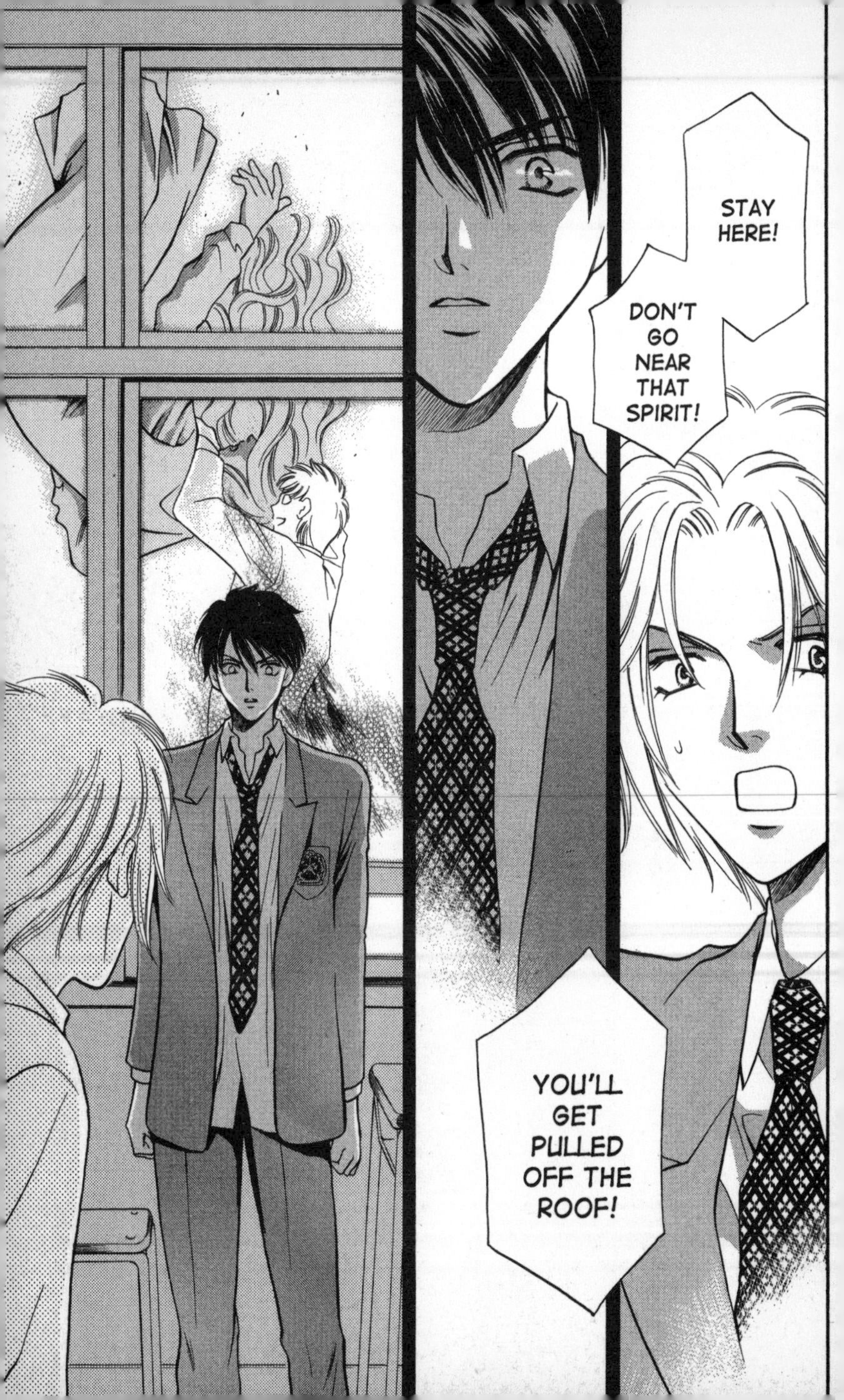
STAY HERE!
DON'T GO NEAR THAT SPIRIT!
YOU'LL GET PULLED OFF THE ROOF!

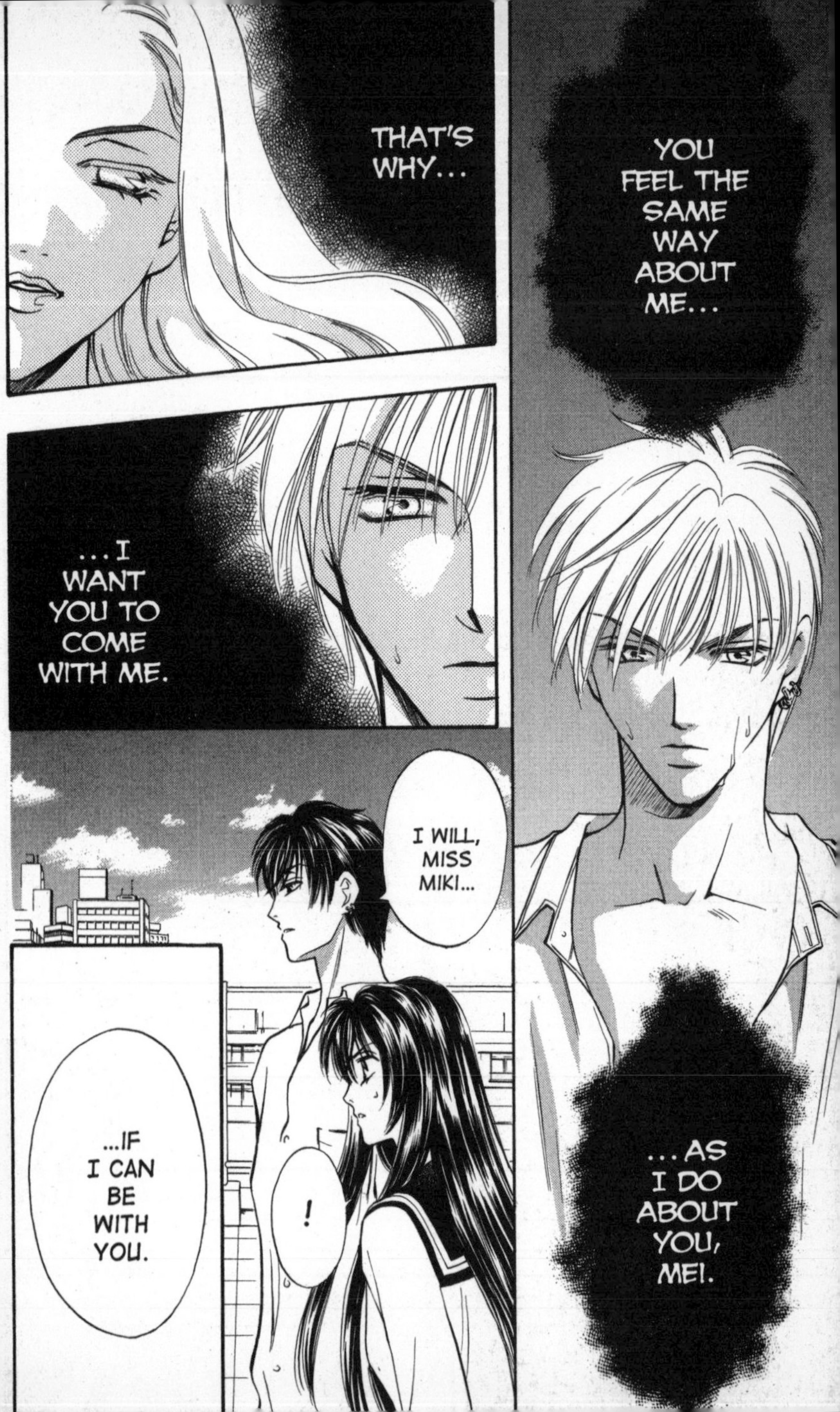
YOU FEEL THE SAME WAY ABOUT ME...
...AS I DO ABOUT YOU, MEI.
THAT'S WHY...
...I WANT YOU TO COME WITH ME.
I WILL, MISS MIKI...
!
...IF I CAN BE WITH YOU.

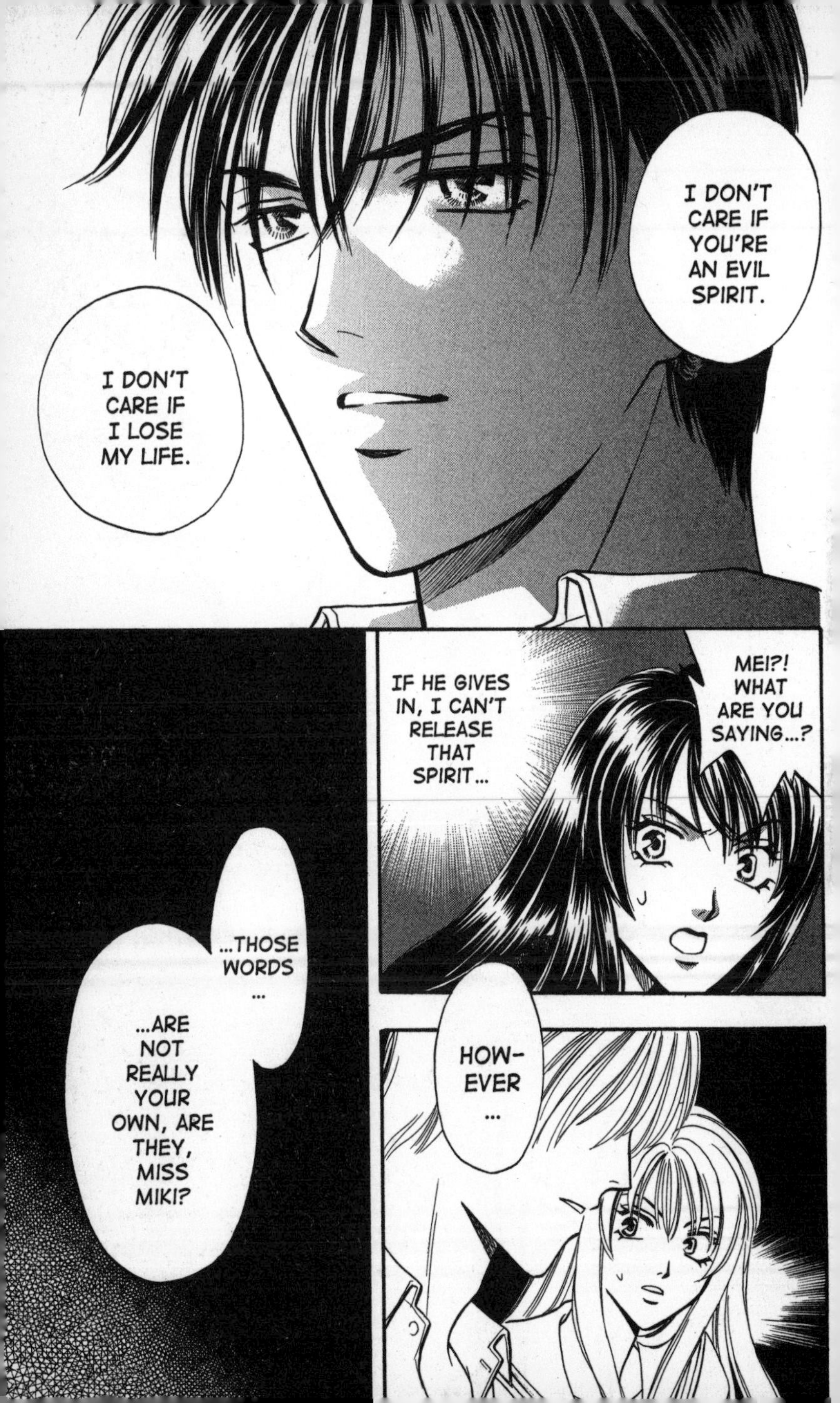
I DON'T CARE IF YOU'RE AN EVIL SPIRIT.
I DON'T CARE IF I LOSE MY LIFE.
MEI?! WHAT ARE YOU SAYING...?
IF HE GIVES IN, I CAN'T RELEASE THAT SPIRIT...
HOW-EVER...
...THOSE WORDS...
...ARE NOT REALLY YOUR OWN, ARE THEY, MISS MIKI?

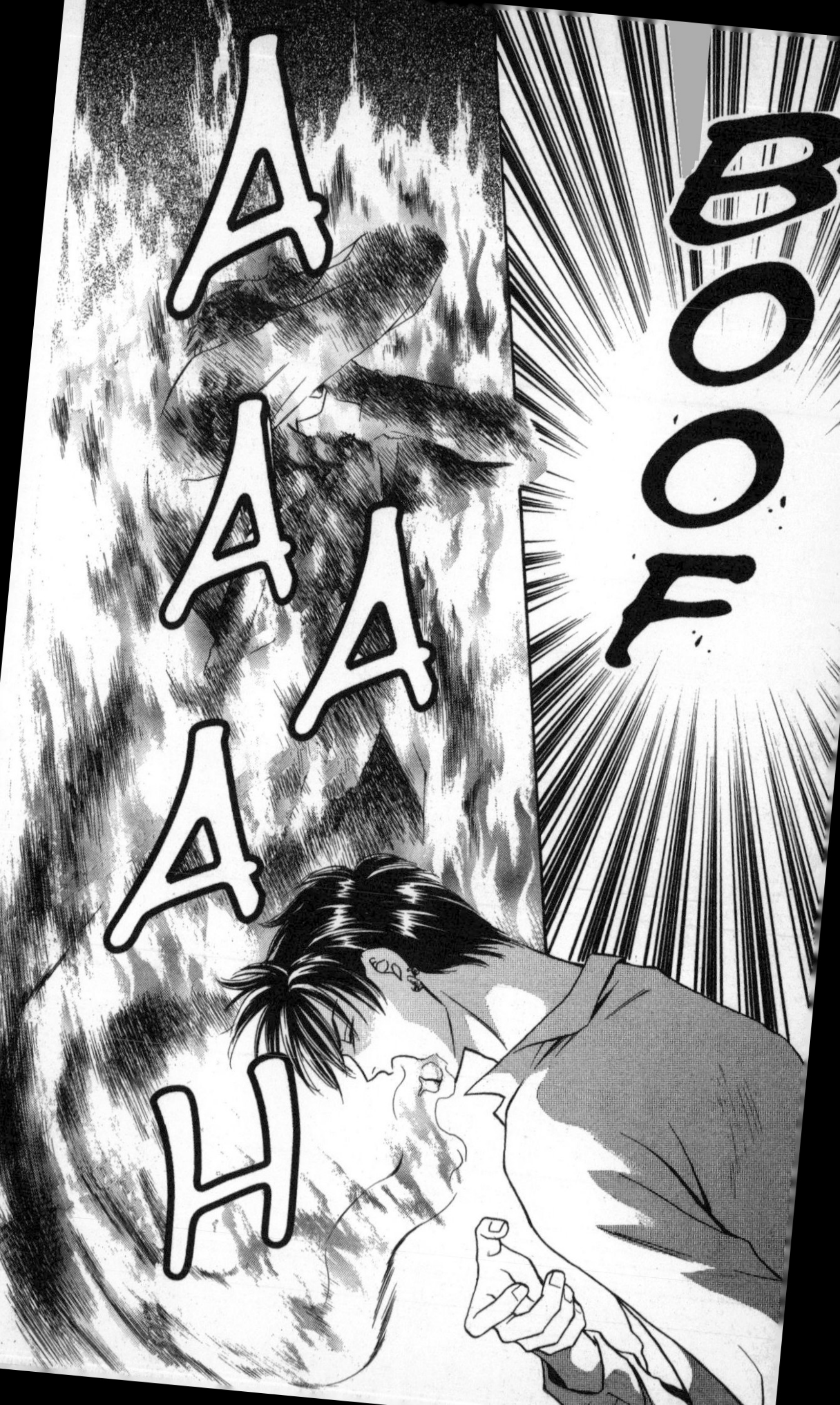
BOOF
AAAAH

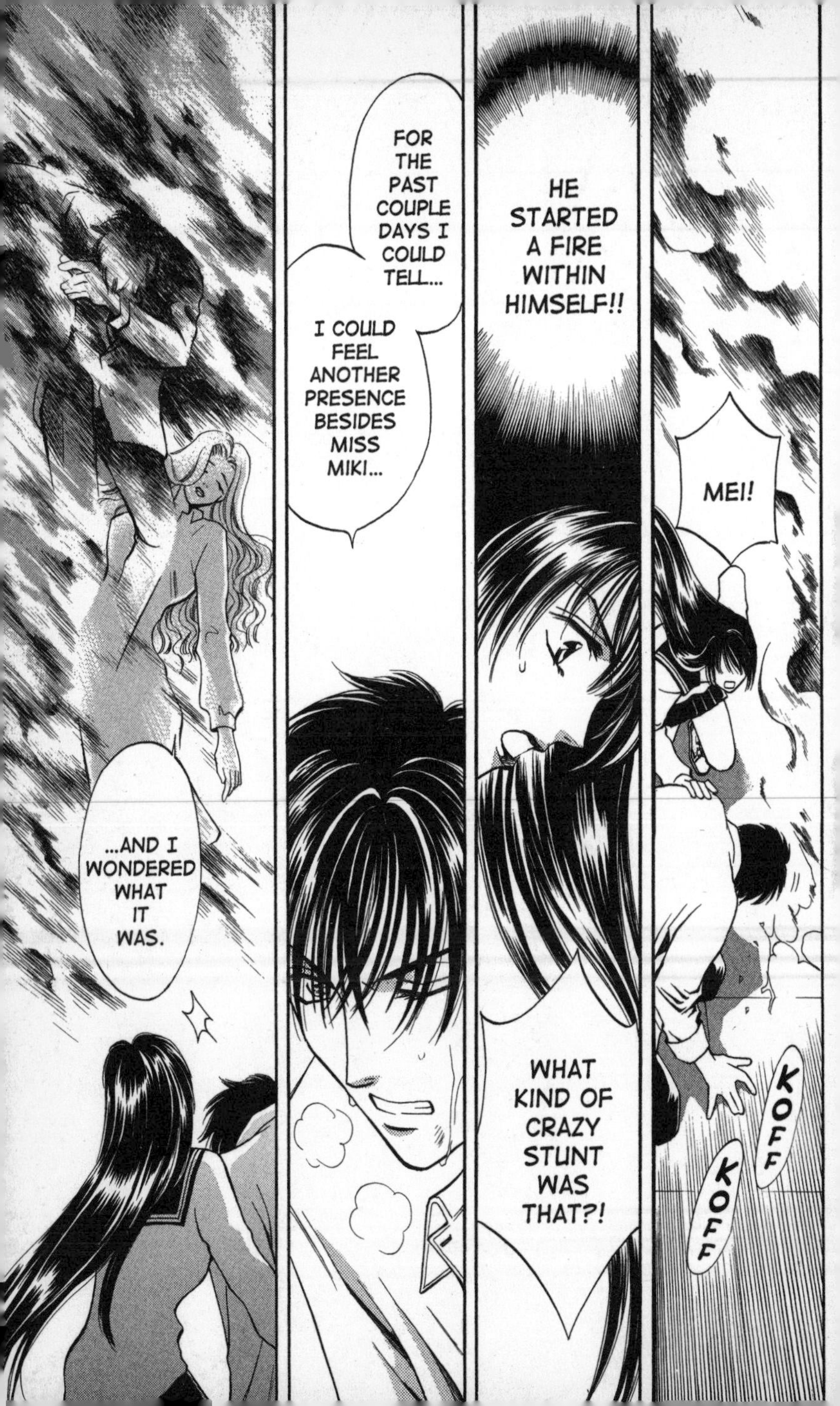
MEI!
KOFF
KOFF
HE STARTED A FIRE WITHIN HIMSELF!!
WHAT KIND OF CRAZY STUNT WAS THAT?!
FOR THE PAST COUPLE DAYS I COULD TELL...
I COULD FEEL ANOTHER PRESENCE BESIDES MISS MIKI...
...AND I WONDERED WHAT IT WAS.

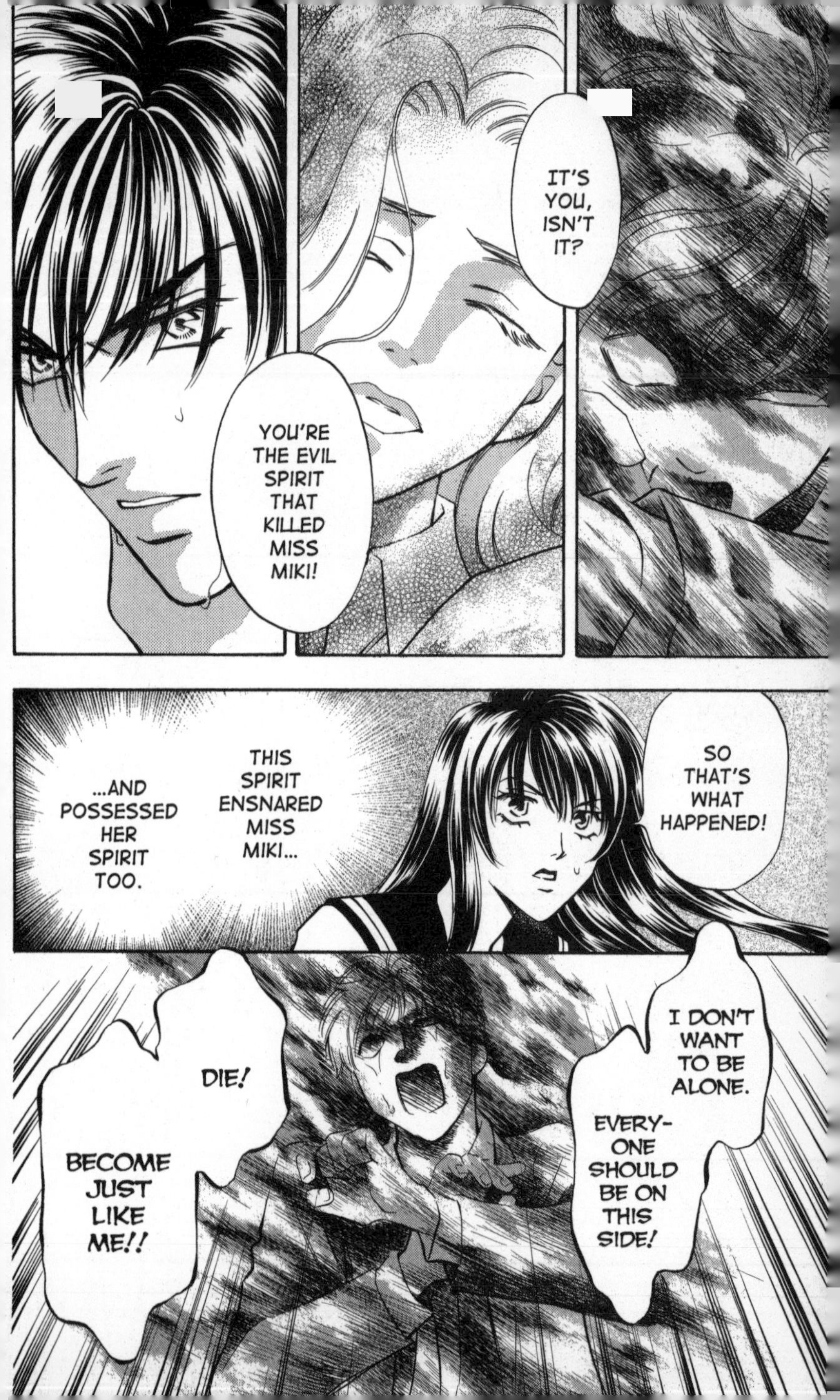
IT'S YOU, ISN'T IT?
YOU'RE THE EVIL SPIRIT THAT KILLED MISS MIKI!
SO THAT'S WHAT HAPPENED!
THIS SPIRIT ENSNARED MISS MIKI...
...AND POSSESSED HER SPIRIT TOO.
I DON'T WANT TO BE ALONE.
EVERY-ONE SHOULD BE ON THIS SIDE!
DIE!
BECOME JUST LIKE ME!!

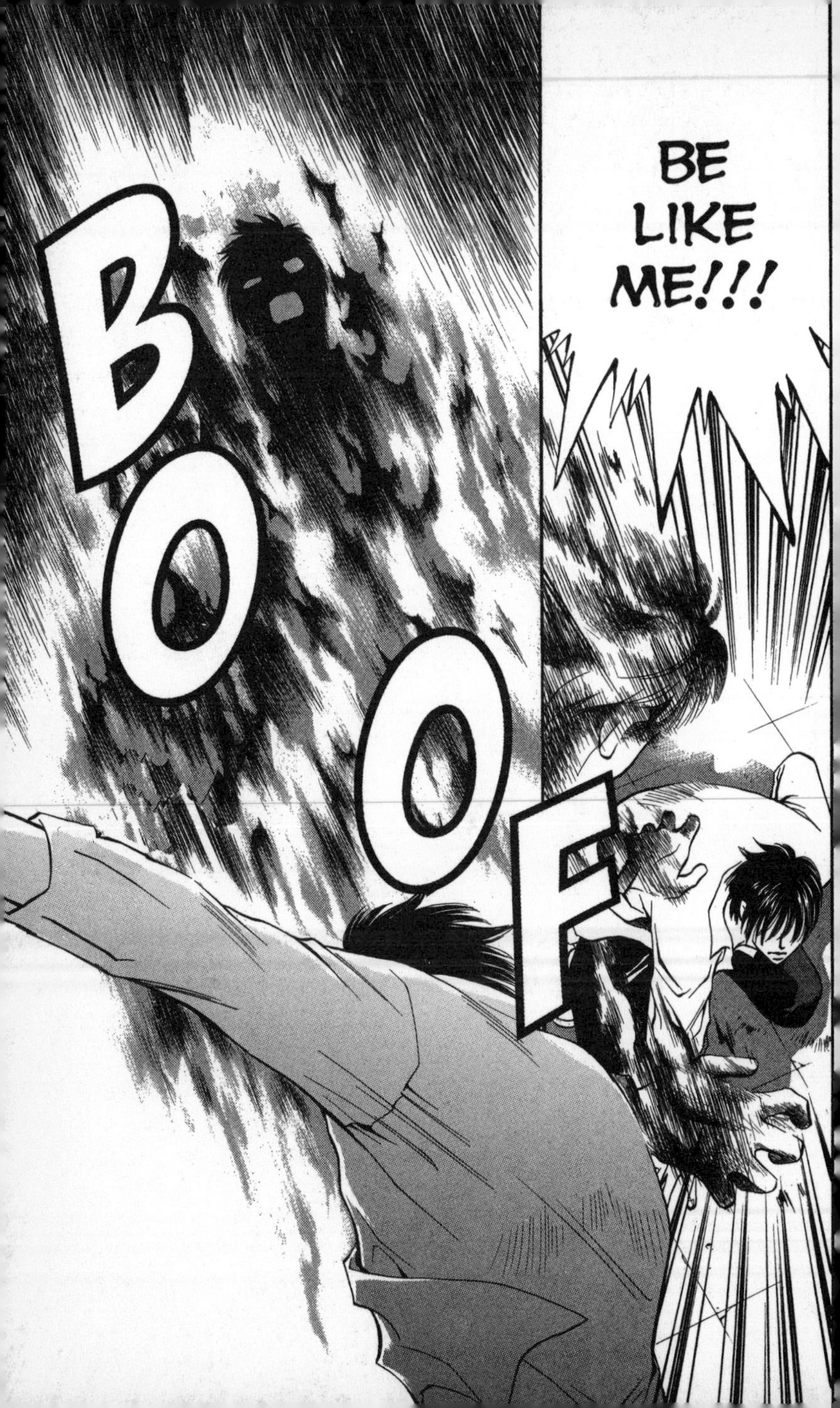
BE LIKE ME!!!
BOOOF

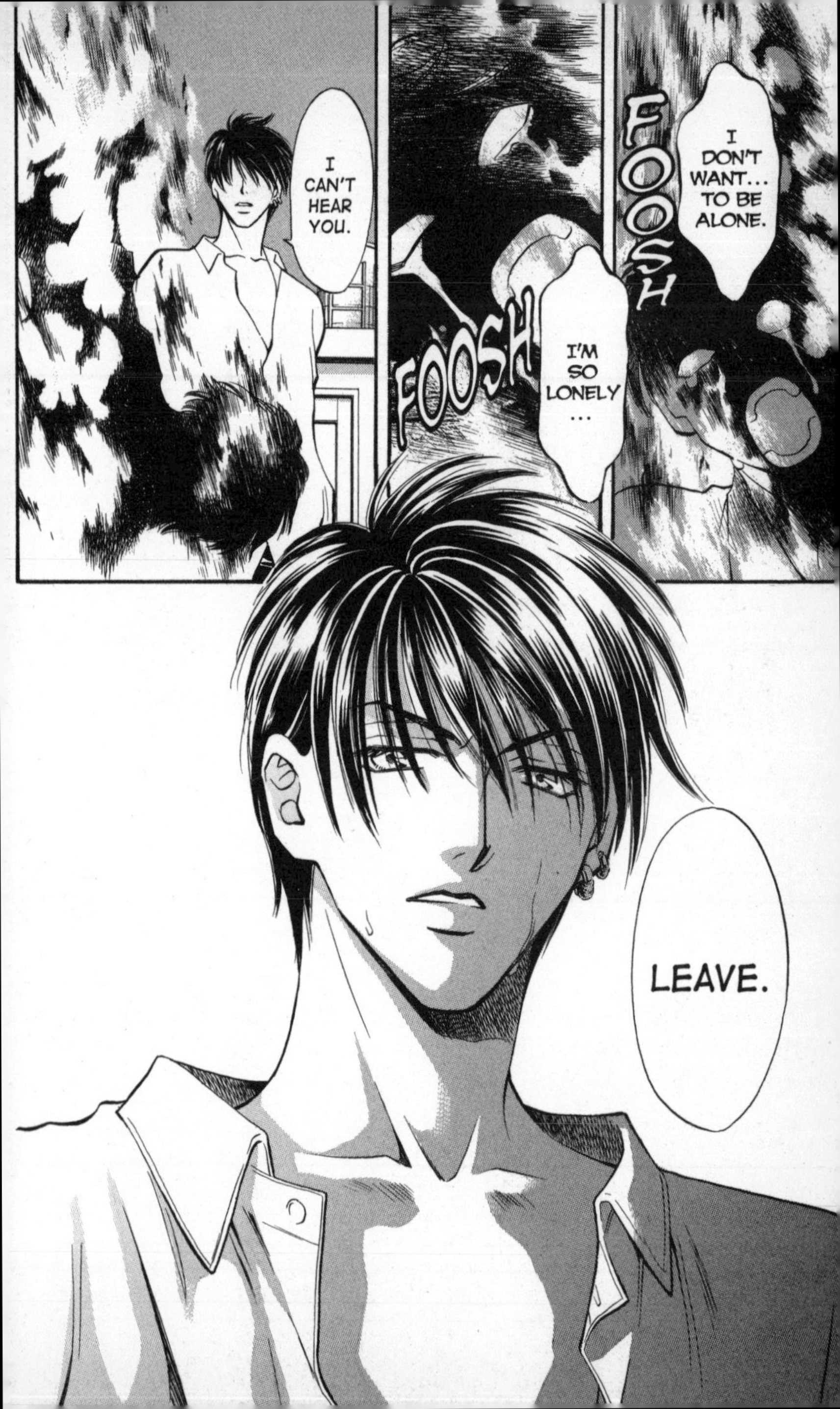
I DON'T WANT... TO BE ALONE.
FOOSH
FOOSH
I'M SO LONELY ...
I CAN'T HEAR YOU.
LEAVE.

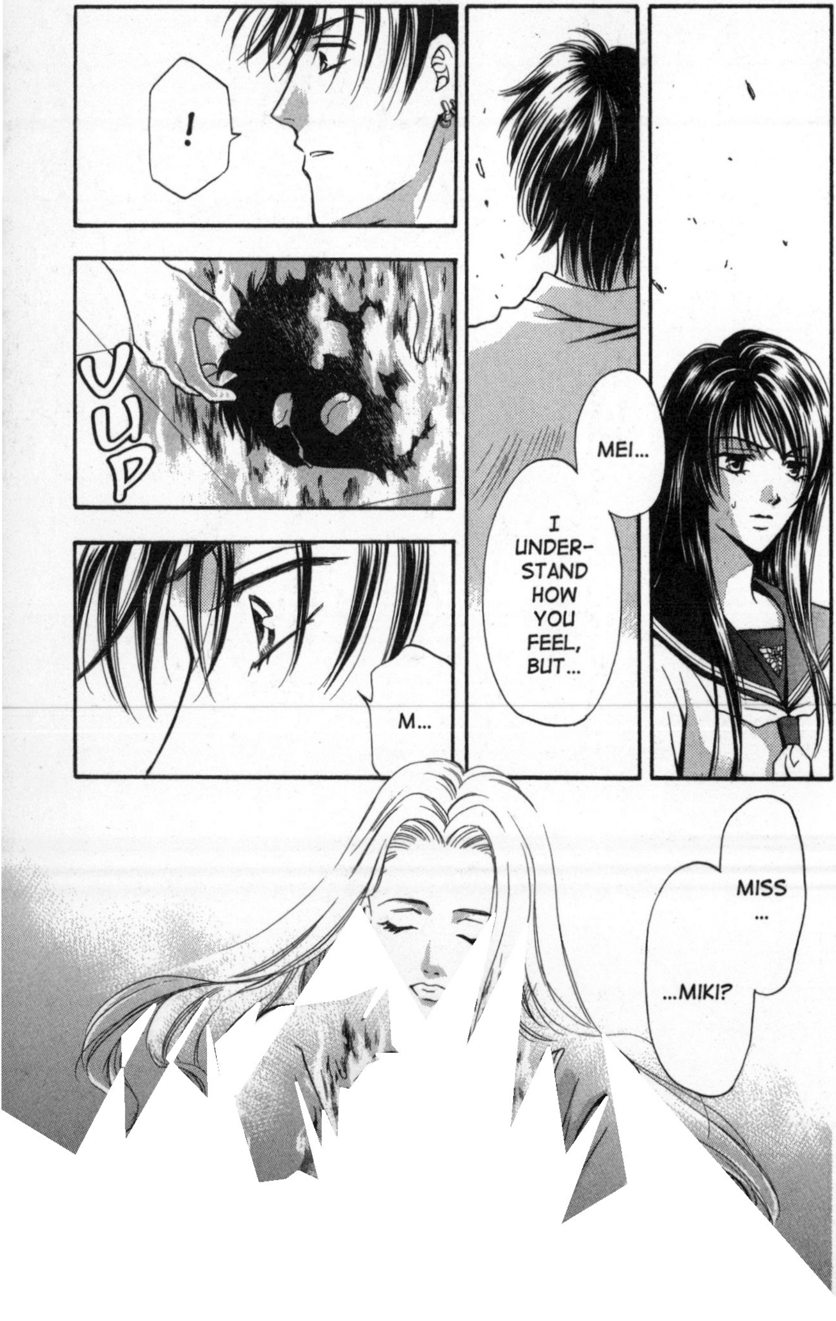
MEI...
I UNDER-STAND HOW YOU FEEL, BUT...
!
VUP
M...
MISS ...
...MIKI?

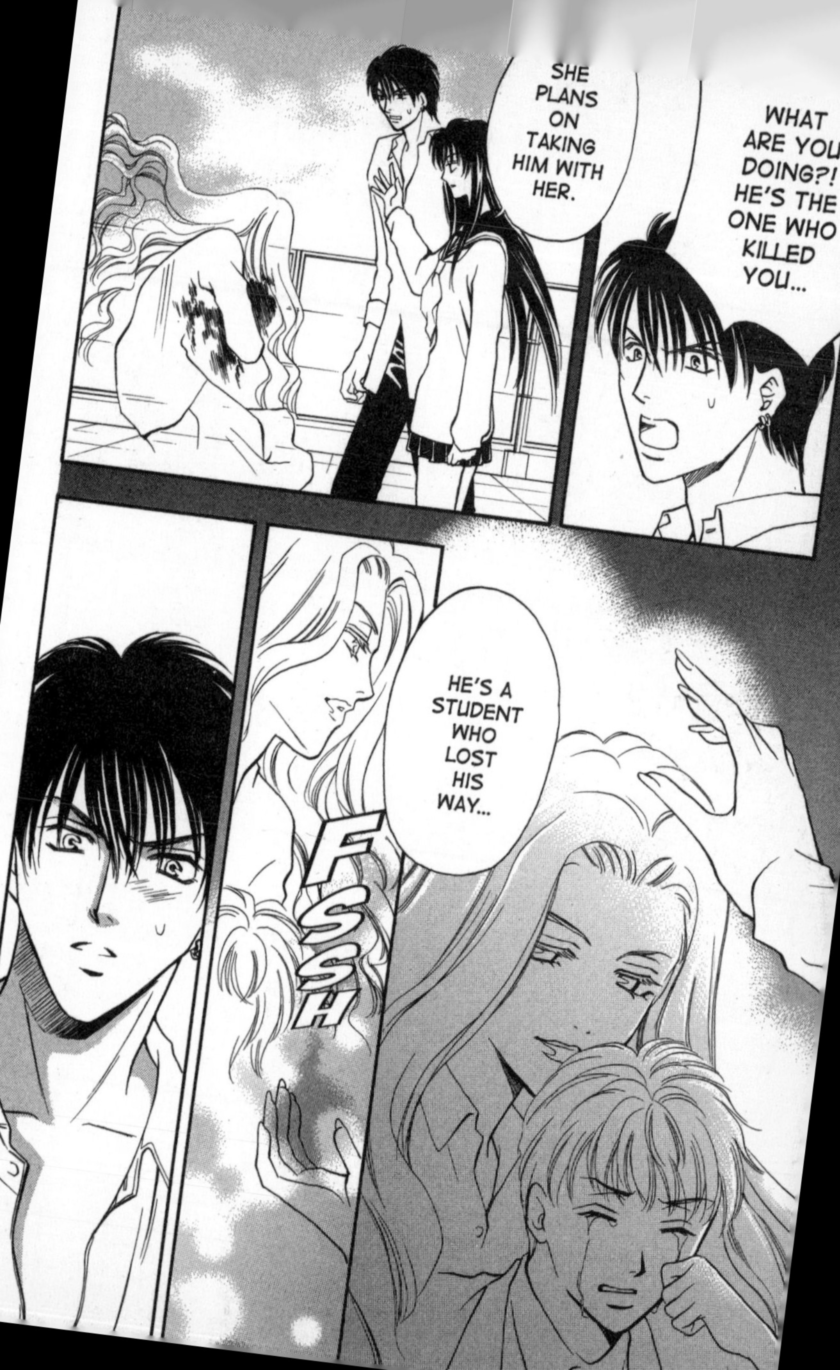
WHAT ARE YOU DOING?! HE'S THE ONE WHO KILLED YOU...
SHE PLANS ON TAKING HIM WITH HER.
HE'S A STUDENT WHO LOST HIS WAY...
FSSH

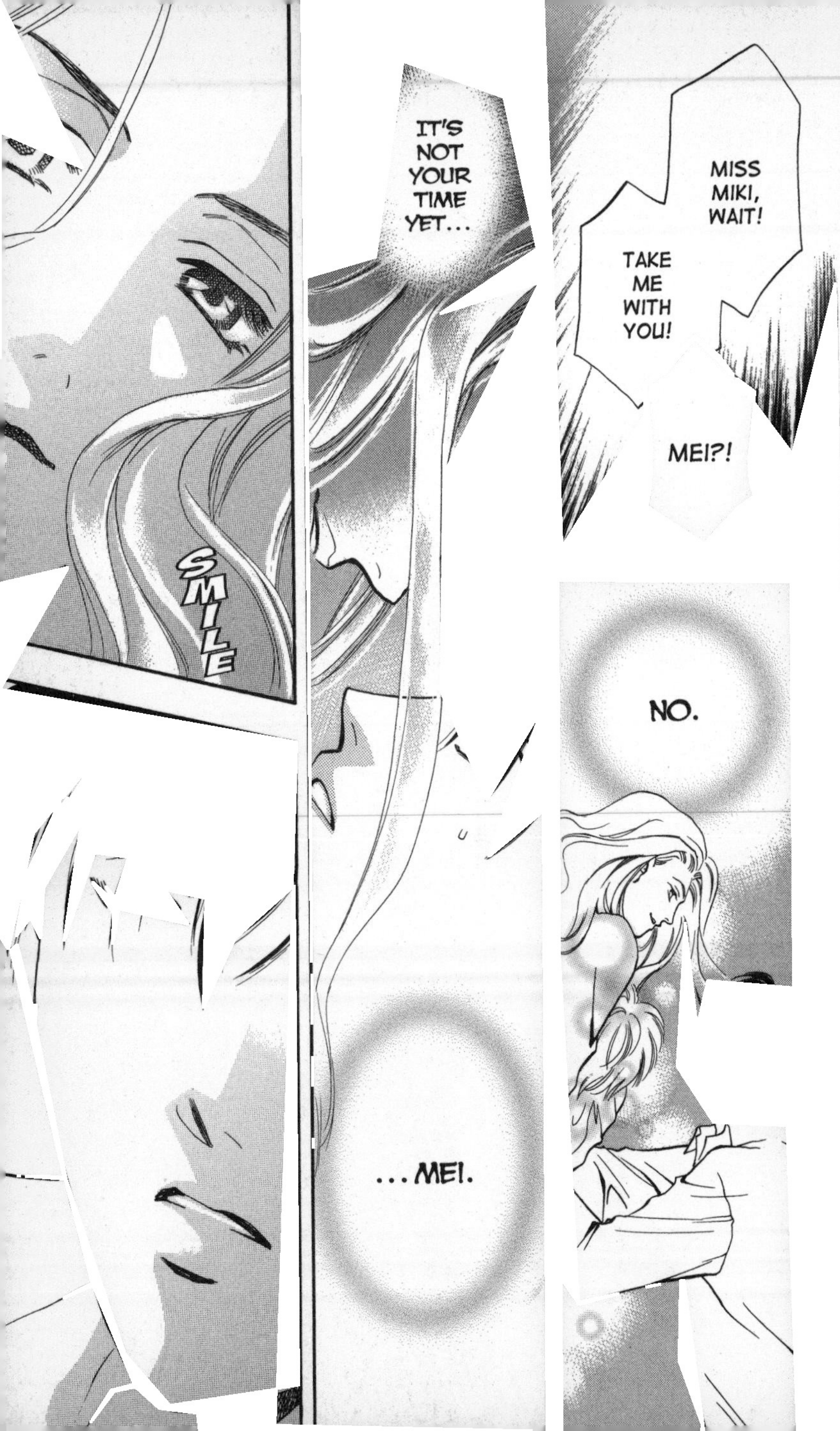
MISS MIKI, WAIT!
TAKE ME WITH YOU!
MEI?!
NO.
IT'S NOT YOUR TIME YET...
...MEI.
SMILE

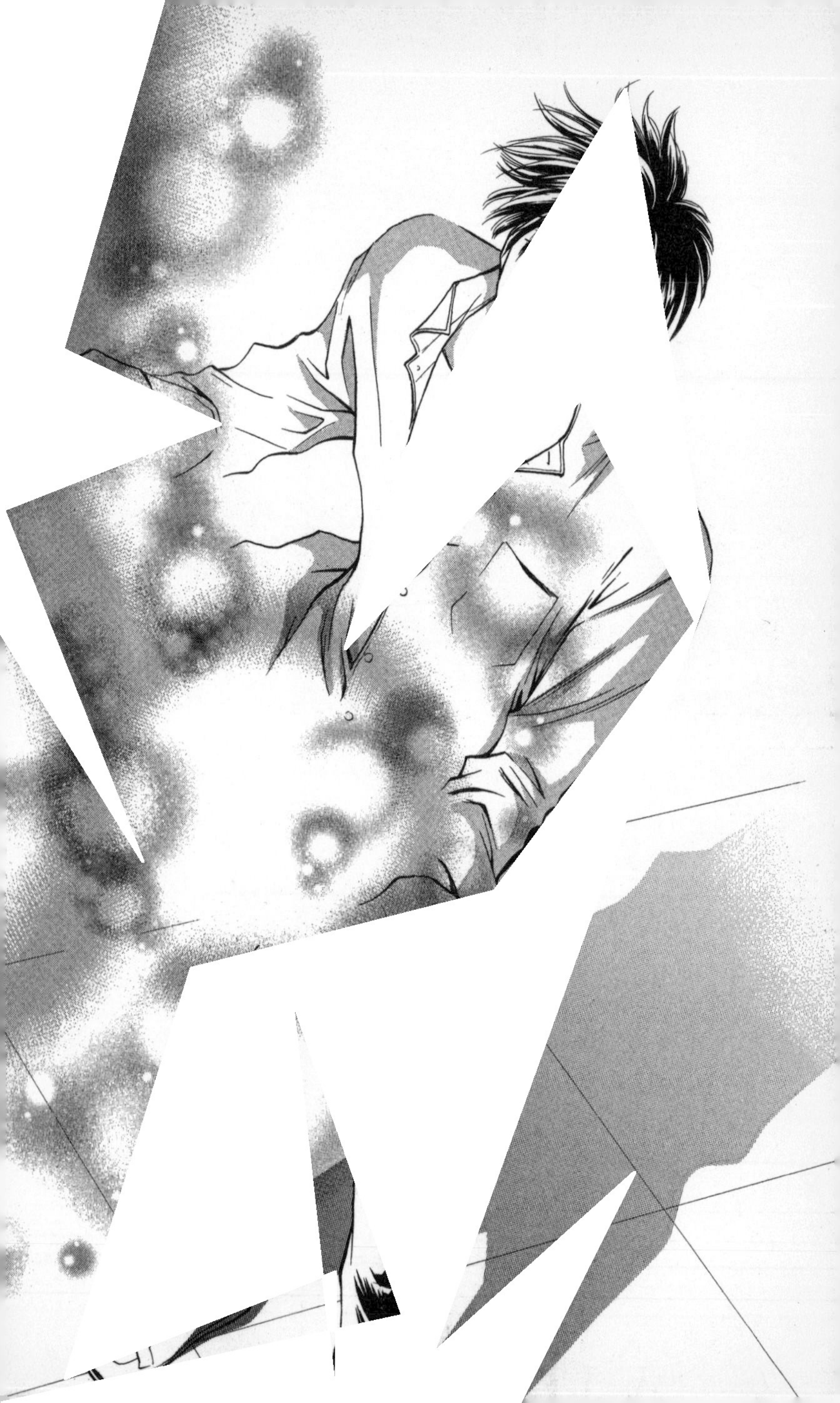

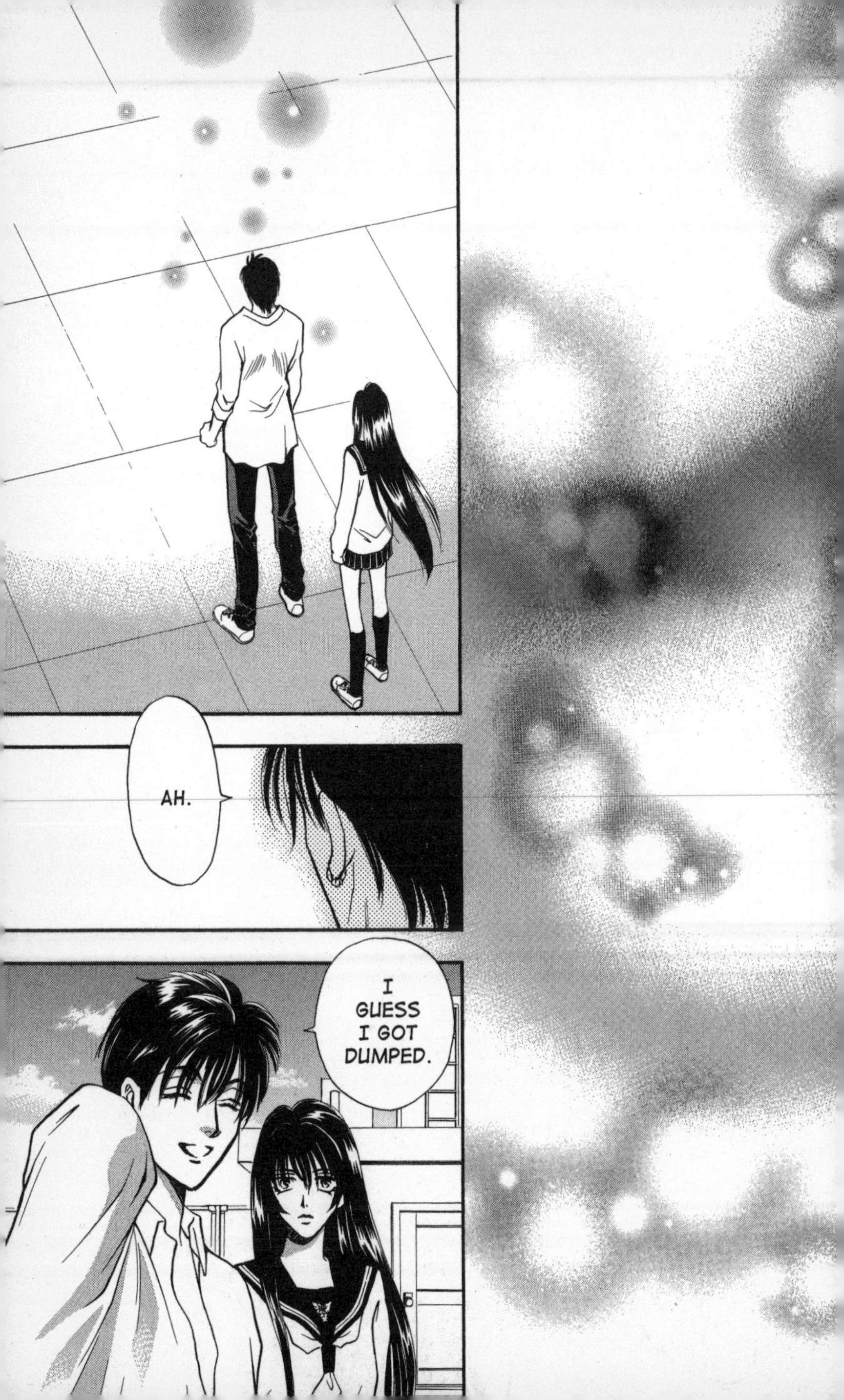
AH.
I GUESS I GOT DUMPED.

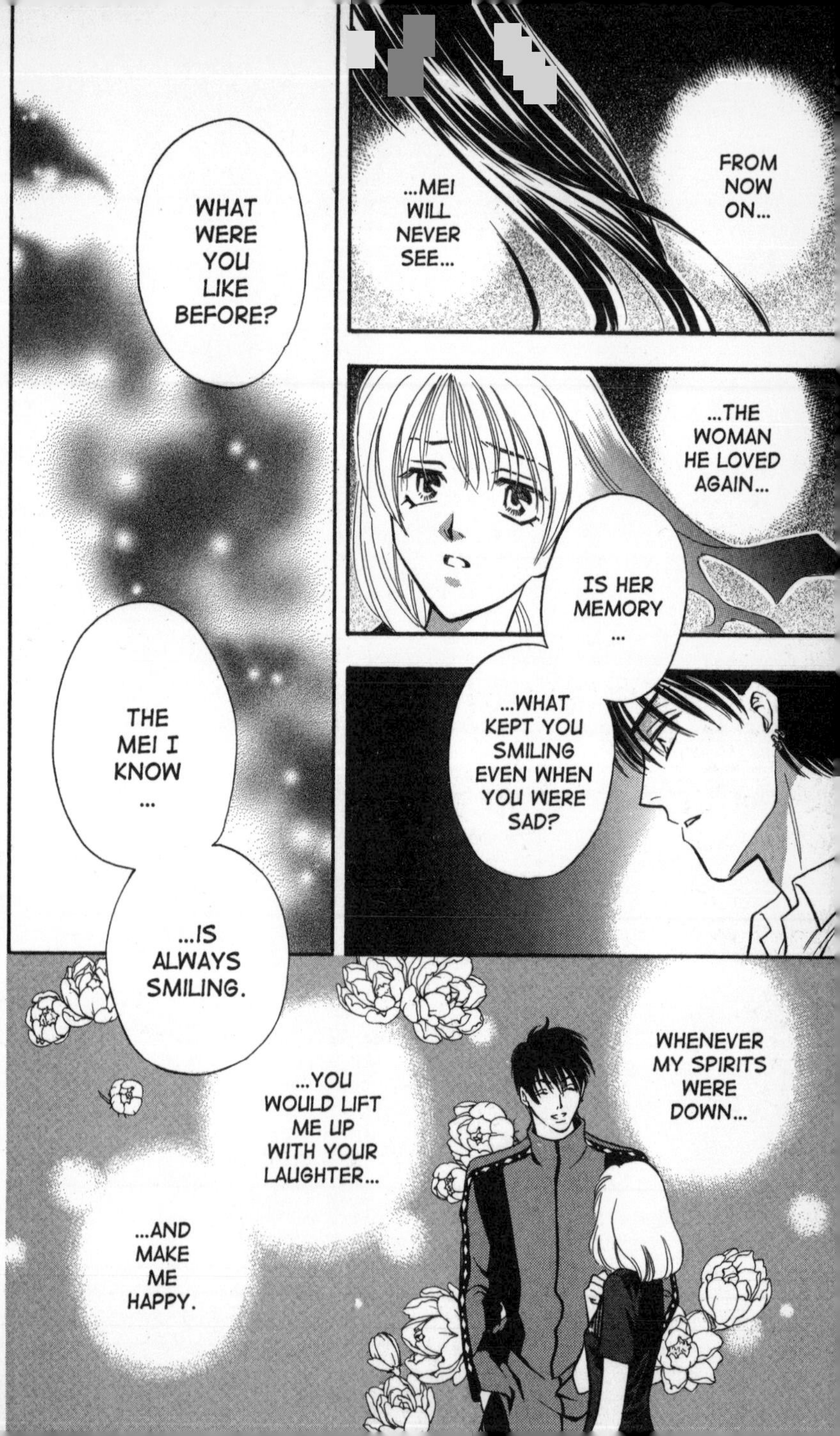
FROM NOW ON...
...MEI WILL NEVER SEE...
...THE WOMAN HE LOVED AGAIN...
IS HER MEMORY ...
...WHAT KEPT YOU SMILING EVEN WHEN YOU WERE SAD?
WHAT WERE YOU LIKE BEFORE?
THE MEI I KNOW ...
...IS ALWAYS SMILING.
WHENEVER MY SPIRITS WERE DOWN...
...YOU WOULD LIFT ME UP WITH YOUR LAUGHTER...
...AND MAKE ME HAPPY.

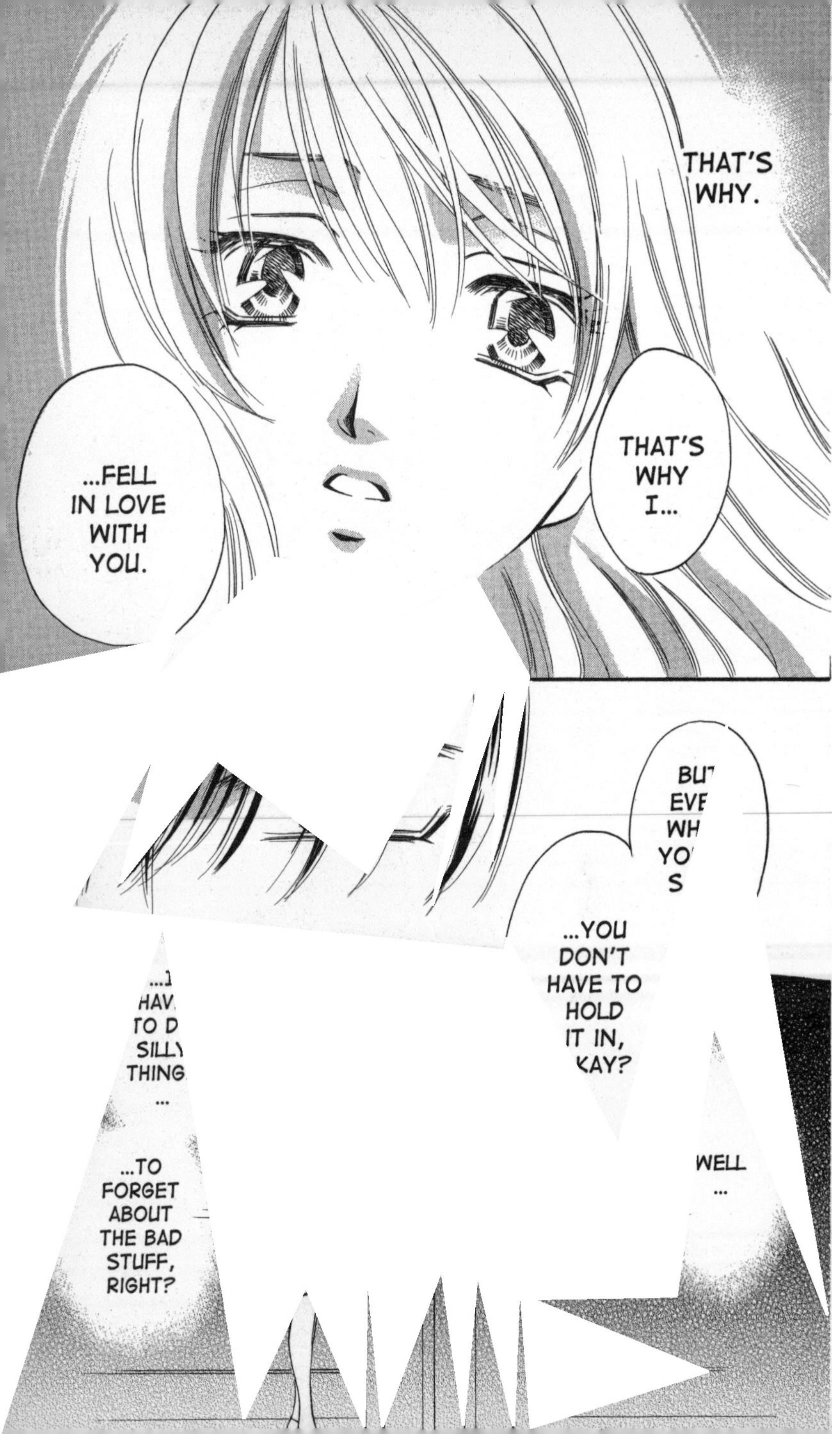
THAT'S WHY.
THAT'S WHY I...
...FELL IN LOVE WITH YOU.
BUT EVE WH YO S
...YOU DON'T HAVE TO HOLD IT IN, KAY?
WELL ...
...I HAV TO D SILLY THING ...
...TO FORGET ABOUT THE BAD STUFF, RIGHT?

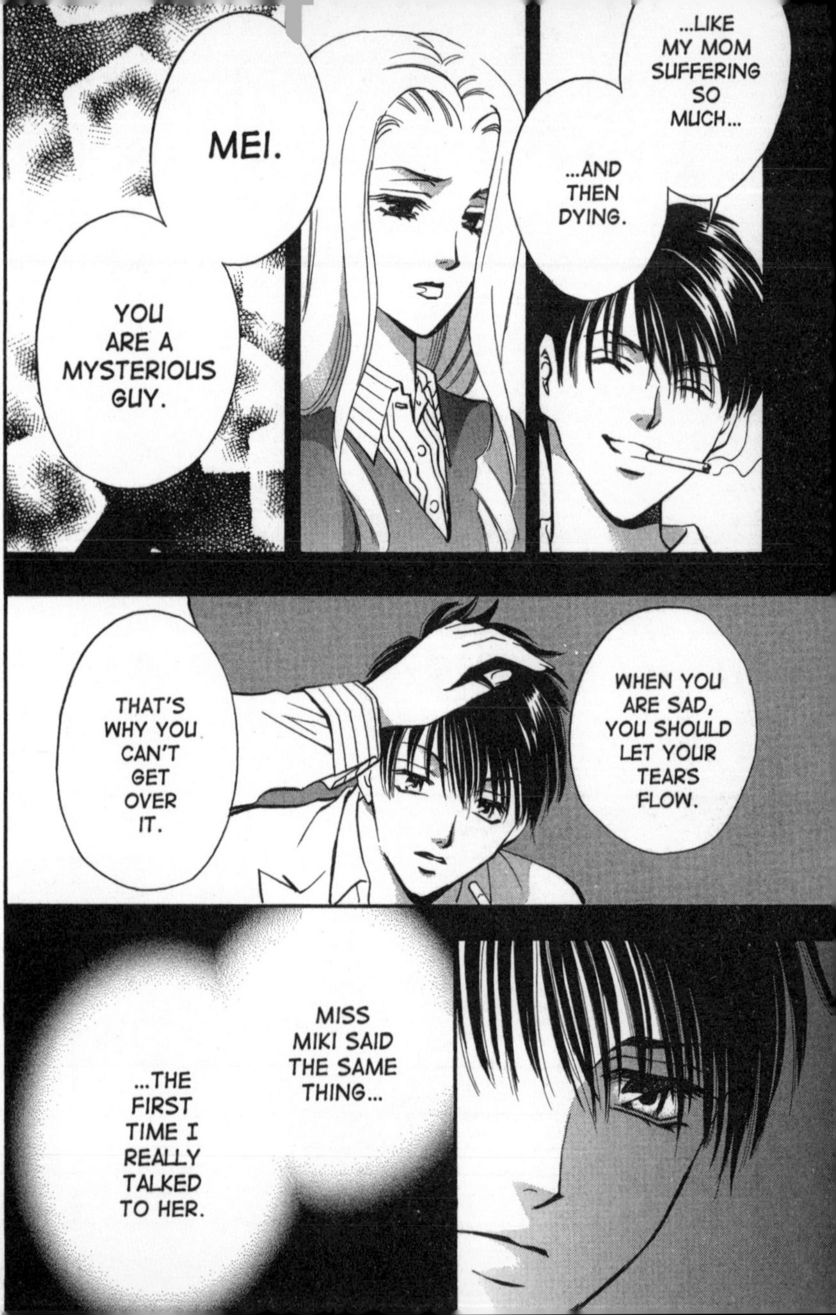
...LIKE MY MOM SUFFERING SO MUCH...
...AND THEN DYING.
MEI.
YOU ARE A MYSTERIOUS GUY.
WHEN YOU ARE SAD, YOU SHOULD LET YOUR TEARS FLOW.
THAT'S WHY YOU CAN'T GET OVER IT.
MISS MIKI SAID THE SAME THING...
...THE FIRST TIME I REALLY TALKED TO HER.

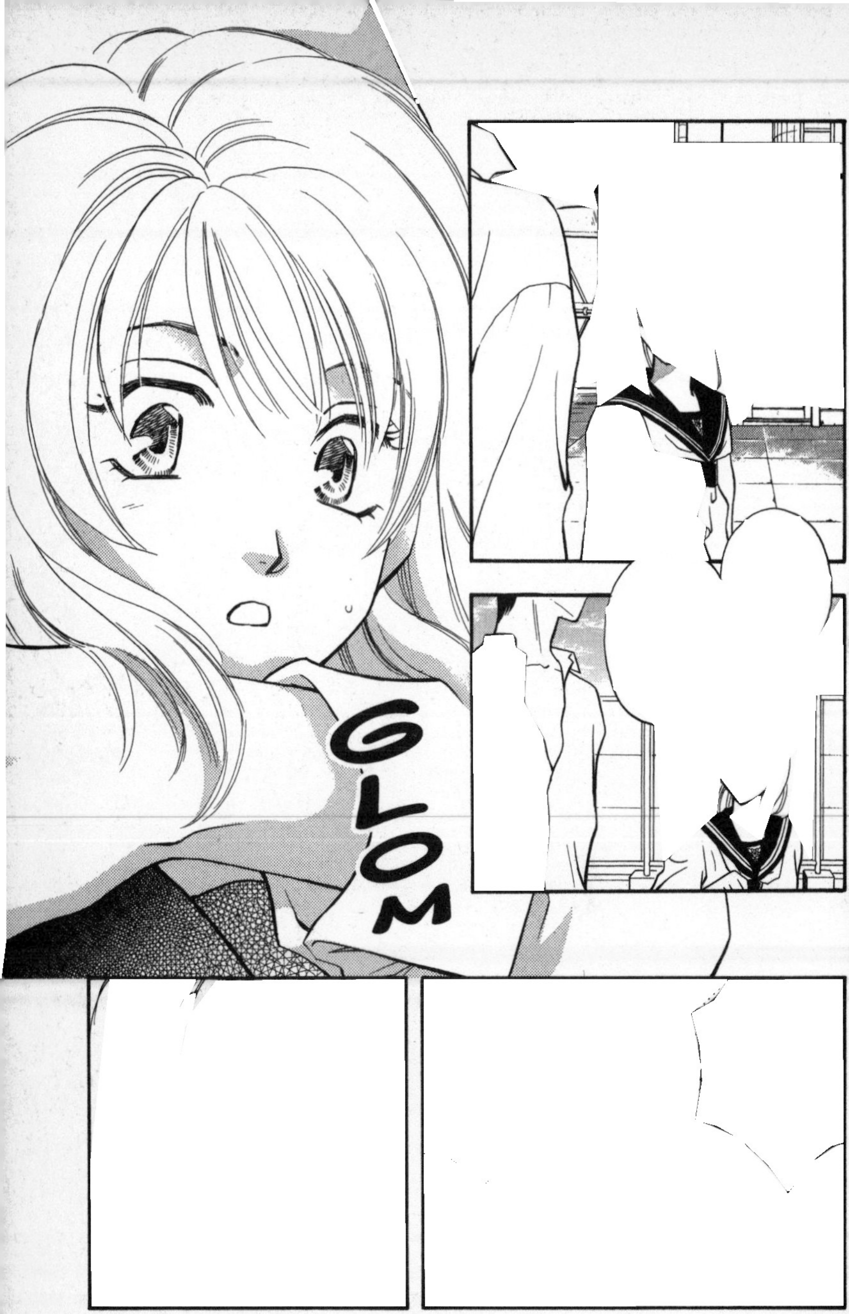
GLOM

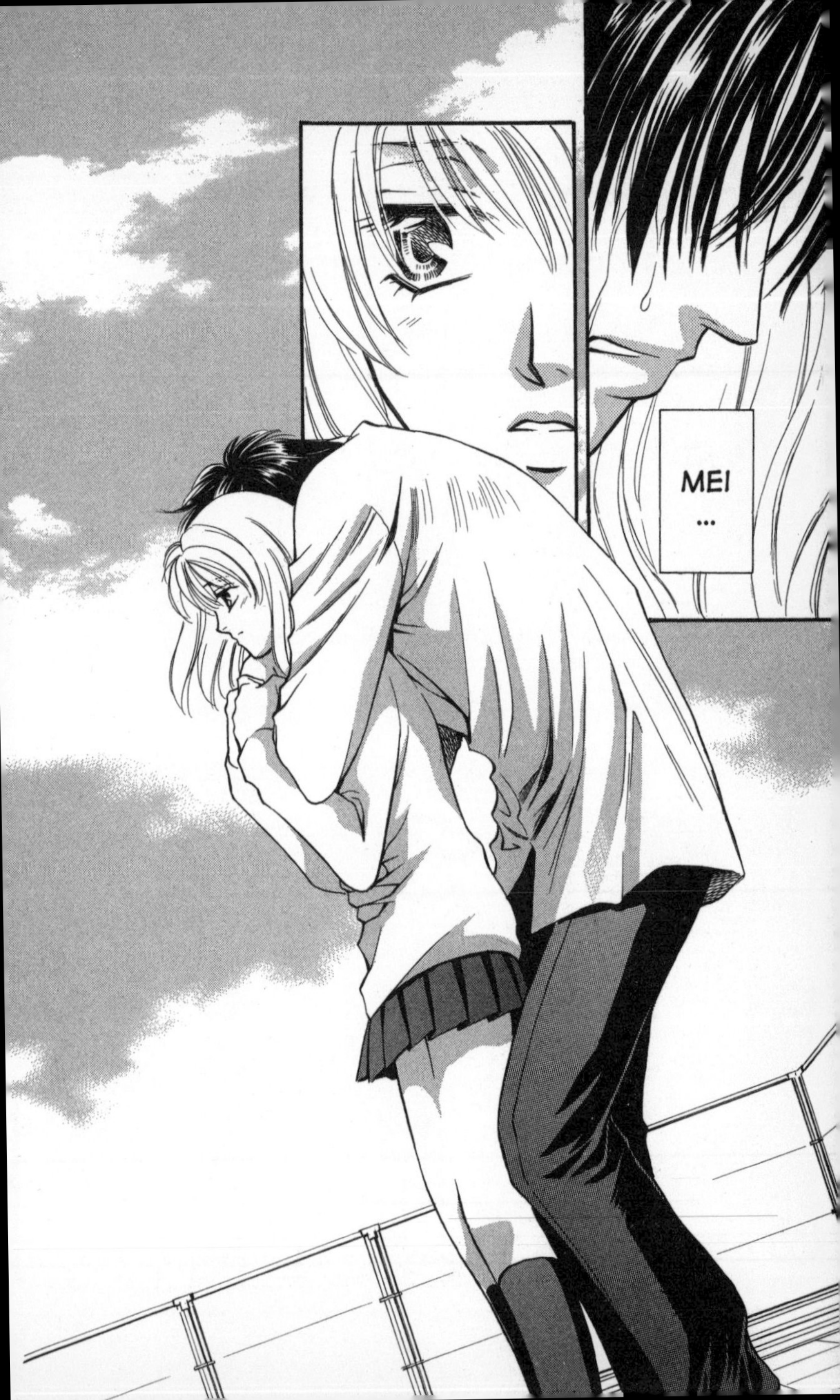
MEI
...

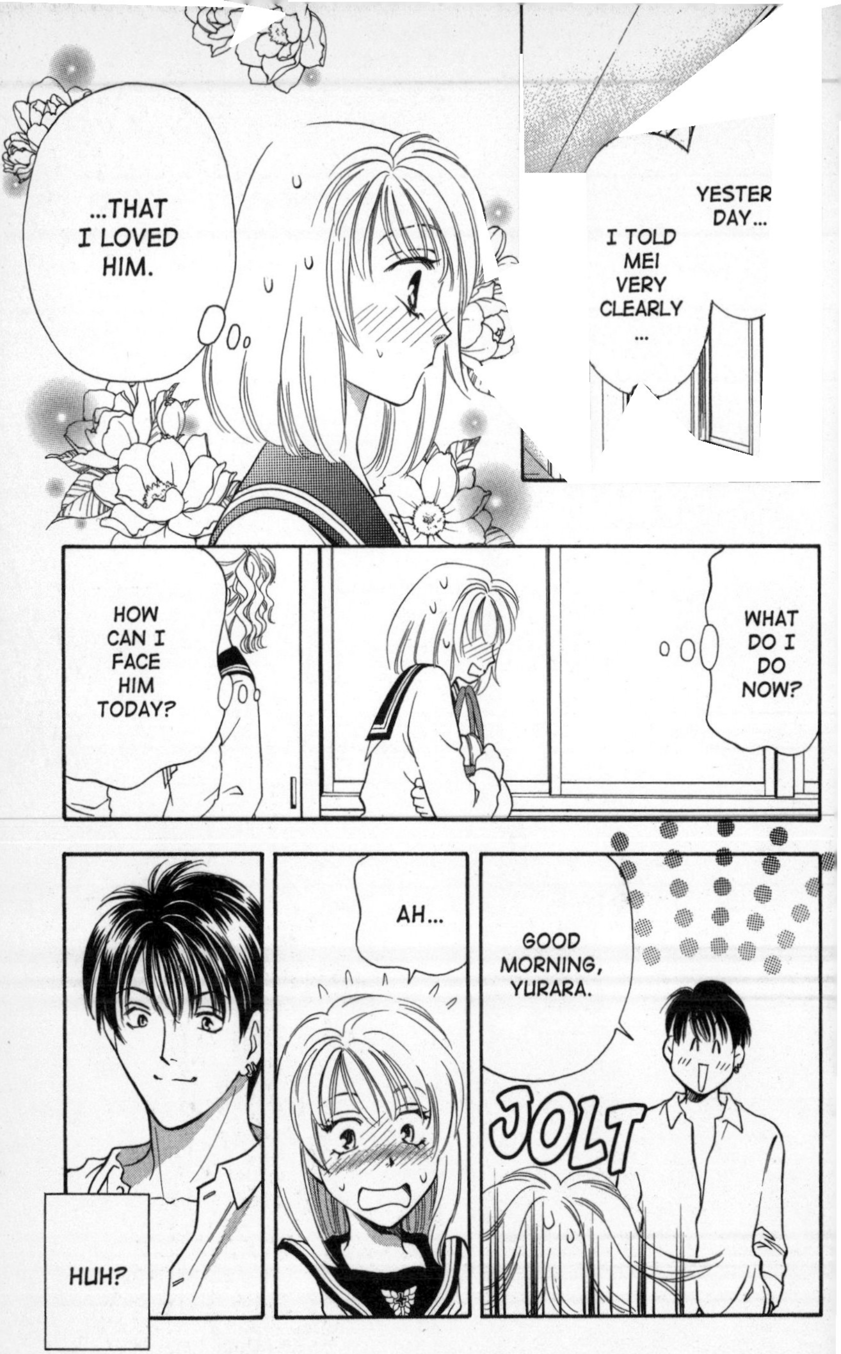
YESTER DAY...
I TOLD MEI VERY CLEARLY ...
...THAT I LOVED HIM.
WHAT DO I DO NOW?
HOW CAN I FACE HIM TODAY?
GOOD MORNING, YURARA.
JOLT
AH...
HUH?

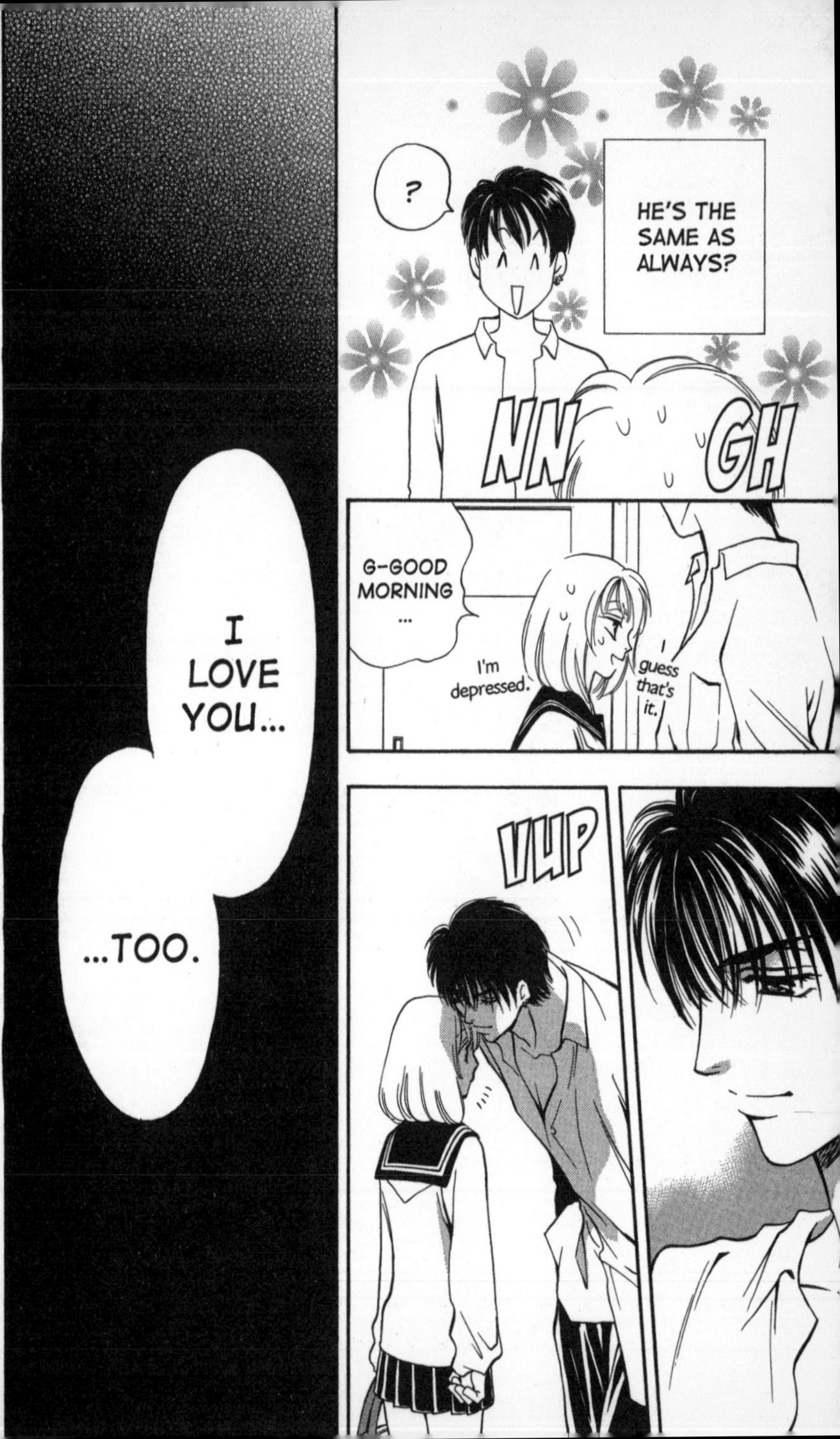
HE'S THE SAME AS ALWAYS?
?
NNGH
G-GOOD MORNING ...
I guess that's it.
I'm depressed.
VUP
I LOVE YOU...
...TOO.

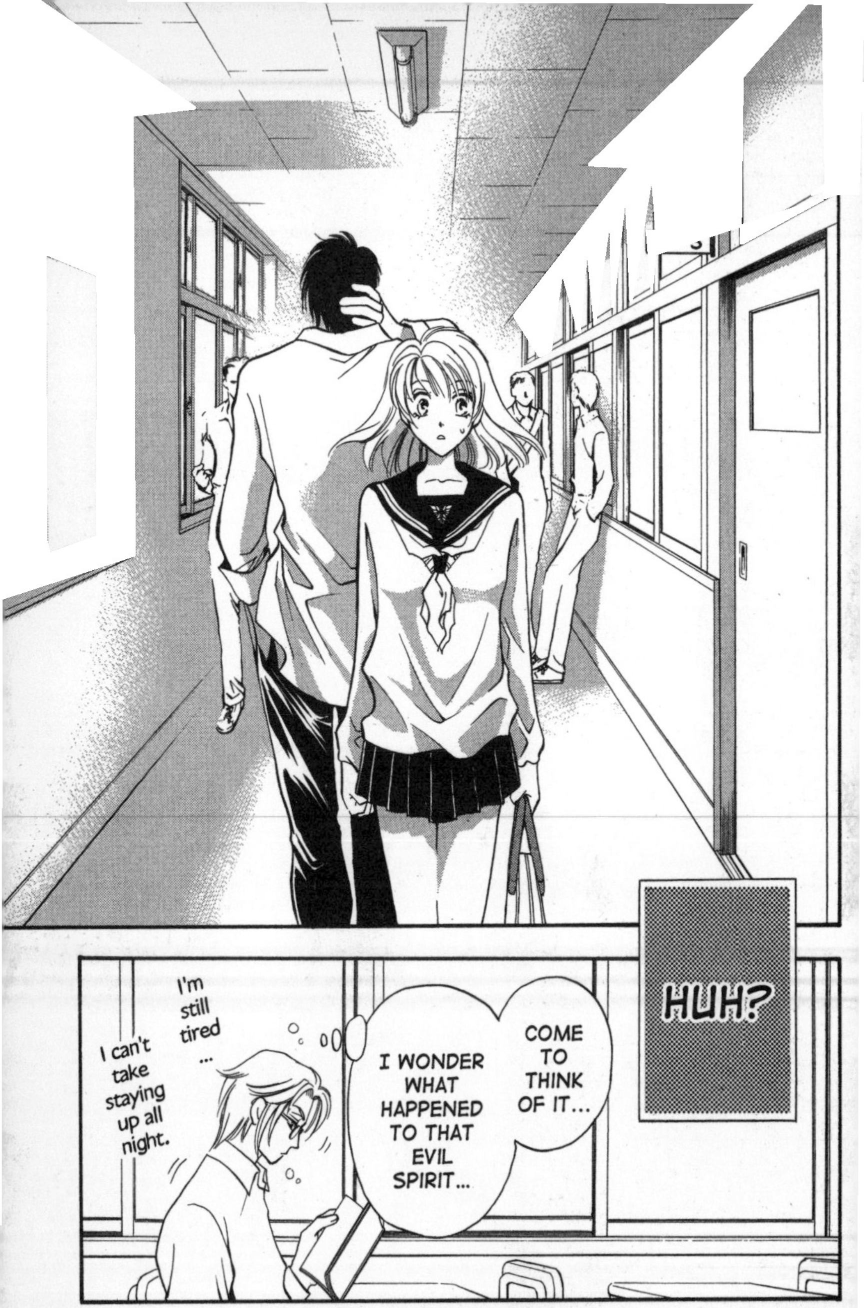
HUH?
COME TO THINK OF IT...
I WONDER WHAT HAPPENED TO THAT EVIL SPIRIT...
I'm still tired ...
I can't take staying up all night.

Yurara Vol. 2/End

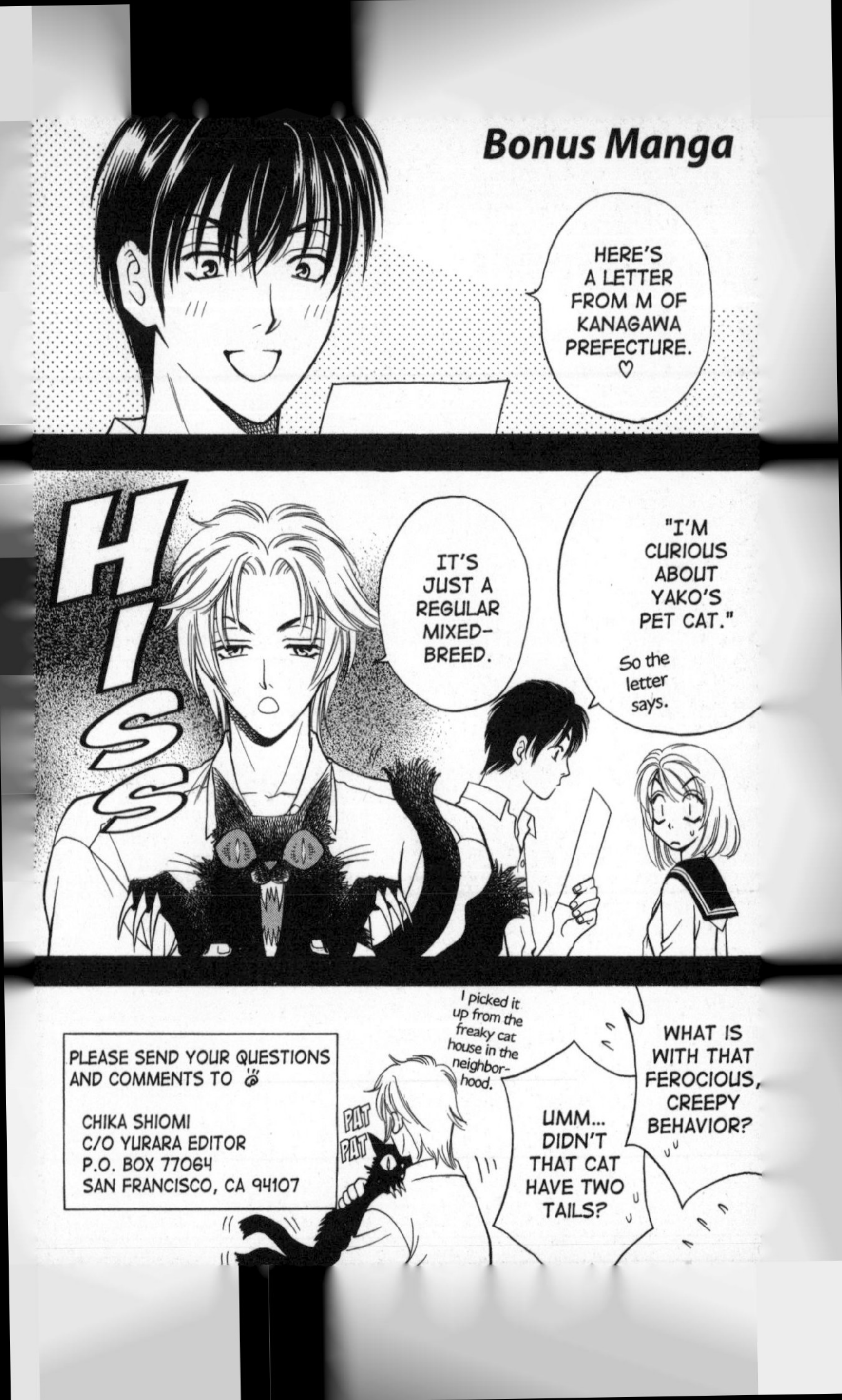
Bonus Manga
HERE'S A LETTER FROM M OF KANAGAWA PREFECTURE. ♡
"I'M CURIOUS ABOUT YAKO'S PET CAT."
So the letter says.
IT'S JUST A REGULAR MIXED-BREED.
HISS
WHAT IS WITH THAT FEROCIOUS, CREEPY BEHAVIOR?
I picked it up from the freaky cat house in the neighbor-hood.
UMM... DIDN'T THAT CAT HAVE TWO TAILS?
PAT PAT
PLEASE SEND YOUR QUESTIONS AND COMMENTS TO
CHIKA SHIOMI
C/O YURARA EDITOR
P.O. BOX 77064
SAN FRANCISCO, CA 94107

Chika Shiomi lives in the Aichi Prefecture of Japan. She debuted with the manga *Todokeru Toki o Sugitemo* (Even if the Time for Deliverance Passes), and her work is currently running in two magazines, *Bessatsu Hana to Yume* and *Mystery Bonita*. She loves reading manga, traveling, and listening to music by Aerosmith, Hyde, and Guns N' Roses. Her favorite artists include Michelangelo, Hokusai, Bernini, and Gustav Klimt.

Yurara

Vol. 2
The Shojo Beat Manga Edition

STORY & ART BY
CHIKA SHIOMI

English Adaptation/Heidi Vivolo
Translation/JN Productions
Touch-up Art & Lettering/Freeman Wong
Design/Izumi Hirayama
Editor/Nancy Thistlethwaite

Editor in Chief, Books/Alvin Lu
Editor in Chief, Magazines/Marc Weidenbaum
VP of Publishing Licensing/Rika Inouye
VP of Sales/Gonzalo Ferreyra
Sr. VP of Marketing/Liza Coppola
Publisher/Hyoe Narita

Published by VIZ Media, LLC
P.O. Box 77064
San Francisco, CA 94107

Shojo Beat Manga Edition
10 9 8 7 6 5 4 3 2 1
First printing, September 2007

store.viz.com

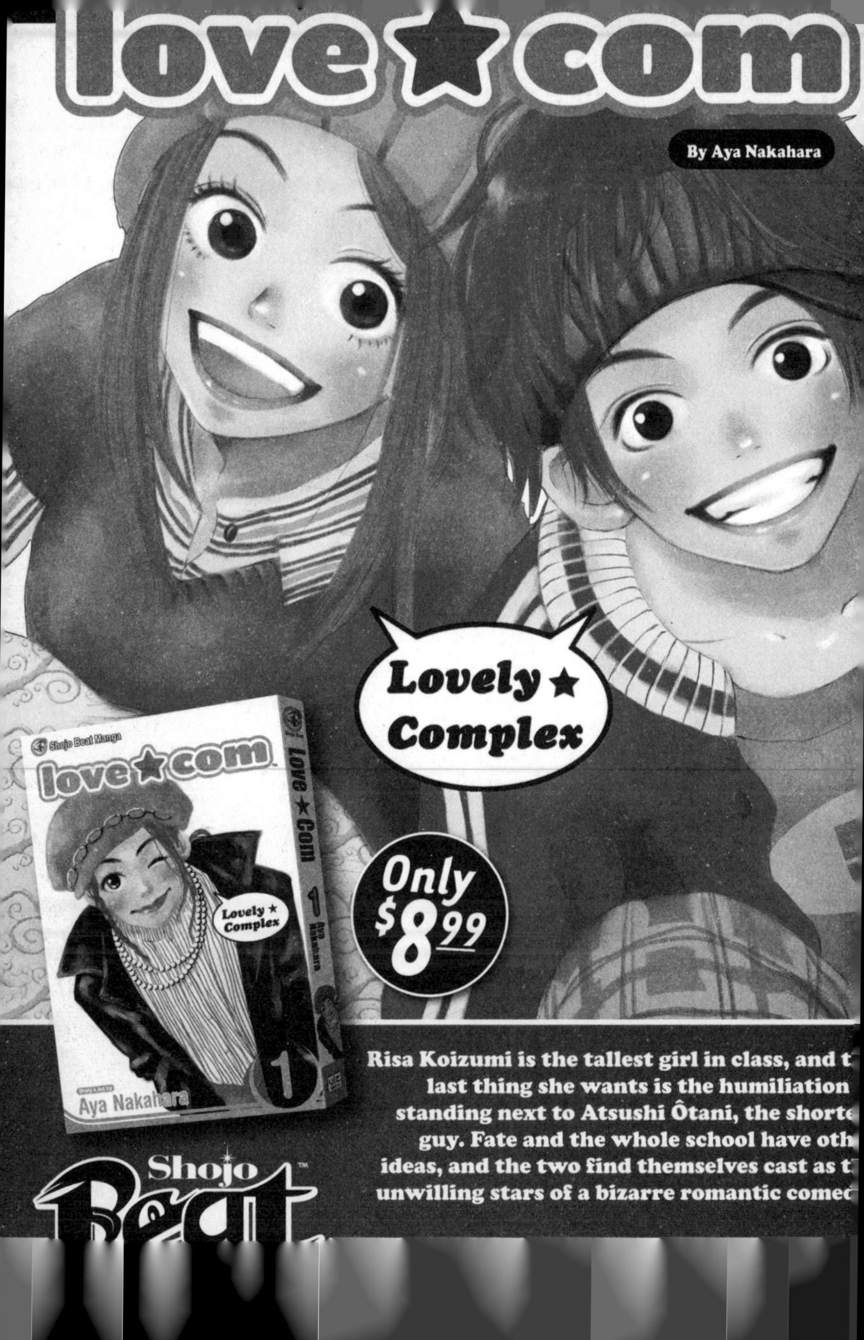
love★com
By Aya Nakahara
Lovely★ Complex
Shojo Beat Manga
love★com
Love★Com
1
Aya Nakahara
Lovely★ Complex
Story & Art by
Aya Nakahara
Only $8.99
Risa Koizumi is the tallest girl in class, and t
last thing she wants is the humiliation
standing next to Atsushi Ôtani, the shorte
guy. Fate and the whole school have oth
ideas, and the two find themselves cast as t
unwilling stars of a bizarre romantic comed
Shojo Beat™

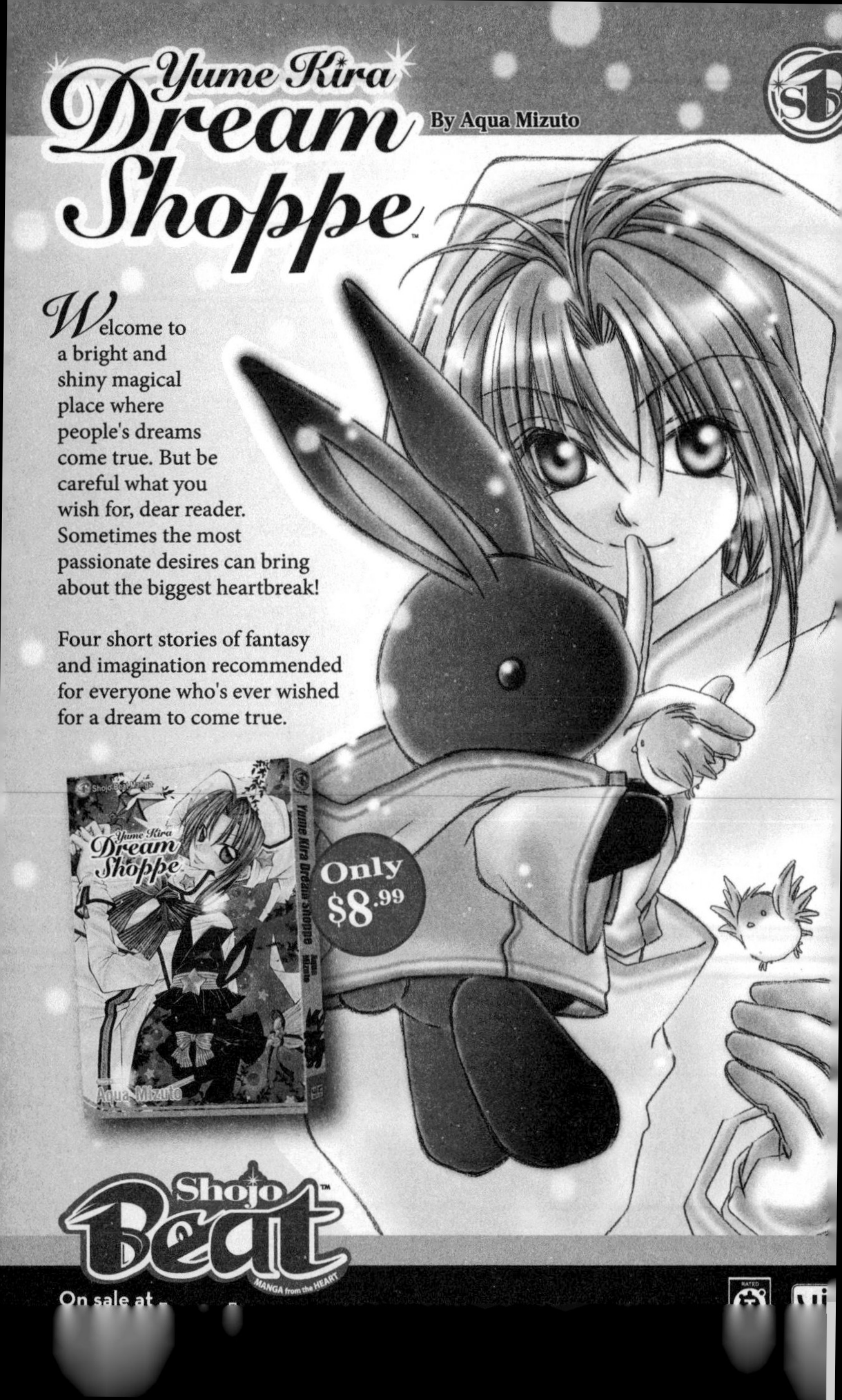

Yume Kira Dream Shoppe™
By Aqua Mizuto
Welcome to a bright and shiny magical place where people's dreams come true. But be careful what you wish for, dear reader. Sometimes the most passionate desires can bring about the biggest heartbreak!
Four short stories of fantasy and imagination recommended for everyone who's ever wished for a dream to come true.
Shojo Beat Manga
Yume Kira Dream Shoppe
Aqua Mizuto
Yume Kira Dream Shoppe
Only $8.99
Shojo Beat™
MANGA from the HEART
On sale at